German Literature on the Middle East

Social History, Popular Culture, and Politics in Germany
Geoff Eley, Series Editor

Recent Titles

The Golem Returns: From German Romantic Literature to Global Jewish Culture, 1808–2008, Cathy S. Gelbin

German Literature on the Middle East: Discourses and Practices, 1000–1989, Nina Berman

Franz Radziwill and the Contradictions of German Art History, 1919–45, James A. van Dyke

Weimar through the Lens of Gender: Prostitution Reform, Woman's Emancipation, and German Democracy, Julia Roos

Murder Scenes: Normality, Deviance, and Criminal Violence in Weimar Berlin, Sace Elder

Changing Places: Society, Culture, and Territory in the Saxon-Bohemian Borderlands, 1870 to 1946, Caitlin E. Murdock

After the Nazi Racial State: Difference and Democracy in Germany and Europe, Rita Chin, Heide Fehrenbach, Geoff Eley, and Atina Grossmann

Work, Race, and the Emergence of Radical Right Corporatism in Imperial Germany, Dennis Sweeney

The German Patient: Crisis and Recovery in Postwar Culture, Jennifer M. Kapczynski

Topographies of Class: Modern Architecture and Mass Society in Weimar Berlin, Sabine Hake

Neither German nor Pole: Catholicism and National Indifference in a Central European Borderland, James E. Bjork

Beyond Berlin: Twelve German Cities Confront the Nazi Past, edited by Gavriel D. Rosenfeld and Paul B. Jaskot

The Politics of Sociability: Freemasonry and German Civil Society, 1840–1918, Stefan-Ludwig Hoffmann

Work and Play: The Production and Consumption of Toys in Germany, 1870–1914, David D. Hamlin

The Cosmopolitan Screen: German Cinema and the Global Imaginary, 1945 to the Present, edited by Stephan K. Schindler and Lutz Koepnick

Germans on Drugs: The Complications of Modernization in Hamburg, Robert P. Stephens

Gender in Transition: Discourse and Practice in German-Speaking Europe, 1750–1830, edited by Ulrike Gleixner and Marion W. Gray

Growing Up Female in Nazi Germany, Dagmar Reese

Justice Imperiled: The Anti-Nazi Lawyer Max Hirschberg in Weimar Germany, Douglas G. Morris

The Heimat Abroad: The Boundaries of Germanness, edited by Krista O'Donnell, Renate Bridenthal, and Nancy Reagin

Modern German Art for Thirties Paris, Prague, and London: Resistance and Acquiescence in a Democratic Public Sphere, Keith Holz

For a complete list of titles, please see www.press.umich.edu

German Literature on the Middle East

Discourses and Practices, 1000–1989

Nina Berman

The University of Michigan Press
Ann Arbor

First paperback edition 2013

Published in the United States of America by
The University of Michigan Press
Manufactured in the United States of America
⊗ Printed on acid-free paper

2016 2015 2014 2013 5 4 3 2

A CIP catalog record for this book is available from the British Library.

Library of Congress Cataloging-in-Publication Data

Berman, Nina.
German literature on the Middle East : discourses and practices, 1000–1989 / Nina Berman.
p. cm. — (Social history, popular culture, and politics in Germany)
Includes index.
ISBN 978-0-472-11751-2 (cloth : alk. paper)
1. German literature—History and criticism—Theory, etc.
2. Middle East—In literature. I. Title.
PT45.B47 2011
830.9—dc22 2010030240

ISBN 978-0-472-03557-1 (pbk. : alk. paper)

To Milena

Acknowledgments

The relevance of contact and social interaction for the development of ideas and the creation of texts is a key focus of my study, and the argument would be incomplete if I were not to acknowledge the impact of my personal network of contacts on my scholarship. My interest in the topic of German–Middle Eastern interaction goes back to my childhood, which was peopled with individuals from Asia, Africa, and the Middle East. The "Orient" was never a mythical place for me, but rather the area where our friends had been born, gone to school, and were working. Presents and photographs from Damascus, Cairo, Jerusalem, Amman, and Baghdad were evidence for the existence of these faraway places. I began my academic studies with a focus on Arabic, German, and history, planning originally to specialize on the Middle Ages. But I made my way through the centuries, and developed an interest in the various dimensions of German–Middle Eastern contact and interaction. Travels to Egypt, Turkey, Jordan, Israel, Morocco, and Syria provided invaluable opportunities to explore the lives of peoples in the area, visit historical sites, and work in archives.

My doctoral work and first book were devoted to the image of the Orient in German literature at the turn to the twentieth century. Gradually, the idea for a far-reaching study on the subject was born. And I was fortunate enough to benefit from the knowledge of generous interlocutors along the way. The Center for Middle Eastern Studies at the University of Texas at Austin afforded me an unexpected arena of growth and collaboration. I am deeply indebted to Abraham Marcus for involving me in the activities of the Center, where I participated in interdisciplinary exchanges and became a great believer in the pivotal role area studies centers can play at a university. I want to thank my former Austin colleagues Kamran Aghaie, Yildiray Erdener, the late Elizabeth Fernea, Bob Fernea, Mohammad Ghanoonparvar, Deborah Kapchan, Esther Raizen, and Yaron Shemer for opening my eyes to many aspects of Middle Eastern studies, and for always being great company. At the Ohio State University I was very fortunate to join the Department of Comparative Studies, which again provided me with an interdisciplinary setting and exhilarating collegiality. I could not have found a better home for my curiosity.

Conferences and symposia have given me opportunities to share my work and to learn from others. Several events stand out in this regard. I want to thank Werner Ruf for inviting me in 2000 to a conference held at Kloster Haydau entitled "Islam and the West," which allowed me to witness the distinct ways in which the topic is discussed in, for example, France, Germany, and the United States. A symposium on the interaction between Europe and the Orient, put together by Georg Stauth and Faruk Birtek at the Kulturwissenschaftliches Institut in Essen in 2004, facilitated a fruitful dialogue with scholars from Turkey. Another productive exchange took place at a conference on German Orientalism organized by Jennifer Jenkins at the University of Toronto, also in 2004. In 2007, I participated in a symposium entitled "Islam and Europe" that was organized by Daniela Flesler and Jane C. Sugarman at SUNY Stony Brook, and in a conference organized by Steve Martinson and Renate A. Schulz at the University of Arizona at Tucson, "Building Bridges: International Conference on Transcultural German Studies." I am thankful to the organizers and participants for affording me invaluable learning experiences.

I conducted research for this study in libraries and archives in the United States and abroad. In Göttingen, Helmut Göbel proved, as always, to be a wonderful host, and in Berlin, I picked up a dialogue begun earlier in Columbus with Horst Wenzel. Thanks also to Michael and Selma Rohrwasser for letting me stay at their apartment. My visit to Damascus, part of an exchange between the Ohio State University and Damascus University that was facilitated by Mahdi Alosh, was a special treat. I am grateful to Abdo Abboud, Nabil Al-Batal and Abdul Nabi Isstaif of Damascus University for inspiring conversations and sharing resources. Naila El Atrash transformed my visit into a marvelous experience: I will never forget witnessing the shooting of a historical film, featuring Khaled Taja and Basel Khayat, in a setting outside the ruins of Tadmor. My stay in Leipzig made me realize that I had to end my study with the year 1989; there I am indebted to Claus Altmayer, Hans-Georg Ebert, Adel Karasholi, Verena Klemm, and Erwin Tschirner for lively exchanges.

My work benefited tremendously from the comments of colleagues and friends who read chapters at various stages of the writing process. I want to thank Philip Armstrong, Andrea Bachner, Marc Baer, Leo Coleman, Dick Davis, Glenn Ehrstine, Bernhard Goldmann, Anna Grotans, Susanne Hafner, Jonathan Hess, David Horn, the late Nick Howe, Julian Anderson, Kader Konuk, Tom Kasulis, Suzanne Marchand, Dan Reff (who was good enough to read every chapter!), Debbie Rosenfeld, Barry Shank, Patricia Sieber, and Etsuyo Yuasa. Frederick Aldama, Snjezana Buzov, Arif Dirlik, Tariq Elseewi, Valentina Glajar, Gregory Jusdanis, Sara Lennox, Morgan Liu, Zaki Al-Maboren, May Mergenthaler, Perry Myers, Manar Omar, Rick Rentschler, Wolfgang G. Schwanitz, Barbara Wolbert, and Joseph Zeidan have been important interlocutors over the years. I also learned much from my former students, especially Erol Boran, Faik Gur, Jarrod Shepherd, and Annett Krause (who also was a fabulous research assistant). Thanks to all of you for sharing your knowledge with me.

I am also indebted to Ellen Bauerle, acquisitions manager, and the staff at the University of Michigan Press for their support, and to Elizabeth Gratch, Natascha Miller, William Heidbreder, Kendra Hovey (who made time for a last-minute round of particularly careful editing), Janice Brill, and the anonymous reviewers of the manuscript for their insightful comments and thoughtful edits.

Research for this study was funded by grants from the Mershon Center at the Ohio State University, the U.S. Department of State, and by several grants and a research leave from the Ohio State University. I am very grateful for having received this support, without which this study would not have been completed. I would also like to acknowledge the financial assistance I received from the College of the Arts and Humanities at the Ohio State University in support of the publication of this book.

My deepest gratitude goes to my daughter Milena, for supporting, inspiring, and challenging me for more than twenty years; she accompanied the genesis of this book almost from the beginning. And to Vicente and Luca Nogueira: I am so glad I found you.

Parts of chapter 2 originally appeared as "Ottoman Shock-and-Awe and the Rise of Protestantism: Luther's Reactions to the Ottoman Invasions of the Early Sixteenth Century," *Reassessing Orientalism in German Studies, Seminar* 41, no. 3, special issue, ed. Friederike Eigler (Summer 2005): 226–45.

Transliterations from Arabic and Turkish follow, with as much consistency as possible, the guidelines adopted by the *International Journal of Middle East Studies.* Diacritics have been omitted.

All translations, unless otherwise indicated, are mine.

Contents

Introduction

> Ideas were like the tides of the sea or the phases of the moon; they came into being, rose, and grew in their proper time, and then ebbed, darkened, and vanished when the great wheel turned. They were temporary dwellings, like tents, and a tent was their proper home.
>
> —Salman Rushdie, *The Enchantress of Florence*[1]

> All social life is essentially *practical*. All mysteries which lead theory to mysticism find their rational solution in human practice and in the comprehension of this practice.
>
> —Karl Marx, *Theses on Feuerbach*[2]

Consider the following snapshots from the history of Germany's interaction with the Middle East:

- Crusaders in the early thirteenth century arrive in the Holy Land surprised to find acculturated European Christians speaking Arabic better than they speak any European tongue.
- In the seventeenth century, as one side effect of Germany's prolonged conflict with the Ottoman Empire, coffee comes to Europe, sobering up the beer-drinking population (on average, Germans drank between one and five liters of beer per day!); perhaps, without this fundamental change German societies would not have been able to industrialize, a process that required alert workers to operate machines.[3]
- In the eighteenth century, even as German states engage in bitter military battles with the Ottoman Empire, their rulers adopt Turkish games, introduce Turkish architectural styles, and enjoy Turkish music.
- During World War I Wilhelmine Germany peddles the idea of a Holy War against the British, French, and Russians to Islamic governments across the Middle East and Asia, and in the post–World War II era,

these initiatives are mirrored in the anti-imperialist foreign policy pursued by East Germany, which works closely at this time with Socialist Arab countries.
- In the last half century the economic, social, political, and cultural histories of Germany and Turkey are so closely bound up with one another that Germany not only adds three million individuals of Turkish origin to its population, but also imports the whole range of Turkey's internal challenges and opportunities.

How do these five snapshots illustrating the social, economic, and political dimensions of German–Middle Eastern relations compare to the image of the Middle East as it emerges, for example, in Wolfram von Eschenbach's medieval epic *Parzival,* Daniel Casper von Lohenstein's seventeenth-century tragedy *Ibrahim Bassa,* Gotthold Ephraim Lessing's eighteenth-century play *Nathan der Weise,* Else Lasker-Schüler's early-twentieth-century narrative *Der Prinz von Theben,* and Feridun Zaimoğlu's recent novel *Leyla*? By asking this question, *German Literature on the Middle East* proposes a refined methodology to evaluate the multiple semiotic layers contained in works of literature and other cultural representations and emphasizes the necessity of considering the wide web of political, economic, and social *practices* when engaging in the interpretative process. In this regard this study asks, what is the place of the literary in light of recent debates over the significance of *practice theory* for scholars in the humanities and social sciences? How can we, as literary scholars, make good use of the models that have been developed in response to the discontent with the determinism of the linguistic turn?[4]

Over the last decade, this frustration with the determinism of the linguistic turn has been articulated in various disciplines and has produced a rich scholarship emphasizing the importance of agency, subjectivity, affect, the body, performance, historical change, and experience. The main charge is that the determinism inherent to the notion of the linguistic construction of the world does not take into account bodily and material practices. The support for practice theory comes from different disciplines: scholars such as the anthropologist Sherry Ortner, the historian William Sewell, and the sociologist Andreas Reckwitz, among others, convincingly show that considering practices significantly enhances our understanding of how human beings operate, create meaning and, through their actions, affect semiotic orders. Sherry Ortner's notion of the "loosely structured actor," for example, illuminates spaces for agency and subjectivity outside of the restrictive conventions of discourse and *habitus.*[5] William Sewell has taken on the question of practice from a different angle and argues that notions of "culture as a system of symbols and meanings" and notions of "culture as practice" are not incompatible.[6] Sewell states that "to engage in cultural practice means to utilize existing cultural symbols to accomplish some end. . . . It [culture] is . . . the semiotic dimension of human social practice in general."[7] Sewell, however, argues that "culture has a semiotic structuring principle that is different from the political, economic, or geographical structuring principles that also inform practice" and thereby makes a distinction to which I do not subscribe.[8] *German Literature on the Middle East* extends Sewell's definition of culture to include all forms of human practice. In this regard, the model of practice theory as outlined by Andreas Reckwitz seems most suited to anchor the approach I pursue in my study. Reckwitz defines practice theory as one of four types of cultural theory, the other three being mentalism, textualism, and intersubjectivism. The four cultural theories have in common that they explain and understand "actions by reconstructing the symbolic structures of knowledge which enable and constrain the agents to interpret the world according to certain forms, and to behave in corresponding ways."[9] Practice theory retains the relevance of the semiotic approach to culture, but shifts away from a Saussurean understanding of language to one informed by, among others, the ideas of Ludwig Wittgenstein who emphasized the importance of practice for establishing meaning.[10]

In explaining the merits of practice theory, Reckwitz draws on the work of, among others, Pierre Bourdieu, Anthony Giddens, the late Michel Foucault, Harold Garfinkel, Judith Butler, Bruno Latour, Charles Taylor, and Theodore Schatzki. Reckwitz emphasizes the importance of the body, the agent/individual, routinization, and the material for cultural analysis, and argues that "practice theory 'decentres' mind, texts, and conversation."[11] In this view "discourse and language lose their omnipotent status. Discursive practices are one type of practices among others."[12] This understanding of discourses is related to an increased recourse to the body and materiality: "A discursive practice also contains bodily patterns, routinized mental activities—forms of understanding, know-how (here including grammar and pragmatic rules of use), and motivation—and above all, objects (from sounds to computers) that are linked to each other."[13] Consequently, practice theory "shifts bodily movements, things, practical knowledge and routine to the centre of its vocabulary."[14]

Literary scholars, including many in the field of postcolonial studies, have been hesitant to absorb these discussions and remain largely committed to what Reckwitz calls "textualism." Perhaps this is understandable in light of the currency literature and language disciplines gained as a result of the linguistic turn. In particular, the centrality of the concept of "discourse" and the presumed ability of texts to influence political, social, and economic action gave literary studies an increased relevance. Following the publication of Edward Said's study *Orientalism* in 1978, the central claim uniting literary studies associated with postcolonial theory has been a belief that literary and other cultural representations not only reflect but also significantly contribute to engendering oppressive structures, such as imperialism. Connected to this understanding of the role played by literary and other textual discourses is the idea that debunking the ideological dimensions of culture can lead to political and social change. As Teun A. van Dijk states in his introduction to the five-volume *Discourse Studies,* "It has become widely accepted that discourse is profoundly embedded in society and culture, and hence, closely related also to all forms of power, power abuse, and social inequality."[15] The goal of critical discourse studies has therefore become to reveal the oppressive structures of cultural discourses and to raise awareness of the power dynamics inherent in the multifaceted manifestations of language.

Yet the focus on the analysis of discourses undertaken by scholars located in literature and culture departments has not gone without critique. As Achille Mbembe points out, "On the pretext of avoiding single-factor explanations of domination, these disciplines have reduced the complex phenomena of the state and power to 'discourses' and 'representations,' forgetting that discourses and representations have materiality."[16] Scholars studying textual and other cultural representations indeed often neglect to explore the specific relationship of these textual discourses to social, political, and economic processes, and to materiality. As a result, a form of idealism—in this case a belief in the power of ideas and beliefs to structure political, economic, and social action—has emerged, primarily in U.S. humanities-based disciplines. Clearly, this turn to the realm of ideas is also connected to the decline of materialist approaches to understanding society, a decline that became more widespread after the fall of Communism in the 1980s and the dramatic transformations of global capitalism that followed. William Sewell links the paradigm shifts in history and other disciplines to the "fundamental transformations of the social forms of world capitalism."[17] While some academic groups, such as the South Asian Subaltern Studies Collective and scholars identified with Latin American subaltern studies, have long insisted that we pay attention to material conditions and practices, the paradigm that became dominant, particularly in U.S. literature and culture departments, has largely omitted these factors.[18]

This rise of idealism in academia is partly rooted in a selective and incoherent reception of aspects of the work of Michel Foucault and other cultural theorists, such as Pierre Bourdieu and Michel de Certeau, and in a related specific use of the concept of "discourse."[19] In the case of Foucault, the incoherence results partially from the fact that Foucault refined his understanding of the idea of discourse over time, although it can be argued that he consistently encouraged the careful exploration of the relationship of textual discourses to social, economic, and political practices in their historical specificity. Initially, Foucault's work is premised on a distinction between the realm of discourse and areas outside of the discursive realm. At the end of *The Archaeology of Knowledge* (*L'Archéologie du Savoir,* 1969) Foucault states, "Discourse is not life: its time is not your time; in it, you will not be reconciled to death; you may have killed God beneath the weight of all that you have said; but don't imagine that, with all that you are saying, you will make a man that will live longer than he."[20]

In his subsequent works, especially *Discipline and Punish* (*Surveiller et punir,* 1975) and the first volume of *The History of Sexuality* (*Histoire de la sexualité,* vol. 1, *La volonté de savoir,* 1976), Foucault increasingly explores "the role of nondiscursive practices."[21] He expands on the notion of discourse by exploring its connectivity to power and knowledge, which entails a more careful understanding of the relationship between discourses and the economic, social, and political spheres. Throughout his work Foucault's case studies, however imperfect they may be, identify specific historical moments, consider economic conditions, and strive to arrive at an understanding of the complexity of how power works through the interplay of institutions, discursive structures, and political, social, and economic processes. Foucault makes a distinction between discursive and nondiscursive contexts, such as "institutions, social relations, economic and political conjuncture."[22] *The History of Sexuality,* for example, reflects the understanding of the complex relationship between discourses and practices that led to Foucault's rejection of the "repressive hypothesis." Foucault's later work, especially *The Care of the Self* (*Histoire de la sexualité,* vol. 3, *Le souci de soi,* 1984), turns to the role of human agency and subjectivity, but this dimension of his work, and Foucault's development in general, is often not considered in analyses that draw on his work.

As a result, and despite the fact that Foucault asks us to pay attention to the tension between textual discourses and nondiscursive practices, the notion of discourse has led to widely different uses of the concept across the disciplines. Sara Mills writes that "Foucault has often been interpreted as saying that there is no non-discursive realm, that everything is constructed and apprehended through discourse." She argues that "Foucault is not denying that there are physical objects in the world and he is not suggesting that there is nothing but discourse, but what he is stating is that we can only think about and experience material objects and the world as a whole through discourse and the structures it imposes on our thinking."[23] Nevertheless, one understanding of especially Foucault's "middle period" writings has led scholars to extend the concept of discourse to include a wide array of practices *beyond* the realm of the linguistic. David Howarth and Yannis Stavrakakis write:

> We take *discourse* or *discourses* to refer to systems of meaningful practices that form the identities of subjects and objects. . . . Discourse theorists . . . affirm the discursive character of all social practices and objects, and reject the idea that ideological practices simply constitute one area or "region" of social relations. Thus, for instance, the distinctions between political, economic and ideological practices are pragmatic and analytical, and strictly internal to the category of discourse.[24]

The expanded definition of discourse proposed by Howarth and Stavrakakis may be interpreted as formulating a semiotic approach to understanding society, but it collapses systems of symbols and meaning and various practices, which, in my view, proves to be an impediment to, rather than a vehicle for, furthering cultural analysis. Here their concept of discourse becomes inclusive and deterministic to the degree that it seems to encompass everything; indeed, the expanded definition of the concept renders it practically meaningless. Alternately, scholars who study primarily literary and other textual discourses often believe in an inherent correspondence between the trajectory of textual discourses and social, economic, and political practices. Generally, the specific historical and geopolitical context relevant to a work of fiction, for example, is assumed to be known. Edward Said, for instance, calls Orientalism "an imperialist tradition" but does not provide his readers with evidence about the workings of imperialism; the reader is expected to know just how European political and economic intervention into, for example, nineteenth-century Egypt took place.[25] Assuming Europe's essential "positional superiority" over the Middle East resulted in another conjecture, namely, the supposed concurrence of textual discourses and social, political, and economic practices.[26] These assumptions have led to an omission of key factors that are relevant to understanding, for example, the colonization of nineteenth-century Egypt, such as various actions of the Ottoman Empire, international debt politics, the modernization plans of the local elites, and the specific infrastructure and raw material situation of the country.[27]

The dilemma inherent to this approach has been acknowledged by critics for quite a while.[28] In fact, Edward Said himself refined his approach in *Cul-*

ture and Imperialism and numerous essays.[29] He went even further when, in 1997, he distanced himself from the field of postcolonial studies because of its disregard of the persistence of political and economic forms of oppression.[30] Of course, in order to do justice to the development of the field, we have to take the historical moment of *Orientalism* into account. In 1978 Said was making a provocative statement when he distinguished between "pure and political knowledge": "I believe it needs to be made clear about cultural discourse and exchange within a culture that what is commonly circulated by it is not 'truth' but representations."[31] In this regard we need to recognize the obstacles Said and other scholars, such as those identified with New Historicism, were facing when they began to expand the notion of textuality and to explore the active role of literature in shaping historical processes. Thus, not only literature and philosophical treatises but also texts such as legal documents, advertisements, and political policy statements, particularly in their interrelatedness, became objects of interpretive study. Extending the semiotic analysis of the textual to include visual representations and other forms of cultural expression, such as music and dance, was a logical next step. These scholars succeeded in raising consciousness about the role of textual discursivity and broadening our understanding of the role of cultural representations, but they neglected to explore the complex and often conflicting relationships between the wide range of social, economic, and political practices on the one hand and textual and other cultural representations on the other hand.

It is at this juncture that *German Literature on the Middle East* makes its intervention. Juxtaposing literary and related textual practices to social, political, and economic practices and materiality does not indicate a desire for a naive realism. Rather, all practices and their engagement of material objects call for interpretation. This approach was already established by Max Weber in the early 1900s, notably in *Economy and Society: An Outline of Interpretive Sociology,* which proposed categories useful to the interpretation of social and economic action.[32] Economic, social, and political practices thus emerge as meaningful and in need of interpretation, just as do literary texts (textual practices) and other cultural representations to which they may or may not be related. The occurrence of a death or a journey undertaken to sell goods may only be known to us through a textual document, but the text is not the death or the journey, and we may understand the action and the discursive statement about the action separately, all the while attempting to acknowledge self-reflexively the discursive boundedness of our own perception of the world. As Theo van Leeuwen writes, "It is important to stress the difference between social practices and representations of social practices. It seems obvious, yet the difference is often glossed over."[33] Acknowledging these distinctions is paramount to practice theory. Reckwitz and other scholars, including cognitive scientists, show convincingly that our perception of the world is determined not only by discourse, but also by the body, affect, and material conditions.[34] Already in 1972 Pierre Bourdieu warned of the pitfalls inherent in "reduc[ing] all social relations to communicative relations and, more precisely, to decoding operations."[35]

Linguists, of course, have also contributed to refining our understanding of the role of language. As John J. Gumperz and Stephen C. Levinson state, "The kind of contextual information that is actually needed [for the understanding of an utterance] turns out to be deeply embedded in practices of speaking, the local conduct of social life, and the social distribution of shared understandings."[36] Clifford Geertz addresses this necessity of considering contextual information when he points out that "code does not determine conduct."[37] In a similar vein, scholars in various disciplines have questioned the dominance of text-centered analyses for quite some time. In the field of religious studies, for example, Thomas P. Kasulis has argued against disconnecting the study of beliefs from the study of practices.[38] In addition, scholars have insisted on the significance of the material world for the development of human consciousness. From the field of cultural studies, Brian Rotman's work shows that understanding the material world's impact on human thought is vital. He writes that "human beings are 'natural born cyborgs'; the 'human' has from the beginning of the species been a three-way hybrid, a bio-cultural-technological amalgam: the 'human mind'—its subjectivities, affects, agency, and forms of consciousness—having been put into form by a succession of physical and cognitive technologies at its disposal."[39] While some studies, such as Tom Lutz's *American Nervousness 1903: An Anecdotal History* (1991) and Daniel T. Reff's *Plagues, Priests, Demons: Sacred Narratives and the Rise of Christianity in the Old World and the New* (2005), have presented innovative models of analysis by drawing on knowledge from different disciplines to sketch the relationship of textual discursivity to political, scientific, and economic practices and materiality, these types of analysis seem to have received limited reception by literary scholars.[40]

The concern regarding the lack of a broader knowledge base to evaluate literary texts motivated Gayatri Chakravorty Spivak to suggest invigorating the field of comparative literature by "consider[ing] the resources of Area Studies."[41] Similar concerns have arisen also in the broader fields of cultural studies and cultural history. In *A Crooked Line,* his account of the last forty years of theoretical and methodological debates in the field of history, Geoff

Eley rightly concludes that "between social history and cultural history, there is really no need to choose."[42] Gabrielle Spiegel says in her commentary on Eley's study that "the book takes a stand among current demands to recuperate the material, in effect, the social, as part and parcel of a belief in the reality and socially significant presence of the past, both in the past and in the present."[43] In fact, with practice theory we are urged to understand the social as located in cultural practices, as it attempts to avoid the trap of linguistic determinism and textualism by opening the field to consider a wider universe of practices in order to arrive at a more complete understanding of cultural processes. Practice theory thus promises new avenues for understanding literary texts.

German Literature on the Middle East brings the debates over the relevance of practices to the study of literature. My case study in this regard is the German literary discourse on the Middle East. Before I turn to the study's outline, it is worthwhile to take stock of how scholars in German studies have responded to Said's *Orientalism,* which remains the point of reference for studies conducted in a wide range of fields. Scholars have both worked within the parameters of Said's paradigm and also expanded and challenged it. As my study draws heavily on the works of these scholars, I will only give a brief overview at this point, categorizing the work that has been done in order to highlight specific accomplishments.[44] Contributions were made primarily in the following areas:

1. Most directly linked to the publication of *Orientalism* are studies on German Orientalist scholarship. In *Orientalism,* Said leveled the charge that the discipline in general is politically corrupt and contributed to establishing imperial and colonial rule in the Middle East. Focusing mostly on French and British scholars, he exempted German Orientalists from the assumed complicity with the imperial project.[45] Several German Arabists and Islamists, such as Tilman Nagel, joined the discussion by defending their disciplines; earlier scholars, such as Rudi Paret, had taken the same stance already in the 1960s, when these charges were first made.[46] Robert Irwin's study, though not exclusively focused on the German tradition, also belongs in the "defensive" camp.[47] For other scholars, such as Holger Preissler, Gernot Rotter, and Ludmila Hanisch, Said's theses inspired investigations of the history of the discipline, without necessarily probing its ideological and political dimensions.[48]

   Clearly in dialogue with Said, however, are analyses by Suzanne Marchand, Ursula Wokoeck, Sabine Mangold, Tuska Benes, Alexander Haridi, and Ekkehard Ellinger.[49] Kai Hafez explored the development of scholarship on the Middle East under the ideological constraints academics faced in the GDR.[50] In addition, recent studies that investigate the role of German Orientalists and other scholars in Turkey (Arnold Reisman, Kader Konuk),[51] show that institutional constraints, material conditions, domestic and international political developments, and a wide range of ideologies (including racism, Christianity, nationalism, civilizationism, communism, and modernizationism on the one end, and universalism and multiculturalism on the other end) structured the work of German Orientalists. While it is possible that the knowledge they produced was appropriated for political and economic purposes at any time, the actual direct involvement of academics in imperial and nation-state politics began, in some cases, toward the end of the nineteenth century. It is noteworthy that Arab-language scholarship tends to absolve German Orientalists and German-language writers from the accusations associated with the Orientalism paradigm and rather celebrates German scholarship and the German literary tradition (ʻAwni ʻAbd al-Raʼuf and Iman al-Saʻid Jalal; Adnan Rashid).[52]

2. A second group of studies focused primarily on literature and its relation to colonialism and imperialism, especially in the aftermath of Said's publications and the emergence of the field of postcolonial studies. Some scholars, such as Andrea Fuchs-Sumiyoshi, attempted to refute Said; others used his framework to illustrate the connections between literary works and the colonial and imperial contexts (W. Daniel Wilson, Nina Berman, Reika Ebert).[53] Andrea Polaschegg's more recent study engages with Said but leaves his theoretical and methodological framework behind. While the study succeeds in assessing an extensive archive of relevant sources, it consists, as the author herself states, mostly of "prolegomena for a history of German Orientalism."[54] Mirjam Weber's study on Orientalism in Goethe's and Heine's poetry emphasizes that the creative engagement with the Orient neither only reproduces nor mirrors existing images, but results in innovation.[55] Some scholars picked up the cue from the Orientalism debate but focused on domestic issues, such as nationalism and gender relations (Todd Kontje, Robert C. Holub, Cornelia Kleinlogel).[56] A number of analyses by, for example, Arlene Teraoka, Leslie Adelson, Nazire Akbulut, Ishrak Kamaluldin, Azade Seyhan, Uta Aifan, Manar Omar, Tom Cheesman, and B. Venkat Mani draw, in one way or another, on the Orientalism paradigm to understand domestic and

transnational power relations, as they emerge in literary texts composed by post–World War II minority and majority authors.[57] Even though Mounir Fendri's 1980 study on Heinrich Heine does not take recourse to Said's paradigm it illustrates that Heine engaged Orientalist topics to define his position in Germany, an aspect also present in the work of Else Lasker-Schüler and other German-Jewish writers and intellectuals (Donna K. Heizer, Nina Berman, Noah Isenberg).[58] Several anthologies and special issues devoted to literary and cultural images of the Middle East include contributions that fall into the various approaches outlined here.[59] In toto, scholarship in this area has attempted to demonstrate (1), that a connection does indeed exist between German literary texts and actual power relations between Germany/Europe and the Middle East, or between majority Germans and minority groups of Middle Eastern descent; and (2), that literary representations signify primarily in their domestic dimension.

3. Related to the second group are analyses that explore German nonliterary representations of the Middle East, especially in the visual arts, film, travel literature, and other nonfiction texts (e.g., Marie Elisabeth Pape, Deniz Göktürk, Almut Höfert, Eugene Sensening-Dabbous, Susan R. Boettcher). Some of these studies refer to the *Orientalism* debate directly, others engage with it indirectly by highlighting the political dimension of cultural representations.[60]
4. A fourth group of studies investigates the nature and implications of the media's image of the Middle East. These studies, including analyses by Sonja Schultheiß-Heinz, Astrib Hub, Samir Aly, and Kai Hafez, by definition illustrate the close relationship between the coverage of actual events and German ideologies.[61]
5. Historians and political scientists, directly and indirectly, contributed to the *Orientalism* debate by focusing on German and Habsburg imperialism, various dimensions of domestic and foreign policies of the Ottoman Empire and other Middle Eastern states, and post–World War II developments. Among the substantive list of studies are works by Francis R. Nicosia, Jonathan S. McMurray, Jennifer Jenkins, Gottfried Hagen, Wolfgang G. Schwanitz, Thomas L. Hughes, Tilman Lüdke, Malte Fuhrmann, Margaret L. Anderson, 'Abd al-Ra'uf Sinnu, Paula Sutter Fichtner, and Carole Fink.[62] In addition, studies by historians and social scientists of the Middle East, such as Taner Akçam, Marc David Baer, Mustafa Aksakal, and M. Şükrü Hanioğlu, are particularly relevant in this regard.[63]

6. Several studies and anthologies focused on German attitudes toward Islam (e.g., Abdoldjavad Falaturi, Detlef Thofern, Werner Ruf, Susan L. Boettcher, Silvia Horsch, Nina Berman, Iman Attia). Here, the results reveal perhaps the most consistent picture, namely, that ignorance about Islam structured German views of the Middle East negatively from the Middle Ages to the present.[64]
7. Finally, studies addressing the relationship between German Jews and Orientalism highlighted dimensions that are often ignored in the *Orientalism* debate, in spite of the fact that Said identified antisemitism as "the secret sharer" of Orientalism.[65] Susannah Heschel and Jonathan Hess assessed the political significance of writings by Jewish Orientalist scholars not only for the development of German Orientalist sciences, but also with regard to the position of the Jewish minority in Germany more broadly.[66] A recent anthology illuminates the significance of Jewish scholarship for critical Koranic studies.[67] The works of Reisman and Konuk on the emigration of German intellectuals to Turkey, which comprised a large number of Jewish scholars, also belong to this group of studies.

As this brief overview demonstrates, German scholarship made a unique contribution to the *Orientalism* debate by working within Said's model, but also by expanding and transcending it. Scholars explored territories ignored or not addressed in the 1978 publication, including the interaction between the Ottoman Empire and German-speaking countries, the tremendous impact of Christianity on scholarship as well as imperial developments, the active roles played by German Jews in German–Middle Eastern matters, various domestic dimensions of literary and cultural representations, and the ties between German Orientalist scholars and the imperial German state. When considered collectively, these contributions by scholars from different disciplines also shed light on the relationship between various social, economic, and political practices and material aspects on the one hand, and textual and other representational practices on the other hand. That is, this body of scholarship allows us to modify the Orientalism paradigm by considering the relationship between these different kinds of practices that are shaped by a broad range of ideas and textual discourses but that also emerge from factors such as epidemics, war, specific technologies, commodities, and institutions.

My study thus draws on and adds to this body of scholarship through an evaluation of the *longue durée* of German Orientalism and by providing a comparative dimension, which yields a number of original insights. My study shows that literary and related nonfiction texts on the Middle East may but do not *necessarily* tell us much about causality, about the *origin and course* of social, political, and economic events. Discriminating between textual discourses and nontextual practices is essential to my approach. The assessment of the tension between discourse and practice remains bound to the realm of the textual, as practice is accessible to us only through textual representation. But texts documenting practices and material reality (such as information regarding the number of pilgrims, trade statistics, legal treatises and their execution, data on intermarriage, and immigration data) need to be juxtaposed with autobiographical accounts of pilgrimages, eyewitness reports on military confrontations, and fictional accounts related to historical events. Of course, data about practices and material reality may be unreliable, even fabricated, and need to be interpreted. Our grasp of complexity is dependent on the accuracy and comprehensiveness of our data, and on our ability to interpret it.

Building on the rich scholarship of the past two decades, my study outlines the complex web of factors relevant to understanding Germany's relationship to the Middle East. This complexity of modes of identification and ideologies that inform literary and other textual representations (such as religion, local belonging, class, gender, ethnicity, and age), understood in combination with political, economic, and social factors, troubles the presumed semiotic unit expressed by the Orientalism paradigm. As stated earlier, I do not intend to promote a naive realism by juxtaposing literary representations to "reality." Rather, I argue for putting into dialogue cultural, social, political, and economic data, all of which need to be interpreted. This extended study of German literary discourses on the Middle East, seen in their relationship to other cultural representations and a wide range of social, political, and economic practices, allows me to identify several key aspects of German-Middle Eastern relations:

Shared History. Rather than presenting a history of divisions, my study highlights a history of contact and exchange between Europe and the Middle East/North Africa. Interestingly, this shared history comes to the fore most clearly when we consider practices such as pilgrimage, conversion, trade, intermarriage, migrations, and war. Even war entails interaction beyond the hostilities. Examples include prisoner taking and exchange, collaboration (as Ian Almond has shown in *Two Faiths, One Banner*), and the establishment of new boundaries through territorial annexations that lead to new shared living spaces.[68] The literary imagination and other areas of cultural production (e.g., architecture, music, painting) may or may not reflect these practices of interaction and exchange. In this regard, *German Literature on the Middle East* contributes to the growing number of scholarly works that emphasize aspects of "coexistence" and "contact" in their analyses of European–Middle Eastern history.[69]

Much of this shared history is preserved in literary texts, but the lack of knowledge about the history of contact impedes a more nuanced comprehension of the literary material. The nobility of Wolfram von Eschenbach's imaginary knight Feirefiz (his speckled body a metaphor for his mixed European-African parentage) tells us that Europeans clearly knew about the achievements and grandeur of Arab chivalric culture. Yet, the accepted usage of the term *noble heathen* downplays this awareness and relegates the figure to the realm of pure imagination. In fact, however, the noble heathen corresponds to facets of reality just as much as does the image of the brutal Turkish warrior of the sixteenth and seventeenth centuries.

Intra-European Rivalries. Related to this aspect of circulating cultural material is the fact that European political and economic relations with the Middle East were significantly and perhaps decisively determined by intra-European strife and competition, rather than by actual interactions with Middle Eastern states. Hence, it was Frederick II's struggle with the pope that spurred his refusal to participate in an early thirteenth-century crusade. Likewise, the French alliance with the Ottomans in 1535 was carried out in defiance of their German competitors; Venice constantly shifted alliances to secure its interests; and Ottoman/Turkish alliances with German powers continue to impact intra-European strife to this day. Seen in light of these events and power constellations, the idea of a seemingly monolithic Europe is untenable.

Heterogeneity of Discourse and Interests of Social Groups. The study of literary discourses in their larger historical context shows that individual literary texts and sometimes entire textual genres correspond to the interests of specific social groups. With the constant waxing and waning of politically powerful groups, literary and cultural discourses prove to encompass the entire range of special interests; rarely do we find coherence with regard to the sum of the textual material or with regard to the actions of possible actors at any one time. Thus, whether a discourse becomes hegemonic depends on specific and ever-shifting power constellations. In this regard, my study confirms findings of George Steinmetz's intriguing study, *The Devil's Handwriting,* about the relationship between precolonial ethnography and colonial native policy.[70]

Oppressive Hypothesis. Analogous to Foucault's critique of what he termed the "repressive hypothesis," the long-term interdisciplinary study of German discourses on the Middle East reveals that the presence of oppressive discourses does not necessarily indicate oppressive action—and that the opposite is also true: the absence of oppressive discourses and the presence of discourses of tolerance and acceptance does not necessarily translate into emancipatory practices. This aspect has mostly to do with the fact that political power often acts in ways that do not correspond with dominant opinion. Frederick II's arrangement with Sultan al-Kamil, *Turcomania* in Saxony at a time of still intense conflict with the Ottomans, and the supposed tolerance of contemporary liberal Germans who meanwhile deny Muslim residents of Germany their basic civil rights all exemplify this point.

The next points relate more specifically to the status of literature:

Translation, Archive, and Politics. Much of the material that makes up the German literary discourse on the Middle East came into German culture via translation from other European languages. The plots of many medieval epics, such as the *Rolandslied* and *Parzival,* were adopted and adapted by German writers via translation from the French language, just like much of the material for Baroque plays and novels, Enlightenment narratives, and nineteenth-century poetry came into German from other languages. Although German translators and rewriters often changed the material in decisive ways, many times they did not substantively alter the basic messages of the source text. In spite of this broadly shared literary archive, however, the political and economic relationships of individual European societies to the Middle East were distinct. This simple insight fundamentally challenges Said's claim regarding the interrelatedness of cultural discourses and political-economic developments.

Most of my analysis focuses on German cultural material, but the connections established here highlight just how crucial the field of translation studies is to investigations of national, transnational, and intercultural discourses. How can we make a claim about a distinctly "national" imaginary when much of the literary and cultural material in Europe is shared? I envision subsequent studies that will complete the unfulfilled promises of this study by shedding light on aspects that I am unable to pursue here in depth. Comparative studies of German and French sources in any of the periods studied here, for example, will allow us to arrive at a better understanding of how material that is circulated in translation corresponds to particular national imaginations and practices. These comparative studies would effectively, in Ute Frevert's words, "Europeanize" German, French, and other histories.[71] Conceived even more broadly, comparative studies will enable us to develop a global consciousness. As Emily Apter suggests, "A new comparative literature, with the revalued labor of the translator placed center stage, expands centripetally toward a genuinely planetary criticism."[72]

Large gaps exist in European studies because of the predominant focus on English, French, Spanish, Italian, and German material, and so here, too, is an area that deserves scholarly attention. I was unable to read sources that exist, for example, in Croatian, Hungarian, and Polish, yet repeatedly stumbled across material that had first been published in these and other languages but that has not been factored into the writing of European histories. Spivak's plea for paying attention to the relevance of "the languages of the Southern Hemisphere" easily applies to the minor languages of Europe as well.[73]

Memory. Another aspect that emerges in my study is the importance of understanding cultural and collective memory, especially as it develops over centuries. How is it possible, for example, that imagery that was largely dormant since the early modern period reemerged so readily in the late twentieth century? The archive of German images about the Middle East is best understood as a palimpsest, in which cultural and literary periods form in layers, with subsequent periods having access to the imagery of earlier periods. From the Middle Ages to our contemporary period German culture harbored imagery that corresponded to major belief systems of respective time periods. Religion, culture, universal humanism, civilization, nation, race, and modernity informed the ideological content of the imagery. Images conceived in earlier periods later reappeared, taking on new meanings but also drawing on their established potential as signifiers. The persistence of a specific archive of images—from religious enemy to noble heathen, from debauched, violent, and hypersexed Arab to wise and amiable Oriental—resonates with Jan Assmann's ideas regarding cultural memory. He writes that cultural memory "exists not only in us and in others who remember, but also in things, such as texts, images, and practices. . . . [Cultural memory is] that tradition in us, those texts, images, and rites, all of which ossified through a process lasting generations, centuries, even millennia, and which shape our consciousness of time and history, our view of ourselves and the world."[74] The archive of German Oriental imagery, largely "ossified" in the sense of Assmann's definition, remains accessible over time. The quality of the images' durability can be explained by the fact that they are displaced from their original historical context, with their anachronistic quality creating tensions. But this archive is not "just there"; rather, it functions as a repertory, allowing for variation in the process of replaying images. This process corresponds to Maurice Halbwachs's ideas regarding "collective memory":

> We preserve memories of each epoch in our lives, and these are continually reproduced; through them, as by a continual relationship, a sense of

> our identity is perpetuated. But precisely because these memories are repetitions, because they are successively engaged in very different systems of notions, at different periods of our lives, they have lost the form and the appearance they once had.[75]

What Halbwachs suggests here for the process of individual and collective remembering may be extended to cultural remembrance. Germany's cultural memory of its greater than thousand-year history with the Middle East has resulted in a vast repertory of images, partially ossified in Assmann's sense, and perpetually reproducible and changeable, as Halbwachs suggests. The conclusion will return to this question by considering insights from cognitive neuroscience.

Images of the Self. Interpreting the meaning of Oriental imagery reveals that the Orient is a place of images of the self—the idealized self, utopian self, problematic self—as much as, in Said's view, it is "one of its deepest and most recurring images of the Other."[76] The imagery may present the self in disguise, but it is clearly the self. Wolfram von Eschenbach's Feirefiz is the ideal knight and Sultan Saladin the ideal ruler, just like Ibrahim Bassa is the despot under attack by Enlightenment thought and Hofmannsthal's son of a merchant the decadent fin de siècle aesthete. Consequently, Oriental imagery also needs to be understood as a vehicle that can be used to express the changing issues of German societies in particular historical moments.

Occidentalism and Orientalism of the East. Another aspect that deserves fuller attention in future works is the Occidentalism of the East. Middle Eastern culture produced its own discourse on the West, from the historians of the Crusades to the intellectuals of the nineteenth and twentieth centuries. This discourse continues to function in much the same way that the European discourse on the Middle East and Islam operates. And just as the European discourse on the Middle East means different things depending on the actual power relations that exist at a given point in time, the Middle Eastern discourse cannot be fully understood without considering these same power relations.[77] In addition, and this may be surprising, much of the European imagery of the Orient that is most closely associated with the Orientalism paradigm—images of violence and sexuality, of luxury and asceticism—has roots in the Middle East's very own Orientalism: the stories of Sinbad the Sailor's journeys to unknown exotic places or the Islamic prejudice against polytheistic and nonurban cultures, among other topoi, emerge as a repository for European fantasies about the East. Other stories have been shared for centuries, such as the legends around Alexander the Great and various religious traditions. In more than one way imagination and social contact are linked in the common history of Europe and the Middle East.

A few remarks about key terms are in order. *Germany* is a shifting signifier, referring to a range of empires and states over a thousand-year period. The focus on "Germany" is legitimated through a textual archive that exists in the German language, beginning here with Middle High German texts from the middle of the eleventh century. This archive of literary texts and other writings in the German language was written and read by people who often valued their regional or religious identity more than belonging to an empire or nation-state, and often would not have self-identified as "Germans." Because a German nation-state came into being for the first time only in 1871, for most of the period being investigated here, "Germany" existed in the form of the Holy Roman Empire and the Habsburg Empire. This study pays little attention to Switzerland as a political entity but includes writings by Swiss authors when relevant.

Just like *Germany* is more of a heuristic device than a stable signifier, the term *Middle East* does not refer to a clearly identifiable territory or political constellation. The Middle East, as referred to in this study, includes what is today known as the MENA region, the areas of the Middle East and North Africa. For the period under discussion this includes some but not all of the territories of the ʻAbbasid Empire and the Ottoman Empire (and later the Republic of Turkey, whose geopolitical belonging has been contested for quite some time). The Middle East, in the Western understanding of the term, includes areas inhabited by Arabic-, Persian-, Turkish-, and Hebrew-speaking peoples and by peoples speaking lesser-known languages, such as Armenian. Various European countries employ different terms to refer to the regions, and they do not correspond: the Middle East, as understood in this study, includes areas described by the German terms *Naher Osten* and *Nordafrika.* In the more recent period, and clearly in response to colonial and postcolonial history, *Middle East* (al-Sharq al-Awsat) has become a term used also for self-identification by the people of the region. Also, Ottoman society was multiethnic and multireligious; neither the term *Muslim* nor *Turkish* appropriately describes it. In the following discussion I use the words *Turk* and *Turkish* whenever they are employed in the sources I discuss, but also alternate with *Ottoman.* The status of the term *Istanbul* is also complex; I use *Constantinople* for the period before 1453, and *Istanbul* afterward, even though the former term and many others were used simultaneously until 1930.[78]

The individual chapters of this book concentrate on five periods that differ greatly in length, and also differ greatly in terms of distinctive ideological, social, economic, and political factors. Chapter 1 covers the years from 1000 to 1350. Even before the Crusades began, tens of thousands of pilgrims traveled to Palestine each year, and because of their literal interpretation of the Bible, the area's eschatological significance was a tangible reality for medieval Germans. German emperors considered themselves rulers of the Holy Land, not only as Christians, but also as successors to the Roman Empire. During the course of the Crusades, however, German political leaders were increasingly more interested in contemporaneous expansion into eastern European territories, or, like Frederick II, they participated in the Crusades reluctantly and largely for political reasons. Literary texts from the period include examples of explicit propaganda literature and texts that articulate a critique of the Crusades. The reality of intercultural encounters is articulated in epics and poems, German and Arabic travel accounts, and the writings of Arab historians.

Chapter 2 addresses events that took place from about 1350 to 1683, the Second Siege of Vienna. Beginning in the fourteenth century, the Ottoman Empire advanced steadily north- and northwestward into Europe, laying siege to Vienna in 1529 and 1683. The fall of Constantinople in 1453 coincided with the invention of the printing press, and some of the earliest printed materials articulate fears of the invading army. As a result of the encounter with the Ottoman Turks, and in contrast to the primarily religious discourse of the Middle Ages, German representations of the Ottomans (plays, broadsheets, songs, and newspapers reporting events from the battlefront) increasingly included images of cultural difference. The fact that during this period the Ottoman Empire posed an actual threat explains the general absence of positive images in German depictions of the Ottomans; interestingly, many Turkish sources about the conflict echo the German portrayals of military conflict and violence experienced by the civilian population. Concurrently, a deep interest in Ottoman culture, reports about conversions, and developing economic relations coexisted alongside the negative view of the enemy.

Events that occurred between 1683 and 1792, the beginning of the French occupation of Germany, are at the center of chapter 3. The Second Siege of Vienna marks the beginning of the Ottoman Empire's slow but steady loss of control over its European territories. In conjunction with the universalism and humanism of the Enlightenment and the call for social change in Europe, multiple challenges to established power structures (including the Christian church) affected German images of the Turks. The *Turquerie,* or *Turcomania*—an interest in Turkish food, clothing, carpets, and other products—that had first begun in France, reached Prussia and Austria in the late 1760s. The popularity of Middle Eastern sources (*One Thousand and One Nights,* among others) reflects a growing interest in the region, which enabled the founding of Orientalist disciplines. By the end of the eighteenth century new types of "enlightened" Turkish and Arab Muslim characters appeared in German plays, operas, and other writings. This new climate facilitated the beginning of Prussian-Ottoman (and later German-Turkish) cooperation, which was paralleled by shifts in French and British relations with the Middle East, among others.

Chapter 4 reviews the events from the end of the eighteenth century to 1945. Although German states did not emerge as colonial powers in North Africa and the Middle East, Habsburgs and Prussians were active in the areas of infrastructure development, banking, and military advising (and even military intervention in a few instances). Economic, military, and political developments were paralleled by an expanded interest in the Middle East by Orientalist scholars, painters, writers, and, later, filmmakers. German Jews were concurrently identified as the internal Oriental other. Writings that conveyed a programmatically positive image of the Orient (e.g., anthroposophy and cultural Zionism) departed from articulations inspired by a sense of German racial superiority, modernization, and progress. This particular tradition of positive identification with the Middle East/Orient—from Wolfram to Goethe, Buber, Steiner, and Hesse—appears to have no equivalent in French or British culture. By considering the actions and writings of Middle Eastern intellectuals and elites, I acknowledge their critical stance toward European domination of the Middle East but also the existence of a dialogue on modernization.

Chapter 5 discusses the period from the end of World War II until 1989. Throughout the postwar era, East and West Germany, Austria, and Switzerland entertained strong economic and political relations with Israel and other Middle Eastern countries. Noteworthy are the distinct political relations that East and West Germany developed with Middle Eastern states and the history of immigration. The GDR established close alliances with Socialist Arab countries, whereas the FRG emerged as a partner to Israel. These interstate relations significantly shaped institutions, media, and cultural representations. The large-scale labor migration changed West Germany in particular; curiously, this important development is largely invisible in highbrow literature produced by writers without immigrant backgrounds. Beliefs established in earlier periods, however, continued to persist. Alongside this mainstream neglect toward the transforming society, literary and other cultural works by authors and artists with immigrant roots altered the cultural landscape in innovative ways.

The concluding pages revisit key findings of the study with regard to the importance of actual intercultural contact; the interdependency of cultural, political, and economic factors; and the role that literary discourses and cultural concepts play in these processes. The concluding section also considers research in cognitive neuroscience that sheds light on patterns relevant to understanding the circulation of cultural memory across time and space. The section ends with an analysis of Zaki Al-Maboren's artwork *Kaaba—Das eckige Haus,* which is interpreted here as a sophisticated commentary on intercultural coexistence.

What my study seeks to accomplish, from the perspective of a literary scholar, is to provide a model for more careful contextualization of literary and other textual discourses. The approach I advocate here raises the question of interdisciplinary competence: To acquire expertise even within one discipline is a challenge, and any steps outside the familiar parameters of disciplinary training may convey an air of transgression. We feel vulnerable when we leave familiar turf, and we are. The potential charge of dilettantism prevents most scholars from exploring the space beyond disciplinary boundaries. But upon leaving familiar territory, we begin to see the limits of disciplinary work. It is with an awareness of the potential and actual weaknesses of this attempt to cover a thousand years of intercultural history that I invite my readers to consider the relationship between Germany and the Middle East in new ways. The role played by textual discursivity in specific historical moments and geopolitical situations does not follow a predictable pattern. This aspect comes to the fore most clearly by way of a long-term and cross-cultural analysis that considers the connections between textual discourses, various practices, and materiality.

The fourteenth-century scholar Ibn Khaldun begins his study of world history by detailing what it takes to write history.

> The (writing of history) requires numerous sources and much varied knowledge. It also requires a good speculative mind and thoroughness, which lead the historian to the truth and keep him from slips and errors. If he trusts historical information in its plain transmitted form and has no clear knowledge of the principles resulting from custom, the fundamental facts of politics, the nature of civilization, or the conditions governing human social organization, and if, furthermore, he does not evaluate remote or ancient material through comparison with near or contemporary material, he often cannot avoid stumbling and slipping and deviating from the path of truth.[79]

As contemporary scholars, we stay away from claiming to write the "truth," feeling more comfortable with Clifford Geertz's notion of "guesses" and "better guesses": "Cultural analysis is (or should be) guessing at meanings, assessing the guesses, and drawing explanatory conclusions from the better guesses, not discovering the Continent of Meaning and mapping out its bodiless landscape. . . . Cultural analysis is intrinsically incomplete."[80] In this spirit I present my (at this point) best guesses at understanding the significance of literary discourses within the context of the long history of Germany's social, political, economic, and material relations to the Middle East.

CHAPTER 1

Pilgrims, Crusaders, Knights, and Settlers (1000–1350)

During the Middle Ages, Europe's relationship to the Middle East was structured fundamentally by the Christian worldview, according to which the Holy Land figured prominently. Geopolitical belonging was clearly not as relevant as religious group identity, and in this regard we need to understand the term *Europe* as a heuristic device that allows us to talk about developments that occurred in a specific geographical space during the Middle Ages and the early modern period. The pivotal importance of religious belonging inspired pilgrimages to Jerusalem from the fourth century onward, and it provided the ideological impetus for the Crusades. Most of Europe, including Germany, shared this preoccupation with the Holy Land, yet different European societies were connected to the Middle East in distinct ways. The Muslim presence in Spain and Sicily; the geographical proximity of southern European states to Muslim territories; the central role played by, for example, merchants from Genoa and Venice in the long-distance trade; and the competition between various European powers are among the many aspects that constitute the complex web of relations between European and Middle Eastern societies. Instances of cross-cultural and interfaith collaboration—in Europe, North Africa, and the Middle East—defied the notion of a strict division between Europe and the Middle East, between Christianity and Islam.

The German view of the Middle East needs to be seen in the context of this web of inner-European and cross-Mediterranean connections. Germany's contact with the Middle East, exemplified first and foremost in its political, economic, and cultural relationship to the Holy Land, was expressed in both religious and secular writings. Because the period predates the arrival of print media, we know very little about the ways in which the issue was debated in popular culture, and only have access to texts composed by a tiny fraction of educated individuals. Whereas most of the religious writings were composed in Latin, the secular writings at the center of our investigation were written in the German language. The views articulated in these German-language writings were often similar to those expressed in other European societies; in fact, much of the material about the Middle East and Islam came into German culture in the form of translations, with German authors modifying the translated material to differing degrees. In spite of the large extent to which particularly the literary archive was shared across Europe, a trend occurred in the later Middle Ages in which German authors of fiction were more critical of the Crusades than writers from other European societies. This critique was expressed through images that rendered German and Middle Eastern societies compatible by envisioning a cross-cultural space defined by shared values and behaviors associated with knighthood and kinship. The cultural critique of the Crusades was reflected in political actions of some German secular rulers and growing disenchantment with holy wars, including those led against Christians within Europe. In addition, the German-language material resonates with evidence of social interaction, of the reception of various aspects of Middle Eastern civilization in German culture, and of exchanges taking place between the two spheres in the realm of material culture. In spite of an increased access to knowledge about Islam and the Middle East, however, a majority of fiction and nonfiction writings did not absorb new knowledge or reflect the many instances of actual contact, and continued to promote clichéd views.

Before the Crusades: Pilgrims, Merchants, *Reconquista*, and Growing Aspirations

In 1064 Bishop Gunther of Bamberg led a group of more than seven thousand pilgrims (by some accounts, as many as twelve thousand) on a pilgrimage to the Holy Land.[1] Significantly fewer returned the following year; the biography *Vita Altmanni* (ca. 1130), written in East Franconian dialect, lamented the stress of the long journey and the substantial loss of life due to disease and skirmishes with Muslims.[2] According to available records, the 1064 pilgrimage was the largest single group of Europeans, most of them German, to travel to Jerusalem, a place that was central to European Christians at the time. But it was just one among countless such groups; during this period, a steady flow of German (and other European) pilgrims moved back and forth between Europe and the Holy Land.

How do we explain the determination with which European Christians embarked on their journeys to Palestine? What was the extent and nature of the interaction between Europe and the Middle East during the period leading up to the Crusades? More specifically, what was Germany's relationship to the region at the time?

Since the third century, the pilgrimage to Jerusalem had been central in the lives of Europeans. The Christianization of the Roman Empire under Constantine the Great had turned Palestine into a Christian area and fostered the establishment of pilgrimage rituals. From the beginning, pilgrims, such as the early fourth-century so-called Bordeaux pilgrim and the nun Egeria, who traveled in the 380s, reported about Jerusalem as "a thoroughly Christian place," leaving out any aspects representing the pre-Christian era.[3] Accounts of these early pilgrimages document the existence and development of a sophisticated network accommodating European Christian travelers.[4] Over time the pilgrimage to Jerusalem was sustained by an elaborate infrastructure that facilitated this early form of mass tourism. In the early phase, pilgrims—who were generally guaranteed the right to shelter, fire, water, and bread—were able to lodge in *xenodochia,* care houses originally donated by bishops and other church dignitaries that emerged in the fourth century and were intended to fulfill multiple functions.[5] In the eleventh and twelfth centuries, when for various social, political, and economic reasons pilgrimages turned into a mass movement, hospices designed especially for pilgrims were founded in many places and along the busiest pilgrimage routes, namely, those leading to Rome, Santiago de Compostela, and Jerusalem.

Over the course of the twelfth century the lodging and provision of pilgrims became increasingly commercialized; whereas in the earlier phase pilgrims often brought their own provisions along with them, they were now able to lodge, eat, and drink in private inns and taverns that were independent from the network of religious institutions.[6] Special guides provided the pilgrims with detailed information regarding routes, inns, restaurants, and visa conditions, even alerting travelers to the avarice of landlords. The legal status of pilgrims was regulated by laws, such as permits granting the right to undertake a pilgrimage, visas for entry into specific territories, laws regarding inheritance in case of death, dress codes, donations, and specific stipulations if the pilgrimage was undertaken as punishment. These various types of regulations often included consideration of the sex and social status of the pilgrim.[7] Pilgrimage in general, and the pilgrimage to Jerusalem in particular, was thus a highly codified and widespread feature of medieval German society. German pilgrims relied on a network of hospices, inns, and restaurants all the way to the Holy Land, and, beginning with the commercialization of pilgrimage traffic, German beer and bread were available in many places between Germany and Palestine.

For medieval Germans the Holy Land was a more significant, and perhaps more "real," place than it is for today's Germans, in spite of the easier access made possible through modern travel and media coverage. At the time the spiritual center of the world was Jerusalem, and biblical history was thought of as world history. The Bible was read as a historical text, and believers understood their lives to be along a time line that began with the creation of the world and would end with the apocalypse, as laid out, for example, in the last chapter of the New Testament, the Revelation of Saint John the Divine. Relevant to the medieval view of history were the teachings of Augustine (354–430). His theory of *aetates mundi* (Ages of the World) divides history into different ages, from Adam to the Flood, from Noah to Abraham, from Abraham to David, from David to the Babylonian exile, and from the Babylonian exile to the birth of Jesus Christ. According to this model, the duration of the sixth age, which began with the birth of Christ, is not known; this age would be followed by the seventh age, the Sabbath, which would then be succeeded by the age of God.[8] Speculation about the actual date of the end of the world was popular during the Middle Ages. Interpretations of the book of Daniel, for example, led Christians to believe in the impending end of the world; the second chapter of that book describes four kingdoms, which are followed by the heavenly kingdom. Medieval (and later) commentary on this passage equated the kingdoms with the reigns of Babylonians, Persians, Greeks, and Romans and concluded that the end of the world was near. Eschatological ideas, in fact, both fears and hopes, about the impending end of the world were widespread among people of different social standing.[9] Just like space was conceived as holy space, time was experienced as religious time.[10] Even if interpretations of biblical history did not result in apocalyptic visions, medieval Germans viewed time as sacred and history as the actualization of the divine message. Thus, in their conception of time and space, medieval German Christians were tied to the Holy Land in fundamental ways.

Medieval maps illustrated the Christian geographical interpretation of the world: the so-called T-map and other world maps, such as the *Ebstorfer Weltkarte* from the middle of thirteenth century, placed Jerusalem at the center of the world. The physical reality of the Holy Land was proof of the veracity of the Christian faith, and pilgrimages to the Holy Land allowed believers to experience for themselves the actuality of biblical places. All major religions share traditions according to which pilgrimages are viewed as a way to achieve holiness in one's lifetime.[11] Traveling across space is seen as a religious act bringing the traveler closer to God.[12] Pilgrimages were undertaken as imposed or self-imposed penance or as an act of pure devotion. Medieval Christians went on local, regional, and long-distance pilgrimages, but the journey to the Holy Land was the dream of every pious Christian.

Whereas the steady flow of pilgrims to the Holy Land tied Germany to the Middle East in an intimate way, the connection to the area was also expressed in political terms when Germans founded a new empire in 962, with Otto I as the first emperor. This political structure signaled a twofold claim to sovereignty over the Holy Land. By 983, continuing Carolingian traditions, German emperors were addressed as Roman emperors, and in 1034 the phrase *Romanum Imperium* became officially part of the empire's title. By invoking the Roman Empire, Germans asserted the Holy Land as an integral part of the new empire's political structure. The title *Sacrum Imperium* was added in 1157 and emphasized the religious dimension of this twofold claim to sovereignty. Palestine, to use the Roman-coined term for the larger area, had been controlled by Greek and Roman rulers for many centuries. Hellenistic rule of the area began with its conquest by Alexander the Great in 332 B.C.E. and continued under the Ptolemies and then the Seleucids. After close to a century of Jewish autonomy under the Hasmonean dynasty, the Romans captured Jerusalem in 63 B.C.E. While the Hellenistic era was one of multicultural coexistence, Roman rule and increasing Christian influence destroyed the Jewish sovereignty over the area. After the partition of the Roman Empire in 395, Byzantine rule continued until the Persian invasion of 614, followed by the Muslim conquest of Palestine beginning in 634. With Arab Muslim armies occupying the area, a period of more than eight hundred years under the rule of Europe-based empires came to an end.

German emperors of the Holy Roman Empire, who aspired to carry on the legacy of the Romans, thus also laid claim to Palestine. This twofold claim to legitimate rule over the Holy Land, through Roman and Christian legacies, was actualized by way of the pilgrimages. A contingent of Germans was always present in the Holy Land, and through the pilgrimages news traveled back to Germany, relating details about the journey, the stay in Palestine, and the current living conditions in the area. Germany's relationship to the Holy Land was therefore by no means imaginary; through pilgrimages and the belief in the actuality of the Christian message, the lands of the Bible occupied a special presence in the minds of German and other European Christians.

Germans were also connected to the Middle East by way of another point of contact: the Muslim presence in Spain. After invading Spain in 711, Muslims had extended their rule to southern France. The onslaught came to a halt when Charles Martel defeated the invading armies at Tours and Poitiers in 732, but "for nearly three centuries . . . the Muslims continued to maintain a series of relatively isolated presences in regions of Western Europe outside the Iberian Peninsula."[13] The following centuries saw the constant struggle over the recovery of Spanish territory by Christian armies; the actual phase of reconquest (*Reconquista*) began with the recapture of Toledo in 1085 and ended with the expulsion of Muslims and Jews in 1492. News about these confrontations between Muslims and Christians traveled north, and Germans followed the events closely.

The poem *Pelagius* by Hrotsvit of Gandersheim, for example, reveals German awareness of the conflict in Spain. This text, written about 959 in Latin hexameter, was based not on an older legend (as were most of Hrotsvit's comparable poems) but on an eyewitness account.[14] The historical event on which the story was based—the martyrdom of a young Spaniard named Pelagius, who is venerated in Spain to this day—had occurred thirty years earlier. Hrotsvit's text tells the story of the young man, who was claimed as a lover by the Muslim ruler Abderraham but rejected his suitor and was tortured to death. The sexualization of the conflict is Hrotsvit's addition; historical sources give Pelagius's refusal to convert to Islam as the reason for his cruel death.[15] Hrotsvit's *Pelagius* shows that news traveled through personal contacts. Pilgrims to Santiago de Compostela—which, next to Jerusalem and Rome, was one of the most popular destinations for medieval pilgrims—played an important role in this regard, as they ensured the exchange of information between northern and southern Europe. In fact, the propagation by Cluniac clerics of Santiago de Compostela as an important destination for pilgrims, rivaling Rome in this respect, illustrates the connection between pilgrimage and ideological as well as practical support of the *Reconquista.*[16]

In addition, long-distance trade facilitated contact between the regions and brought not only goods from southern to northern regions, but also news about Muslim areas.[17] Because of their role in transporting much-sought-after wares and sharing "useful information about possible enemies and allies," traders "were granted privileges by rulers, such as exemption from heavy ship's duties, tolls on vehicles and pack-animals, fees for passes, and other dues, and through special protection."[18] Beginning in the late eleventh century, in the context of greater social and economic mobility, these privileges were expanded throughout Europe, which furthered trading activities. Whereas traders had originally returned to their points of origin, thus following "a circular migration pattern," increasingly they began to settle temporarily or permanently in central trading places, such as Constantinople, Venice, and Alexandria, and thus gradually established permanent trading outposts.[19] The foreign communities were often significant in number: "Some 3,000 Italians, overwhelmingly travelling traders, were in Alexandria in 1215."[20] Documents illustrating the work of notaries who wrote contracts for merchants, in particular *commenda* contracts, attest to the collaboration between sedentary investors and their traveling associates.[21]

Initially, items of trade were mainly luxury goods, such as precious metals and slaves; the Bohemian capital, for example, was a center of the slave trade. Cotton was imported to northern Europe from Aleppo, and raw silk reached Montpellier "from no less than eleven different areas."[22] Over time items such as grain, hides, and raw materials used in the manufacturing industry were traded regularly. The development of the financing and banking system also played a significant role in refining the economic system that extended from the British Isles to Asia. By the twelfth and thirteenth centuries, as Janet Abu-Lughod shows, Europe had achieved its connection to the "numerous preexistent world-economies," and "neither the violence of the Crusades nor the repeated Papal injunction enjoining Europeans from trading with Muslims could interfere with the prosperous trade that in the twelfth and thirteenth centuries traversed the middle route."[23] As David Abulafia states, "The political, cultural, and religious barriers across the Mediterranean proved permeable; cotton, indigo, and alum were the agents binding together east and west."[24]

Arab-language geographical and historical works of the medieval period attest to the traffic between north and south that already existed in the period preceding the Crusades. The account by Ibrahim ibn Ya'qub, dated roughly 965/973, brought information to the Middle East about the northern regions, including central German-speaking territories, such as today's Saxony, Hesse, and Westphalia. Details taken from his report are cited in the works of various geographers and historians, such as Abu 'Obaid 'Abdallah al-Bekri (d. 1094), al-Qazwini (d. 1283), and Ibn Dihya (d. 1235).[25] This account also documents the pivotal role played by Jews, who acted as traders, translators, and advisers during this period and ensured the flow of knowledge and goods between the areas.[26] Letters kept at the Cairo Geniza, which shed light on the Mediterranean and the India trade, also provide us with invaluable insights into the lives of medieval Jewish traders and their contemporaries.[27]

Understanding the extent of this exchange of information and goods, as well as the pervasiveness of pilgrim travel is important in examining the situation that preceded the Crusades. These wars did not develop out of nowhere; they did not represent a radical break with a prior state of affairs but, rather, in light of pilgrimages, *Reconquista,* and religious and political claims on the area of Palestine, an intensification of something that had been developing for decades, even centuries. As noted earlier, the number of pilgrims increased steadily over the course of the tenth and eleventh centuries, which has led scholars to describe the shift from pilgrimage to crusade with the phrase *armed pilgrimages.*[28] That is, the Crusades fit into a continuum of previously existing pilgrimage conventions and the German Empire's, and more generally Europe's, claim to sovereignty over the Holy Land. In addition, violent campaigns against Christian heretics escalated throughout the eleventh century, marking a change among religious leaders in their condoning of the use of violence.[29] When Pope Urban II called for a crusade in 1095, a number of factors made engaging in a military conflict abroad appealing. European countries struggled with a series of problems. The eleventh century, in particular, was marked by famine, agricultural crisis, and social fluidity. Gradually, changes in the inheritance law increased the land available for agriculture, which was revolutionized by new inventions. New and larger settlements, an increase in trade volume, the growing importance of money, the development of an advanced economic infrastructure, and other factors marked the large-scale changes of the period. The steady rise in population until the end of the thirteenth century was leading to a population density that, after the decline beginning in the middle of the fourteenth century, would not be reached again in some areas until the nineteenth century.[30] Joachim Bumke has emphasized that the period around 1200, when German courtly literature reached its peak, was marked by internal wars and public distress. In light of this perhaps paradoxical situation, Bumke suggests that the ideals developed in courtly literature functioned as a utopian vision to counter the negative aspects of reality.[31] Similarly, as a response to widespread economic, political, and ecological crises, a holy war provided a welcome escape from unfortunate circumstances.[32] In addition, receiving absolution for their sins by participating in the Crusades appealed to medieval Germans in fundamental ways, and mobilized large numbers of them to participate in religiously sanctioned wars.[33] These participants and, "from the later twelfth century, contributors . . . earned spiritual privileges . . . as well as the Church's protection for their property, immunity from repayment of debt, and delays on law suits."[34]

Another factor was the unifying appeal this common project articulated to European Christianity, which was divided on the basis of religious, political, and economic conflict and constantly struggled with secular powers. Theological disputes were often grounded in real-world interests regarding political and economic gains. The investiture controversies (1076–1122) highlight this struggle between religious and political powers; an earlier reform movement sparked by teachings promoted by the monastery of Cluny speaks to the same phenomenon. In addition, the Great Schism of 1054 had finalized the split into Western Catholicism and Eastern Orthodoxy. The call for a crusade thus, in effect, masked the various divisions within the Church. The fact that the Crusades were ultimately not successful in creating unity over time is documented by the growing conflict with Byzantium and the numerous sects, such as Albigensians, Petrobrusians, Henricians, and Waldensians, that grew in number and importance over the course of the twelfth century

First and foremost, however, the church presented the call for holy war as a response to the Seljuk invasion, in which the Byzantine Empire had suffered significant defeats and that made travel by European pilgrims to, and within, Palestine more difficult. Although the Byzantine Empire was certainly threatened by the Seljuks, the effects of their presence in terms of access to the holy sites in Palestine is still debated. Sources from the period suggest that the steadily increasing number of pilgrims itself posed logistical problems in the Holy Land. This might have been a factor bringing about the attacks on the large German pilgrimage of 1064/65, even before the Seljuk capture of Jerusalem in 1071; as mentioned earlier, of the seven thousand or more participants, only two thousand returned home. The extent of this disaster seems to have played a role in mobilizing energies for the Crusades even thirty years later; the most detailed description of the atrocities has come down through the account of Ingulphus, the secretary of the earl of Normandy, who was one of the survivors of the expedition.[35] Since the Arab invasion of the seventh century, the Christian sites of the Holy Land had been primarily under the supervision of the Byzantine Empire, while Rome played only a marginal role.[36] The Crusades were thus also an attempt by the Western church to strengthen its significance in the area vis-à-vis Constantinople; the liberation of Jerusalem, rather than support of the Byzantine Empire, became the rallying cry of the Crusades. The fact that the Western church's motivation for the Crusades differed substantially from that of the Eastern church was evident from the beginning and would over time lead to dramatic inter-Christian warfare.

The Crusades were one of various expansions under way at the time. In the West the Spanish continued to regain territory from Muslim conquerors. Germans set out to Christianize and colonize areas in eastern Europe. The Mediterranean Sea was the stage for incessant battles between Europeans and Arabs, including Arab pirates. The kingdom of the Normans in southern Italy, Sicily, and—for a short period—a part of northern Africa emerged in the eleventh century as a transitional zone, where Christians and Muslims, Europeans and Arabs, coexisted in relative tolerance, somewhat comparable to the situation in Muslim Spain.[37] The Crusades brought these various expansive ambitions farther south. Whereas the Crusades were certainly a European undertaking and were not led by one specific nation, the German case (complicated as it is to even argue such a case) demonstrates that over time individual secular rulers, representing power structures such as the Holy Roman Empire or individual kingdoms, pursued distinct courses.

The First Crusade, though announced in France and led mainly by French aristocrats, was enthusiastically supported by German rulers and subjects alike. Accounts tell of fanatical German masses under the leadership of charismatic popular preachers. In fact, the so-called Peasants' Crusade (or Crusade of Poor People) preceded the official First Crusade by a couple of years and was led by popular figures, including Peter of Amiens (also known as Peter the Hermit). Peter preached in Cologne and other German cities, drawing throngs of impoverished peasants and all kinds of destitute people from the Rhineland, middle and East France, and the Netherlands. Although, as Christopher Tyerman emphasizes, the participation of poor people in the Crusades was not the norm, they tended to fervently support the First Crusade.[38] According to some estimates, fifty to seventy thousand fanaticized individuals followed Peter to Constantinople.[39] Most of his followers were beaten by Seljuk troops in late October 1096; "probably nearly twenty thousand of them . . . were exterminated."[40] Peter himself managed to return to Constantinople and ultimately participated in the First Crusade, but the Peasants' Crusade had come to an end, and, as Hans Eberhard Mayer points out, it did not leave a positive first impression on the Byzantines.[41] Other "troops" who had departed under the leadership of various preachers and ambitious noblemen never made it to Jerusalem, and, in another ugly dimension of the Crusades, many began their holy journey by turning their wrath on the Jewish populations of Worms, Speier, Mainz, Trier, and other cities, expropriating money from the communities and murdering and plundering in the name of Christ. The official army followed soon afterward, departing from several cities in Europe throughout 1096 and 1097.

Conquest

By the time of the First Crusade, Germany's relationship to the Holy Land was thus by no means fictional or imaginary. The lands of the Bible occupied a special presence in the minds of Germans (and other European Christians), and the Holy Land was not understood only in a metaphorical way. Rather, the actuality of the Christian message was confirmed through the pilgrimages and the Crusades, and the reality of the biblical lands proved the veracity of the Christian message.

In spite of broad cultural, political, and economic exchange, and in spite of close contact in Spain and Sicily, knowledge of Islam was rudimentary in most areas of Europe. In contrast to the Christians of the Middle East, who were well aware of the connections between Islam, Judaism, and Christianity, most Germans, like other European Christians outside of Spain and Sicily, knew very little about Islam during the period leading up to the Crusades. For the most part Islam was not understood as a monotheistic religion, and Christianity did not develop an attitude of tolerance toward other religions that was comparable to the Islamic idea of the "People of the Book," which allowed non-Muslim (mostly monotheistic) minorities to attain the status of *dhimmi,* that is, protected minority under Muslim rule. This attitude created a legal framework that allowed Muslims to live side by side with Christians and Jews in the Middle East and enabled them to be familiar with other religions in a way quite unlike the experience of European Christians.[42] The European propaganda that supported the call to arms against Muslims, however, depicted Islam as a heathen religion, and many instances of absurd claims about Muslims, such as their supposed reverence for idols called "Apolle," "Mahound," and "Tervigant," surfaced in epics of various literatures.[43] By associating Muslims with pigs, dogs, and alcohol, European Christians ridiculed Islamic laws about cleanliness and abstinence.[44] According to Robert Irwin, some "clerics who sought to understand Islam better only did so in order to have more material with which to refute its errors," while other ardent Christians rejected the study of Islam on principle.[45] In contrast, Middle Eastern Christian commentators on Islam discussed actual features of that religion.[46] Christian Arab apologetics played an important role, often facilitating interfaith dialogue.[47] Nevertheless, some commentators held a negative view of Islam. St. John of Damascus (d. ca. 749), to mention an earlier example, tied Islam to Arianism and thus regarded it as heretical. Over time, Spain and, later, Sicily became staging grounds for debates about the nature of Islam.[48] Not until the beginning of the twelfth century did European Christians engage with Islam in a serious manner. The first translation of the Koran into Latin by Robert of Ketton in 1143 signaled a new stage in the engagement with Islam (even though it was commissioned with the intention of improving the critique of Islam), but, as Irwin states, "Ketton's rendering . . . [was] soon forgotten." In spite of the growing awareness about Islamic philosophy and science across Europe, his translation did not raise the general knowledge about Islam.[49] Even the "proximity to the Muslims in Palestine and Syria did not at first encourage any understanding of Islam" among European Christians.[50] Texts documenting serious theological disputes between Muslims and Christians were not uncommon, but most were not widely disseminated.[51]

The lack of knowledge about Islam has to be acknowledged as a cornerstone of successful propaganda for the Crusades. The European views of Islam as polytheist or heretical formed the basis of the holy wars. But how was this view of Islam conveyed to the population? We have very little knowledge of the actual wording of sermons used to inspire participation in or financial support of these holy wars. But chronicles, annals, and letters shed light on recruitment practices and legal provisions that made the Crusades attractive. Sermons either appealed to people's individual failures as sinners and offered spiritual rewards or aimed at "exciting their anger, rage, and aggression toward the enemy of the faith against whom the crusade was preached."[52] Reports about fanatical masses suggest that preachers, such as the aforementioned Peter the Hermit, another called Gottschalk, and a figure known as Volkmar, were tremendously successful at gaining recruits.[53]

Recruitment and related practices also changed over time. Military orders were introduced in the first decades of the twelfth century, which marked a radical digression from earlier "prohibitions against the use of armed force by clerics of all grades and dignities, even including bishops."[54] The military orders played a crucial role during the last century of the Crusades. As historian Christoph Maier writes, "During the first half of the thirteenth century, the crusade was transformed into a most sophisticated institution. By developing such aspects as recruitment, finance, liturgy, and the legal rights and duties of crusaders the Roman Curia managed to make the crusade an immensely versatile, and a potentially effective, instrument of papal politics."[55] Because local clerics were seen as unreliable because of their "local political and social ties," an independent network was set up in the thirteenth century that drew on the service of religious orders and mendicant friars.[56]

By the end of the twelfth century participation in the Crusades was also possible through donations, and by the early thirteenth century crusaders were allowed "to commute their vows by sending proxies and encouraged 'anyone who wishes' to redeem crusade vows for money according to means."[57] Through their inclusion in liturgy, sermons of mendicant friars, and legal and financial stipulations, the Crusades were omnipresent in medieval Europe, even affecting the lives of those who did not actively embark on journeys to the Holy Land.

Propaganda and Exoticism in Literature and World Chronicles

In the wake of the first call for a crusade and after the successful conquest of Jerusalem in 1099, this new dimension of European presence in the Holy Land was discussed in various forms of fiction writing and songs. Even before 1095, most of the writing had been dedicated to religious topics; the earliest testimonies in German were closely tied to the continuous Christianization of Europe itself, which continued in the eastern regions of Germany well into the ninth century. Many texts from the early period were written in Latin, others were composed in Old High German dialects; the *Heliand,* for example, written around 830 in Old Saxon, is a testimony to the Christianization of the Saxons.[58] Between 900 and 1050, according to extant records or the lack thereof, very little was written in German; many of the surviving texts are translations from the Latin or heavily influenced by Latin rhetoric and vocabulary. The *Ezzolied,* a world chronicle reviewing the time from the creation of humans to the death of Jesus Christ, is considered the first text that was composed in early Middle High German. Central stories of the Bible were retold in numerous versions, and apocalyptic thought dominated the religious discourse. Vernacular versions departed at times from the Latin text of the Bible, the *Vulgata* (the canonical Latin version, which had remained the authoritative text since the eighth century), and shifted the emphasis on selected stories or biblical motifs.[59] Stories about paradise and the heavenly Jerusalem were highly popular; they functioned as utopian promises of a better life.[60] In addition, they were central to the spreading of Christian ethics and values, the idea of reward being crucial in this regard.

On their pilgrimages to the Holy Land, pilgrims sang religious songs or recited poems to keep up their spirits. One such song is the *Ezzolied,* which is thought to have been sung during the vast pilgrimage of 1064/65. Once the idea of the Crusades turned into reality, religious propaganda literature, often composed in Latin, was circulated widely. (We should remind ourselves that Latin was key to the connection between the Middle Ages and Rome; by using this language, Germans declared their commitment to Christian Rome and the Roman Empire. Latin, however, also facilitated the existence of a European literate culture, one that defies a view of different societies in national terms.) This propaganda literature supported the call to arms and extolled to Christians the benefits of participating in the religious wars. Sermons, admonitions, and hymns, composed in both Latin and vernacular languages, called upon believers to take up arms to defend the holy sites of Christianity. The glorification of suffering and sacrifice as well as disdain for the bodily existence of human beings that marked Christian rhetoric at the time culminated in the propagation of a notion of holiness that was to be acquired through the martyr's death. Melodies set to these texts encouraging participation in the Crusades made them easier to memorize and indicate clerics' efforts to popularize the message contained in the verses.[61]

The famous collection *Carmina Burana* consists of songs that were written in Latin in different parts of Europe during the twelfth and early thirteenth centuries, and a number of the songs stress the need for unity among Christians and advertise the prospects of eternal salvation for those who join the struggle.[62] "De cruce signatis," which begins with the words "Fides cum Ydolatria" and was composed in Germany before 1149, shortly before the Second Crusade, glorifies the death of martyrs who die for Christianity and contains apocalyptic imagery combined with references to practical matters, such as an admonition to be careful to ensure the well-being of one's wife and children before departing to the Holy Land.[63] Songs of this nature were also composed in vernacular languages throughout Europe.[64]

The Crusades were also promoted in epics and poems, and again the German examples are not unique, but part of a shared heritage that existed in variation across Europe. The *Rolandslied,* an epic composed by Pfaffe Konrad around 1170 and received quickly and broadly in Germany, revisits the confrontation between Muslims and Christians in eighth-century Spain in order to mobilize Christian forces.[65] The epic is an adaptation of a French chanson de geste, the *Chanson de Roland* (ca. 1090), which is based on the historical battle of Roncesvalles on August 15, 778, in which the rear guard of Charlemagne's retreating Franks, after waging successful battles against the Muslims, was attacked by Basques. The *Chanson,* among other changes, transforms these Basques into Muslims. The German version retains these alterations but emphasizes the religious dimension of the war against the Muslims, as the German emperor and other knights are called upon by God to fight the heathens. Critics assume that Heinrich der Löwe commissioned the writing of the epic.[66] An epic glorifying the Crusades (and Charlemagne, who was claimed by Heinrich as a foundational ancestor) was very much in tune with the goals and political ambitions of this ruler, who not only supported the Crusades against the Muslims (and went to Jerusalem in 1172) but also played an important role in the war against "heathen" Slavs (Wenden) in 1147.[67] This military expedition against the Slavs was officially recognized as a crusade and thus included the promise for absolution from sins and the benefits that came with dying as a martyr.

The *Rolandslied* exemplifies a mind-set in which the demands of religious and secular leadership are merged harmoniously in the idea of the *miles Dei,* the soldier of God. Other texts from the period, such as the *Kreuzlieder* (Crusading Songs), articulated a different stance in this regard. For example, Friedrich von Hausen, Albrecht von Johansdorf, and Hartmann von Aue, who were otherwise known for their courtly love poetry, raised the question of how to reconcile ideals of courtly knighthood with those of religious service, and voiced a range of differing views of the problem. "Swelch vrowe sendet lieben man . . .," the poem by Hartmann von Aue that dates from the end of the twelfth century, may serve as an example of the attempt to reconcile ideals of worldly knighthood with those of religious knighthood. Here, *minne,* the notion of courtly love that inspired deeds in the service of a woman, serves as the mediating principle that allows the wife to support her husband's participation in the Crusade.[68] Friedrich von Hausen, in a song dated from 1188/89, presents the problem as one of body versus heart: "My body would like to fight the heathen, but my heart has chosen a woman."[69] Other poems by the same author repeat the lament about this conflict (only one of his songs about the Crusades is clearly dedicated to religious ideals).[70] Poetry about the Crusades by Albrecht von Johansdorf, also written in 1188–89, similarly expresses the tension between desires for earthly love and religious duty.[71]

Heinrich von Rugge, on the other hand, who also wrote his poems at the end of the twelfth century, clearly praises the martyr death. His poem "Kreuzleich," for example, written after the death of Frederick I in 1190, expresses frustration about the emperor's death. Yet the poet attempts to find a new attitude, challenging those who lament the present situation and implicitly referring to the dire outlook the crusaders were facing. He states, "Whoever now takes the cross does what is appropriate to a hero and acts with manly courage"; especially in light of the fact that life is short and nobody knows how long he might live, he argues, one should take the cross, embark on the journey, and not fear death.[72] Heinrich von Rugge stands out as an ardent supporter of the crusaders' mission. Similar poems, many of them attempting to reconcile ideals of courtly life and love with crusading ideology, were composed across Europe.[73]

Walther von der Vogelweide also continued to promote the legitimacy of the Crusades at a moment when, as we will see, the German emperor Frederick II was already pursuing a different course. Walther, however, did criticize specific crimes committed by crusading armies, such as the sacking of Constantinople in 1204. He did not discuss the conflict between *minne* and serving God; he asserted secular over religious leadership, bemoaned certain practices of the church, and, in some ways foreshadowing the position later developed by Martin Luther, argued that the Crusades should be led by the emperor. Yet the legitimacy of the idea of a holy war remained intact.[74] Poets from the later period who advanced the crusading spirit in their works include Bruder Wernher and Rubin (both from the early thirteenth century). Poetic writing calling for a holy war against Muslims did not diminish even with the fall of the last Christian bastion in 1291; in fact, the practice was resumed with renewed vigor during the confrontations with the Ottoman Empire.

Many poets, including Neidhart von Reuenthal, Rubin, and Tannhäuser, participated in a crusade. Hartmann von Aue might have participated in the Crusade of 1189, and Friedrich von Hausen died in it; Otto von Botenlauben lived for twenty years in Palestine. The fact that actual experience informed the writings about the Crusades is clear in the shifts that occurred over time—when, for example, critical voices began to emerge in response to the changing political and military situation in the Holy Land, alongside writings that continued to promote the Crusades.

Apart from religious and secular propaganda literature, the German claim to biblical lands was also formulated in texts that focused on the life of Alexander the Great, whose empire united European, North African, Middle Eastern, and Asian territories. The figure of Alexander inspired reworkings across diverse cultures and historical periods and in a range of literary genres. Indeed, texts about Alexander played a central role in Greek, Roman, Islamic, Christian-Syrian, Ethiopian, Medieval French, Latin, German, and other literatures.[75] In each case the material was adapted to the specific context: Alexander was conceived, for instance, as a hero of Islam and as a hero of Christianity. Medieval Latin versions of Greek and Latin Alexandrian romances influenced Middle High German renditions of the story, which modernized and adapted the topic according to the ideas prevalent at the time. The earliest among the significant German versions of the material dates from around 1150, when the *Alexanderlied* was composed by Pfaffe Lamprecht, who renders Alexander as an impressive hero but also includes a critique of his quest for power. Later adaptations of this text reflect the rise of courtly culture and emphasize the knightly qualities of the emperor. The *Alexander* by Rudolf von Ems (ca. 1230–40) views Alexander as having been sent by God in order to punish mankind for its sins. The *Alexander* by Ulrich von Etzenbach (ca. 1280) presents Alexander as a model ruler. A late fourteenth-century version, the *Große Alexander* (also know as *Wernigerode Alexander*), depicts Alexander as both a model of a heroic ruler and a memento mori. In this work his adventures in the East lead him to ever more grandiose schemes, for which he is finally punished. Versions of the Alexander tales continued to be composed throughout the fifteenth century.

While the various renditions of Alexander's life articulate the encounter between Europe and the Orient, the omnipresence of the material attests to the cultural ties between Europe and the Middle East, including North Africa. Some of the writings about Alexander's adventures were based on Greek and Roman sources; other stories derived from the Sinbad cycle and other seafaring tales of Arab and Persian provenance that celebrate marvels of the East.[76] In regard to these Middle Eastern sources, we need to acknowledge that much of Europe's "Orientalism" is in fact based on the Orient's own exoticizing of the East. The Alexander topos was only one of several themes of antiquity that were picked up by German authors. Whereas the *Aneid* received less attention (with only one adaptation by Heinrich von Veldeke [*Eneas,* 1170–90]; Latin versions, however, were widely read), the Trojan War was a popular theme into the late Middle Ages. Interestingly, in Konrad von Würzburg's widely received rendition of the *Trojanerkrieg* (1281–87), various Oriental people align themselves with the Trojans; this conception of a battle between Orient and Occident might have been inspired by the centuries of crusading warfare. The story of King Apollonius of Tyre (for example, in the version by Heinrich von Neustadt, *Apollonius von Tyrlant,* ca. 1310) also leads its audience into adventures in areas of the Middle East. The versified narrative of *Eraclius* (from the early thirteenth century) by an author known as Otte contains an episode in which Emperor Eraclius calls for a crusade against the Persians, who are said to have stolen the Holy Cross from Jerusalem.[77]

Through the legend of Alexander the Great and other stories drawing on Greek and Roman material, medieval Germans fantasized about ruling Oriental territories. Long before the Renaissance, Germans thus appropriated Greek and Roman epics and legends—which were read as historical texts, not as fiction[78]—as a vehicle to express their own fantasies about empire. It is important to realize that, because of the geographical expanse of the Greek and Roman empires, almost all of the related literary and mythological material that was passed down over the centuries by definition involved Asia and Africa. Another textual genre tying Europe and Orient together through narrative plots, the *Spielmannsepen,* combined love and adventure stories with a more serious narrative framework, often related to issues of domestic politics. Here, at times, the religious dimension of the conflict seems like a mere ploy to relate the ultimately more entertaining pursuits of the German knights who abduct and liberate Christian captives and who face many challenges on their voyages. The authors use the Middle Eastern setting more or less as a staging ground for the presentation of topics rather unrelated to the Crusades.[79]

Herzog Ernst (1170), for example, does not foreground the religious conflict but articulates a contemporary struggle between central imperial and local particular power in its frame story. The protagonist's journey in the Orient reads like a medieval version of *Star Trek:* he encounters many of the mythological beings and monsters associated with the East that were known from the writings of Pliny the Elder (in particular his *Natural History*), Herodotus, Homer, and Isidore of Seville (*Etymologies*), among others. In India, Herzog Ernst almost falls in love with a Christian princess who had been captured and tortured (and eventually killed) by beings who are described as a blend of human and cranes.[80] Some of the mythological material was also based on tales from the *One Thousand and One Nights* and on the Sinbad cycle, which, as mentioned earlier, draws on stories related by Arab and Persian seafarers. (The fact that Middle Eastern literature also employs this shared archive of topoi is exemplified by the thirteenth-century Arabic epic *Sirat 'Antar,* which incorporates popular stories that were conceived over several centuries about contacts between the various peoples of the region.[81] This story of a mixed-race knight features many of the motifs found in the *Spielmannsepen* and other European medieval epics staged in the Orient.)[82] Jacques Le Goff has identified a noteworthy characteristic regarding the centrality of marvels in many of the European epics: courtly culture, according to Le Goff, "was bound up with the class interests of a rising but already threatened social stratum, namely, the lower and middle ranks of the nobility, the knightly strata. It was the desire of this group to oppose the culture of the Church and its ally, the aristocracy, by erecting not a counterculture but an alternative culture that was more its own, hence more amenable to its wishes. . . . That the marvelous plays such a large part in courtly romance is no accident. It is intimately associated with the idealized knight's quest for individual and collective identity."[83]

The image of the ideal knight is also a significant theme in the earliest of these epics, *König Rother* (written after 1152). Here the plot regarding the abduction of a princess mirrors the conflict within the Christian world: the princess is the daughter of the Byzantine emperor, and the confrontation between the two political spheres demonstrates ideas regarding the positive (Roman-German) versus the negative (Byzantine) ruler. Various contemporary events inspired the epic, such as Roger II of Sicily's courting of a Byzantine princess and his various wars against Constantinople (1143–49). The epic does not foreground themes related to the Crusades; rather, its central question concerns the optimal balance between ideals of worldly and religious leadership.

In *Salman und Morolf* (1160/90) Princess Salme, the daughter of a heathen ruler, is abducted, baptized, and married to King Salman, the Christian ruler of Jerusalem. The abduction motif does not appear only once: in separate episodes, two heathen rulers succeed in abducting Salme, but the king's brother, Morolf, a particularly cunning and cruel trickster, wins her back and ultimately puts an end to the string of abductions by killing the beautiful Salme. The bitter tone of the epic is fed not only by hatred for heathens but also by anti-Jewish and misogynist sentiments.

Among these epics *Orendel* (ca. 1190) displays the most direct connection to the Crusades. The text was based on a simple legend that tried to prove the legitimacy of the claim of Trier's bishop that he owned an important relic, namely, the "grey frock" of Jesus Christ. The epic includes another abduction story but also a number of episodes involving baptisms and the liberation of Jerusalem and other holy sites. A further variation within the genre is presented in *Sanct Oswald* (ca. 1170), in which a raven plays a pivotal role in the struggles between Christian and heathen armies, again combining abduction of a woman and baptisms of heathen. As in *Orendel,* the sexual component of the abduction plot is transformed into a parable of ideal conduct because the royal would-be lovers, after beholding visions of an angel, decide to abstain from carnal love and earn their place in heaven.

The *Spielmannsepen* thus highlight the connectedness of literary texts to political events of the time. The Crusades, but often even more important, regional politics, inspired many of the narratives; at the same time, the love and adventure stories woven in with the religious and political dimensions of the narratives reveal multiple dimensions of the fascination with the Middle East. The many luxury goods and other novel items that appear in these narratives attest to the presence of material objects from the Middle East in Europe. But regardless of how grounded in reality they are, these narratives move seamlessly from aspects of reality into the realm of fantasy and myth.[84]

Chronicles reveal a similar blend of fact and fiction. These texts, which strengthened the Christian and German claim to territories in the Middle East, narrate world history from the point of view of Christian eschatology but place different emphases on sacred and secular history. The universal history (*Historia de duabus civitatibus,* 1132–46) by Otto von Freising, for example, tells (in Latin) world history from the beginning of creation to the Roman Empire and then turns to the succession of popes and emperors who carried on the tradition of the Roman Empire. Similarly, Jans Enikel's *Weltchronik* (ca. 1276–84) begins with the creation of the world and reviews historical events up to the contemporary period, in this case the death of Emperor Frederick II in 1250. His rendition of world history, however, reflects the influence of courtly and also city culture (Enikel was based in Vienna) and thus the specific expectations of these audiences; it incorporates information about the economy and life in the cities and is narrated in a somewhat emotional and humorous style.[85]

Not every world history began, however, with the creation of the world. The *Kaiserchronik* (1135–55), for instance, foregrounded political genealogy from the Roman Empire to contemporary German times. Generally speaking, when the participation of specific German rulers was being recounted, the Crusades were included. The unfinished *Weltchronik* (1250–54) by Rudolf von Ems, one of the mostly widely read books of the German Middle Ages, was commissioned by King Konrad IV, who had inherited the crown of Jerusalem through his mother, Isabella of Brienne, the daughter of King Johann of Jerusalem. In the context of this overview, it is interesting that Rudolf von Ems made this genealogical connection central to his work by reviewing Jewish kings and praising Konrad as king of Jerusalem.[86] Foregrounding sovereignty over Jerusalem was a strategic move, intended to establish the legitimacy of Konrad's embattled rule, a feature that also appears in other epics that are unrelated to the Crusades, such as *Wilhelm von Orlens* by Rudolf von Ems (ca. 1238). Because world histories were dependent on the specific aspirations of their aristocratic, clerical, and other sponsors, the perspectives presented in these texts varied greatly.[87]

World histories thus functioned in ways similar to the stories surrounding Alexander the Great or the *Spielmannsepen,* in that they articulated a political and religious claim to the territories of the Holy Land yet stressed various topics, from love and adventure stories to local events. In comparison to religiously inspired writings, most of these texts displayed a less hostile attitude toward the Muslim enemy. Almost never do we encounter the slander that distinguishes the secular propaganda literature, particularly of the early phase of the Crusades, and the religious literature of the time.

Defeat and Coexistence

If the Crusades were intended to unify European Christianity, the use of military confrontation to battle heresy within the Church reveals the true extent of internal friction. Crusades were led not only against Muslims and Jews (in the latter case, through pogroms and perpetual harassment and violence) but also against Christians who were in conflict with official doctrine, as defined by Rome, or who were political enemies of the church for a variety of reasons. Violent campaigns against heretical and politically undesirable Christians occurred throughout Europe and took place from about the middle of the eleventh century to the end of the fifteenth century, shortly after which the confrontation between Protestants and the Catholic Church would result in another two hundred years of religious warfare in Europe. In Italy "the belief that the eradication of heresy was inseparably linked with action against the public authority which had permitted its growth or hindered its early repression" was particularly widespread.[88] Some of the most violent intra-European Crusades occurred in France. The battles against the Cathars, known as the Cathar or Albigensian Crusade, are among the most well-known examples of internecine warfare among Christians. Beginning in 1209, with an army of, according to some reports, about thirty thousand soldiers descending on the Languedoc region in southern France, the conflict lasted for almost forty years and became notorious for its unprecedented violence. Entire villages were destroyed, their populations slaughtered, and the land devastated. For decades after the wars, the Inquisition tortured, executed, and dispossessed thousands of heretics in its effort to destroy the movement.[89] Participation in the Crusades against Catharism was, as in the case of the wars against Muslims, rewarded by indulgences promising eternal salvation through the absolution of one's sins.[90]

Another noteworthy aspect to consider within this context is the increasing number of European Christians who settled in various areas of the Mediterranean. As Europeans established their rule over the Holy Land, they also founded several states, namely, the County of Edessa, the Principality of Antioch, the Kingdom of Jerusalem, and the County of Tripoli. During the Third Crusade the Kingdom of Cyprus was founded, and, after the sacking of Constantinople, the Byzantine Empire was divided into several states connected to the crusaders. The European Christians who settled in these crusader states became acculturated to various degrees, which often created friction with the newly arriving crusaders.

Against this background of struggles between religious and secular leaders, various groups of Christians, and local and translocal interests, as well as defeats in the Holy Land, Germans and other Europeans became increasingly critical of the Crusades. Their criticisms, including expressions of sympathy and admiration for Muslim culture, mark the beginning of a new tradition, which is particularly prevalent in German culture and persists to this day.

Critics voiced a number of arguments against the Crusades, reflecting military defeat but also a growing conflict between the ambitions of religious and secular leaders, including dissension among worldly rulers, who had different priorities. Even though the main impetus for these wars had emerged in

France with the First Crusade in 1096–99, German kings, noblemen, and their armies (including impoverished and poorly equipped mobs) had enthusiastically supported them. By the Second Crusade (1145–49) the German role was becoming less certain. Initially, Bernard of Clairvaux followed the pope's plan to exclude the Germans, but ultimately he was unable to bypass the already fanaticized German masses. German and French preachers (such as one Cistercian monk called Radulf, who moved back and forth between northern France and western Germany) had succeeded in stirring unrest among ordinary people, and many impoverished and desperate Germans were ready to leave for the Holy Land. In preparation for Holy War, they once more first turned their hostilities on the local Jewish populations.[91] The German king Konrad III was much more reserved, however, regarding the mission. In addition, Saxon noblemen were more interested in a crusade against the Slavs, which they ultimately carried out after negotiations with the pope, thereby further advancing the German colonization and Christianization of eastern Europe.[92] When the German king finally decided to lead an army of crusaders (together with Louis VII of France), he was able to draw on the support of a broad alliance of German leaders. The enterprise, however, ended in chaos: actions of German soldiers created tensions with the Byzantine emperor, Manuel Komnenos, and the German army was defeated in its first battle with the Seljuks. King Konrad III, wounded in battle, fell ill by the end of 1147 and had to return to Constantinople. Finally arriving in Jerusalem in 1148, Konrad supported what Mayer has called the "unbelievably stupid decision to attempt the conquest of Damascus," an endeavor that failed thoroughly.[93]

A turning point came when Saladin and his troops retook Jerusalem in 1187. Saladin had succeeded in creating a forceful alliance of Muslim rulers. The main reason for his fame as a just ruler, in both Europe and the Middle East, lay in the fact that the "reconquest was nearly bloodless"; even the victory in Jerusalem proceeded without massacre and plundering.[94] Saladin's reputation as a measured military and political leader is mirrored in the celebratory writings of Arab historians.[95] This positive image was also transmitted and picked up extensively in literatures across Europe. The thirteenth-century French romance *La Fille du Comte de Pontieu,* one of many literary examples in this regard, suggests a genealogical linkage between Saladin and the counts of Ponthieu; a later testimony to this positive transmission in German culture is Gotthold Ephraim Lessing's play *Nathan the Wise* (1779), which depicts the Muslim leader as a model of wisdom and humanism (see chap. 3). Saladin is celebrated not only in literary representations, but also in an extensive corpus of scholarly investigations. Tyerman paints a more sober picture of Saladin as "the most calculating of politicians."[96] But the appeal of the twelfth-century leader as a positive symbol for East-West contact has not waned over time; an extensive exhibition, "Saladin und die Kreuzfahrer," that was shown in the German cities of Halle, Oldenburg, and Mannheim in 2006 pays tribute to his legacy.[97]

Medieval Europeans, however, reacted to the fall of Jerusalem with desperation. A song composed in 1188, probably in Germany and included in the *Carmina Burana* collection, expresses the anguish: "Alas, with lamenting voice I am forced to tell about a calamity that recently happened overseas."[98] The song is interesting because it describes Saladin's army as an assortment of heathens, an alliance made up of a range of peoples associated with the lands of the Bible and the marvelous East. The lament does not say anything favorable about Saladin; here the battles are cruel, the heathen army massacres Christians arbitrarily, and the "land of the Christians" is defiled and laid to waste.

The fall of Jerusalem inspired renewed ambition among European crusaders that would prove to be disastrous, especially for German participants: Emperor Frederick I Barbarossa led one of the largest armies in the Third Crusade (1189–92), which, according to contemporary (and most likely exaggerated) estimates, consisted of up to 100,000 men. But the ambitious plans came to an abrupt end when Barbarossa, while leading his troops across a river, drowned in Anatolia in 1190, and the German crusade fell apart. The death of the charismatic emperor was traumatic for Germans (as mentioned before, the *Kreuzleich* by Heinrich von Rugge clearly expresses the anguish), and, because of it and facing steady defeats of crusading armies, rising interest in colonizing eastern Europe, and internal power struggles, German secular leaders grew increasingly disillusioned with Christian warfare.

The growing opposition to the Crusades also had to do with the gruesome reality of these wars. Here the reports of Arab historians offer an important counterpoint to the idealizing representations of European knights drawn up in various European literatures and nonfiction writings throughout the twelfth century. From the beginning, reports of unprecedented cruelty practiced by the crusaders sent shock waves through the Arab world. According to the historian Ibn al-Athir, carnage followed the taking of cities, as evidenced by the defeat of the city Ma'arrat an-Nu'man during the First Crusade, when "for three days the slaughter never stopped; the Franks killed more than 100,000 men and took innumerable prisoners."[99] According to the same historian, 70,000 Muslims were slaughtered during the 1099 sacking of Jerusalem in the al-Aqsa mosque alone.[100] Other sources offer similar figures.[101] The various reports echo one another in their descriptions of the slaughter of large numbers of civilians after the defeat of cities and villages. Treaties were broken, prisoners were executed en masse, cannibalism was performed as a scare tactic, and women and children were sold into slavery.[102]

The crudeness of European military practice was also mirrored in other areas of contact. The Syrian nobleman Usama Ibn Munqidh, for instance, exposes in detail the outlandish practices of Frankish doctors and marvels at the backwardness of European medicine. In his account, which dates from roughly 1180, Ibn Munqidh describes grotesque scenes during which a Frankish doctor, for example, hacks off the leg of a knight, who dies on the spot, and cuts a cross onto the skull of a woman, who also dies immediately. He contrasts these kinds of approaches to the much less invasive practices of Arab doctors, who used herbal poultices and understood the effects of dietary changes. In addition, Ibn Munqidh points out other European practices that left Arabs incredulous: the reliance on "judgments of God," for example, such as tests of fire and water torture, were seen by Muslims as pagan rituals.[103]

European knights were also feared by indigenous Christian populations of the occupied territories. Since the arrival of crusader armies they "suffered a double oppression . . . : their Western coreligionists suspected them of sympathy for the Saracens and treated them as subjects of inferior rank, while their Muslim compatriots often saw them as natural allies of the invaders."[104] The hostility and occasional violence experienced by Middle Eastern Christians, however, were surpassed by the suffering of Byzantine Christians during the sacking of Constantinople in 1204 and its aftermath. This incomprehensible event, facilitated by a coalition of various European powers (among whom the Venetians played a crucial role), blatantly unmasks the unholy aspects of these holy wars: the city was plundered, its inhabitants were killed, maimed, and raped, and Emperor Alexius III was deposed.[105] The loot brought back to Europe from what is said to have been at that time the richest city of the world became the subject of legends. Only "an empty ruin" was left.[106] After the crusaders plundered Constantinople and massacred its population, they carved up the empire, assigning Constantinople and about a quarter of the former territory to a leading crusader (who was voted new emperor) and dividing the remaining three-quarters among crusaders and Venetians.[107] In the aftermath of these developments a number of settlements were created in the larger Aegean area that were held by western Europeans for as long as three hundred years.[108]

After losing sovereignty over parts of the Holy Land as a result of Saladin's reconquest of Jerusalem, and again after the sack of Constantinople, the entire crusading enterprise became less and less appealing to segments of the

European, and particularly German, nobility. This opposition grew especially strong under Emperor Frederick II. Even though he had taken the oath to go on a crusade in 1215, he had delayed participating for a number of reasons. In 1220, after he was crowned emperor, Frederick II returned to his original homeland of Sicily, which still contained a large Muslim population. Scholars have interpreted the emperor's policies toward the Arab Muslims of Sicily in different ways; Norman Daniel, for example, concludes that "it was Frederick who destroyed the Arabs of Sicily."[109] At the core of Daniel's criticism was Frederick's resettlement policy; after years of military campaigns against Muslim populations, who had secured a great deal of independence on the island during the years of Frederick's absence (and were thus defiant not only as Muslims but also as independent nobility who had conquered territories previously owned by Christian dynasties), he moved Arab Muslims from various areas in Sicily, especially the mountains, to Lucera in Apulia. From among these Arabs he recruited troops for service in the imperial army. Frederick II also introduced laws that forced Jews to wear distinctive clothing. In a departure from Daniel's assessment Frederick's policies, however, can be seen as diplomatic strategies that ultimately protected both minorities from more extensive persecution. The situation of Jews in Europe had worsened ever since the First Crusade, and whereas Frederick introduced new laws using dress codes as a means of setting Jews and Muslims apart, he did not enforce other laws that, for example, criminalized sexual contact between members of different religions. The economic activities of Jews in Sicily were virtually unlimited, and, apart from the dress code, the status of Jews in Sicily defied several decrees passed by the third and fourth Lateran Councils.[110] The Arab population of Lucera, in spite of the fact that it functioned as a military colony, generated a thriving culture. Frederick allowed Muslims to practice their religion and follow their cultural traditions. Distinguished Muslim scientists became his advisers, and Arab soldiers served in his army. The situation was very complex, but clearly offensive to the church, which strongly criticized Frederick for his policies.

His role in the Crusade of 1228–29 was equally controversial. In 1225 Frederick II married Isabella of Brienne, the daughter of the king of Jerusalem. This marriage gave a new dimension to the crusade that Frederick II was supposed to lead and which he postponed repeatedly. The question has been raised whether Frederick's expedition can even be called a crusade, as he broke with several features central to crusading ideology.[111] In 1227 he finally left for the Middle East but became ill and returned to Sicily. As a result, Pope Gregor IX banned the emperor. Defiantly, Frederick II decided to embark on the Fifth Crusade in 1228. To the surprise of the pope and other leaders, he fought the crusade with political means: he negotiated a peaceful handover of Jerusalem with Sultan al-Kamil. Perhaps the accounts of Arab historians are the most credible evidence that Frederick's policies were aimed at promoting peace between Muslims and Christians. One anecdote relates that the sultan ordered the muezzins of Jerusalem to cancel the call for prayer during the Christian ruler's stay in the city. According to the testimony, which is recorded in several historical sources, Frederick II complained the next morning that the muezzins had not called for prayer. The *qadi* Shams al-Din replied: "'It is I who prevented them from doing so, out of respect for Your Majesty.' 'You should not have acted thus,' the emperor said, 'for if I spent this night in Jerusalem, it was above all to hear the muezzin's call in the night.'"[112] Other accounts by medieval Arab historians, as well as contemporary Arab scholars, reflect the great appreciation for the emperor that comes across in this anecdote.[113]

Literary Commentary on Defeat and Coexistence

This political background and perhaps also the growing realization that Muslim culture was sophisticated and contained notions of ethics that were shared by medieval German courtly culture explain why criticism of the Crusades was articulated more and more frequently. Critical voices in Germany found expression beginning toward the end of the twelfth century. *Graf Rudolf* (ca. 1170–85) is an early example of a text that features favorable Oriental figures. Here the Christian protagonist forms an alliance with Girabobe, one of the heathen leaders, who reveals himself to be more noble than the Christian king. The Christian king is criticized for his abominable treatment of the civilian population, in particular his scorched-earth strategy, according to which "women and children were slaughtered like cattle."[114] Girabobe wins a strategic standoff and then offers peace, which the king and his knights accept after Graf Rudolf's pleading. The narrator laments the loss of life on both sides.[115] The intercultural collaboration exemplified by Rudolf and Girabobe finds further expression in episodes that introduce additional heathen characters who are either educated in courtly culture or desired in marriage. Rudolf succeeds in winning the heart of a Syrian princess, who converts to Christianity. The couple nevertheless faces many adverse situations; toward the end of the fragmented manuscript the lament "Alas! Why was I born in such terrible times!" powerfully expresses the frustrations of the crusading experience.[116]

Graf Rudolf documents the reality of historical events in more than one way: it discusses the tension between newly arriving crusading knights and locals, including the king of Jerusalem; acknowledges conflicts between kings and their vassals; reflects the practice of arranged marriages between Christians and Muslims; and mirrors the intermittent political interventions of the Byzantine emperor. Whereas the protagonists of this particular story are not historical, the topics articulated through the narrative closely resemble historical developments of the era.

Most German texts critical of the Crusades were composed after the battle of Hattin, which led to the loss of Jerusalem in 1187. This holds true for writings in Latin as well as in Middle High German.[117] The most well-known critique of Christian endeavors in the Middle East is articulated in epics by Wolfram von Eschenbach. In *Parzival* (ca. 1200–1210) the connection to the Crusades is implied in various encounters between (European) Christians and various non-Christian characters. The account of the adventurous voyages of Parzival's father, Gahmuret, which sets the tone of the epic's multicultural contacts, is Wolfram's addition to the French main source text, *Perceval* (*Le Conte du Graal*), by Chrétien de Troyes. After his father's death, Gahmuret leaves home to serve the Baruc of Baghdad, who is described as the mightiest and most respected ruler of the time. Gahmuret excels in this function and on one of his assignments travels to Zazamanc. Here, Gahmuret serves and falls in love with the black queen Belakane and fathers a child. He leaves Belakane before the child is born, supposedly because she is not baptized. The narrative makes it clear, however, that Gahmuret uses this reason as an excuse to move on—after all, the story needs to continue. Years later the offspring from this relationship, a black-and-white checkered knight called Feirefiz (who thus bears some features of the mixed-race Arabic knight 'Antar), meets his half brother Parzival in a joust and emerges as an exemplary knight: when Parzival loses his sword, Feirefiz does not take advantage of the situation but, rather, offers reconciliation. He ends up converting to Christianity, but the narrative reveals that his ultimate goal is to marry Parzival's aunt Repanse. Feirefiz promises to do whatever is necessary and declares, "Brother, I believe in the God of your aunt and in her!"[118] This conversion borders on heresy and makes it clear that Wolfram wanted his readers to consider the idea of what constitutes a noble human being: in his view it is ethical and spiritual conduct, rather than nominal heritage or formal membership in a religion, that determines the true nobility of individuals.

This message was also put forth in *Willehalm* (ca. 1215), an epic that directly addressed the question of the Crusades and which was "immensely popular in the German Middle Ages."[119] Wolfram adapted the story from a French source, a chanson de geste, describing an encounter between Muslim and

Christian armies that occurred in the south of France in the early eighth century. But, as he did in *Parzival,* Wolfram changed the message substantially: the epic is a lament of the unfortunate loss of life on both sides. The central character is Gyburc, an Arab princess whose original name was Arabel, who had fallen in love with the French knight Willehalm, left her family and her country, and converted to Christianity (the conversion of a "heathen" woman to Christianity and her ensuing marriage to a Christian man was a popular topos in European literatures at the time). The war was instigated by her Muslim family in an attempt to bring her home. In his epic Wolfram not only acknowledged the nobility of both heathen and Christian knights, but he allowed Gyburc to utter the central message of the text: that all human beings, having been born as yet unbaptized, were heathen at some point and are thus equal to one another. She refers to characters of the Old Testament to make the point that central figures venerated by Christians were not baptized (a point that also addresses the anti-Judaism of the Middle Ages), and, in the name of a humanist perspective that was directly at odds with the official teachings of the church, she encourages both sides to stop fighting.[120]

Wolfram's criticism goes farther than that of any other text transmitted to us from the period, and questions remain regarding his references to Arabic place-names and his intimate knowledge of Arab culture.[121] Wolfram may well have had contact with some learned Muslim or Jewish scholar; although we have no documentation of such an exchange, it is realistic to presume that—in light of the significant traffic between north and south—personal contacts were at the core of Wolfram's knowledge and his unorthodox views of the Islamic world.

Next to Wolfram, other critics of the Crusades pale not only in terms of their overall aesthetic achievement but also with regard to the extent of the critique they articulate. Nevertheless, these texts are significant because they indicate that Germans debated both the ideological framework and the practice of crusading. Arthur Groos's assessment of Wolfram's *Parzival*—he wrote that "Wolfram's narrative secularizes clerical crusading discourse on the East, thereby destabilizing its narrow religious perspective"—applies to other texts as well.[122] One such example is Reinmar der Alte's poetry. These poems, composed at the end of the twelfth century, differ from earlier examples of *Kreuzlieder* in that they express an ambivalent attitude toward the Crusades. Reinmar questioned the collective experience and highlighted the conflict between worldly pleasures and the joy of fighting for spiritual reward. Unlike other poets, such as Hartmann von Aue, Reinmar contested the compatibility of these different goals and clearly favored the pursuit of worldly pleasures.[123]

Otto von Botenlauben expressed similar views in his poetry, which he wrote in the period around 1200. In "Waere Kristes lôn niht alsô süeze," for example, he emphasizes the conflict between earthly and heavenly love by expressing his hesitation to leave his lover, whom he calls his "heaven." The woman's voice responds that because he made her his heaven, she selected him to be her God and that his loss would destroy her happiness forever.[124] Appropriating religious imagery to express worldly concerns might have bordered on blasphemy, but doing so allowed Otto von Botenlauben to illustrate clearly the tension between courtly and religious value systems. The role of the female voice is central here. William E. Jackson has shown that "there exists no medieval poem in any language in which a female persona is portrayed as speaking out in support of crusading."[125] Given the central role played by women in courtly literature, as catalysts and role models for inducing exemplary behavior, this aspect may highlight the critique expressed through the use of the female voice, but it may also, as Jackson argues, speak to the "concerns of women who viewed themselves as crusade victims," as they and their children were abandoned by crusading men.[126] A critique of the dominant idea of holy war was also expressed by Ulrich von Lichtenstein in a poem contained in his *Frauendienst* (Service to Ladies, ca. 1255), where he presents the holy war as a function of serving a woman, rather than God.[127] Whereas poetry from the end of the twelfth century, such as that of Albrecht von Johansdorf, had already expressed the conflict between competing loyalties—namely, to the world (embodied in love for a woman) and the realm of the religious (embodied in the love of Christ)—the shift in emphasis on the worldly relationship, as articulated by the later poets, challenged crusading ideology.

Increasingly, the *Kreuzzugsklagen*—that is, laments about the Crusades—of the thirteenth century articulate the fatigue many Germans displayed in light of new calls for crusading. Often poets drew on their personal experiences: in the first third of the thirteenth century Neidhart von Reuenthal, who is said to have fought in Egypt, wrote two songs about the Crusades in which he expresses concerns about the meaningfulness of the Crusades. He laments the harsh reality of warfare and the strenuous journeys, openly expressing his desire to return home to Germany, and ultimately questions the benefits of Christian warfare.[128] In a poem from 1228–29 that begins with the words "Wol ime, der nu beizen sol," Tannhäuser details the adverse conditions of the journey, namely, the harsh winds, waves, unsavory meat, and moldy wine. The last two lines of the poem express ambivalence: "Because of God I traveled away from home, and I was not asking the question of how hard it would be for me."[129] This statement can be read as a final acceptance of the hardships in light of the ultimate motivation, but the poem as a whole nevertheless focuses mainly on the many challenges crusaders faced.

Whereas some of these poems maintained an ambivalence between their ultimate support of the Crusades and their concerns about a range of problems associated with these wars, a number of interpretations are possible, depending at times on the ordering of stanzas, which new editions of manuscripts suggest in some cases. It is also unclear whether a final statement of support of the Crusades at the end of a poem is a concession to the expectations of the audience or perhaps even an ironic reference to those expectations, something a knowledgeable and worldly audience might have greeted with laughter. Apart from these aspects, which lead us in most cases to conjecture, the extent and trajectory of the critique becomes evident by comparing the later poems to earlier examples of the genre. The sheer fact that hardships are mentioned, in some cases extensively, distinguishes these poems from early propaganda literature. The disillusionment with the Crusades, as a result of the continuing defeats of crusaders and the reality of physical challenges, clearly motivates the later works. In addition, these poems contain a complexity that deserves to be mentioned here; they refer to other literary works and genres, such as love poems (*Minnelieder*), through allusions and puns, which an educated audience would have been able to appreciate. The last two lines of Tannhäuser's "Wol ime, der nu beizen sol," for example, may be interpreted as an allusion to the central question that needs to be asked by Parzival in his search for the Grail.[130]

Freidank added another dimension to the reality of the crusaders' woes in his poem "Akkon-Sprüche": he lamented not only disease, death, and the greediness of the crusaders, but also the conflict between the crusading armies coming from Europe and local Christian settlers. In Freidank's view the local settlers took advantage of the soldiers coming from overseas. He also bemoaned the way that Christians and heathens stuck together in Acre, united by the fact that they spoke the same language, namely, Arabic. His frustration is expressed quite directly: "One heathen is more dear to them [the local Christians] than two or three Christians."[131] Freidank's poem ends with an exhortation that is clearly supportive of crusading ideology: "Whoever dies there [in Acre] in the right way will be saved."[132] The detailed description of daunting challenges facing the crusaders suggests an ambivalence that is not resolved by the programmatic declaration about the ultimate benefit of the martyr's death in Acre.

Freidank's poem addresses a complex dimension of the historical situation that pits ideology against practice; increasingly, the reality of the crusading experience created a gap between new recruits coming from Europe and settlers in the crusader states. We should not forget that the seven or eight expeditions that are counted by historians as distinct events were only the largest identifiable military campaigns; in addition to these larger campaigns, a steady flow of crusaders moved south. In the course of the twelfth century a rhythm was established: departing from Italian and French port cities, "seasonal crusaders" left for Palestine twice a year, usually in the spring and fall, and supplied the crusader states with new troops.[133] Because of their ignorance regarding local conditions, these regular arrivals of new crusaders and pilgrims, whose numbers increased in the course of the thirteenth century, were a mixed blessing for the European Christians who had settled in the region. As documented in Muslim accounts from the period, Christians and Muslims managed to live peacefully with one another, which irritated European Muslim and Christian travelers alike. Ibn Jubayr, a Muslim pilgrim from Andalusia who traveled through Palestine in 1184, expressed his amazement at observing instances of peaceful Christian-Muslim coexistence.[134] But even during the early period of the Crusades odd alliances between Christians and Muslims occasionally sprang up, reflecting internal divisions in both camps. The conflict between Baldwin and Tancred over the city of Edessa, which led Baldwin temporarily to support the Muslim leader Jawali Saqau against Tancred, is one such example.[135]

In fact, these kinds of alliances had become a necessity, especially in the economic realm, because too few crusader knights had permanently settled after the conquests of the early phase. Already in the early twelfth century, Muslims were encouraged to remain on or return to their land and to cultivate it, for the benefit of both occupiers and the native population.[136] In addition, as Norman Daniel has pointed out, shared notions of knighthood provided a link for Muslims and European Christians to communicate with each other. The most visible area of difference, apart from religion, was the status of women in society. Notions of *largesse* and *courtoisie,* however, enabled both sides to interact.[137] Acculturation also played a role: Usama Ibn Munqidh reported on "Franks who have settled in our land and taken to living like Muslims. These are better than those who have just arrived from their homelands, but they are the exception, and cannot be taken as typical."[138] Ibn Munqidh's account includes a description of a visit to the house of one such orientalized European, who, when offering food, assures his Muslim guests that "no pig's flesh ever comes into my house."[139] It is not surprising that newcomers from Europe reacted with shock and disbelief to such instances of cultural assimilation; English sources, for example, describe Europeans dressed in Arab garb and speaking Arabic.[140] Other sources document concerns "about future crusader inhabitants of the East 'going Saracen.'"[141] The fact that Arabs recorded these positive encounters more frequently than their European counterparts has been noted by scholars.[142] Perhaps fiction texts written by Germans and other Europeans can be seen as providing further evidence of cross-cultural contact and interaction.

Another aspect of the material reality that structured the relationship between Muslims and Christians, namely, the significance of trade, is articulated in an epic poem by Rudolf von Ems, *Der gute Gerhart* (written after 1215).[143] Gerhart, a successful long-distance trade merchant, gets drawn into the conflicts between Christians and heathens, and proves himself through selfless behavior. By placing a merchant at the center of the action, the story also reflects the emerging consciousness of the new class of influential burghers.[144]

A later example of this group of texts that were critical of the Crusades and which document the historical reality of Muslim-Christian interaction is the epic *Reinfried von Braunschweig* (ca. 1300). This epic attempts to revive the ethics of courtly culture by suggesting the Crusades were led for the wrong reasons and fought by knights who did not display exemplary behavior. In *Reinfried,* as in the epic *Graf Rudolf,* the policy of scorched earth was questioned.[145] Whereas the text seems at first to have been designed to promote the proper values necessary to lead crusades, it gradually presents possibilities of intercultural collaboration on the basis of a shared code of ethics. A Persian nobleman, for example, is not forced to convert and ends up becoming Reinfried's companion.[146] The two friends then embark on a series of adventures in the East. In this environment of shifting perspectives the Muslim sultan is portrayed as a model preferable to the unreasonable and debauched Christian knights.[147]

The negative image of crusaders appears also in texts written outside of the German context by, for example, William of Tyre and James of Vitry. But the critique that was expressed across Europe was directed primarily at the conduct of crusaders, at the acculturation of European settlers, and at various secular and religious leaders, and did not entail an appreciation of Arabs or Muslims comparable to what we find in German sources.[148] As Trotter states about the French tradition, "It is rare, and surprisingly so, to find the crusades themselves the object of criticism. It is either their mishandling or misuse which incurs poetic wrath. Secondly, even this reason for invective against the leaders of crusades is very often merely a pretext for, and ammunition in, the more general anticlerical struggle."[149] Distinct geopolitical constellations inspired rhetorical shifts in different contexts. As Jaye Puckett has shown, the changing views of the Crusades in thirteenth-century songs of French troubadours, for instance, can be linked to the failure of the Fourth Crusades but also to the Albigensian Crusade.[150] But here, critique of crusading did not result in the invention of positive Middle Eastern characters. Along these lines, the use of Oriental metaphors in, as an example, Dante's work does not share the appreciation so clearly expressed in Wolfram's and other German epics.[151] Geraldine Heng's discussion of what she terms the "Constance Group" of medieval romances demonstrates in exemplary fashion that in the British tradition favorable portrayals of interfaith and interracial relations were mostly unthinkable.[152] The German tradition seems to be unique in this regard.

Nevertheless, even while diplomatic solutions were attempted in the Holy Land and criticism was voiced at home, some German poets and other writers continued to champion the Crusades. As suggested earlier, songs by Walther von der Vogelweide, Rubin, and Bruder Wernher, which were written right around the time of the Fifth Crusade, resume the enthusiastic rhetoric of the early period and stress the duty of Christians to serve God by defending the Holy Land. But things were unraveling quickly in the course of the thirteenth century; the crusader states were lost one after another, and Acre, the last Christian stronghold, fell in a terrible siege in 1291. Texts from the middle of the thirteenth into the early fourteenth century by, for example, Hawart, Meister Alexander (also known as Wilder Alexander), and Barthel Regenbogen affirm the realization that the time of the Crusades was over.

Calls for crusades to recover the Holy Land did not subside, however, with the fall of Acre. As Antony Leopold shows in his evaluation of crusade proposals of the late thirteenth and early fourteenth centuries, "the recovery of the Holy Land was regarded as an attainable goal for forty years after the fall of Acre."[153] These treatises were written by monarchs, clerics, and even merchants, and range in length and style. To a large extent they were inspired by the activities of the popes of the period, who attempted to renew their leadership, often in opposition to secular leaders. Based on the material compiled in Leopold's anthology, it seems that during this period German leaders did not raise their voices in favor of further crusades in any significant way.

The claim to political and religious sovereignty over Palestine, however, continued to determine the relationship between German-speaking countries and the Middle East in significant ways. Although Germans did not participate in political action in the Holy Land again until the middle of the nineteenth century, the centrality of the holy sites was kept alive through pilgrimage rituals and the circulation of texts about Palestine, including highly popular travel reports by pilgrims and other visitors to the area. One of these late medieval texts is a romance entitled *Wilhelm von Österreich;* the earliest and most relevant version of this story was completed in 1314 by Johann von Würzburg. A mix of love, jousting, and conversion episodes, not reflecting a particular religious or even political stance, the text picks up themes laid out in writings from the preceding 150 years.[154] In this story Wilhelm dies in an attack carried out by heathen who were baptized after Christian victory, and who were led by a relative of Wilhelms's wife (who also converted before her marriage to Wilhelm). Neither baptism nor kinship resolves the conflict between Christians and Muslims. The fact that *Wilhelm* did not convey a clear political or religious stance may be interpreted as a reflection of the general ideological confusion in light of the failures of the Crusades and actual intercultural contact. The text was copied and reworked in manuscripts and prints published into the sixteenth century.

In addition, German travelers such as Wilhelm von Boldensele (1333) and Ludolf von Sudheim (1350) left behind valuable accounts about their pilgrimages to the Middle East. These narratives transcend the focus of the religious aspect of the pilgrimage and signal the emergence of a new textual tradition that displayed a new consciousness concerned with geographical and anthropological information (see chap. 2).

Amnesia

In reflecting upon the events that connected Germany and the Middle East during the Middle Ages, we can highlight the following aspects. The Christian claim to sovereignty over territories located in the Middle East, mainly in Palestine and surrounding areas, was part of a Christian eschatological understanding of space and time. In addition, identification with Greek and Roman history and their longtime presence in areas of Asia Minor and North Africa validated the belief that European Christians were entitled to control those areas. German rulers of the Holy Roman Empire drew on both traditions in staking their claim to the Holy Land. (Jewish history was effectively erased in this constellation of historical claims.) The reality of extensive travel by pilgrims long before the First Crusade also bolstered Germany's, and more generally Europe's, belief that its presence in the region was incontestable. In all these instances, religious and political ideology (communicated orally through, for example, sermons and courtly poetry, and textually, albeit to a very small group of educated individuals) played a significant role in motivating action, such as the Crusades.

The Crusades need to be seen, however, in the context of larger expansive movements into southern and eastern regions. In all cases the rationale for military conflict was inspired by a blend of religious, political, and economic motivations. In Spain, crusader ideology could be seen in the activities that led to the eventual reclaiming of the country from Muslim rule. In eastern Europe, Germans were interested in expanding their political and economic control and employed crusading ideology to pursue these goals. Crusading ideology was also used to fight heretics within Europe; the wars in southern France are the most devastating example of attacks on religious minority populations and also reflect the convergence of religious and political ambitions. Local conditions determined the specific investment of different communities in the Crusades; distinct political and economic policies pitted individual European powers against each other on a regular basis, challenging the notion of a unified Christianity fighting the world of Islam. In addition to the strife among secular leaders, the motives of religious and secular leaders often conflicted as well; that tension became evident as European crusaders began to lose territory to Muslim rulers in the mid-twelfth century. Over time the failures and losses led to an eventual critique of crusading ideology, and this critique was articulated by German-language poets in distinct ways.

The textual archive that informs the analysis presented here expressed, reflected, and influenced the varying ideological positions that motivated political actors, both religious and worldly, and their critics. This archive, which shares similarities across Europe, also documents the complex relationship between ideas, as expressed in literary and other texts, and various practices and material dimensions. The outstanding example in this regard is the interaction between acculturated European Christians, Middle Eastern Christians, and Muslim Arabs living side by side in Palestine as well as in Muslim Spain and Sicily.[155] Reactions to that coexistence, voiced by Christians and Muslims from Europe and the Middle East, highlight the clash between official doctrine and people's lived reality. As Michael A. Köhler has convincingly demonstrated in a significant study, the numerous alliances and treaties between European and Muslim rulers in Palestine and surrounding areas document that extensive interaction.[156] Michael Lower's study on the complex alliances between various Christian and Muslim powers in the late thirteenth-century French Crusade against Tunis is another case in point and demonstrates that political alliances were often not based on religious affiliation.[157]

In conclusion I would like to call attention to two points to inspire further reflection. Both concern the relation of textual discourses to social, economic, and political practices and materiality. First, we have to acknowledge the distinctness of the German tradition. At the beginning of the Crusades, German textual images of Muslims were entirely religiously motivated, and negative as such, but became more differentiated over time (particularly so in comparison to textual traditions of other European cultures). Regarding the views of Middle Easterners in European accounts, the German material reveals the shifting perspectives and the influence of social interaction, from pure fantasy to images that reflect social contact. In the early phase of the Crusades, the idealized knight is juxtaposed to the debased heathen, but over time Germans articulated a critique of crusader ideology and expressed shared ideals through the figure of the noble heathen, male and female, especially in secular texts.[158] This image should thus not be seen as a romanticized fabrication. Rather, it documents knowledge about shared features of European and Middle Eastern cultures, the political and military failures of the Crusades and the tremendous loss of life,[159] admiration for aspects of Arab Muslim cultures, and the fact that European settlers living in Palestine coexisted with their Arab neighbors. It also pays tribute to instances of divergent interests of worldly and religious powers. Even though scores of clerical as well as political leaders continued to call upon Christians to participate in holy wars throughout the thirteenth century, the enthusiasm of the early phase had been lost. By the thirteenth century European Christians served as mercenaries in Muslim armies, trade between the spheres—cyclical patterns of growth and decline and shifting centers of trading activities, notwithstanding—was active, and conversions to Islam were common.[160]

The tension between cultural representations, practices, and material reality is also tangible in the writings of Middle Eastern historians of the Crusades who often pursued a more fact-oriented approach. They were also critical of Muslim leaders, and their accounts have been verified, for example, by Byzantine sources and material evidence. Documentation of systematic rapes of captured Christian women by Muslims, for instance, acknowledges the harsh reality of warfare for women whose fate generally received little mention.[161] According to these sources, crusaders were more likely to massacre than to rape Muslim or Jewish women, as "sexual abuse would contaminate the purity of the Crusader."[162] In light of this kind of multifaceted data the actions of crusaders stand in stark contrast to their idealized self-representation in most European literature of the time.

However, Arabic literary and historical sources, as well as literary texts by Germans and other Europeans who were critical of the Crusades and who assumed that social interactions between Arabs and Germans were possible, paid tribute to the reality of coexistence in Palestine and other areas.[163] In this regard the thirteenth-century Arabic epic *Sirat 'Antar* offers additional evidence for the complex collaboration between Middle Eastern and European knights: as the leader of the Byzantine army, 'Antar opposes the "Franks" in battle but also collaborates with them. Interactions between Muslims and European Christians in the epic, in spite of the often clearly unhistoric nature of the narrative, have inspired scholars for decades to speculate about the genesis of this outstanding example of Arabic literature.[164] Other examples of Arabic heroic literature incorporate themes related to the interaction between Middle Eastern and European rulers and their armies, often displaying surprising historical inaccuracies but perhaps thereby more accurately rendering constantly shifting and perplexing alliances.[165] Numerous contemporary Arab poets also commented on these complex, ever-changing events.[166]

Whereas the absorption of Middle Eastern cultural materials—stories, genres, images—is acknowledged for central authors of the British and Italian tradition, such as Chaucer and Dante (both of whom wrote at a later point and thus require a different geopolitical contextualization), the *appreciation* of aspects of Middle Eastern culture that we find mostly in thirteenth-century German epics and songs seems to be rather unique in the European context.[167] The figure of the noble heathen existed in literatures across Europe, but the German textual tradition—which, like the English tradition, was commonly based on French sources—goes farther in imagining cross-cultural compatibility and interfaith collaboration.[168] On the one hand, the number of German epics that promoted this notion of interfaith and intercultural understanding is relatively small; on the other hand, based on the number of extant manuscripts, *Willehalm* and *Parzival* were the most popular German texts in the Middle Ages and inspired countless reworkings and extensions.[169] Nevertheless, this appreciation was limited to elite circles, expressing the attitudes of limited groups of a somewhat secularized nobility, and does not reflect the thinking of dominant religious circles or—as far as we can conclude from accounts of medieval popular religiosity—the population at large.

What explains the fact that this particular German tradition is unique? Was it facilitated by German-Italian dynastic connections, by flows of political power that related Germans to an Islam-friendly Sicily at a moment when disenchantment with the Crusades was rising and other interests were emerging, namely, with regard to eastern Europe? Perhaps, in contrast to the English and French tradition, the Muslim Middle East did not provide the negative foil to develop ideal notions of Germanness because at the time Germany was not united by a national consciousness. The transnational nature of the Holy Roman Empire, with its strong regional leaders, may have precluded the emergence of a binarism that pitted German Christians against Arab Muslims, as both Heng and Calkin have argued for the (somewhat later) British tradition. In light of the available insufficient evidence, however, I hesitate to venture a conclusive answer; further comparative research may shed some light.

Second, in spite of the extensive interactions between the two cultural spheres, awareness of the extent and repercussions of cross-cultural interaction and knowledge transfer remains minimal to this day. The memory of the Crusades has remained highly inaccurate over the centuries and continues to serve various ideological functions. Much of what was related to cultural contact left only scant traces in the memory of Germans/Europeans: whereas some areas of knowledge transfer from the Middle East have been acknowledged (for example, with regard to the role the Arabs played in translating Greek and Roman sources), the sophisticated knowledge that Muslim geographers acquired regarding the settled areas of Asia and Africa, for instance, was not integrated into the European understanding of the world. In spite of the translation schools in Muslim Spain, the collaboration between scientists in Sicily, and the two hundred years of coexistence in Palestine, Europeans continued to spread fables about mythical beings and monsters located in Asia—areas that were well known to Muslims.[170] While the Muslim scholar al-Biruni presented a sophisticated analysis of Hindu religion and society in 1030 (*Kitab al-Hind* [The Book of India]), European notions of India remained mythological well into the early modern era. The fable about the Christian realm of Prester John in India (and later China and Ethiopia) circulated up until the sixteenth century.[171]

In other areas, however, we have evidence of the integration of Middle Eastern knowledge into European culture, yet this evidence is not part of European memory. The fact that central epics and stories of European literature—such as, but certainly not limited to, the German epic *Herzog Ernst*—drew on material from works such as *One Thousand and One Nights* is at best acknowledged in specialized scholarship but remains limited to these expert circles. Evidence for the reception of Arab scientific thought has been demonstrated for Chaucer but is not widely known.[172] Admiration for the dress and weaponry of Middle Eastern knights, a central topic of many German epics, illustrates that not only were tales brought home by the crusaders but also cloth and other items from the Middle East. In Israel, Palestine, Jordan, Lebanon, and Syria remnants of crusaders' castles remain visible today as constant reminders of the past.[173] Various artifacts documenting the artistic heritage of the crusaders also remain present in the area as well as in European churches, libraries, and museums.[174] In Europe, however, the presence of Islamic civilization is less easily detectable. The influence of Arab mathematics, medicine, technology, chemistry, astrology, astronomy, warfare, clothing, architecture, pharmacology, cooking, and many other cultural achievements has been demonstrated clearly, but its significance for the development of European sciences and economies, its actual presence in European civilization, is not widely acknowledged beyond a small circle of scholars.[175]

The tension between the reality of social contact, material exchange, the textual archives, and subsequent memory is not unique to the Middle Ages. Beliefs and transmitted histories clash with the actuality of intercultural social, political, and economic interaction and coexistence. Ideology determined the mental map of the world and kept Europeans from acknowledging their assimilation of knowledge and skills from the Middle East and the incorporation of the region's goods and techniques. This paradox would emerge again and would propel much of the discovery of the New World and the subsequent colonization of the globe. For the time being, however, Muslim empires ruled the world immediately adjacent to Europe and controlled parts of Europe itself. In fact, the threat of Muslim rule over European, including German, territories intensified with the rise of the Ottoman Empire, which shall occupy us in the next chapter.

CHAPTER 2

Conflict with the Ottoman Empire (1350–1683)

The last Christian bastion in Palestine was retaken by Arabs in 1291, but by the beginning of the fourteenth century European Christianity was confronted with an enemy on its own territory. For the next few centuries, German interaction with Arab rulers and their populations was negligible. While British, French, Spanish, Italian, and other European peoples were affected in significant ways by, for example, the slave raids of North African corsairs, German attention was turned toward the Ottoman Empire, which posed a serious threat to central Europe.[1]

After a brief review of the early phase of the Ottoman invasions our discussion first centers on fiction and nonfiction material that continued to be devoted to the Holy Land and adjacent areas. This material reworked aspects and themes integral to medieval writings but is also distinguished by innovation. By the early fifteenth century and culminating in the two sieges of Vienna in 1529 and 1683, the Ottomans took center stage. Reactions to the Ottoman invasions were articulated in a wide range of publications, including theological texts, nonfiction writings (particularly newspapers and autobiographical accounts), and fictional representations of the Ottomans. The analysis of this varied material reveals a distinct shift to include substantially more and—especially in nonfiction material—often correct information about culture and society in writings on the Ottomans. The last section evaluates the German discourse in relation to the larger European discourse on Turks and Muslims at the time.

From the Holy Land to the Ottoman Invasions

The Ottoman onslaught began in the early fourteenth century when Ottoman troops advanced steadily north- and northwestward into European territory. In the second half of the fourteenth century Thrace, Macedonia, and Bulgaria were captured, and in 1389 the Ottomans defeated the Serbs at Kosovo, leaving Constantinople cut off from other European countries. A European coalition organized in reaction to the Ottoman invasions was defeated in 1396 at the Battle of Nicopolis. Nearly fifty years later, in 1444, another broad alliance of European rulers was defeated at Varna. These victories in European areas prepared the way for the capture of Constantinople in 1453, which marked a turning point in the history of the Ottoman Empire and led to the administrative, fiscal, and military consolidation of Ottoman rule.[2] Serbia became a tributary in 1459, and, after the occupation of Bosnia, Herzegovina, and Albania, the Ottomans began their incursions—in 1473, 1476, 1478, 1480, and 1483—into Austrian areas.[3] By 1504 they had acquired the Romanian principalities.

Europeans sought to fight the Ottomans by establishing political coalitions and, in keeping with traditions of previous centuries, drew on established patterns of crusading rhetoric. This rhetoric, however, did not succeed in uniting Christians from different regions to lead a large-scale attack against the Ottomans. The lack of enthusiasm, particularly among secular leaders, can be tied, to some extent, to the humiliating defeat in the Crusades. More significant, however, was the fact that Europe was politically divided, with leaders involved in territorial disputes across the Continent. The beginning of the Hundred Years' War between France and England (1337–1453), for example, effectively prevented collaboration between the two powers. Other regions were similarly divided; in the Latin East, for instance, Venetians, Genoese, Frankish states, Cyprus, Rhodos, and "various duchies and lordships in eastern Greece and the Aegean islands . . . presented anything but a united front."[4]

The Church, however, continued to build on earlier ideas and practices. In light of the Ottoman invasions, a new series of military expeditions that were promoted as crusades began with an attack on Smyrna in 1344. A century later, on August 12, 1451, Pope Nicholas V issued a Bull of Crusades that "covered all Catholic Europe with the exception of Iberia" and granted indulgence to those who participated in the defense of the kingdom of Cyprus, whose strategic importance was significant.[5] The sale of indulgences served as an important fund-raiser for the Church, although most European rulers did not respond to the appeal.

Calls for crusades to recover the Holy Land were mainly commissioned by popes and other clerics and were composed by monarchs, clerics, and even doctors and merchants for several decades following the fall of Acre. After the start of the Hundred Years' War, although they were no longer being produced, these treatises continued to be copied and circulated throughout the fourteenth and into the fifteenth centuries. They differed from earlier calls for crusades in that they were "mostly very practical in tone, offering considered advice on how a recovery crusade should proceed." A number of historians, according to Antony Leopold, "have viewed the proposals as being the most distinctive feature of crusading in the early fourteenth century and as a phenomenon new to the period."[6] In line with developments from the twelfth century, calls for crusades were issued for fights against various non-Christian enemies. As mentioned earlier, crusade treatises did not succeed in unifying European powers; in particular, rulers and even clerics from Germany did not promote the idea in any notable ways. Nevertheless, various military expeditions were staged as crusades, such as the 1365 attack on Alexandria by Peter I of Cyprus (who had also recruited in Germany); the attack ended with a Muslim victory after the city was looted by the crusaders. Another case of an expedition promoted as a crusade was the French siege of Mahdia in 1390, carried out with support of the Genoese. German rulers, however, did not actively contribute to these activities.

The period up to the fall of Constantinople was thus characterized by internal political strife and the Church's attempt to unify Europe. The reluctance by Europeans to respond to the new enemy is recorded in the textual tradition; material preserved from the fourteenth and early fifteenth centuries continued to focus on the Holy Land and an imaginary Orient. It is also important to acknowledge the reduction in literary output in the second half of the fourteenth century as a result of the devastating plague of the mid-fourteenth century in which about 33 percent of Europe's population died. "Between 1347, when the plague arrived in Sicily, and 1352, when it appeared in the plains in front of Moscow," according to John Kelly, "the continent lost twenty-five million of its seventy-five million inhabitants."[7] The plague's impact on the economy and social infrastructure of Europe was tremendous; with regard to the economy, Şevket Pamuk has argued that "modern economic growth and the Black Death are the two events that led to the most significant changes in wages and incomes during the last millennium."[8] Repercussions from this disaster curbed textual production for several decades.

Much of the literary material familiar from the High Middle Ages continued to make its way into popular narratives. The Alexander novel was retold in multiple versions throughout the fifteenth century. Johann Hartlieb, for example, followed Leo's *Nativitas et victoria Alexandri Magnis regis* but reworked the material so that Alexander was conceived as a role model for German rulers. Composed in 1444 in accessible language, Hartlieb's extremely successful work was printed for the first time in 1472, reached a large audience, and continued to be reprinted throughout the sixteenth and seventeenth centuries. Hartlieb's and similar texts use the Oriental material for entertainment and to comment on local conflict and contemporary events at home, but do not directly address political conflicts between Europe and the Middle East. It is perhaps not surprising, then, that epics such as *Wilhelm von Österreich* and *Reinfried von Braunschweig,* which identified the prolonged absence of rulers during the Crusades as the reason for increasing problems at home, were adapted and widely circulated in the post-Crusade era. Hans Sachs, who rewrote many medieval texts featuring Oriental topoi, later used Hartlieb's *Alexander, Wilhelm von Österreich,* and also *Reinfried von Braunschweig* as bases for his plays.[9]

Alongside the fictional literature that drew on the medieval material without much enthusiasm for the Crusades or the Middle East in general, new information entered the German textual tradition through travel accounts. Writings in Latin about pilgrimages to the Holy Land existed since the earliest pilgrimages, undertaken, for example, by the so-called Bordeaux pilgrim and the nun Egeria in the late fourth century; notable in the German context is the account of Saint Willibald, a German cleric who traveled to the Holy Land at the beginning of the eighth century. All of these texts focus on the description of the holy sites in Palestine and other important stops on the way to and from the Holy Land. Around 1165 Johannes von Würzburg, for example, composed one of the many accounts following the model of the Latin "descriptiones terrae sanctae," which portrayed the holy sites of Palestine according to biblical and other traditions of antiquity. In the late Middle Ages, Wilhelm von Boldensele also used this model to write about the pilgrimage he undertook around 1334–36. His account was translated into German in about 1350 and was significant in making this material accessible to a larger audience. Other German-language autobiographical accounts of journeys to the Holy Land also date from the middle of the fourteenth century and, together with Boldensele's text, represent the beginning of a new genre in terms of style and content. They drew on the established Latin-language traditions but increasingly included ethnographic and historical information about contemporary events.

The account "Ein niederrheinischer Bericht über den Orient," for example, dates from the mid-fourteenth century. Based on the dialect of the text, its author is assumed to have hailed from Cologne. He traveled through Egypt in 1338 and apparently spent the following decade in several locations throughout the Middle East. The author conveys knowledge about the Middle East in systematic fashion. Even though the text itself is not consistently categorized according to specific subjects, the author relates information in areas previously not addressed in the German textual archive and certainly not in the German language. He includes information about geographical locations (e.g., names of countries and cities); political events and actors; religion (e.g., about different groups and sects within Christianity, Judaism, and Islam); customs (e.g., clothing and appearance); and animals, plants, and agricultural products. He describes the fact that "Christians and heathen, who live in those cities, get along well, and do not concern themselves much with the faith of the other."[10] The account also includes references to mythological lore, such as Prester John and monstrous peoples who were commonly associated with India. These topoi appear in most accounts about the farther Orient, and it seems that they were so widely considered factual that they functioned to authenticate texts about the areas. That is, even in the case of an account based on an actual journey, these mythological topoi had to be mentioned. This phenomenon continued well into the sixteenth century. Adhering to textual traditions was a crucial element structuring accounts composed in the Middle Ages, and thus the gradual departure from these conventions, beginning in the mid-fourteenth century, indicates larger social developments.

These travel accounts contained significant errors; the author of the "Niederrheinischer Bericht," for example, confuses ethnic and religious communities and seems to know very little about the different languages spoken in the Middle East and adjacent areas. On the other hand, documenting the changes in the content of travel narratives, the text communicates a significant amount of factual information—about specific rules and practices of Islam, for example, as well as the diversity of Christianity in the Middle East. We thus witness a novel attempt to provide information about Middle Eastern countries based on firsthand observation.

Ludolf von Sudheim traveled in the Middle East roughly around the same time as the author of "Niederrheinischer Bericht," about 1336–41. Von Sudheim's account, like that of Boldensele, was also first written in Latin and then translated into vernacular German. Sudheim clearly copied directly from Boldensele; this convention of copying one another's work, even when authors were reporting about a journey they had undertaken themselves, was widespread and speaks to a textual tradition that values the written text more highly than the individual experience. This literary practice inspired another author to fabricate an account that drew entirely on texts composed by others yet to present it as reflecting his own travels. As we know today, John Mandeville, who wrote the most popular travelogue of the later Middle Ages and Early Modern period, never left Europe. His book of travels, which was written anonymously in French around 1357, relied on the accounts of actual travelers, including

Marco Polo, Boldensele, and Sudheim, and added standard topoi from the mythological and folkloristic traditions about India and the Far East.

German-language travel accounts of the fourteenth century often contained several direct references to the Crusades. In some cases the loss of the Holy Land is acknowledged and the desire to recapture it expressed, but the issue is not given much thought beyond what is stated in a few sentences. In Sudheim's account, however, the disastrous destruction of Acre takes up a significant portion of the text, filling ten out of sixty-six pages.[11] He also talks about Turkish attacks on Rhodos, thus recognizing the increasing threat posed to European Christians by the Ottoman invasions.[12]

A late fifteenth-century text exemplifies structural changes that pilgrimage accounts underwent during this period. Bernhard von Breydenbach's memoir about his 1483–84 journey conveys a wealth of information in a coherent and accessible narrative. Breydenbach (who composed his account first in Latin) describes the individual stops along the journey, particularly the sites of the Holy Land, but also customs of different religious communities. His text includes illustrations of Muslims, Jews, and Oriental Christians in typical dress, and one illustration depicts various animals, such as the crocodile and the camel; a picture of a unicorn is also included. He offers a description of Cairo's architecture, its slave market, population, bathhouses, and an Oriental massage. Reproductions of different alphabets (Arabic, Hebrew, Greek, and Syriac) and an Arabic-German glossary at the end of the text are also included, which suggests that interest in Oriental cultures had reached another level.

Breydenbach laments the devastation he observes in the Holy Land, and his condemnation of the state of affairs in the Orient includes Greek-Orthodox Christianity, which is "especially unruly" because of its wrong beliefs.[13] He berates "the cursed law of Muhammad" and also condemns Jews for insisting on their faith.[14] Among the peoples and religious groups of the Middle East, only Abyssinian Christians find his—still conditional—approval. The Ottoman threat is highlighted in the final paragraph of the account in which the author reports on Ottoman attacks on Rhodos in 1480 and warns that the Ottoman "tyrant increases his might and strength from day to day."[15] Other travelers who accompanied Breydenbach, such as Felix Fabri and Konrad von Grünemberg, also published widely circulated accounts, in Latin and German, of the same journey.[16] Additional travelers from the fifteenth century who left portrayals of their pilgrimages to the Holy Land are Dukes Johann and Albrecht of Brandenburg, Wilhelm II of Thuringia, Hans Tucher, and Sebald Rieter.

These accounts remained focused on the Holy Land and played an important ideological role in articulating European Christianity's continuing attachment to the Christian sites. A significant number of these texts were written in the late Middle Ages; according to one statistic, over 120 accounts about journeys to Palestine were composed in the German language (and mostly authored by noblemen) between 1320 and 1500.[17] A statistic based on Röhricht's bibliography, *Bibliographia Geographica Palaestinae,* and Mieck's *Témoignages oculaires,* which include most western European pilgrimage narratives, suggests that 262 accounts about pilgrimages to the Holy Land were written between 1301 and 1540.[18] A recently published bibliography pays tribute to the large corpus of extant manuscripts.[19] The accounts were popular; 32 manuscripts of von Boldensele's account are known to exist, as well as 54 of von Sudheim's.[20] Bernhard von Breydenbach's account was translated into various European languages, and widely disseminated in print versions.[21] The popularity of these writings further influenced the development of the genre and promoted the shift toward including new kinds of information. In addition to providing pilgrimage accounts, chronicles kept crusading ideas alive—an example is Sebastian Brant's *History of Jerusalem,* published in Latin in 1495 and in German translation by Kaspar Frey in 1518. Other chronicles, mostly written in Latin, were composed by Johannes Gast, Thomas Ebendorfer, Heinrich Pantaleon, Celio Agostino Curione, and Sebastian Herold.

The amount of ethnographic and political information contained in the texts reveals the increasing knowledge transfer regarding information about Islam and the peoples of the Middle East. In addition, the fact that the travel account, a genre with specific conventions, gradually allowed for the personality of the traveler to emerge represents a significant shift in the narrative tradition, one that heralded the greater value attributed to observations made by individuals.

Breydenbach's warning against the Ottoman threat in his description of the battle for Rhodos reveals that Christian Europe was clearly involved in a new struggle. But, while appeals to unite a Christian army against the Ottomans remained fruitless, a turning point came with the fall of Constantinople in 1453. The terror experienced by the inhabitants of Constantinople during their last days under Christian rule is described in graphic terms. According to the *Chronicon Maius* by Georgios Sphrantzes, dead bodies were piled up high throughout the city, and scores of men, women, and children were taken into captivity.[22] The city had not been able to withstand the Ottoman onslaught; according to the contemporary account of Michael Kritoboulos, who details the various stages of the siege, Ottoman strategies, and the final takeover, the army had roughly 300,000 troops, not including the supporting personnel.[23] Kritoboulos, who constructs his work as Ottoman history and dedicates it to Sultan

Mehmet II, depicts in detail the atrocities committed by Ottoman troops and argues, in an elaborate comparison, that the destruction of Constantinople was far worse than what had been experienced by Troy, Babylon, Rome, Jerusalem, and other cities.[24] News of the fall of Constantinople quickly spread throughout Europe.

Immediate Danger: 1453–1683

The fall of Constantinople in 1453 has been widely acknowledged as the beginning of the European Renaissance, as the influx of scholars from Constantinople introduced new intellectual horizons to European cities. From Italy the knowledge and skills of these Greek scholars slowly traveled into northern territories. Orthodox Christian refugees brought with them a particular image of the fall of Constantinople as well as a fierce hatred for the Ottoman invaders, along with, as Bisaha shows, some sentiments of "accommodation and even admiration." Dominant, however, was the desire to recapture the homeland, and thus "Italy soon became a seedbed of Greek protonationalist thought."[25] The standing of Orthodox Christians within European Christianity was initially challenged, due to the long history of adversity between Eastern and Western Christianity, but in 1453 a new Christian solidarity began to emerge.

The Christian perspective of Constantinople was visible, for example, in maps of Istanbul. Ian Manners has shown that extant fifteenth- and sixteenth-century maps of Istanbul convey differing images of the city. In most instances the Christian heritage is emphasized, in a clear attempt to claim the city as a Christian site. These maps do not acknowledge the transformation the city underwent following its conquest in 1453 through the building of "fortresses, shipyards, mosques, palaces, cemeteries, markets."[26] Another tradition, which did pay tribute to the historical changes, was much less widely circulated. Manners argues convincingly that "as cultural constructions, the maps play a role in the reappropriation of that contested city for Christianity."[27] Maps of Istanbul were included in different types of texts, such as world chronicles. One of the most well-known of these chronicles, the *Liber Chronicarum* (1493) by Hartmann Schedel from Nuremberg, contained a map typical of this attempt to reappropriate Istanbul for Christianity. On the map "the city appears as it may have looked before the conquest: the gates are decorated with the Byzantine double eagle; in the city there are no Islamic buildings; and outside there are no Ottoman troops with cannons, as appear on similar contemporaneous pictures that show the conquest."[28]

Following the fall of Constantinople came renewed calls for a crusade. The number of indulgences distributed for participation in the struggle against the Ottomans increased, and, in order to meet the demand for producing these important documents, they were commissioned to be printed, putting the means of the revolutionary innovation that had been (re)invented in the early 1450s to immediate use.[29] In fact, of the early products to come off the new printing presses, these one-page documents were the first that could be dated exactly. Printing became an important tool in gathering support against the Ottomans. The earliest preserved pamphlet, for example, is devoted to the conflict with the Ottomans. This so-called *Türkenkalender: Eyn manung der cristenheit widder die durken* was printed in Mainz in 1454, and, although neither author nor printer has ever been identified with certainty, scholars agree that it was printed in the workshop of Johannes Gutenberg. The general thrust of the text is an exhortation to Christianity's leaders to gather their forces in order to fight the Turks in unified fashion.[30] Printing changed the flow of information drastically. Information made available through newspapers and other pamphlets reached groups of the population that previously had only limited access to such knowledge. Newspapers were read in public, and information was passed along to large groups of people, especially in cities. Both factual information and polemics about the Ottomans and Islam were spread this way.[31]

While the *Reconquista* ended Muslim rule in Spain in 1492, increasingly the Ottomans attacked European Christianity on its own territory. Europe continued to be divided, and those powers whose territories were not immediately affected—namely, Britain and France—showed the least concern. Changes were also brought on by the discovery of the New World, which boosted the self-esteem of the powers involved in this enterprise at the time, particularly Spain and Portugal. The rise of the Spanish Empire affected power constellations in Europe: after 1516 the Habsburg dynastic connection with the Spanish Empire resulted in a political axis of the Holy Roman Empire and Spain, whereas France, caught geographically in the middle between these spheres of influence, developed a tense relationship with these powers that further precluded a unified European front against the Ottomans.

The Ottoman expansion continued with renewed vigor under Selim I, who conquered Syria and Egypt in 1517. His son, Suleiman the Magnificent, took power in 1520 and continued the conquest. In 1521 he invaded Hungary and Serbia. In 1526 the Ottomans waged another large-scale operation in the area, defeating the Hungarian army in the Battle of Mohács, during which King Louis II Jagellon was killed, and pillaging Buda. The Hungarian defeat and the death of the king had major repercussions: the Hungarians elected

János Zápolya as king, challenging the dynastic politics that had united Hungarian and Habsburg rule, and secured economic stability in the area.[32] One month later, however, another group of Hungarian noblemen elected Ferdinand of Habsburg as king. Both laid claim to the Hungarian crown, a fact that enabled the Ottoman sultan to find a collaborator in Zápolya. Zápolya accepted the sovereignty of the sultan, and Hungary became a tributary of the Ottoman Empire. This alliance was further strengthened later, when France, which was formally allied with the Ottomans after 1536, recognized Zápolya as the legitimate king of Hungary in 1535.[33] Hungary was from then on divided into three areas: Transylvania (Siebenbürgen), which became Protestant by the 1550s and had secured independent status; the middle part of the country, which was a tributary of the Ottomans; and the western part, which belonged to the Habsburg Empire.[34] Apart from France and parts of Hungary, other states also entered into alliances with the Ottomans, such as the Venetians, who signed separate peace treaties with the Ottomans in 1540 and 1573. The Ottomans were able to maintain their presence in Central Europe until the end of the seventeenth century, when in 1699 they lost Hungary in the Peace Treaty of Karlowitz.

A host of attitudes about the Ottomans was vocalized in publications across Europe, on a spectrum described by Kissling as ranging from "Türkenfurcht" (Turkish fear, i.e., fear of the Turks) to "Türkenhoffnung" (Turkish hope, i.e., hope for the Turk).[35] Some humanist thinkers, especially in Italy, came to see the Turks as "barbarians," which, as Bisaha argues, "provided one more avenue for conceptualizing the Turks via ancient sources" and allowed them to dehumanize the Ottomans and to express their own sense of cultural superiority.[36] Other attempts at understanding the Ottoman invaders included seeing them more neutrally as powerful political adversaries or even favorably as admirable opponents. John of Segovia and Nicholas of Cusa engaged with the Ottomans on a theological level and took a scholarly stance toward Islam. Bisaha explains that "both believed that the key to solving the problems posed by Islam lay in the study of textual sources—namely the Qur'an."[37]

But attitudes were certainly influenced by the geopolitical location of writers of any kind, and specific political, economic, religious, and other ideological factors determined the view of the Ottomans. Until the Hungarian invasion German leaders had not perceived the Ottomans as a threat to their own territory. The situation changed with the Battle of Mohács; the Hungarian defeat made German (particularly Habsburg) territories much more vulnerable to Ottoman conquest and, indeed, ultimately led to the First Siege of Vienna in 1529.

The conflicts with the Ottoman Empire were discussed in all areas of cultural production. Theologians and authors of fiction commented on the hostilities and used the threat of Ottoman invasion to articulate a range of positions. Secular and religious leaders debated their political and military options.[38] Songs as well as woodcuts and paintings with Ottoman themes were extremely popular.[39] Secular and religious rituals were invented that allowed the population to process its fear of the Ottomans.[40] Tournaments staged fights between Germans and Ottomans throughout the fifteenth to seventeenth centuries. Helen Watanabe-O'Kelly has argued that the representations of Ottoman warriors in these games reveal that Ottomans were respected and admired; in spite of several instances in which derogatory images of Ottoman fighters during such jousting events were reported, these reenactments of military conflict reveal that attitudes toward the Ottomans were marked by both fear and admiration.[41] On an economic level, taxes, known as *Türkensteuer,* were introduced to raise money for the fight against the Ottomans.[42] *Türkenhilfe* (help against the Turks) was another term used to refer to these taxes and, in some instances, the actual troops that were sent to fight the invaders. Various German states ordered their populations to fast and pray on specific days in support of the troops, and public prayer hours were held in various places.

In German-speaking areas a flurry of publications were written (often first in Latin), particularly in response to the growing threat following the First Siege of Vienna. In light of the wealth of material, the following sections consider three select groups of German-language material about the Ottoman invasions: theological writings, secular nonfiction writings, and fictional material. Each group of texts reveals a somewhat heterogeneous picture of attitudes, but also unifying tendencies. Whereas the early period of the conflict with the Ottomans is characterized by images that draw on medieval ideas about Islam, the actual encounter with the Ottomans, in battle and other forms of contact, brought an entirely new set of images to the discussion. Over time a fictionalization of some topoi can be observed, in nonfiction as well as fictional writings.

Theological Writings: The Case of Luther

Taken together, religious writings from the period express an attitude that Susan R. Boettcher has compellingly summarized as "religious superiority in an age of military inferiority."[43] Quite in contrast to the Saidian paradigm, religious writings from the period express a sense of superiority not at a moment of actual political might, but, rather, in times of increasing crisis and defeat.

Perhaps one could argue that a sense of superiority is a structural element present in all religions, but, given that we have evidence of moments of peaceful coexistence and collaboration among different religions across time and space, generalizations are not fruitful here. German Christianity voiced differing attitudes toward the Ottomans in sermons, prayers, pamphlets, theological disputations, prophecies, and religious songs. In spite of these diverse viewpoints, the underlying attitude was one of superiority, which confirms Boettcher's argument. The Ottoman invasions were interpreted as the beginning of the Apocalypse: Ottomans were seen as God's punishment for Christian failures; preachers used the Ottoman threat as a vehicle to push specific teachings; certain aspects of Ottoman culture were seen as exemplary and were used to teach negligent Christians a lesson; and Protestants positioned themselves with Ottomans in various ways.[44] Some theologians set out to promote the conversion of Muslims; as Göllner has shown, in contrast to ideas voiced by theologians across Europe, missionary thought was not widespread in Germany.[45] Actual journeys of missionaries to the Ottoman Empire did not begin in significant ways until the seventeenth century and even then "must be seen as part of the movement known as the Counter-Reformation," aimed at encouraging "Ottoman Christian groups to submit to Papal authority."[46]

Knowledge about Islam was increasingly brought into the discussion, even though it had changed little since the Middle Ages. The twelfth-century Latin translation of the Koran by Robert of Ketton (1143) continued to be the standard work and was the basis of the first printed translation, which was edited by the Zurich theologian Theodor Bibliander. A corpus of texts that greatly contributed to creating negative perceptions of Islam consisted of outlandish legends involving the prophet Muhammad.[47] Various refutations of the Koran circulated since the early fourteenth century, such as Riccoldo de Monte Croce's *Confutatio Alcorani* (ca. 1300), which Luther translated into German in 1542. These and other refutations by, for example, Thomas Aquinas, Nicholas of Cusa, and John of Segovia, attempted to engage with Islam on a theological level and were often more factually oriented. But it was not until 1616 that a German-language version of the Koran appeared; still, this work, produced by Salomon Schweigger, was based on an Italian translation that was full of mistakes and omissions and is so highly polemical that it might not qualify as a translation. Information about Islam was also conveyed through various sources based on extended stays of prisoners in the Ottoman Empire. Johann Schiltberger's account of his thirty-year stay among Ottomans and Mongols, Georgius de Hungaria's *Tractatus de moribus, conditionibus et nequicia turcorum* (1481), and Bartolomej Georgijević's *De afflictione tam captivorum* (1544) circulated widely, the originally Latin texts translated into German (and other European languages) soon after their publication.

Theologians drew on these various sources to make their arguments, which were often primarily concerned with bettering Christians at home, rather than fighting the Ottomans per se. In order to understand the reasoning presented in the religious literature of the time, it is worth examining select writings of Martin Luther. Luther was one of the most prominent voices in the public call for unity against the Ottomans. His views differed substantially from those of other European humanists, such as Segovia and Cusa, but were in line with thinkers such as the Italians Petrarch, Salutati, and Leonardo Dati.[48] His opinions were discussed in both Protestant and Catholic churches and came to influence political and religious events across and beyond German territories. An analysis of Luther's writings about the Ottomans sheds light on the constant shifting of alliances and counteralliances between various German secular powers, European secular powers, and the different groupings within the church. It also highlights topoi and motifs central to the larger German discourse on the Ottomans.

The position Luther articulated in several texts from 1529, before and after the First Siege of Vienna, differed quite substantially from his earlier positions. In December 1518, for example, Luther had stated that the pope was a greater menace than the Turks and was unwilling to support a call for war against the Ottomans. In the following years he insisted that the Turk was fought best by introspection and repentance and by leading a life in the spirit of Christianity.[49] In particular, Luther fought renewed calls for a crusade against the Ottomans and the connected practice of selling indulgences. Even after Mohács, he continued to see the Ottoman invasions as God's punishment for the dismal state of Christianity and refrained from calling for war against the Turks. His views were not only contrary to those of both secular and religious leaders, but also largely out of touch with public opinion.[50]

The general fear of renewed Ottoman intervention finally motivated Luther to speak out publicly. This move occurred, however, under pressure from the Protestant princes and cities, which used the conflict with the Ottomans to extract concessions from the emperor in return for their military support. It should be pointed out that independence from Rome not only contained religious dimensions but also carried political and economic benefits.[51] In this conflict between Protestant rulers and the Habsburg emperor and his allies, Luther's writings played a central role.

Luther worked on "Vom Kriege wider die Türken" (On War Against the Turks) between fall 1528 and spring 1529. The text was printed in April 1529, only a few months before the First Siege of Vienna and at a moment when the Second Diet of Spires was in session, deliberating, among other questions, resistance to the Ottomans.[52] The First Siege of Vienna produced a large corpus of texts, as did the Second Siege, and Luther's "Vom Kriege" needs to be understood in the immediate context of this traumatizing event.[53] In "Vom Kriege" Luther pursues two main trajectories: first, he details his new position with regard to taking up arms against the Ottomans; second, he uses his condemnation of the Turks to attack the papacy. Luther acknowledges that he had indeed preached against fighting the Turks but that he had gained new insights "about temporal authority" that implicitly justify his altered position.[54] Luther's revised understanding of the difference between temporal and spiritual authority—he had first elaborated on these concepts in "Von weltlicher Obrigkeit" (On Temporal Authority, 1523)—figures prominently in this argument. He sharply attacks the notion of a holy war and argues that the war against the Turks must be led by the emperor.

Luther blames Islam for attempting to spread its teachings not through preaching but, rather, by the sword. He recounts practices of the Ottoman army, such as selling captives into slavery and the murder of civilians, which, as we will see in the next section, correspond to historical events. Luther discounts reports that under Ottoman rule Christians have the option to keep their faith and argues that Christians are forced, instead, to comply with definite restrictions. Those instances of Christian captives who "become altogether Turkish" pose a particular problem for Luther (121). Here the theologian is addressing the situation of a large number of converts. According to Pál Fodor, up to 30 percent of volunteers in the sixteenth-century Ottoman army can be identified as first-generation renegades, which also "tallies with the ratios experienced within the Ottoman forces of the border areas."[55] These renegades and those Christians who fared relatively well under Ottoman rule concerned Luther greatly. Only through deceit and violence, claims the theologian, are these people kept in a confused state in Ottoman lands (121). Those who voluntarily join the Turks, says Luther, become complicit in the Turks' actions. Luther's ultimate verdict about Turkish religion and customs is unequivocal condemnation, for "the Turk is the irate rod of our Lord God and the slave of the angry devil" (116). In his discussion the only rival to the Turk's purported evilness is the pope, who, he claims, is "the antichrist, just like the Turk is the living devil" (126). Such comparisons pervade the text and culminate in the conclusion that one has to fight the pope just as much as one has to fight the Turks.

Regardless of the pressing historical situation, which explains the urgency of the polemic, we have to acknowledge its ideological purport. The main target of Luther's elaboration is the pope: strengthening the role of the emperor by arguing that only the worldly leader is entitled to lead the army against the Ottomans is primarily aimed at disqualifying the pope. His critique of Islam and the Turks is indeed an attack on religious and cultural difference, but simultaneously provides Luther with ammunition in his struggle against the papacy.[56]

Luther's second text from 1529, "Heerpredigt wider den Türken" (Military Sermon Against the Turk), in which he calls for war against the Turks, was written only months after the publication of "Vom Kriege."[57] The immediate cause propelling Luther to write once again about the topic was the fact that the Ottomans had invaded German lands and laid siege to Vienna. In "Heerpredigt," Luther sets out to highlight religious dimensions of the conflict with the Turks. In order to prove his point that the Turks continue to be a threat, he picks up the apocalyptic tone that appeared at the end of "Vom Kriege" and invokes the prophecies in the seventh chapter of the book of Daniel.[58] Luther's exegesis of biblical passages consistently associates the Ottoman Empire's invasions with the Apocalypse. Accordingly, Luther exhorts his fellow Germans to follow his instructions regarding proper behavior in light of the impending end of the world. Luther repeats what had been the central argument in his previous publication: that the Turks should be fought, first of all, spiritually by Germans behaving like good Christians and by accepting the leadership of the temporal ruler with regard to the military struggle. That the war was not to be fought as a crusade and in the name of Christ comes as a surprise after the detailed association of the Turkish threat with the prophecies of the Bible. This tension, which may be perceived as an internal contradiction, begins to make sense when considered in light of Luther's conflict with the pope: he has to reject the notion of a crusade in order to continue his defiance of papal orders. He justifies his choice of the emperor as the only legitimate leader of a war against the Turks by referring to Romans 13:1 and Titus 3:1, the biblical passages that (in Luther's interpretation) demand ultimate obedience toward the temporal ruler, who is appointed by God.

In light of these concepts, war against the Turks is legitimate. As Luther states, a Christian fighting under the leadership of the emperor should not worry about spilling innocent blood among the Turks, as the Turk is the archenemy of Christianity. And, if a Christian should die at the hand of the Turks, what better fate can happen to the believer than to become a martyr, to die an "honest holy death" (175)? Again, we can detect dissonance within Luther's view of the role of the temporal ruler as leader of the military campaign against the Turks. In spite of his appeals to secular leadership, the idea of dying a martyr's death resonates with crusading rhetoric. In fact, this idea figures quite centrally in Luther's elaboration; over several pages Luther details the advantages and importance of martyrdom (174–80). Even if war against the Turks is not a crusade, it remains a holy war, a war understood in religious terms, because Luther's notion of temporal government is solidly placed within sacred history.

Luther's "Heerpredigt" restates several of the arguments made in "Vom Kriege," but here the emphasis lies in the eschatological dimension of the conflict with the Turks. Whereas Luther quickly identifies reports regarding the cruelty of the Turks as deeds of the devil, he struggles with accounts of commendable aspects of Turkish culture that were based on eyewitness accounts. Another challenge for Luther is that, although the Ottomans were indeed cruel invaders, their army included Christian soldiers and renegades. In addition, as individual European powers (such as Hungary, Venice, and France) entered into alliances with the Muslim invaders, it became increasingly difficult to see this conflict as one exclusively between Christians and Muslims. Luther, however, in order to strengthen his appeal to Germans to join the fight against the Ottoman army, stages the conflict in religious and even apocalyptic tones.[59] As he did in the first text, Luther draws comparisons between Turks and Jews in order to amplify the gravity of the blasphemous behavior he criticizes (186). Using the tools of polemic and propaganda, he ignores or reinterprets conflicting evidence and simplifies the situation by rendering the struggle as one between good and evil, even if reality were more complicated and actual events on the ground defied easy categorization. Luther's discourse distorts not only Ottoman society and Islam but also the actions of European religious and political leaders.[60]

The analysis of Luther's support of war against the Ottomans highlights the ways in which the rise of the Reformation movement, the development of national consciousness (particularly through Luther's use of the German language), and the conflicts with the Ottoman Empire were related. Acknowledging this nexus, historian Stephen Fischer-Galati argues that the Ottoman invasions were the main factor bringing forth the success of the Reformation movement.[61] In addition, the invention of printing was an important factor in disseminating ideas about both the Ottomans and Protestantism. As Mark Edwards states, "It is the magnitude of the effort, and the overwhelming use of the vernacular, that justifies designating this [i.e., the Reformation's use of the possibilities of printing] the West's first large-scale media campaign."[62] In this regard the conflict with the Ottoman Empire had a significant impact on developments within Germany. The image of the cruel invading Ottoman army became crucially tied to Germany's self-image. Opposing viewpoints developed in different parts of Europe: Erasmus of Rotterdam, for example, as a "strong proponent of Christian nonviolence . . . challenged contemporary European notions of holy war and the Infidel."[63] Erasmus changed some of his views after the First Siege of Vienna; nevertheless, in his *Consultatio de bello Turcis inferendo* (1530) "Erasmus did not cease in his attacks on crusade and his calls for more charitable views of the Turks."[64] Generally, however, Luther was more representative of the dominant attitudes being voiced in Germany and variously across Europe.

Luther's sermons were based on existing sources about Islam and the Ottomans, and had a formative function for subsequent texts about the Ottomans.[65] His discussion of converts and renegades; his interpretation of commendable aspects of Ottoman culture as ruses of the devil; his description of Turkish atrocities; his view of the Turk as Satan; the great importance biblical prophecies have in his analysis; the refutation of specific aspects of Islam—these and other topoi were picked up in scores of texts published throughout the sixteenth and seventeenth centuries. Luther's writings were at once part of the discourse on the Ottomans and also played a crucial role in its further development.[66]

Nonfiction Writings: Information about the Ottomans

Newspapers, pamphlets, and travel accounts were the primary sources reporting events at the front and information related to immediate contact with the Ottomans. The large number of printed materials about these topics illustrates the extent to which these topics occupied Central Europeans at the time and, as mentioned earlier, the printing press was immediately put to use to provide commentary about matters central to religion and politics. Göllner's two-volume compilation of sixteenth-century documents about the Ottoman invasions, which are collectively titled *Turcica,* gives insight into both the content and the prevalence of material about the conflicts with the Ottomans. Göllner records 2,460 prints, of which about 1,000 were written in German.[67] Translations, often word for word, were common and document the high degree to which Europeans shared this textual archive across linguistic boundaries. Göllner describes the number of prints published at different times as comparable to the movements of flood and tide; that is, a large number of prints were produced in moments of immediate danger and confrontation, with fewer prints published in the interim periods. Between 1522 and 1523, for example, 80 prints were published on the issue of Rhodos alone, which was embattled at the time; during the following two years, however, Göllner registered only 14 prints on Turkish themes.[68]

Newspapers supplied commentary on the main military conflicts with the Ottomans. After the Battle of Mohács (1526) and the First Siege of Vienna (1529), the major military engagements were the Battle of Lepanto (1571), which ended with a defeat of the Ottoman fleet; the Habsburg-Ottoman war of 1593–1606, which followed a period of relative stability in the aftermath of the Peace of Edirne (1568); the battle of 1664 at St. Gotthard-Mogersdorf; and the Second Siege of Vienna (1683). The latter two events are widely considered turning points that led to the gradual demise of the Ottoman presence in Central and southeastern Europe. In addition to coverage of concrete events, newspapers and other types of texts reported about Ottoman customs, religion, and the fate of individuals who had traveled in the Ottoman Empire, or who had been captured by the Ottomans.[69]

These diverse types of German-language writings that commented on the military confrontations with the Ottomans—excluding the religious writings that I discussed in the preceding section, but which technically also belong to the category of Turcica—were often based on eyewitness reports; others, however, were composed from hearsay. The accounts, which often included maps and illustrations, were written mostly by diplomats, pilgrims, and former captives. Plagiarism was common, and certain topoi became widespread and were often repeated word for word. The ideological gist of the accounts is heterogeneous; their ideological trajectory cannot be reduced to a simple message, such as the Christian rejection of Islam. Rather, we see a more complex picture emerging. Whereas textual traditions from the time of the Crusades are also distinguished by diverging attitudes toward Muslims—ranging from rejection on the grounds of religion to acceptance based on universal notions of knighthood and kinship—texts from the early modern period are heterogeneous in different ways. In contrast to the work of Luther and other religious writings, the religious aspect is less relevant in accounts that were based on actual encounters with Ottoman military practices and/or experience of living under Ottoman rule. The overwhelming power of the invaders sparked curiosity about their strength, which resulted in a desire to know more not only about the Ottoman military and their government but also about their general customs and religion. We should not forget that scores of captured Christians decided to convert to Islam, that especially Protestant and Orthodox Christians experienced a much greater degree of tolerance under Islamic rule, and that several European states decided to align themselves with the Ottomans. This complex situation made it more difficult to reject the Ottomans in simplistic ways.[70]

One early example of such accounts, which would become an influential model for reporting about the Ottomans, is that of Johann Schiltberger, who was captured by the Ottomans at the Battle of Nicopolis in 1396 and spent the following thirty years in the service of Ottoman and Mongol rulers. Upon his return home in 1427 he wrote about his life in the Middle East and Central Asia. This account, which became extremely popular, contains significant ethnographic, socioeconomic, and political information about the various societies Schiltberger got to know during his forced exile. Schiltberger reported about agriculture, religious customs (including an informative section on the life of the prophet Muhammad and one on the Islamic reservations regarding the Christian concept of the Holy Trinity), and the life of nomads. Schiltberger's memoir included significantly more factual information about Islam and cultural practices of the region than had previous texts. The account, however, is most relevant with regard to the Ottoman invasions. His detailed portrayals of brutal military practices and torture methods of the Ottomans certainly shaped German ideas about those cultures.[71] As will become evident, Ottoman historical sources confirm the accuracy of the information that Schiltberger provides about Ottoman military practices. Generally, the account stands out for its descriptiveness; only rarely do we encounter any form of derogatory speech. Schiltberger, similar to Georgius de Hungaria, another famous captive who composed an account of Ottoman culture, was clearly impressed with much that he learned about the areas he describes; he does not fail to acknowledge the grandeur of the architecture, landscape, and peoples whenever he finds it warranted.[72] Nor is his criticism reserved for non-Christians: Christians living at the Black Sea who sell their children as slaves to Muslims are just as much criticized for this practice as Turks or Mongols who brutally slaughter their enemies. Schiltberger's text became a model for countless German-language reactions to the Ottoman invasions and was a best seller for many decades after its first publication.

Schiltberger's memoir clearly reflects the influence of other European travelers who reported on their journeys to Asia, such as Giovanni da Pian del Carpine (ca. 1247), William of Rubruck (ca. 1256), Marco Polo (1298), Giovanni di Monte Corvino (1305–6), and Odoric de Pordenone (ca. 1330), as well as the pilgrimage accounts from the fourteenth and fifteenth centuries discussed earlier.[73] Whereas most of these travelogues continue to feature sections on the "marvels" of the East, they stand out for including new ethnographic and economic information. Whether on diplomatic assignments or sent as missionaries, however, the majority of travelers still operated within the Christian paradigm of viewing the world. In contrast, Marco Polo's account illustrates a shift away from traveling to and writing about places that occupy a central space in Christian salvation history, such as the Holy Land, or for reasons connected to the interests of Christianity. Europe's economic expansion brought about a need for new kinds of information. In this regard, Marco Polo's text includes only few of the marvels and none of the "monsters" known from antiquity; rather, he introduced Europe to new wonders, such as paper money.[74]

Arnold von Harff's memoir of his journey to the main sites of medieval Christianity (Rome, Jerusalem, Santiago de Compostella), in spite of belonging to the genre of pilgrimage accounts, is another example of the increased interest in factual information about other cultures and places. Von Harff traveled from 1496 to 1498 and wrote his account in the year following his return to Germany. The author displays an acute awareness of his role as the narrator of his experiences, and his motivation for traveling goes beyond that of the pilgrimage. He is clearly interested in relating information about the various cultures he encounters and includes more than twenty glossaries of European and Middle Eastern languages, several alphabets, and a large number of illustrations. He reports about the architecture of the places he visited, the layout and size of cities, the veiling of women, the size of populations, the pyramids, animals, agriculture, and slave markets. In Cairo he spent time with two German Mamluks, an interesting indication of the fact that German-born men were often found in the service of Arab (and other) rulers. In von Harff's discussion of Istanbul he mentions a German convert to Islam who takes von Harff to meet with the sultan, where our traveler is evidently offered employment but manages politely to decline the invitation.[75] In several instances von Harff voices criticism of Islam, but generally his account of the Islamic world consists of matter-of-fact descriptions. He expresses respect for the piousness of Muslims, various rituals of Islam, the abstinence from alcohol, and the beauty of mosques.[76] Other autobiographical accounts of Ottoman society are also rendered in a neutral tone, such as those by Teodoro Spandugino and Captivus Septemcastrensis, whereas others reflect the religious propaganda against Islam that flourished in Europe at the time.

Like Schiltberger and Breydenbach, von Harff emerges as a personal and personable narrator but includes topoi that functioned over the centuries to authenticate accounts of the Orient. For example, he includes a section detailing his supposed travels through India and Africa, drawing on the long tradition of folkloric and mythological tales about these areas. Nevertheless, von Harff's account, like Schiltberger's, reflects the emergence of a new consciousness that is expressed via a new textual tradition.[77] This shift is clearly indicated stylistically, with the use of first-person singular or plural and the organization of the material around the events of the author's life.[78] Another account that should be mentioned in this context is that of Johann Wild, who hailed from Nuremberg. Wild was captured by "anti-Habsburg Hungarians at Szentendre (S. Andrea) and soon sold to a Turk. He was resold repeatedly," and in the course of traveling with various owners saw Istanbul, Cairo, Damascus, Mecca, and Medina.[79] An account of his life was published in 1613.

The focus on Ottoman atrocities was a prominent topic in times of direct military confrontation. A text by Peter Stern von Labach from 1530 reports on the sieges of Ofen and Vienna and clearly functions to render a tale of the heroic resistance of the Viennese and their survival in the face of several weeks of shelling and burning, from September 24 to October 14, 1529.[80] The strength of the Ottoman army has been estimated at over a quarter-million people, with about 80,000 to 120,000 troops. No supporting army came to the assistance of the Viennese, but the Ottomans did not succeed in taking the city. Yet, by the time the Ottomans finally retreated, in part due to the early onset of winter and the lack of food sources from the areas they had laid waste, tens of thousands of soldiers and civilians had been killed or wounded.[81] Women, children, and many of the notables and well-off had fled Vienna but were captured by the Turks. Grisly descriptions give a sense of the brutality of the battles: heads of captured Viennese on pikes; children cut out of their mother's wombs, thrown away, or impaled; and virgins, whose bodies were lying in the streets, raped to death.[82] These kinds of descriptions became standard topoi incorporated into countless reports about battles with the Ottomans.[83] The Saidian paradigm would have us treat such images of cruel Ottomans as European fabrications. But how does the image of Ottoman atrocities rendered in these accounts fare in light of comparative historical evidence?

According to available European and Ottoman sources, the Ottoman army was feared because of the widespread destruction it inflicted on local populations, settlements, and agricultural land. The first and most gruesome phase of devastation was brought about by unsalaried troops of volunteers and by contingents of enlisted raiders. These units preceded and collaborated with the salaried and more disciplined regular troops and "mount[ed] punitive expeditions outside periods of formal warfare."[84] Numerous German-language writings of the era expressed fear of these troops, which often invaded in large numbers; the volunteers alone made up at least 20 percent of the Ottoman army.[85] The unsalaried troops lived off the booty they pillaged and were thus especially ambitious in their actions. The enlisted raiders' income also came mostly from booty.[86] In addition to the loot made from plundering and selling individuals into slavery, the volunteers were often remunerated for their actions with prebends, monetary rewards, and other forms of compensation.[87] To prove the successful slaughter of the enemy, heads were cut off and presented to the army leaders, who then set the reward for the accomplishment. Impaled heads were displayed in public places and became grisly symbols of Ottoman warfare. These practices are confirmed by historical sources written by both German and Ottoman authors of the period.[88] Descriptions of war are rendered, for example, in the chronicle of 'Aşıkpaşazade, who covers events of the fifteenth century, and Oruç, who reports about expeditions carried out under the leadership of Sultan Bayezid I (1481–1512). The portrayal of brutal violence certainly functions as proof of military strength, tangibly so in descriptions that boast, for example, about high towers made of the heads of enemies.[89] Another example of the omnipresence of the theme of severed heads in seventeenth-century German culture is a military game called "Kopfrennen" in which fighters on horseback attempt to cut off fake heads of poles, using pistols, bows and arrows, or swords. A historical account from the seventeenth century claims that the game originated in Ottoman culture and that the Ottoman version used actual heads.[90] Whether this claim is true or not, in light of actual Ottoman practices the existence of this game indicates that beheadings were widely known about and feared.

The atrocities committed by the Ottoman army sent waves of fear through Central European areas, even though, as Göllner points out, we have to recognize that the Ottoman atrocities did not differ from practices common to wars generally at the time.[91] Descriptions by Franz Christoph Graf von Khevenhüller (also known as Khevenhiller), who created a monumental historiography with his twelve-volume *Annales Ferdinandei,* confirm that severing the heads of enemies was also practiced by Habsburg military. Especially grisly is the account of the fate of French mercenaries who had rebelled against their Habsburg employer. The captured French troops were slowly killed through

> thails spissen, Radbrechen, an die Hacken werffen, die haimbliche Glider ausschneiden, sengen, braten, Riemen aus ihren Leibern schneiden, mit Eßig, Salz und Peffer darein sprengen lassen, andere mit Zindtstricken brennen, mit Pech troepffen, mit Bulffer sprengen, biß an die Haelß in die Erden gegraben, und mit Eysernen Kugeln umb Geldt darnach schieben lassen, auch viel derselben zusammen gekuppelt, und in einen Ring gestelt, welche, wie einer nach dem andern von dem Scharpffrichter seines gefallens heraus genommen, unnd mit manigfaltiger Peyn hingrichtet worden, zusehen muessen.[92]

The list of unthinkable atrocities continues, including the roasting of mutineers, whose bodies were then fed to their fellow mutineers. Accounts of this kind certainly put the portrayals of Ottoman atrocities in perspective; war was fought brutally on both sides, in ways that are difficult to imagine today. Even if many of the widely circulated reports from the front were recycled and not based on firsthand information the image of the Ottomans as cruel and reckless soldiers needs to be acknowledged as an image based in reality. The number of casualties was high; according to some estimates, approximately 100,000 civilians lost their lives during the First Siege of Vienna, when large regions were burned and looted.[93] The unceasing invasions of the Ottomans throughout the fifteenth, sixteenth, and seventeenth centuries led to depopulation in some areas. The cruelty of the volunteer troops, raiders, and other army units was a frequent topos: they plundered and destroyed villages, burned the fields, killed scores of soldiers and civilian men, captured women and children, and sold captives into slavery.[94] At times the local population was saved in order that they might become future subjects who would pay taxes.[95] In the course of the sixteenth century new weapons came into use, and guns and mines increased the number of casualties even more.[96]

Ottoman military terror was generally followed by an offer of peace in exchange for tribute under relatively lenient conditions. The local population was allowed to retain the legal and administrative structures of its society (although differences existed with regard to the specific status of the territory) and those not converting to Islam had to pay an additional tax in return for attaining "the status of *ahl al-zimma,* i.e., protected subjects of the Muslim state in accordance with Islamic Law."[97] This strategy, which amounts to a kind of shock-and-awe strategy by the Ottomans, was successful; as mentioned earlier, the Ottomans annexed large territories over the course of a couple of centuries in Europe, North Africa, and Asia Minor, and many of the former Christians converted to Islam. In Europe the Ottomans solidified their influence by pursuing "an active diplomacy . . . , everywhere supporting forces opposed to the Papacy and the Habsburgs, such as the Calvinists in France, Hungary and the Netherlands, the Moriscos in Spain and the rising national monarchies in France and England."[98]

German accounts from the period express the fear of Ottoman military might, such as a text dating from 1532 that records an interrogation of two Ottoman prisoners who are asked thirty-five questions on various issues. Their—at times divergent—answers are presented without commentary. The questions relate exclusively to the military situation, particularly the size and location of the army; the number and kind of weapons and other military equipment; the different kinds of troops and their numbers; the situation of specific cities; plans of the Ottoman army to move toward Vienna; the morale of the troops; hunger; disease; payment of soldiers; and future plans and strategies. The text also comments on the high number of prisoners that had been taken by the Ottomans and claims that female prisoners got their hair cut, were dressed in male clothes, and were used in battle on the front line. A description of the siege of the city of Guenns, of the negotiations between the warring parties, and a mention of the Turkish sultan's offer to withdraw in exchange for tribute conclude the account. The text ends on the ominous note that the army was now "sechs meyle von Wien."[99]

The primary function of this account is clearly to inform readers about the current situation, but the print dates from 1532, and the urgent tone is not only related to events of the past. The terminology used to refer to the two opposing parties is noteworthy: the Turks are never referred to as Muslims, in fact, there is not a word about their culture or religion. Different groups of Europeans, however, are referred to as Christians.

A text from 1533, which includes a number of visual representations, is staged as a conversation between a soldier, a "Landfarer" (priest), a poet, and a student ("eyn Römischer Student"). The soldier describes the Ottoman state and army as very disciplined and orderly and relates that many of the state employees were compensated through property instead of salary, which he compares to the allotting of fiefs in the feudal system. His descriptions include details about the expanse of the empire, the hierarchy of the army, the elite troops, and different units of the army—including the Ottoman soldiers' equipment and clothing—as well as the army's means of transportation and its organization of supplies. The soldier stresses that the Ottoman army was inspired by ideological unity: its soldiers were patient, modest, did not scream when they fought, and were very disciplined. Ottoman subjects were obedient and did not gamble. He also claims that the Ottomans pursued their scorched earth policy only in areas that were not considered valuable. He talks about horses and their treatment and the tricks and strategies of warfare, and also relates at length certain aspects of Ottoman history, such as the origin of the Turks in Inner Asia and the fall of Constantinople. Another section of his account deals with Turkish ideas of the afterlife. When the account moves on to include the voices of the poet, priest, and student, the conversation reveals more personal information about the soldier, in particular how he had acquired his knowledge about the Ottomans, where he had traveled, and his views about the current and future situation. The text closes with an appeal to the emperor to unite the different parts of the "Christliche nation," that is, European Christianity.[100]

There is very little information in this text that focuses on Islam directly, confirming that, as in the previous two examples, its primary focus was to get a grasp of the military situation. The Ottomans are primarily seen as Turks, not as Muslims; Europeans, however, are defined in religious terms through the idea of a united Christian army.

A text from 1542 paints a gruesome picture of the brutality of the Ottoman army and captures particularly well the helplessness of peasants. It describes specific events that took place in August and September 1541, including the capture of Buda (Ofen), and details numerous instances regarding the torture of civilians, among them women and children. The author vividly relates scenes of plundering and describes the Ottoman practice of leaving behind scorched earth. He also reports on agreements between King Ferdinand and the Ottoman sultan, which are not honored by the occupying army of Ofen. The Ottomans are said to mistreat the population, for example, during the wine harvest, which is then followed by retaliation by Christians. At the end of the narrative the anger and disappointment of the Hungarian narrator is clearly expressed: just as Germans and other peoples of the empire let Hungary fall victim to the Turkish army, the same thing could also happen to Austria, Moravia, and Bohemia, to all those who now watched the disaster in Hungary without sending help to their Christian brothers.[101]

Several texts from 1582 and 1583 report about the circumcision ceremony of Mahmet, the son of Sultan Murad III, which had taken place in 1582.[102] The ceremony was celebrated with great pomp, demonstrating the sultan's power. Many Christian European state representatives were invited, and a Persian embassy attended as well. Clearly a popular topic, the event was described in numerous writings for decades. A 1595 version gives a glowing account of the festivities and describes jugglers and artists who, for example, insert knives into their bodies and have horseshoes nailed to themselves. The author describes extravagant shows, including musical performances, fireworks, dances, jousting, and displays of horses; he talks about Sufis and dancing dervishes; he mentions the food and lavish decorations; he reports about the goods that merchants and representatives of different trades were selling and how people were fed; and he provides a numerical accounting of the different groups of participants. The author includes a graphic description of the actual circumcision ceremony, which clearly drew the attention of European audiences. The text also includes a list of marvels, "Wunderwerck," in Constantinople. The list of seventeen marvels includes 4,492 big streets, each with a mosque; 100 hospitals; 895 public bathhouses; 582 mills; 12 big marketplaces; 418 inns; and 515 distinguished schools. The question of accuracy notwithstanding, the list betrays an interest in realia about the achievements of Ottoman civilization.[103]

Some of the most popular texts that circulated in Europe were based on Ottoman sources, such as the various versions of texts by Hans Lewenklaw (also known as Löwenklau and Leunclavius) that drew on chronicles composed by Ottoman authors. In 1584 Lewenklaw was invited by the nobleman Heinrich von Lichtenstein to accompany him on a diplomatic mission to Istanbul and remained for more than half a year in the Ottoman capital. The stay in Istanbul from October 1584 to April 1585 inspired Lewenklaw to engage with Ottoman history. While he himself did not translate the Ottoman sources he compiled, his studies were comprehensive and allowed him to compose erudite annotations. In 1588 he published *Annales Sultanorum Othmanidarum A Turcis Sua Lingua Scripti,* a Latin translation of the Turkish chronicle of Muhji ed-Din Gemali.[104] Two years later he published the extensive volumes *Neuwe Chronica Tuerkischer Nation / Von Tuercken selbs beschrieben and Neuwer Musulmanischer Histori Tuerkischer Nation.* In these publications Lewenklaw acknowledged Hans Gaudier, also known as Spiegel, as collaborating translator. The publications from 1590 are based on the *Annales* of 1588 but include information gathered from additional Turkish manuscripts.[105] As Dieter Metzler points out, important information contained in Lewenklaw's texts can be traced to manuscripts owned by Antun Vrančič, Archbishop of Esztergom, primate of Hungary and later Cardinal, and also known as the humanist scholar Antonius Verantius.[106]

Lewenklaw's renditions of Turkish sources and his commentaries on Ottoman history were disseminated across Europe, and the circulation of these texts highlights the fact that European-Ottoman history can only be accessed meaningfully by paying attention to the complexity of this shared textual history.[107] An example of a text that draws on Lewenklaw's works, and thus implicitly on those of Ottoman historians, is the 1595 broadsheet "Vom Tuerckischen Reich." The title of the text refers to Lewenklaw but does not mention Turkish sources.[108] A reference to these sources, however, is made at the beginning of the actual section on the Ottoman Empire, entitled "Bericht Vom Türkischen Reich" (which is preceded by a preface and followed by a "Prognostico" from 1480 that predicts the end of Muslim rule), but the account does not acknowledge specific Ottoman texts, as Lewenklaw does in his longer works.

"Bericht Vom Türkischen Reich" is a short review of only fourteen pages, covering information discussed in detail in Lewenklaw's comprehensive texts, but lacking a tangible relation to Ottoman sources.[109] The discussion begins with information about religion. Religious unity is said to be a dominant value among Muslims and ensures that everybody is equal during religious services.

The notion of religious freedom also receives attention and is acknowledged as one element that inspired people to live under Ottoman rule. Other sections discuss knowledge; wisdom among the rulers; the writing of history (the author stresses that Turkish historiography allows criticism of its rulers); the importance granted to scientific study; the unifying effect of the sultanate; the significant role given to public welfare; various features of the army and military system (e.g., elite soldiers are well trained and disciplined); and the justice, reliability, and strictness of the Turkish legal system. On the latter topic the author acknowledges that, unlike "Barbaric peoples," Turks have a legal system that treats everybody the same, and he praises the Ottoman system over the European one, in which disputations are endless. In contrast, the Turkish legal system is described as simpler, faster, more strict, and more effective.

After this discussion, which largely points out laudable aspects of Ottoman society, the author lists those aspects that he considers signs of weakness that could bring about the demise of the empire. He lists heresy and political dissent; the great number of Christians; the long duration of the empire, which, according to Christian messianic ideas, points to its end; the decline of the empire's administration; the loss of respect for rulers; cultural decay and widespread cruelty (which contradicts what the author says earlier about the reliability of the legal system); arrogance, stinginess, and greed; unreliability toward allies; and high and unjust taxes, which alienate parts of the population, state apparatus, and clerics. In his summary the author stresses that, though there continues to be reason to be afraid and prepared for further attacks from the Ottomans, there is also some room for hope that things might change; it is better to assume the worst and to be prepared, he suggests, and to think of new strategies for fighting the Turks.

This account illustrates the degree to which factual information was passed on as well as the interest in learning about the Ottoman Empire and the level of admiration for Ottoman accomplishments.[110] At the same time, the reader is presented with an analysis suggesting possible scenarios for further developments, based on information about the internal problems affecting the Ottoman Empire. The fact that this information was based in large part on Ottoman self-representation—an aspect ultimately invisible in this particular text—is crucial: the reception of Ottoman sources and their further incorporation into countless texts in German and other European languages defies a simplistic understanding of the image of Turks in German and other European textual histories.

In a comparative study of select European newspapers from the seventeenth century, Sonja Schultheiß-Heinz showed that coverage of international conflict was central, constituting 68.4 percent to 77.8 percent of the texts.[111] Schultheiß-Heinz also asserted that more than 90 percent of the coverage was neutral—that is, in spite of clear attempts to depict a negative image of the respective enemies, a focus on the facts seemed to have prevailed in most instances.[112] This holds true for both newspapers and pamphlets, even though many of the stories were based on eyewitness accounts. The study by Schultheiß-Heinz thus confirms, alongside the present discussion, that, with regard to newspapers and pamphlets about the Ottomans, the ideological slant notwithstanding, these printed materials conveyed a significant amount of information beyond mere political or religious propaganda.

The select newspapers and pamphlets discussed here convey a sense of the actual encounter with the Ottomans by Germans. These texts fulfilled various functions, including informing the population about ongoing and past military confrontations; sharing information about cultural and religious customs of the Ottomans and about the Turkish language, often in neutral terms; popularizing knowledge about Islam that was previously restricted to elites; providing entertainment value with stories about warfare, unknown places, strange customs, and survival; promoting the idea of Christian unity; and helping to shape a sense of a German-language reading community and thus, much like Luther's writings, promoting the growing sense of a shared German culture. Information about trade corroborates the high level of social interaction documented by these texts. In spite of the centuries of hostilities (though apart from the years of intense warfare), historians have emphasized that trade between Ottoman and Habsburg territories was not negatively affected by the hostilities.[113] After periods of intense fighting, the two spheres of influence reestablished economic relations,[114] and trade increased over the centuries.[115] As Halil Inalcik points out, "Trade with Austria . . . did not fully flourish until the eighteenth century, mainly because the sultans did not grant the Habsburgs the same trade freedom which the 'friendly' nations such as the French or English enjoyed."[116] Even if Ottoman-Austrian trade did not expand until the cessation of military hostilities, historical sources about the existence of economic and social institutions involving Ottomans and Europeans document economic collaboration.[117] Capitulations, that is, trade agreements that regulated the privileges of foreign merchants, facilitated the expansion of trade between various European trading partners and the Ottomans.[118] On this level cultural discourse not only has to be measured against political and military action but also put into perspective in light of economic relations, which at times run counter to political and military events.

But how do we understand the apparent interest in information about Islam and Ottoman society, which differs from the theological disputations encountered in the previous section? The newspapers and various types of accounts about the Ottomans betray a desire to understand the powerful empire and to learn about it in order to gain knowledge that might be useful to fight it. This curiosity can also be related to what has been termed *Türkenhoffnung,* that is, a hope that the Ottoman Empire might bring positive change to people's lives. This attitude was most prevalent in the very early phase of the Ottoman invasions; Göllner states that it was mainly merchants who seem to have held this attitude.[119] The idea of *Türkenhoffnung* must also be seen in the context of defections of, for example, Protestants, who were able to practice their religion under the Ottomans, and with regard to conversions to Islam, which, as mentioned earlier, were widespread. Jean Delumeau suggests that conversions ranged in "the thousands" and that, "between the years 1453 and 1623, at least 33 out of 48 grand vezirs were renegades."[120] Some conversions were highly publicized, such as that of Adam Neuser, a Unitarian theologian who was persecuted for his anti-Trinitarian views and found refuge in Istanbul in the 1570s as a convert to Islam. Gotthold Ephraim Lessing later used the case of Adam Neuser to argue his position on religious tolerance.[121]

Apart from religious motivations, individuals joined the Ottoman Empire for a range of sociopsychological, political, and economic reasons, such as ideas of belonging, state coercion, and the attainment of economic and social privileges.[122] One highly spectacular case of soldiers defecting to the Ottoman army was that of a unit of French mercenaries within the Habsburg army (mentioned earlier). Whereas the employment of French mercenaries in the Habsburg army has been identified as "an aberration," particularly in light of French-Ottoman collaboration, the fact that soldiers defected to the Ottomans was not unusual at all. In this case it provided the Ottomans with "a pool of soldiers skilled in the use of the up-to-date weapons which were to be vital thereafter in the conduct of war."[123] The defection occurred as a result of a mutiny over the Habsburgs' failure to pay the mercenaries. The extremely brutal events are documented in a large number of European and Ottoman sources (such as the report contained in F. C. Khevenhüller's *Annales Ferdinandei*), and comparing these sources proves once again just how important such comparisons are. In contrast to the European accounts, which sought to convey an image of total defeat of the mutineers, the Ottoman sources "indicate clearly that the Habsburg forces did not kill all the mutineers."[124] Various sources, such as pay lists, document French renegades connected to the mutiny involved in numerous battles across the Ottoman front lines.

The issue of renegades was clearly a hot topic in the conflict with the Ottomans. Apart from gaining strategic information in order to combat the Ottomans, perhaps the great interest in factual information about Ottoman culture and Islam that we detect in writings of the period is connected to the real-life appeal that the Ottoman Empire had for Protestants, mercenaries, and certain social groups—even for entire countries (such as parts of Hungary and other Balkan states)—who benefited from the Ottoman system in one way or another. The curiosity observable in these fact-oriented writings, along with theological motivations, also spawned the beginnings of Orientalist sciences, a development that will be discussed in more detail in the next chapter. In addition, trade relations and other forms of social action pay tribute to the real-life interaction that existed between Germans and Ottomans in spite of warfare and religious adversity.

The Ottomans in Fiction

The threat of Ottoman invasion and the nature of Ottoman society were thematized in all literary genres of the period, including Latin epics and poems (which will not be considered here).[125] As with the theological and nonfiction material discussed thus far, fictional representations of Turks commented on the conflict itself, but also used it as an opportunity to make points about internal political issues or to express a general view of life.[126] All across Europe the Ottoman threat lent itself to fantasies about a dualistic view of the world, and it easily evoked crusading rhetoric. At a moment when Europe was struggling to once again unite against an Oriental enemy, the epic *Gerusalemme liberata* (1581) by the Italian poet Torquato Tasso retells the story of the First Crusade. Received widely and translated into many languages (into English in 1601, by Edward Fairfax, as *Godfrey of Bulloigne;* and into German in 1626, by Diederich von dem Werder, as *Gottfried von Bulljon*), the story called for religious and political unity at a moment of widespread division. The issue of the Ottoman threat resurfaced in literatures everywhere; the Portuguese national epic *Os Lusíadas* (*The Lusiads*), by Luís Vaz de Camões, was published in 1571 (additional editions were published in 1572), the same year (in fact, month) in which the Ottomans were defeated in the Battle of Lepanto by a coalition that included, among others, the papacy, Spain, Venice, the Republic of Genoa, the Duchy of Savoy, and the Knights of Malta. A testament to the significance of this European victory, the epic also reflects the self-confidence resulting from colonial Portugal's overseas successes. Similarly, other European plays and epics from the period—such as Shakespeare's *Othello, Moor of Venice* (1604);

the Croatian poet Ivan Gundulić's early seventeenth-century epic *Osman; The Conquest of Granada* (1670–71) by John Dryden; Molière's comedy *Le Bourgeois Gentilhomme* (1670); and Racine's tragedy *Bajazet* (1672)—comment in geopolitically specific terms on the conflicts with the Ottoman Empire.[127]

Already in the early fifteenth century, German carnival plays focused on the Ottoman threat. The 1454/56 play *Des Turken Vasnachtspil,* which has been attributed to Hans Rosenplüt, employed the alterity of the Turkish sultan to articulate a strong critique of the existing social order. As Glenn Ehrstine has shown, *Des Turken Vasnachtspil* differs markedly from the virulent anti-Jewish plays of the period, but Ehrstine cautions us against assuming that its author had been particularly friendly toward the Turks. In fact, other writings by Rosenplüt as well as publications and events in Nuremberg betrayed anti-Turkish attitudes and active participation in warfare against the Ottomans.[128]

Hans Sachs made good use of the controversial topic and discussed Ottoman matters in carnival plays, comedies, poems, and other writings of his extensive oeuvre.[129] Sachs draws on information from newspapers and pamphlets of the period; in fact, much of the paraphrasing is styled closely after the original sources and betrays a formulaic discourse that repeats certain images, such as the cutting-up of pregnant women and the impaling of heads (which can also be found almost word for word in Luther's sermons). It is noteworthy in this regard that scholarship on the depictions of the Turks in Sachs and Rosenplüt, for example, tends to treat these representations as fantasies, ideas, and polemics—the fact that Ottomans were indeed cruel invaders who engaged in torture, rape, and pillaging is not taken into consideration.[130]

Jakob Ayrer incorporated Turkish topics into three of his plays, which were part of his *Opus Theatricum* (1618)—namely the comedies *Comedia vom Soldan von Babilonia* and *Ramus,* and the tragedy *Machumet und Hircavena.* Each play presents a different view of the Turks: the first comedy renders a positive image of a sultan during the time of the Crusades; the second one presents Turks as characterized by excessive sexuality; and the tragedy pairs sexual deviancy with the idea of Turks as oppressors of Christianity. The different ways in which Ayrer uses the Turkish material provides an example of how, by the beginning of the seventeenth century, Turkish topoi became indeed fictionalized, and were used to discuss topics that were divorced from the actual threat of Ottoman invasion. Cornelia Kleinlogel emphasizes this process of abstraction whereby Turkishness became a motif and a vehicle to convey German political, ethical, and social ideas.[131]

Jesuit plays from the mid-seventeenth century also made use of the Ottoman material and emphasized the religious dimension of the conflict in plays such as *Constantinopel Oder Constantinus der achte Griechische Kayser* (1649), *Maria Exhilaratrix* (1660), and *Prodigiosus Deiparentis Favor* (1696). Kleinlogel shows that *Maria Exhilaratrix,* for example, draws heavily on graphic depictions of Ottoman atrocities contained in newspapers and travel accounts from the period.[132] Regardless of their groundedness in historical conflict, however, Turkish-Muslim characters featured in these plays are primarily reprehensible models of excessive sexuality, and serve to articulate norms and ideas of proper ethical Christian behavior.

In the middle of the seventeenth century the Ottoman threat once again intensified. And again, Central European countries were much more concretely affected by the events. Fighting with the Ottoman Empire flared up in the latter part of the century, under the leadership of Grand Vizier Köprülü Mehmed Pasha and then his son, Fazıl Ahmed Pasha. Military excursions were frequent, especially to assert Ottoman rule in Transylvania. After initial successes, an expedition in 1663 and 1664 suffered a tremendous defeat in 1664 at St. Gotthard-Mogersdorf. By the 1660s European countries formed a broad alliance; even France joined Central Europe's push against the Ottomans. Despite victory in 1664, the threat was not yet averted; with the Treaty of Vasvár (Eisenburg), the Ottomans, with the help of French diplomacy, negotiated conditions that were favorable to Ottoman interests, an outcome that led to alienation between the Habsburgs and the Hungarians.[133] The court historian Hasan Aga accompanied Fazıl Ahmed Pasha during the expeditions of 1663 and 1664, and his writings provide us with an Ottoman view of the devastating warfare of the time. Throughout the account we read about severed heads, which were the basis of soldiers' remuneration; soldiers who took prisoners were awarded a higher amount, but severed heads were probably easier to come by.[134] Several descriptions contained in the account are particularly grisly; Hasan Aga reports, for example, that in one instance the number of severed heads and prisoners was so great that it became impossible to cross a bridge with them. Large piles were constructed of heads and dead bodies. Heads were often displayed on the walls of cities.[135] It is not surprising, in light of these Ottoman descriptions—which mirror accounts written by Hungarians, Germans, and other Europeans—that the fear of Ottoman siege rose once again, especially in the period leading up to the siege of Vienna.

In this climate of intensified conflict, several plays by German authors reflect the political concerns of the day and express the anti-Ottoman stance by drawing on the dualistic worldview that distinguished the Baroque period. In the play *Catharina von Georgien* (1651) Andreas Gryphius juxtaposes an idealized Christian queen, Catharina, against an irrational Persian ruler, Abas, who wants to marry her and force her to convert to Islam. Sarah Colvin has argued that Catharina's strength conveys masculinity, while Abas's addiction to sexual desire feminizes him; through this construction, a Christian woman usurping a masculine position, "the danger of the Orient and of the rival religion, Islam, is lessened."[136] However contrived the story may seem, the plot was based on historical events: the actual Queen Ketevan of the eastern Georgian kingdom of Kakheti died in 1624 as a result of a most brutal torture ordered by Shah Abbas of Persia. Gryphius draws on French renditions of this gruesome event; in the play, as in real life, rather than giving in to the advances of Shah Abbas, Catharina remains steadfast in her beliefs and dies a martyr.

Daniel Casper von Lohenstein, who had drawn on Roman materials for several of his literary works, wrote two tragedies featuring Turkish characters. Both *Ibrahim* (also known as *Ibrahim Bassa* [1653]) and *Ibrahim Sultan* (1673) convey images of Muslim rulers who are cruel, oversexed, fanatical, and irrational. Peter Skrine points out how much more "brash and discordant" Lohenstein's Turkey is in comparison to the "delicate refinement of passion and of its linguistic expression, which is such a notable feature of Racine's tragedy."[137] *Ibrahim,* inspired by a translation of the four-volume historical novel entitled *Ibrahim ou l'illustre Bassa* (1641) and considered to be a collaboration between Madeleine de Scudéry and her brother Georges, depicts Oriental despotism through the story of a military leader named Ibrahim.[138] Ibrahim is unjustly killed by Sultan Soliman after an unsuccessful attempt to woo Ibrahim's lover, Isabelle. Whereas the French version ends happily, Lohenstein imagines a tragic ending. In the later play, *Ibrahim Sultan,* Lohenstein roots political despotism in an uncontrolled and reckless sexuality and in greed for power, and paints a most gruesome image of Oriental debauchery and violence. Interestingly, August Adolph von Haugwitz revisits the same material a few years later, in *Obsiegende Tugend oder der bethörte doch wieder bekehrte Soliman* (1684), and follows the French model, presenting a happy ending, in which reason wins out over lust.[139]

The religious merges with the cultural and the political in this ideological rejection of Ottoman Turks, and the result is a Manichaean allegory that reflects on all areas of life. As Skrine points out regarding the later of Lohenstein's Turkish plays, "Its atmosphere of concealed menace and claustrophobic tension, torrid lust and sexual decadence, cogently conveys exactly what Lohenstein's Turkey stood for: the incarnation of slavery in both the physical and psychological sense."[140] The grounding of the reproachable character of the Ottomans in their addiction to physical pleasures, especially in excessive sexuality, can already be observed in the earliest representations of Turkish characters and includes texts produced in Latin, such as Humanist plays (e.g., *Spectaculum de Thurcorum Rege* [1497] by Jacob Locher, also known as Philomusus). Over the course of the seventeenth century this nexus of sexuality and alterity became a central topos of fictional representations of Turkish characters. Kleinlogel's study *Exotik-Erotik,* which focuses on this topic, shows convincingly just how dominant this topos was in German-language material.

In these fictional portrayals Turks are characterized by behavior that interlinks religion and culture. Muslims are no longer primarily judged on the basis of their religious beliefs, indeed the falsity of their beliefs is verified through their abominable cultural behavior. In this view ideas of universal knighthood or kinship and the notion of the "noble heathen," concepts that were widespread in the Middle Ages, have no place. The dominant images in the dramatic literature of the mid-seventeenth century also do not correspond to the more complex images we find in the nonfiction material from the same period. These fantasies from the late seventeenth century are, of course, also a reflection of the devastation and tremendous cruelty brought on by the Thirty Years' War; the confessional wars between Protestants and Catholics reduced the European population by 30 percent. In light of this decimating war depictions of Ottoman Muslims also speak to intra-European conflict: Ottoman Muslims appeared as the reincarnation of evil at a moment when Europeans needed to process the violence they had inflicted on each other. The plays by Gryphius and Lohenstein, for example, while written at a time of intensified fighting between Ottomans and Europeans, also provide commentary on internal despotism, abuses of power, and the lack of social and ethical cohesion.

Like Haugwitz's play, however, other fictional material from the sixteenth and seventeenth centuries did not convey such dark images of Oriental rulers. An interest in realia, such as information about specific places located in the Orient, and action-driven narration defy the didactic impulses that structure epic texts from the period. Turkish and other Middle Eastern topoi were incorporated into, for example, *Historia von D. Johann Fausten* (1587), the narrative precursor of Goethe's famous play about the historical Johann Georg Faust (ca. 1480–1540). In the popular narrative Doctor Faustus travels to the Orient, spends time at the court of the Turkish sultan, and bewitches the sultan and his courtiers. In fact, Faustus transforms himself and appears to the sultan as Muhammad, upon which the sultan falls to his knees and honors the false prophet. Faustus continues his gimmick the following day in the sultan's harem and impresses the women with his skills as a lover, which ultimately makes the sultan doubtful about the true identity of the prophet (who was also said to speak a language unknown to the women). After his stint in Constantinople, Faustus travels through Cairo across India and gets close to Paradise, which remains ultimately off-limits. The figure of Faustus allows the reader to imagine the limits of Turkish imperial, religious, and human power, and to feel superior. Compared to the dramatic tradition, however, the approach here is much more playful.

German novels from the seventeenth century were often based on French sources but, like the adaptation of French plays, were reinterpreted by the German authors and translators. *Ibrahim ou l'illustre Bassa* (1641), by Madeleine and Georges de Scudéry, was translated in multiple versions; Philipp von Zesen translated the text in 1645 as *Ibrahims, oder, Des durchleuchtigen Bassa und der beständigen Isabellen Wunder-Geschichte;* another version appeared as *Ibrahim, deß durchleuchtigen Bassa und der beständigen Isabellen Wunder-Geschicht* in 1667. Kleinlogel points out that Zesen's translation betrays a greater focus on specific ethical ideas, especially the notion of "constantia."[141] Other novels from the seventeenth century also reflect a focus on normative ethics, as they are mediated through sexually excessive and violent Ottomans depicted in plays.[142] Novels by Eberhard Werner Happel (*Der Asiatische Onogambo* [1673]; *Toroan* [1676]; *Der ottomanische Bajazet oder so genannte Europäischer Geschicht-Roman auf das 1688. Jahr,* in four volumes [1688–89]), for example, use the Turkish material as a background for the author's lengthy tales of adventure and, like the dominant dramatic traditions, employ topoi about the excessive sexuality of the Turks to affirm German/Christian ethics.

Other novels, such as Hans Jakob Christoffel von Grimmelshausen's *Der Abenteuerliche Simplicissimus Teutsch* (1669), are closer to the model represented by *Historia von D. Johann Fausten,* in which the Orient serves mostly as a backdrop to the hero's journey of spiritual development. In one episode, Simplicius ends up on a Turkish galley used in a conflict between Ottomans and Venetians and is set free once the ship is captured by the Venetians.[143] In a part of the "Continuatio" Simplicius embarks on a pilgrimage to Jerusalem but ends up in Cairo "indem der türkische Bassa zu Damasco eben damals in armis begriffen und gegen seinen Kaiser rebellisch war."[144] Not able to reach Jerusalem, he enjoys his time in the Egyptian city, which is described as the most populous city he has seen. On his way to acquire some mummies he is captured by Arabian robbers and is then exhibited by them for money as a curious attraction, dressed only with a piece of moss across his loins. Material reality and actual social interaction of the time period are quite tangible in this account (pilgrimage, Cairo, trade, robbery, fights between Ottomans and Venetians), but there is less sense of a particular ideological slant against Muslims or Turks. In similar ways, a fictional but seemingly historical novel by Herzog

Anton Ulrich von Braunschweig entitled *Die durchleuchtige Syrerinn Aramena* (1669–73) paints a positive picture of an Arabian princess who serves as a role model in a lengthy story about ideal statehood and human virtue.

In contrast to narrative and dramatic literature, poetry from the sixteenth and seventeenth centuries rarely focuses on the Ottomans in explicit ways. Only a few poems linger on the subject of the Ottoman Empire; for example, "Über das gute Lützen," a poem by Ernst Stockmann (1634–1712), refers to Turkey as a battleground but mentions it as part of a broader discussion of wartime hardships. The Thirty Years' War, however, is explicitly addressed in poems by, for example, Friedrich von Logau (1604–55), Paul Fleming (1609–40), and Johannes Klaj (ca. 1616–56). While some of the many poems of the period that talk about war in general may be related to the conflicts with the Ottoman Empire, examples that specifically thematize these battles in ways comparable to the poetry about the Thirty Years' War are rare. On the other hand, songs that refer to the conflicts with the Ottomans were abundant. As mentioned earlier, studies by Şenol Özyurt and Bertrand Michael Buchmann document the extent to which the Ottomans were part of the popular imagination in songs rendering a predominantly negative image of the Ottomans.

By way of conclusion we may acknowledge that actual political and military confrontations certainly inspired negative fictional representations of Ottoman society and Ottoman individuals, but internal German and European crises generated these dark images just as much as the battles with the Ottomans. In addition, Ottoman characters served as vehicles to articulate ideas about the proper kind of government, Christian ethics, and normative cultural behavior. As German writers drew on the large archive of sources on the Ottomans, they fictionalized aspects that were based on social interaction and material culture and created a vast repertoire of Ottoman-related topoi.

Changing Paradigms after the Second Siege of Vienna (1683)

In the aftermath of the events of 1664 Kara Mehmed Aga was chosen to travel to Vienna as an ambassador of the Ottoman sultan in order to bring letters and presents to the emperor. Traveling with him was the famous Evliya Çelebi, whose accounts of forty years of journeying through Ottoman and adjacent territories are invaluable sources about the period. He visited Vienna in 1665 and was full of praise for the Austrian city. Although his account contains fictional additions and unresolved contradictions, his commentary on Vienna gives a sense of the deep impression the city made on the traveler. Evliya Çelebi admires the architecture of palaces, fortresses, churches, and other buildings; he describes inns, marketplaces, and the workshops of merchants, and he enjoys the clean air, bathhouses, and various kinds of entertainment in the city. Evliya Çelebi does take issue with some aspects of Viennese culture—for example, the presence of women in the public sphere, which he suggests is related to the importance of the Virgin Mary for Christians.[145] He also berates the emperor for his ugliness and clothing.[146]

Clearly, Vienna was the prize most desired by Ottomans at the time.[147] Once again, at the end of the seventeenth century, Ottoman armies attempted to capture the Austrian capital. The newly appointed grand vizier, Kara Mustafa, a brother-in-law of Ahmed Köprülü, sought to extend Ottoman influence in Europe and turned his armies toward Vienna. The Ottomans advanced at a difficult moment for the Austrians: a pest epidemic had just devastated the area, and 10 percent of the Viennese had lost their lives in 1679, leaving a weakened population to face the enemy.[148]

The Second Siege of Vienna lasted from July 14 to September 12, 1683. The Ottoman army, with 200,000 troops, was about twice the size of the forces against which the Viennese had successfully defended themselves in 1529.[149] Whereas the Viennese had survived the First Siege without external support, help was clearly needed now. It took the European alliance—which brought together Austrian, Polish, Venetian, Saxon, and Bavarian troops, with papal support and under the leadership of Polish King Jan III Sobieski—two months to mobilize and then arrive in Vienna. In the days immediately before the arrival of the European troops, the Ottomans had succeeded in destroying strategic parts of the ramparts. In a dramatic sequence of events designed to prevent the detonation of mines, the Viennese were able to thwart the Ottoman plan. The European army, with 70,000 troops, three times smaller than the Ottoman army, fought the Ottomans by using tactics developed by the Polish military. The failure to detonate the city's walls and win the battle led to a hasty Ottoman withdrawal.[150] The accounts of killings on both sides document another grisly episode, and, once again, Ottoman chronicles of the invasion and siege of Vienna in 1683 mirror the reports given in the German-language accounts.[151] Ottoman authors carefully registered the number of severed heads that were delivered by volunteer troops to the vizier, who compensated them for their accomplishments.[152] Three months after the withdrawal from Vienna, the leader of the Ottoman army, Kara Mustafa, was ordered killed by the sultan for his failure to capture the city.

The victory of the Christian alliance at Vienna was a turning point in the centuries-old conflict between Ottoman and European troops. It took another century of continuous battle before the Ottoman Empire was significantly weakened and Austria aligned itself with its former enemy against the Russians. The next chapter will discuss the repercussions and broad dimension of these historical shifts, which were reflected in new attitudes in the political, economic, and cultural spheres.

More than three hundred years of intense conflict with the Ottoman Empire left a large corpus of texts that reveal the range of ideas held by Germans about the Ottomans at the time. Religious rhetoric and thought continued to structure much of the way in which Germans responded to the Ottomans. Yet much had changed since the Middle Ages.

Beginning in the fifteenth century, and clearly related to the revolutionary effects of the printing press, Germans began to gain broader knowledge about the peoples they were fighting. Christian polemics, newspapers, travel accounts, and various genres of fiction all convey the encounter with the Ottomans in a more tangible way than can be seen in the medieval material. Firsthand information about Islam and Ottoman culture was incorporated into German-language texts in fundamentally new ways. Although ideological slants structure the discourse on the Ottomans, visible particularly in texts driven by religious propaganda, a good deal of factual information was now passed along, especially through newspapers and travel accounts. The negative images that dominated the larger discourse were based on the actual and justified fear of an Ottoman invasion, and over time these images and topoi became standard elements in nonfiction and fictional writings. The fact that a great deal of neutral information about the Ottomans was also conveyed, however, bespeaks both fear of and admiration for the powerful invader. During the period discussed in this chapter the discourse on the Middle East moved from a focus on Muslims to a focus on Turks as the Oriental other. The shift to culture as the primary signifier of difference foreshadows the invention of physiognomy and racial science, which in turn paved the way for the development of racist ideologies in the nineteenth century.

Various European powers entered into political alliances with the Ottomans, and individuals and groups of Europeans also formed relationships with the empire. The existence of political alliances, defections to the Ottoman army, and conversion reflect the ideological fluidity of the age. The economic, political, and religious suffering of individuals and the desire for personal well-being made it possible for Germans and other Europeans to abandon their original religion and culture and to find a place within multicultural Ottoman society. Primary examples are the Austrian and Hungarian renegades who served as interpreters.[153] Also, the desire to learn about other cultures and religions is evidenced in accounts of travel to the Arab Middle East of the time; these texts document the fact that Germans were able to move in and out of Middle Eastern spaces, either on pilgrimages or during their enforced or voluntary service in Ottoman society. The accounts of those who spent years in the Middle East document the existence of a multicultural world, in which religious and cultural differences structured social and economic interaction in ways that were less restrictive than has often been assumed. Reading Schiltberger alongside Luther, and Lohenstein next to Johann Wild and Evliya Çelebi, allows us to gain a deeper understanding of the extent of social interaction during the period. Trade, conversions, travels, and the multicultural makeup of the Ottoman army give us a sense of the nature of human interaction across cultural and religious divides.

How does the German attitude toward the Ottomans compare to attitudes prevalent in other European societies? Clearly, each state or empire had a distinct relationship to the Ottomans, and, depending on their proximity to the military events, news from the front and about the Ottomans were more or less significant. The textual material about these events, however, was widely shared: as Göllner's collection of *Turcica* illustrates most pointedly, translations made the most popular texts accessible in most European languages. As we have seen, stories from individuals of various national backgrounds were prominent, such as those by Johann Schiltberger, Teodoro Spandugino, Georgius de Hungaria, Nicolas de Nicolay, Ogier de Busbecq, Guillaume Postel, and Bartolomej Georgijević. These firsthand accounts, written, for example, by diplomats and former Ottoman prisoners, differ in ideological outlook but were circulated widely across Europe. Religious treatises and fictional works were also shared through translations. In this regard we can clearly speak of a European discourse about the Turks that illustrates the interconnectedness of the European imagination.

In spite of this shared textual history different states pursued very different policies toward the Ottomans. Political, religious, geographical, and cultural factors played a role. Hungary, like the Habsburg Empire, was immediately affected by the Ottoman invasions. The tremendous archive of Hungarian sources chronicles the Ottoman invasions, covering three hundred years of military conflict, occupation, and alliances.[154] As we have seen, however, different parts of Hungary negotiated distinct political arrangements with the Ottomans. Italy, in comparison, was home to many Greek Orthodox refugees from Constantinople who certainly had an impact on views of the Ottomans, but Italy itself was not homogeneous, and, as Bisaha has shown, a range of different views existed there.[155] Different Italian states opted for specific arrangements; Venice, for example, pursued its own course. France, another important player, was not immediately threatened and over time became allied with the Ottomans, primarily to counter Habsburg hegemony. Some of the most neutral accounts were written by French diplomats, such as Guillaume Postel. Yet, as Klaus Malettke has shown, the idea of a crusade against the Turks was present in the French public imagination. The predominance of negative attitudes toward the Turks explains, for example, the hostile reaction of the French population, which was not at all receptive when Ottoman emissaries visited France in 1534.[156] That the image of Ottomans was more generous in the fiction of highbrow writers such as de Scudéry, Molière, and Racine perhaps reflects an elite consciousness that identified with the dominant political course.[157]

England was farthest removed from the battlefront, and Ottoman topics did not attain the significance there that they had in continental Europe. Luc Deitz has attributed this relative disinterest to the lack of firsthand travel accounts about the Ottomans, the general lack of information about them, and the fact that the British did not directly fear an Ottoman invasion. Newspapers, so widespread in Central Europe, were few in number and existed mostly in the form of translations from other European languages. Nevertheless, the image of Turks in British literature, including in Shakespeare, was undoubtedly negative, which supports the contention here that dominant cultural discourse on the one hand, and social and political action on the other hand, need not match up.[158] Daniel Vitkus addresses this seeming contradiction when he writes that "one might assume that people in England felt safely removed from any direct Islamic threat, but in fact English authors of the sixteenth and seventeenth centuries frequently refer to the menace of the Ottoman conquerors in terms that express a sense of proximity and immediacy."[159] The negative image of Turks was reinforced by the generally negative image of Muslims in British literature: "John Milton depicted Satan in *Paradise Lost* as a Muslim potentate surrounded by Eastern trappings and minions."[160] In spite of these negative images, "Queen Elizabeth herself maintained diplomatic relations and official correspondence with Moroccan and Turkish rulers. Her primary purpose was to request loans or military aid from these Islamic potentates or encourage trade, not to chastise them for their infidel ways."[161]

Whereas England was not directly threatened by the Ottomans, battles were fought in the Mediterranean and the Atlantic in conjunction with the expansion of English commerce. By the early seventeenth century "Barbary pirates began to raid the English coastline and take captives."[162] Conversion of captives became an acknowledged phenomenon and generated phobic reactions. On the pragmatic level, English rulers attempted to engage the help of "the Ottomans to restrain the Barbary pirates' predations on English shipping," which shows quite clearly that distinctions were made between different Muslim powers.[163] Nabil Matar stresses the contrast between "*actual* interaction between Britons and Muslims" and "the creation of . . . alterity . . . within literary and theological contexts."[164] In the sixteenth century, "thousands of Turks and Moors visited and traded in English and Welsh ports, and hundreds were captured on the high seas and brought to stand trial in English courts. In addition, scores of ambassadors and emissaries dazzled the London populace with their charm, cuisine and 'Araby' horses," and an even "greater number" of "Britons were going to North Africa and the Levant," all of which is recorded in letters, government and economic documents, and other materials from the period, illustrating, once more, that different discourses coexisted and contradicted each other.[165]

Other European countries, such as Poland, Spain, and the Netherlands, also possess distinct political and military histories with the Ottomans.[166] Even though there was a cultural discourse on the Ottomans and Muslims that was shared across Europe—one that was largely negative and polemical but which also revealed an acute interest in factual information about the Ottoman Empire and about Islam—different European states pursued distinct strategies toward the Ottoman Empire. Alliances were entered into for political and religious reasons, often reflecting internal European power struggles, and the economic advantages of such alliances is beyond doubt. Economic relations played an important factor in determining the nature of relations. As Kate Fleet has argued, the

> Ottoman ability to utilise the skills and money of outside traders may in some way have played a part in the successful early development of the state, for while it is true that without military success there could not have been an empire, it is also true that military strength alone cannot be the sole explanation for the continuing Ottoman success. Another factor in the successful creation of a lasting state may well have been Ottoman ability to absorb from those they conquered systems that were in place and which worked, and to use the capital and know-how of foreign merchants.[167]

In spite of these mostly state-led alliances and economic interactions, the general image of the Ottomans reflected dominant religious attitudes, experiences of actual warfare, and various needs to construct images of cultural and religious alterity. Nuances in the cultural and literary discourses that are observable with regard to specific states, such as the more positive image of the Ottomans held by French elites, correspond to distinct political relationships toward the Ottomans. The eighteenth century would turn some of these relationships upside down and bring new political alliances and changing views of the Ottomans to Europe.

CHAPTER 3

A Moment of Equilibrium (1683–1792)

The Ottoman invasions brought new information about Islam and Ottoman culture to Europe. Whereas the image of the Middle East during the Crusades was primarily determined by a religious view of the world, greater knowledge about Ottoman society inspired reflection upon cultural differences. Both fictional and nonfictional writings on the Ottomans included not only dismissive but also curious and sympathetic responses, even at the height of the conflict. After the Second Siege of Vienna and before power relations between Europe and the Ottoman Empire finally reversed themselves, an interest in Ottoman culture—its clothing, weapons, music, flowers, and food products—flourished throughout Europe. By the end of the eighteenth century ongoing Ottoman losses, along with the proliferation of Enlightenment ideas about religious and cultural tolerance, generated a brief moment of equilibrium between the two spheres. This phase in German–Middle Eastern relations was characterized by the so-called *Turcomania,* the rage for things Turkish, even as political and military events continued to define formal relations between Europe and the Middle East. Enlightenment thought, Orientalist scholarship, translations, fictional works, and travel accounts circulating in and across Europe at that time influenced German discourse about Ottoman culture and allowed for the emergence of new Middle Eastern themes in fictional representations.

Turcomania

The interest among Germans for greater knowledge about Ottoman culture and society began to grow in the sixteenth century—especially during relatively peaceful periods, such as the years between 1566 and 1593, when ambassadors and other travelers moved back and forth between the areas, bringing information back to Austrian and other German territories. The ambassador David Ungnad Freiherr zu Sonneck, for example, lived in Istanbul from 1573 to 1578 and had drawings made of the Ottoman court. Departing from conventions associated with maps and other portrayals that attempted to erase the Ottoman presence, these visual representations enabled Germans to get a sense of what the city looked like.[1]

The growing interest in Turkish realia was visible in the many popular collections of Turkish weapons, such as those of Ferdinand II of Tyrol (1529–95) and Christian I of Saxony (1560–91). The collection in Dresden known as the Türckische Cammer is considerable to this day. The Ottomans greatly valued intricately decorated weaponry, and the German/European fascination with exquisite Ottoman weaponry is reflected in the contemporary trend to imitate its styles. Three different groups of weapon makers borrowed the Ottoman style: European craftsmen who sold them to Europeans; craftsmen who lived in the Christian-Muslim border areas and who made weapons for a diverse group of buyers; and European craftsmen who produced weapons for Ottoman buyers.[2]

This interest in Ottoman weapons, as well as other aspects of Ottoman culture such as architecture and art, expanded after the Second Siege of Vienna. What has become known as *Turcomania,* a fascination with and embrace of things Turkish, emerged in all areas of culture. It is noteworthy that this appreciation of Turkish goods and enthusiasm for Turkish themes coexisted with hostility toward Turks and Muslims in religious discourse and German highbrow literature, and can be described as a tension between discourse (albeit heterogeneous) and social practice (as manifested in the acquisition of material goods and the de facto interaction between antagonistic parties). Part appropriation, part identification and emulation, these seemingly contradictory encounters with and relations to an "enemy culture" shape cross-cultural relations in contexts throughout time and space. In this regard it is noteworthy that, as Paula Sutter Fichtner points out, in those Habsburg territories that were affected most by the Ottoman invasions, the fad emerged somewhat later than in the rest of Europe and Germany.[3]

With increasing contacts between Ottomans and Europeans, previously unknown goods of all kinds were brought from Turkey to Europe. One of these novelties was the tulip, which reportedly was grown in the Bavarian city of Augsburg as early as 1559. Tulips became one of the most coveted luxury items in Europe, initiating an investment frenzy that has become known as *Tulipomania.*[4] Across Europe individuals were willing to pay tremendous amounts of money for the bulbs, equaling tens of thousands of dollars in today's value per bulb.[5] The economist John Kenneth Galbraith has identified the tulip frenzy as "the first of the great speculative explosions known to history. It remains to this day one of the most remarkable."[6] When the market for tulips crashed, "the resulting impoverishment had a chilling effect on Dutch economic life in the years that followed."[7]

Festivals and tournaments with Turkish themes were already popular in the sixteenth century. Often conducted during times of war, they reflected a mix of fear and admiration for the enemy.[8] Weddings, some of them high-profile, were often celebrated with Turkish themes; the wedding of Ludwig von Württemberg and Dorothea Ursula von Baden in 1575 included "Turkish music" (in this case neither instruments nor music were of Turkish origin), and fierce Turkish warriors in glamorous attire participated in an allegorical play.[9] The festivities for the 1719 wedding of Frederick August II of Saxony and Erzherzogin Maria Josepha of Austria in Dresden lasted throughout the month of September and represented a high point of *Turcomania* in Saxony.[10] Ottoman themes embellished clothing and the accessories of guests, soldiers (including 315 "Janissaries"), and servants. Among the servants, for example, were twenty-one Africans who had been bought for this occasion in Portugal.[11] An especially choreographed festival was announced as "Türkisches Fest" and occupied a central place at the wedding; among other Turkish themes, a reproduction of a harem allowed visitors to play out their fantasies about life at an Ottoman court.

Turkish music became a serious subject of study over the course of the eighteenth century.[12] Significantly, Turkish musical instruments were integrated into military music during this period. In 1650 the music corps at the court of Dresden adopted Turkish bass drums and small shawms, which Ralf Martin Jäger identifies as early evidence for the integration of authentic Turkish musical instruments into a European military music ensemble.[13] The uniforms worn by musicians often followed Turkish models. Turkish music was part of carnival parades and other local festivities, and frequently the term was used synonymously with "Janissary music." Originally, the elite Janissary corps was composed of non-Muslim, often Christian captives, who converted to Islam, which might have contributed to their special place in the popular imagination. The Janissary music corps, the *mehterhane,* played a very distinct style of music, using instruments such as bass drums, oboes, trumpets, bells, triangles and cymbals. Often its appearances in European countries were arranged as a present by the Ottoman sultan;[14] only rarely, however, was Turkish music actually played by Turks themselves.[15] The reception of Janissary music was mixed; listening to Janissary music during the visit of Ahmed Resmi Efendi in Berlin in 1763, a German witness called it "dreadful."[16] But the interest in Janissary music was considerable and its use for representational purposes widespread. Beyond the influence of Janissary music on military music, Turkish musical themes were most prominent in the so-called Turkish operas, which will be discussed later. Instruments and themes associated with Turkish music also were incorporated into European instrumental music.

The grandeur of the Ottoman court put a lot of pressure on European elites, who felt compelled to find new forms of representation to impress Ottoman ambassadors.[17] Often, Ottoman-German relations had very personal dimensions: in 1701 the Saxon king August II (1670–1733) began a relationship with a Turkish woman by the name of Fatima, who bore him a son in 1702 and a daughter in 1706.[18] August popularized Turkish themes enthusiastically, for example, in architecture. In 1705 construction of the Taschenbergpalais, built as a "Türkisches Haus," for another one of his lovers, Countess Cosel, got under way. The remodeled "Lusthaus" in the "Türkischer Garten" also drew on Turkish motifs, although the Turkishness was mostly visible in the interior.[19] August II also introduced various Turkish elements into his military and courtly context, such as a Janissary battalion (recruited in Saxony, Poland, and Lithuania, under strict guidelines), uniforms styled after Ottoman models, servants dressed as Turks, and elements of Ottoman military and courtly ceremonies.[20] Ottoman tents became popular symbols for the appropriation of Ottoman culture, especially in the aftermath of the victory of 1683.[21]

Ottoman ceramics and textiles, which are fixtures of German museums and private collections, also document the presence of Ottoman crafts in Europe. Turkish porcelain was collected and exhibited, although not every "Turkish" piece was indeed of that origin; often East Asian pottery was presented as such.[22] In return, Turkish demand also affected the porcelain production in Meißen: in 1732 manufacturers in Meißen received "the first commission over 24,000 cups and agreed to manufacture 43,200 pieces annually."[23] Oriental carpets, a valued commodity since the Middle Ages, continued to garner high prices on the European market but also faced competition from European manufacturers, who tried to imitate them.[24] Also noteworthy are the so-called *Kostümbücher*, illustrated volumes about Turkish culture which included drawings and woodcuts of Turkish scenes. They date back to the late sixteenth century but became popular in the course of the eighteenth century. These illustrations conveyed ethnographic information and enabled Germans to gain a visual image of Turkish life.[25] Yet, as Maria Elisabeth Pape points out, most artists who reproduced Turkish themes in their art had never visited the Ottoman Empire.[26] Following the model of mostly French and Italian artists, German artists produced woodcuts, paintings, etchings, and drawings. Popular themes were Turkish women and scenes from the Ottoman court, particularly the harem. In 1719/22 Johann Christoph Weigel (1654–1726) etched a series entitled "Wahreste und neueste Abbildungen des türkischen Hofes," in which he followed a cycle often imitated and originally produced by the French artist Jean-Baptiste Vanmour (1671–1737). Increasingly, especially after the 1740s, European aristocrats had themselves painted as Turks, dressed in rich Oriental garb.[27]

Nothing, however, parallels the effect that the introduction of coffee and tea had on European societies. The drinking of coffee had been established in Arabian countries during the fifteenth century and made its way to the center of the Ottoman Empire in the context of the Ottoman conquest of Arab lands. The first coffeehouse was opened in Istanbul in 1554 by two merchants from Syria, and Europeans who visited Istanbul and Arab countries brought news of this exotic drink back home. In Germany coffee was known as "der Türkentrank." Following other European countries, the first coffeehouses opened in the 1670s in Bremen and Hamburg. A coffeehouse that opened in Würzburg in 1697 was run by a baptized Turk.[28] In Vienna the first coffeehouse was founded right after the Second Siege, when ingenious entrepreneurs made good use of five hundred sacks of coffee that had been captured from the withdrawing Ottoman troops. Although Prussian aristocrats had already been drinking coffee since the 1670s, the first public coffeehouse opened in Berlin only in 1721. Tea, known to Europeans since the thirteenth century, grew in popularity at about the same time; in England tea became the drink of choice by the middle of the eighteenth century, a development that, according to Wolfgang Schivelbusch, "still remains an unexplained phenomenon."[29]

Schivelbusch has shown how these drinks gradually replaced beer and other alcoholic beverages and, by sobering up the population, allowed for new behavior to emerge that was crucial to the functioning of new forms of production, particularly in industries and offices. At first consumed primarily by the upper and middle classes, coffee and tea created new cultural institutions that transformed society. The coffeehouse, for example, was a space from which women were excluded and that gained importance "as a *social* center": "It was *the* site for the public life of the eighteenth-century middle class, a place where the bourgeoisie developed new forms of commerce and culture."[30] Johann Sebastian Bach's "Coffee Cantata," one of his roughly fifty secular cantatas, was composed between 1732 and 1734; the fourth Aria, "Ei! wie schmeckt der coffee süsse," is a playful testament to the popularity of the drink.

How can we explain this fascination with Ottoman culture, particularly the adoption of Ottoman motifs and products by German and other European cultures? Several factors seem to have played a role. First, the interest in things

Ottoman clearly is a form of appropriation of enemy culture, especially once the enemy threat had receded. Appropriation and the desire to imitate can be identified as a ritual of empowerment, a ritual that was already present at a time when the Ottomans were the superior power but which became widespread once the Ottomans were losing. As David Spurr has argued, colonial discourse often "seeks to dominate by inclusion and domestication rather than by a confrontation which recognizes the independent identity of the Other."[31] The appropriation of the culture of conquered peoples functions to control and often eradicate them. After the Indian Wars of the nineteenth century, white Americans adopted many symbols of Native American culture, some of which remain visible today in the language, logos, mascots, and other symbols used in American sports. Second, curiosity and the desire for novelty certainly contributed to the fascination with Ottoman goods. Third, there was money to be made; trade for Ottoman goods and exports to the Ottoman Empire were serious business. The case of coffee and tea clearly links interest in these and other goods and novelties to the rise of a new economic order that was characterized by new forms of consumption and production. The commercial aspect, which draws on the desire for novelty but more importantly facilitates the performance of class distinction and social empowerment, may have been the most forceful drive behind Europeans' interest in things Ottoman.[32]

But not only goods and fads made their way north and northwest: Turkish individuals also lived in Germany. In the aftermath of the Second Siege of Vienna a large number of captured Ottomans settled in German countries. Hartmut Heller has traced the life stories of about five hundred such cases; he claims that this number is only "the tip of the iceberg."[33] These captured Turks were almost always baptized, a phenomenon that was known as *Türkentaufen.* Data about these baptisms, which often were celebrated with great pomp, is one source of information about Turks in Germany during the period. Tombstones, church registers, and local chronicles provide additional information. Among those captured in battle were women and children; Heller estimates that about half of the captured individuals were children, while the other half consisted in equal parts of young men and women.[34] Sometimes captured Turks were brought home as "trophies" and presented to friends and notables to win favors. In Vienna it was fashionable to have a baptized Turk for a servant.[35] While many did work as servants, others learned a trade and, in some cases, attained a respected social standing.[36] Intermarriage was common, especially after the immigrant Muslims were baptized. Often within a few generations traces of their Ottoman past had disappeared.

Ottoman sources document the lives of several of these individuals who were captured by German troops and who lived in German countries for extended periods of time. ʻOsman Aga, for example, was captured in 1688 and suffered gravely as a prisoner before he attained a more bearable social standing serving Graf Stubenberg in Steiermark and, later, General von Schallenberg in Vienna. ʻOsman Aga's time under Austrian owners came to an end in 1699, when he escaped, masked in the uniform of an Austrian officer and protected by false papers. In Temesvár (Timişoara) he used his knowledge of German to secure a position as a translator. He served in this role for several diplomatic missions and then settled in Istanbul in 1724.[37] Another account from the same period is the chronicle of Cafer Pasha, written by Ali of Temesvár (*Tarih-i Vak'aname-i Cafer Paşa*), which covers the period from 1688 until 1697. Cafer Pasha was governor of Temesvár during this time, and his account describes in vivid detail Ottoman-Habsburg hostilities and other nonviolent contacts.[38]

Just as Europeans were fascinated with Ottoman culture, Ottomans were interested in the arts and crafts of Europeans. Orhan Pamuk's 1998 novel, *My Name Is Red,* for example, notes the growing interest of Ottoman court artists in portrait painting and other forms of representational art during the sixteenth century.[39] Items that were part of yearly tribute payments also led to the cross-cultural exchange of goods. In addition to financial obligations, tribute payments included silver- and goldsmiths' works, precious textiles, rare raw materials, and other luxury items unavailable in Turkey at the time.[40] High-priced items such as clocks, particularly automatic clocks, were decorated for the Ottomans with Oriental motifs. A similar cross-cultural influence occured in other areas of cultural life, including architecture and music.[41] Knowledge was transferred through original works composed in Ottoman Turkish, such as geographical manuals and embassy reports, and through translations; scientific studies in the fields of geography, astronomy, and medicine from across Europe were quickly picked up by Ottoman translators.[42] In 1726 the first Ottoman printing press was in operation, contributing greatly to a proliferation of scientific knowledge.[43]

Political, Economic, and Military Developments

After the Second Siege of Vienna, the influx of Turkish wares and omnipresence of Turkish themes rose even further, even though hostilities were far from over. Between the Second Siege of Vienna and the Peace Treaty of Jassy, in 1792, the Ottomans were at war with either Russia or the Habsburgs, or both, for almost four decades.[44]

Following their defeat at Vienna, the Ottomans lost against the Holy League (Holy Roman Empire, Poland, the Venetian Republic, and Russia) in land and sea battles. The Treaty of Karlowitz in 1699 finalized the Ottoman loss of Hungary (except the Banat of Temesvár), Transylvania, Croatia, and Slovenia to the Habsburgs (other areas went to Venice and Poland).[45] Several areas were recovered by the Ottomans over the next fifteen years. As the power of Russia grew, however, wars between Russia and the Ottoman Empire gradually contributed to the weakening of the Ottomans in Europe. The Ottomans defeated Russia and signed a peace treaty in 1712, returning—among other provisions—Belgrade to the Ottomans. The Treaty of Passarowitz (1718) reversed this outcome, and the Habsburgs gained the Banat of Temesvár, northern Serbia (including Belgrade), northern Bosnia, and Lesser Walachia (Oltenia). Venice, which was a third party in these negotiations, had to give up several Greek territories. The following decade brought peace; during these years of relative calm, Ottoman ambassadors were sent to various European capitals.[46] Fighting flared up again in the 1730s, however, and most territories captured by the Habsburgs were lost again in the 1739 Peace of Belgrade. The turning point came with the Russian-Ottoman War of 1768–74, which brought Catherine the Great into the picture. This war was a turning point in more than one way: in 1771 Austria negotiated with the Ottomans against the Russians, who were threatening to invade the Balkans. The divisions of Poland (in 1772, 1793, and 1795) played an important role in the struggle between German powers and Russia. This Habsburg-Ottoman cooperation from 1771 marks the beginning of alliances between various German and Ottoman–Turkish powers.

The Treaty of Jassy (1792) concluded the Russian-Ottoman War of 1787–92 favorably for Russia. Wars between Russia and the Ottoman Empire continued throughout the nineteenth century, but for the Habsburg Empire, the Ottomans were no longer the main enemy. The cooperation between Habsburgs and Ottomans was followed by Ottoman-Prussian alliances. Part of the changing power constellations in Europe was the increasingly hostile relationship between Prussia and the Habsburg Empire. Since 1706 Prussian troops had fought alongside the allied powers of the Grand Alliance and were therefore no longer under the command of the Holy Roman Empire. These new developments, in the context of tension between France and Britain over sea routes, led to the establishment of diplomatic relations between Prussia and the Ottomans. Contacts initially were facilitated with Hungarian help and developed slowly over the course of several decades. When Prussia sought Ottoman support during the Seven Years' War, the Ottomans hesitated to send military help but agreed to a *Freundschafts- und Handelsabkommen* (Friendship and

Trade Agreement), negotiated by Adolf von Rexin, who became the first consul to represent Prussia in Istanbul.[47] A Turkish-Prussian agreement against the Habsburgs fell through when Catherine II of Russia took power. Catherine put an end to the Prussia-friendly politics of her husband, who had promised not to intervene in case of an Ottoman attack on Hungary. The 1763–64 attempt to agree on a defensive treaty between the Ottomans and Prussia also did not come to pass, largely because of agreements between Russia and Prussia.[48] But in 1790 these attempts were renewed, and a military agreement between Prussia and the Ottomans was worked out that enabled the Ottomans to negotiate more forcefully with Habsburgs and Russians.[49]

Thus, by the end of the eighteenth century both Habsburgs and Prussians had developed cooperative relationships with the Ottoman Empire, which no longer immediately threatened German areas. In particular, Prussia became a model for the Ottomans, who sought to reorganize their military and to carry out reforms to keep up with the developments of the time. In fact, the restructuring of the Ottoman army is one of the areas that demonstrate Prussian-Ottoman cooperation. A pamphlet from 1718 stands out as one of the earliest texts documenting that the Ottomans considered European models to restructure their army, especially after the losses of the previous decades. The text is designed as a dialogue between an Ottoman and a Christian officer.[50] The suggestions offered in this treatise were not actualized; a generation later, however, the first attempts were made to reorganize the Ottoman army. Significant here were the efforts of Claude Alexandre, comte de Bonneval (1675–1747), a French army officer who had first fought for the Habsburgs against the French and the Ottomans before defecting to the Ottoman army. Bonneval converted to Islam and became known as Humbaraci Ahmed Pasha. Historians disagree on his role, and while the Ottomans ultimately came to distrust the flamboyant figure, he is credited with having reformed those parts of the Ottoman army that contributed to bringing about Ottoman victory in the war of 1736–39.[51] Heinrich Benedikt acknowledges Bonneval as one of the first political players to envision collaboration between Prussia and Germany and the Ottoman Empire and Turkey.[52]

Reform of the Ottoman state, economy, and military was indeed necessary to keep up with European expansionism. Several factors suggest that the decline of Ottoman power was related to internal developments. Failed or incomplete attempts at reorganizing economic, political, social, and military structures are among those factors. In addition, however, the global expansion of European states and empires challenged Ottoman control over sea and land routes, which led to a loss of state income and trade activity. As Donald

Quataert argues, "Global market forces may have affected the eighteenth century Ottoman economy more powerfully than state policies."[53] France and Britain competed with Holland, Spain, and Portugal over controlling and exploiting areas around the world. Britain established dominance in India in the second half of the eighteenth century; the United States achieved independence in 1776. These and other global developments challenged Ottoman power across Asia, the Middle East, North Africa, and Europe.[54]

Trade with the Ottomans had increased over time, regardless of military confrontations, and often was fostered by the fact that different European nations had quite distinct diplomatic and economic relations with the Ottomans. England was the most important trading partner of the Ottoman Empire in the seventeenth century. The French, building on their alliance with the Ottomans since the early sixteenth century, dominated trade with the Ottomans throughout the eighteenth century. With regard to power relations between French and Ottoman trading partners, "the situation . . . was still one of quasi-equality and . . . a true *dominant-dominé* type of relation was yet to come."[55] The period from the 1720s until the end of the 1760s was particularly stable and favorable to trade.[56]

German states gradually increased their imports from and exports to the Ottoman Empire, and by the end of the eighteenth century the Habsburg Empire received 24 percent of Ottoman exports, while France still dominated with 36.5 percent (Britain, 9.2 percent; Holland, 18.3 percent; Venetian Republic, 12 percent).[57] Quataert states that "Ottoman exports to the Habsburg Empire nearly equaled and sometimes even exceeded imports from that state during the 1830s through the 1870s."[58] For a brief period of time political alliances were reflected in economically balanced relations. The political changes of the nineteenth century, which brought about political collaboration between Habsburgs and Ottomans, and Prussians and Ottomans, created the conditions for subsequent close cooperation.

Age of Enlightenment

In addition to the influence of political and economic developments, images of the Middle East and Islam were shaped by four factors, namely the emergence of new thought, as formulated during the Enlightenment period; translations of literary and nonliterary writings into German; the development of German Orientalist sciences; and the circulation of new information from travel accounts. The influence of French and British cultures in this regard is essential; much of the material that inspired German cultural production came from France and Britain and, to a lesser degree, from Italy.

Ideas that we generally associate with the Age of Enlightenment greatly shaped novel perceptions, not only of Turks, but of the Orient and Islam more broadly. In the seventeenth century Johannes Kepler (1571–1630) and Galileo Galilei (1564–1642) prepared the ground for new scientific thinking; the contributions of René Descartes (1596–1650), Francis Bacon (1561–1626), and Isaac Newton (1642–1727), among others, created methods of scientific thinking and made discoveries that shattered beliefs that had been central to European and Christian views of the world. In conjunction with changing modes of production and the expansion of European empires, new ideas about the globe, religion, culture, and political life entered the public sphere. As political institutions no longer fit the reality of an economy that was propelled by a rising middle class, demands for political participation expanded. Thomas Hobbes (1588–1679; *Leviathan* [1651]) and John Locke (1632–1704; *Two Treatises of Government* [1690]) offered new ideas of the state, and the critique of religion was expressed, for example, in Pierre Bayle's *Dictionnaire historique et critique* (1697). In this secularizing world, the power of the Church was challenged and gradually restricted, although we need to stress that in Germany, the Enlightenment movement was closely tied to Protestantism. Over time ideas about and the actual implementation of the separation of state and church led to greater tolerance for different forms of religion. Rulers across Europe realized that change was necessary; following the lead of French kings, such as Louis XIV (1638–1715), and Britain's Glorious Revolution of 1688, Frederick the Great (1712–86), Maria Theresa of Austria (1717–80), and Catherine the Great of Russia (1729–96) pursued social, political, and economic reforms of varying degrees. Later, American Independence (1776) and the French Revolution (1789) prompted calls for political change across German lands.

The call for religious tolerance and new forms of governance and social norms was mediated by engaging with, among other subjects, Islam and Middle Eastern cultures. As we will see, the literary and cultural discourse on the Middle East highlights the tension between competing ideas of inclusion and exclusion that characterize Enlightenment thought.

Translation and Cross-Cultural Reception

Over the course of the eighteenth century, operas featuring Oriental themes gained popularity throughout Europe. Turkish operas had been staged in

France, Italy, and Britain since the seventeenth century and employed themes such as Turkish violence, excessive sexuality, and despotism. Gradually, new Turkish characters were added to the cast of actors and conveyed new themes. In particular, the figure of the enlightened sultan and characters who appeared laughable revealed that the once threatening Ottomans were no longer considered so formidable. Negative qualities were often transferred from major to minor characters, who stood in contrast to the central, positively conceived sultan. These new Turkish characters functioned to articulate a range of ideas and ethical concerns that preoccupied European societies at the time.

Turkish operas also contributed greatly to creating a visual image of the Orient as a place of luxury, abundance, and splendor. Costume designers were inspired by authentic drawings and paintings that displayed a high degree of accuracy, which "were popularized by inexpensive single-sheet engravings, and engraved albums of oriental costumes published in various European countries were collected in aristocratic libraries."[59] These images served as models not only for opera and play costumes but also for the popular masked costume balls.

One of the earliest Turkish operas was written in 1619, by the Italian Prospero Bonarelli (1580–1659), whose *Il Solimano* (1632) became the blueprint for many eponymous operas and for other operas that employed elements of its plot. *Solimano* is representative of a group of operas that mix political intrigue with interpersonal drama and articulate questions related to political power through the staging of family conflict. Many plays inspired the writing of opera libretti, such as a play by Carlo Goldoni (1707–93), *La sposa persiana* (1753), rewritten for the operatic stage in 1775 by Felice Alessandri (1747–98) and that also thematizes power relations through family conflict.[60]

Just as a cluster of operas focuses on the figure of Sulayman (Soliman), other operas centered on the conflict between the historical Ottoman sultan Bayezid I (1360–1403) and Tamerlane (1328–1405), the fourteenth-century Mongol ruler also known as Timur-i Lang. Tamerlane conquered large areas of western and central Asia and captured Bayezid in a battle in 1402; Bayezid later died in captivity. The historical events became the focus of a significant number of operas and also were known through paintings, plays, and historical writings across Europe. In England Christopher Marlowe (1564–93) popularized the story with his play *Tamburlaine* (1587). According to Walter Preibisch, the first documented operatic version comes from Venice, where in 1689 it was staged to the music of Marc'Antonio Ziani (1653–1715).[61] Several versions produced in the Italian context were followed by an opera composed by George Frideric Handel (1685–1759), which will serve here as an example of the cross-cultural exchange that occurred with regard to the transmission of tales involving Turkish sultans. Handel, a German who worked in England from 1712 until his death in 1759, absorbed cultural productions from all over Europe. The immediate models for his *Tamerlano* (1724), adapted for the composer by Nicola Haym, were two Italian libretti, one by Count Agostino Piovene (1710), the second an adaptation of the same work performed in 1719.[62] Piovene stated that he drew on two main sources for his libretto, namely, Jacques Nicolas Pradon's late seventeenth-century play *Tamerlan ou La Mort de Bajazet* and a history of the Byzantine Empire by Ducas. Both these sources, in turn, followed even earlier models.[63] Pradon's play exemplifies a new trend in depicting Oriental rulers, in that Bayezid's fate and demeanor inspire compassion and respect, and even the cruel Tamerlane appears as a complex character with benign traits. These aspects are emphasized musically by Handel's score.[64] The Bayezid/Tamerlane plot was adapted numerous times throughout the eighteenth century.

Another group of Turkish operas follows the model of the comic opera, which in turn was inspired by comedic traditions, particularly of the Italian and French variety, and adopted many of its themes and characters.[65] The fact that the comic opera was adaptable to Turkish themes shows a radical departure from the grim Turkish tragedies of the seventeenth century, certainly in their German renditions.

Similar to the intent of many operas, French seventeenth-century novelists and playwrights, such as Georges and Madeleine de Scudéry, envisioned Turkish characters in more benign ways, as compared with influential German authors such as Daniel Casper von Lohenstein.[66] Increasingly, comical Turkish figures were introduced, for example in Jean de Rotrou's comedy *La Sœur* (1645) and in several court ballets. Molière's *Le Bourgeois gentilhomme* (1670) also exemplifies this tradition. This comedy, which "plays the resentments of the decadent nobility against the emerging bourgeoisie in its eagerness to claim social prestige based on wealth, rather than privilege," also takes stabs at the shallowness of the nobility.[67] The play features characters who masquerade in Turkish clothes and also presents a mufti, a Turkish dance, as well as Turkish music—all of this explicitly on demand by King Louis XIV, who requested a play involving Turkish elements.[68] Ali Behdad has tied the play to a growing demand for the exotic and explains the masquerading as an attempt to master "the fear and the threat produced by the powerful Ottoman"; Michèle Longino understands the play against the background of complex diplomatic relations between the French and the Ottomans.[69] Both approaches to the play are compatible and highlight the significance of French-Ottoman relations at the time.

One of the first texts that uses an Oriental setting to comment on European societies and which was read across Europe is Montesquieu's *Lettres persanes.*[70] The author, who is also known for his ideas about the separation of powers, published this work anonymously in Amsterdam in 1721, a clear sign that its content was expected to create great controversy. Indeed, its controversial content ensured that many years after its publication it was included in the Vatican's Index of Prohibited Books in 1762. The narrative is written in the form of letters, most of them composed by Usbek and Rica, two Persians who travel through France over the span of nine years and who comment on French and Persian society. Using the outsider perspective, the letters critique controversial aspects of French society, such as the power and decadence of the aristocracy and religious leaders. But the letters also convey distinct ideas about Persia; passages about life in the harem fed European ideas of Oriental eroticism and violence, and the Orient emerges as a site of attraction and repulsion.

Montesquieu also popularized the idea of Oriental despotism. In his 1748 *De L'Esprit des lois* (The Spirit of the Laws) he distinguishes between republican, monarchical, and despotic forms of government. Even though Montesquieu highlights areas of weakness and possible malfunction with regard to republican and monarchical government, despotism clearly emerges as the type of government that is to be rejected.[71] Throughout the text, China, Turkey, Persia, and other Middle Eastern and Asian societies are invoked as examples of despotic governments, which rule through the principle of fear. In order to establish these geopolitical divisions, Montesquieu has to ignore, for example, Islamic legal systems and the reports of missionaries that contradict his idea of Chinese despotism.[72] The idea of Oriental despotism and its projection onto non-European areas allowed Europeans to articulate new ideals of government for their own societies, and it also allowed them to employ the concept in their critique of European absolutism, as embodied, for example, by Louis XIV.[73] With regard to the Middle East and Asia, however, the concept became an ideological tool that served to disqualify its societies in a sweeping manner.

Islam and the Middle East play a considerable role in Voltaire's writings. He evoked the Orient as a vehicle to comment on French society but also made direct judgments about Islam, circulating images that had a significant impact on the cultural and literary discourse on Islam and the Middle East more generally. Voltaire's plays were influential models for Germans: *Zaire,* published in French in 1732, saw at least twelve editions in Germany by 1800. Set at a Turkish court, the play uses a love story between the Christian-born slave Zaire and Sultan Orosmane as a vehicle to discuss questions related to religious tolerance and political despotism. Based on a misunderstanding that arouses his jealousy, the sultan stabs Zaire to death and then, realizing his mistake, kills himself, after he orders the release of his Christian prisoners. The tragedy attests both to ideas of religious tolerance—it is conceivable to endorse marriage between a Muslim and a Christian—and new ideas about the just political ruler, who has to overcome autocratic behavior. The Christian counterpart to the sultan turns out to be the ethically inferior character, a clear stab at Christianity.

Directly offensive to Islam was Voltaire's play *Mahomet, ou le Fanatisme* (1741). After its third performance it was forbidden by the Church, which rightly understood the play as a veiled affront to Christianity. Minou Reeves claims, however, that the play was canceled "after a formal complaint by the Turkish ambassador" but "returned to the stage after popular outcry."[74] Drawing on a repertoire of distortions circulating in Europe since the Middle Ages, the play conveyed an image of Muhammad as a fanatical, sexualized, and power-hungry leader. Voltaire's satire *Zadig, ou La destinée, Histoire orientale* (1747), which used the setting of ancient Babylon, was also translated into German several times. Voltaire's time in Germany from 1750 to 1755, initially at the court of Frederick II, furthered the reception of his ideas in Germany as well. He projects a more appreciative image of the Orient in his *Essai sur les moeurs et l'esprit des nations* (1756) and the satirical novel *Candide, ou l'optimisme* (1759), among other writings. In the latter, the main character, Candide (who is German by origin), and a group of friends settle in Turkey after a worldwide journey replete with violence and disappointment. They live on a farm, and each member of the group excels in pursuing useful activities in the house and garden. Turkey is rendered as the place that finally allows for a life of wisdom and happiness and for pleasures such as "eating candied citron and pistachios."[75] In "A Treatise of Toleration" the Ottoman Empire is praised as a role model with regard to the peaceful coexistence of different religions and sects.[76]

What emerges from this brief review of Voltaire's writings is evidence of the author's contradictory stance toward the Middle East and Islam. Gestures that stress the humanity of Middle Eastern individuals or even societies as a whole are undercut by Voltaire's critique of Islam, although it is important to consider this critique in light of Voltaire's general rejection of religion, an aspect that holds true for other Enlightenment critics of religion as well.[77] Nevertheless, he contributed to the creation and perpetuation of negative images about Islam that circulate to this day. Another well-known French writer who employed the Orient centrally is Abbé Prévost, whose novel *Histoire d'une Grecque moderne* (1740) stages a passionate love story in Constantinople.[78] Jean de La Fontaine, painted a thoroughly idyllic image of life in Turkey in *Ballade sur le mal d'amour* (1750): "Tout est galant, traitable, et gracieux" in this Turkey, which appears as a paradise on earth.

Much like the French, British authors utilized the Orient to comment on social issues at a moment of imperial expansion and "deployed oriental models as both analogue and opposite."[79] And similar to German authors, British writers incorporated and modified themes and motifs that distinguished them from the French-language models. Ros Ballaster has shown how specific tales, often taken from the French translation of a Persian or Arabic original, appeared in distinct versions throughout Europe.[80] But areas of similarity existed as well: Comparable to developments in France and Germany, enlightened Oriental characters emerged in eighteenth-century British fiction. As Ballaster argues, "Oriental narratives provided significant opportunities for the exploration of Enlightenment models of transformation and progress, especially for women writers." Penelope Aubin's *The Strange Adventures of the Count de Vinevil and His Family* (1721), Eliza Haywood's *Philidore and Placentia* (1727), and Frances Sheridan's *The History of Nourjahad* (1765) are examples.[81] British writers often used French models to present their own commentary on society and especially local politics; see, for example, Daniel Defoe's *Continuation of the Letters Writ by a Turkish Spy* (1718) and George Lyttelton's *Letters from a Persian in England, to His Friend in Isphahan* (1735).[82] Other well-known British authors from the period—namely Samuel Johnson (*The History of Rasselas, Prince of Abissinia* [1759]), John Hawkesworth (*Almoran and Hamet* [1761]), and William Beckford (*Vathek: An Arabian Tale* [1786])—also employed an Oriental setting in their narratives.[83]

What these texts and operas, circulated in Europe in the original languages and in translations, have in common is that they use an Oriental setting in one way or another to critique European societies in light of new ideas about politics and religion. In spite of their interest in critically examining European contexts—as well as the fact that they contained a wealth of new detail and historical information largely culled from publications by Orientalist scientists—most of these writings perpetuated clichés about the Orient; sexuality (particularly the rescuing of Oriental or European women from lusting Middle Eastern men) and despotism were central themes. Nevertheless, reflecting the reduced threat from the Ottoman Empire, the figure of the Enlightened Oriental and the comical Turk entered the literature, countering earlier exclusively negative images.

Orientalist Scholarship

Enlightenment thinkers set out to organize knowledge in ways that challenged religious cosmologies. One way to avoid the narrative of salvation history was to catalog knowledge in the form of encyclopedias. The great significance encyclopedias have for the age signals both the quest for knowledge as well as an attempt to organize it systematically and objectively, from A to Z, without integrating it into larger philosophical, and certainly not religious, frameworks. Encyclopedic knowledge was also collected by Orientalists, and in fact, one of the most outstanding works predates the famous *Encyclopédie,* a collaborative work directed by Denis Diderot and Jean d'Alembert that was published between 1751 and 1780, by several decades. Barthélemy d'Herbelot de Molainville (1625–95) worked for most of his life on the *Bibliothèque orientale, ou dictionnaire universel contenant tout ce qui regarde la connoissance des peuples de l'Orient,* for which he drew on Arabic, Persian, and Turkish bibliographies and manuscripts. The work was completed after his death by Antoine Galland (1646–1715), who published it in 1697.

Herbelot's work exemplifies the beginning of serious Orientalist scholarship, but his efforts were preceded by those of still earlier scholars. While scholars such as the Florentine Pico della Mirandola (1463–94) had already engaged with Aramaic and Arabic in the fifteenth century, the French scholar Guillaume Postel (1510–81) is often considered the "first true Orientalist."[84] Appointed from 1538 to 1544 as professor of Arabic in Paris and then in 1554 in Vienna, Postel traveled widely in Europe and the Middle East. He composed the first Arabic grammar and gathered a large number of manuscripts that were bought by Ottheinrich, Elector Palatine; the collection marks the beginning of Orientalist studies in Heidelberg. Other early Arabists include Thomas Erpenius (1584–1624), who published a *Grammatica Arabica* (1613, Leiden); Jakob Golius (1596–1667), who wrote the *Lexicon Arabico-Latinum* (1653, Leiden); and Johann Heinrich Hottinger (1620–67), whose *Historia Orientalis* (1651, Zurich) made a large number of Middle Eastern sources available to scholars. In England William Bedwell (1563–1632) "was the first Englishman to study Arabic since the Middle Ages," and used this knowledge to write anti-Islamic treatises.[85] Another outstanding scholar was Edward Pococke (1604–91), whose translations and manuscript collection furthered Oriental studies in spite of his hostility toward Islam. *The History of the Saracens* (1708–18) by Simon Ockley (1678–1720) was one of the first positive accounts of Arab culture written by a European Orientalist. While the British lawyer and scholar George Sale (ca. 1697–1736), whose translation of the Koran appeared in 1734, was clearly anti-Islamic and anti-Arab, "many of his readers thought his portrait of the Prophet and the rise of Islam much too favourable," thus demonstrating the extent to which the serious study of Islam and Middle Eastern material generally continued to be viewed with suspicion by many.[86]

Throughout the sixteenth and seventeenth centuries Middle Eastern manuscripts found their way to Europe; by the early eighteenth century, for example, three to four hundred Middle Eastern manuscripts were available to scholars in the city library of Leipzig alone. The translation and explication of many of these works greatly expanded European knowledge of the Middle East and Islam and made possible works such as that by Herbelot. Literary works became widely disseminated: Antoine Galland's translation of stories from the cycle known as *One Thousand and One Nights* were published beginning in 1704 and were crucial in popularizing Oriental themes. In fact, so influential were these stories that we can attribute many topoi that have become standard ideas associated with the Middle East to that collection of tales. How reliable this reception is may be understood if one imagines a portrayal of Germany based largely on Disney-like adaptations of German fairy tales.

The official beginning of the academic discipline of Middle Eastern studies is often associated with the founding of the École spéciale des Langues Orientales in Paris in 1795, but centers for the study of Middle Eastern languages and cultures already had appeared across Europe, in Leiden, Leipzig, and Antwerp, among other cities.[87] "Orientalistik," in Germany and across Europe, was born of theological studies, which in the eighteenth century included a growing number of specialists in various Middle Eastern languages. An important next step was separating the study of Arabic, Turkish, Persian, and other Middle Eastern languages from its original association with biblical studies (although, as Suzanne Marchand shows, Christian perspectives remained integral to German Oriental studies into the twentieth century).[88] A leading figure in this regard was Johann Jacob Reiske (1716–74), who published editions and translations of Arabic prose, made initial attempts to systematize Arabic literary history, and acknowledged the importance of Islam.[89] His controversial views ensured that he never received a professorship at a German university. Reiske's approach to Arabic differed substantially from that of Albert Schultens (1686–1750), an influential Dutch philologist who considered Arabic inferior to Hebrew. His translations of the pre-Islamic poet Tarafa and works by historian and geographer Abu al-Fida, for example, were pivotal for Goethe, Herder, and Lessing. Johann Gottfried Eichhorn (1752–1827), professor of theology and Oriental languages in Jena, substantially furthered knowledge of Middle Eastern poetry. Eichhorn's successor was Heinrich Eberhard Gottlob

Paulus (1761–1851), who published an Arabic grammar and an anthology of Middle Eastern literatures, *Neues Repertorium für biblische und morgenländische Litteratur* (3 vols., 1790–91). Johann David Michaelis (1717–91), an expert in Hebraic studies who taught at Halle and Göttingen, approached the Bible as a historically created rather than a revealed document. Although Raymond Schwab states that "the 1771 edition of the *Zend Avesta* marks the first approach to an Asian text totally independent of the biblical and classical traditions," theology-free translations of Arab-language texts by some German Orientalists, such as Reiske, had already been published in the middle of the century.[90] But, as Suzanne Marchand's erudite study on German Orientalists and Jonathan Hess's insightful discussion of Michaelis show, the often-made claim that Michaelis helped liberate Oriental studies from Christian ideology can no longer be maintained.[91] Perhaps Oriental studies became institutionally separated from theology, but Christianity (especially in its Protestant garb, which, following Luther's lead in this regard, was more easily able to pose as secularism) continued to structure the works of many Orientalists for decades to come. The translations by German (and of course French and British) Orientalists made material accessible for the first time, and the gradual institutional liberation from theology promoted an openness toward literary materials. Over time translations such as those by Joseph von Hammer-Purgstall (1774–1856) of the Persian poet Hafis were widely disseminated and influenced a great number of German poets.

In addition to the greater availability of literary material from the Middle East, Germans had access to improved translations of the Koran. The highly problematic translation by Salomon Schweigger (1616) was followed by an equally questionable translation by Eberhard Werner Happel in 1688, and in 1746 by a German translation of Sale's English version. A printed edition of the Koran in Arabic was facilitated by Abraham Hinckelmann, a pastor from Hamburg, in 1694.[92] In 1772 David Friedrich Megerlin (1698–ca. 1750) composed the first German translation of the Koran that was based on an Arabic text. This translation was used by Goethe and other writers and intellectuals of the time.[93]

Writings on the Koran and Muhammad differed across Europe in terms of their ideological import. Humphrey Prideaux's *The True Nature of Imposture fully display'd in the Life of Mahomet* (1697) rendered a highly negative image of the Islamic prophet, whereas Simon Ockley's *The History of the Saracens* (1708/18) and Henri Comte de Boulainvilliers's *La Vie de Mahomed avec des Reflexions sur la Religion Mahometane & les Coutumes des Musulmans* (1730) pursued a more sympathetic approach. German philosophers began to treat Islam as a serious religion. Leibniz's writings on Islam exemplify the emergence of these new points of view. The philosopher has been credited with seeing "Muslims not as animals or savages or political enemies, but primarily as misguided human beings with similar moral/theological frameworks who, for some reason or another, have rejected the truth of Christianity."[94] This shift from a complete rejection of Islam in the Middle Ages to some form of engagement with it as a serious religion (Erasmus, Leibniz) to the idea that it was a legitimate religion that ought to be tolerated (Lessing) was a considerable development. Nevertheless, as we will see in the next chapter, the status of Islam remained contested for many thinkers.

Newspapers and Travel Accounts

Journals and newspapers were crucial in disseminating knowledge about the Middle East. Political and cultural events were well covered; Ali Behdad points out that when the Ottoman ambassador visited France in 1669, "the publishers of the *Gazette* devote[d] the entire December issue to Soliman Aga's visit."[95] In Germany the Ottoman Empire received considerable attention; a Hamburg newspaper focusing exclusively on the conflict with the Ottomans in 1683 and 1684 was received enthusiastically. Editions of the illustrated *Türkischer Estats- und Krieges-Bericht* were fact-oriented and disseminated information about such things as military events, the political organization of the Ottoman Empire, and various aspects of Ottoman culture.[96] Regarding the proliferation of cultural materials, *Neuer Teutscher Merkur,* the *Morgenblatt für gebildete Leser,* and the *Allgemeine Literaturzeitung* are just a few of the leading papers that published translations of Middle Eastern literature. To date, unfortunately, no systematic study has explored the image of the Middle East in the hundreds of German newspapers and journals that were published during the eighteenth century; such an investigation would be worthwhile, particularly in terms of a comparison to literary writings and other cultural representations from the period. Generally, much like the coverage of the Ottoman invasions in the sixteenth and seventeenth centuries, newspapers reported extensively on foreign events and continued to be fact centered; compared to literary and other artistic representations, they generally contained a higher level of accurate information.

As we have seen in accounts from the Middle Ages onward, ethnographic, political, and economic information was conveyed through the writings of individual travelers. Travel accounts were received broadly and cross-nationally: the *Göttingischen Anzeigen von gelehrten Sachen* was one of the most important review journals in Europe, featuring, among other topics, discussions of travel accounts.[97] Even if accounts were not translated into the German language, reviews about them made them available to German speakers. As travelers began to pursue knowledge more systematically, they brought back manuscripts from the Middle East that formed the basis of philological studies and scholarship. One such traveler-scholar whose work is considered groundbreaking was Adam Olearius (1603–71). Olearius wrote two accounts of his travels in Persia, where he served as a secretary to the ambassador sent by Frederick III of Schleswig-Holstein-Gottorp. *Offt begehrte Beschreibung der newen orientalischen Reise,* first published in 1647 and later revised and enlarged, is remarkable for the level of information it provides about Persian literature and culture. The work was translated into French as *Relation du voyage de Moscovie, Tartarie et de Perse* (1656) and inspired French writers, such as Montesquieu. Olearius also provided some of the first translations of Persian literature into German, such as the famous *Gulistan* by the thirteenth-century poet Sheikh Muslih-uddin Sa'di Shirazi; his translation, *Persianischer Rosenthal,* was published in 1654.

The works of Jean Chardin played a similarly important role as those by Olearius. Chardin "had an active life as a jeweller and merchant, ten years of which were spent in Asia, mostly in Persia," where he "was appointed a royal merchant to Shah Abbas II and for whom he executed some jewelry."[98] A first volume based on his experiences was published in 1686; a German translation followed the next year. A complete account of his experiences in the Middle East was published in 1711 as *Voyages du chevalier Chardin en Perse et autres lieux de l'Orient* and was widely circulated. It contained a wealth of information about trade, religion, governance, literature, arts, and crafts. Texts such as Chardin's received substantial attention, often attaining canonical status; some eighteenth-century travel writers copied from these earlier sources, in spite of having their own firsthand experiences. Authors of travel accounts often complained about their lack of access to information; ambassadors in particular seem to have encountered barriers to entering the host culture (perhaps for understandable reasons).[99] The length of stay and the social standing of the travel writer were crucial in this regard; access to insights about non-European societies were greatly dependent on the ability of the individual to enter unfamiliar social spaces, and this aspect made accounts such as those by Chardin invaluable and credible.

Among these exemplary texts the epistolary travel account by Lady Mary Wortley Montagu clearly stands out. She wrote about her experiences in Turkey, where she spent time as the wife of the British ambassador extraordinary to the court of Turkey from 1716 to 1718, in the form of letters intended for publication. Her account was not published until 1763, a year after her death; it was reviewed in Germany in the same year. Montagu deals with topics that were central to other travel writings, such as the character of the Turkish nation, Turkish women, and the politics of the Ottoman Empire. Many of these accounts reveal more about their authors than about Ottoman society, and this may also hold true for Lady Montagu. Whereas Lady Montagu's access to Turkish women's quarters provides the reader with an entirely new kind of information, challenging notions of the objectified Oriental woman, she also uses Turkish women in a way that, as Lisa Lowe has pointed out, "misrepresents and appropriates Turkish female experience for the purpose of defending English feminism."[100] Lowe further argues that "Montagu's *Letters* directly refute the perspectives, rhetorics, and themes of her orientalist predecessors' writing in that tradition."[101] As we have seen, that tradition was not unified and included accounts that valued aspects of Ottoman and Islamic society; with regard to the image of Oriental women, Montagu clearly offered an alternative view regarding the status of women in Ottoman society.[102]

For the German context, and in translated form throughout Europe, Carsten Niebuhr's *Beschreibung von Arabien* (1772, Copenhagen) and his two-volume *Reisebeschreibung nach Arabien und andern umliegenden Ländern* (1774, 1778, Copenhagen) became highly influential.[103] Encouraged by the Orientalist Johann David Michaelis, Niebuhr traveled with an expedition that was proposed by Michaelis and funded by Frederick V of Denmark to survey Egypt, the Arabian Peninsula, and Yemen. Several expedition members died in the Middle East, others on the journey to Bombay, making Niebuhr the only surviving member of the original team. Niebuhr returned via the Middle East, arriving in Copenhagen in late 1767. The focus on the Arab Middle East indicates a shift away from centuries during which the Ottoman Empire, and particularly Istanbul, received primary attention; this new information about the Arab and Persian Middle East that came to Germany increasingly after the middle of the eighteenth century was soon picked up in literature and culture, as the next chapter will show. According to one anthology, fourteen original German accounts based on journeys to Palestine are known from the period under discussion here, a number that was to rise exponentially in the nineteenth century.[104]

The second part of the eighteenth century witnessed a new phase of European control over the world. English rule over India was established in the second half of the century, and France competed with Britain over sea routes and territories in Asia and Africa. In the context of these struggles, accounts about non-European areas were disseminated widely. Even though German states did not govern colonial territories until the end of the nineteenth century (apart from a brief Prussian episode in the middle of the seventeenth century in West Africa),[105] Germans often were part of expeditions or worked in the service of other European colonizers. Georg Forster's account of his participation in James Cook's expedition, originally published in English in 1777 as *A Voyage round the World,* is a notable example. German merchants, especially those based in Hanse cities, also established trading posts in Africa and Asia, even without state support.

Most important, ideas of European entitlement to rule over the rest of the planet were discussed widely across Europe. Susanne Zantop has shown that Germans entertained colonial fantasies even in the absence of a German colonial empire. As we will see in more detail, the contemporaneity of scientific approaches toward understanding the world and calls for political participation and religious tolerance, on the one hand, and European political and economic expansionism, on the other, brought about tension and contradictions.

New Ideas and Images in Fiction and Philosophy

In contrast to the changes observable in material culture, fictional works from the period immediately after the Second Siege of Vienna do not offer much insight into the impending changes in the power relations between German countries and the Ottoman Empire, mostly because until the middle of the eighteenth century very little was written that used Oriental motifs, and most of the texts followed models developed in the seventeenth century. Gradually, however, and primarily through the reception of French, British, and Italian works, new ideas about the Middle East emerged in the German context. The large number of texts that were produced after the middle of the eighteenth century documents the ubiquitous fascination with and the burgeoning use of Middle Eastern topics.

Two basic groups of texts emerge among this corpus of textual material: the first group includes texts that used the Middle East as a staging ground to discuss, and negotiate with, a wide range of topics, primarily those having to do with emerging political ideals and social norms; the second group of texts engaged directly with the Middle East and Islam. Both groups of texts share a feature that is at the core of the tension described by Theodor Adorno and Max Horkheimer in *Dialectic of Enlightenment,* namely, that "rationality bound to identity has always felt compelled to deny, repress and violate singularity, difference and Otherness."[106] As noted in the preceding discussion, Enlightenment thinkers conceived new ideas of both inclusion and exclusion. On the one hand, new positions of religious tolerance and political citizenship were developed; whereas the plea for religious tolerance originated with inner-Christian sectarian violence that had marred Europe for centuries and was directly geared to creating unifying conditions among European Christians, calls for political citizenship were based on changing economic realities and claimed political agency and rights for individuals, who played central roles in the new economies. On the other hand, the emerging sciences, including racial sciences, conceptualized histories and hierarchies that led to the exclusion of non-Europeans from the new ideals of political citizenship and social equality. History, philosophy, and the natural sciences, in effect, took over the role that religion had played in creating and authorizing narratives of inclusion and exclusion. The idea of progress, in particular, allowed Europeans to relegate non-European cultures to an earlier stage of history and precluded their participation in modern developments. Notions of progress, a cornerstone of modernization ideology, replicated the missionary impetus of Christianity, but its professed inclusiveness was undercut by racism and civilizationism.[107]

The Orient as Staging Ground

One group of texts discussed here drew on Middle Eastern imagery—which increasingly included not only Turkish but also Arab and Persian characters—as a way of dealing with changing political, social, cultural, and religious norms within Germany and Europe. Nevertheless, the texts also address the changes in relationship between Germany and the Middle East; a newfound sense of strength and entitlement toward the Ottoman Empire allowed Germans (and other Europeans) to deploy the Middle Eastern imagery with greater confidence.

One way to get a sense of what was new with regard to the fictional image of the Orient is by noting which topics disappeared from the prevailing discourse. With few exceptions, such as Wieland's *Oberon,* which will be discussed in the following section, the absence of crusading rhetoric in fictional material is striking. Unlike views that dominated relations during the Crusades and the Ottoman conflict, the idea of a crusade or the general superiority of Christianity did not occupy any significant space in public discourse. Rather, various authors used religious difference to articulate new views of religious tolerance but also, more generally, new social and political norms. The idea of religious tolerance and the seemingly inclusive gesture toward non-Europeans, however, was quickly neutralized by new paradigms of exclusion.

Turkish operas and plays emerged as vehicles to articulate new social mores and concepts of political leadership. Two earlier Turkish operas that reflect negative conceptions of Turks are documented for the late seventeenth century, namely, *Kara Mustapha* (1682/86) and *Muhamed II* (1696). After a gap of several decades, and responding to the Europe-wide fad, German composers and writers began to create new types of Turkish operas in the middle of the eighteenth century. According to Walter Preibisch, a "Türkische Lustbarkeit" was performed in 1749 in Hamburg, and in 1753 Migliavacca's *Soliman* was performed to the music of Johann Adolf Hasse.[108] This opera became the prototype for a great number of operas adapting the Soliman story. *Soliman* draws on the personnel of earlier versions of the plot, but here the characters are more fully developed and, like the more recent versions of the Bayezid/Tamerlane plot, convey new ethical positions that depart from conceptions of Turks as cruel, erratic, and oversexed. The magnanimity of Soliman inspired similar characters in subsequent operas and plays—for example, Mozart's *Abduction from the Seraglio* (1782). Hasse used percussion instruments, *Timpani turchesi*, which were identified with Turkish music, to achieve a nuanced characterization of the opera's figures.

In 1762 Johann Schwanenberg provided the musical score for the libretto *Solimann* (also known as *Solimano*). Written by an anonymous author, it is a tale of love and political intrigue in which a changed sultan ultimately permits marriages that he had previously seen as a threat to the social order. Similarly, G. F. W. Grossmann's "Schauspiel mit Gesang," *Adelheit von Veltheim* (1780; score by Christian Gottlob Neefe), which was popular in its day, postulates the need to revise social and political ethics. Achmet, pasha of Tunis, is inspired by a female German protagonist to develop a new understanding of love and of his role as a political leader; at the end of the play Achmet releases the women of his harem.

Many German Turkish operas followed a particular scheme, drawing on medieval paradigms in which a European Christian abducts an Oriental princess (mostly understood to be Muslim but at times also Byzantine), who accompanies him voluntarily or involuntarily to Europe, where she usually converts to Christianity. Several eighteenth-century operas reproduced variations of these abduction scenarios, perhaps the best-known among them being Gluck's *La Rencontre imprévue* (1764; the German version is called *Die Pilgrime von Mekka*); Haydn's *L'Incontro improvviso* (1775); and Mozart's *Die Entführung aus dem Serail* (1782), which was based on Gottlieb Stephanie's adaptation of Christoph Friedrich Bretzner's libretto *Belmonte und Constanze, oder die Entführung aus dem Serail* (1780). In addition to these well-known works, other Turkish operas adhered to a similar plot of abduction of a European woman who is then sold to a sultan as a slave.[109] The heroine, however, resists advances by the sultan. In the meantime, her European lover attempts to rescue her, but in most cases the abduction plan is revealed, and the lovers are left to fear the worst. In the final moment, however, the sultan changes his mind and sets the Europeans free, whereby the sultan emerges as an enlightened ruler.[110] Operas designed according to this model—such as *L'italiana in Algeri* (1813) and *Il turco in Italia* (1814) by Gioacchino Rossini, *Les Pêcheurs de perles* (1863) by Georges Bizet, and *Der Barbier von Bagdad* (1858) by Carl August Peter Cornelius—were composed throughout the eighteenth and nineteenth centuries.

Using elements from a wide range of available models, these operas featured figures such as an enlightened sultan who is juxtaposed to a character most often called Osmin, who retained many of the negative traits of previous Turkish characters. At times Osmin (or a character like him, such as Gripon, Omar, Albumazar, or Barac) is rendered as a primarily comical figure; in other versions he is violent and deceitful. Haydn's canzonetta "Il Profeta Maometto," for example, pokes fun at Islam's injunction against alcohol, and Osmin's negative characteristics are related to the fact that he is a Muslim.[111] Osmin enjoys wine excessively and thus seemingly proves the hypocrisy of Muslims, an element that Mozart also included in his *Abduction.* Indeed, Mozart's deep involvement in the creation of the libretto, particularly with regard to the conceptualization of Osmin, is well documented.[112] The enlightened sultan of Mozart's opera *Pasha Selim* becomes a mouthpiece of the composer's humanism.[113]

Like other composers before him, in his Turkish operas Mozart used instruments and musical patterns associated with Turkish music to amplify the scene; interestingly, he also drew on these elements in other works that have nothing to do with Turkish themes. In *Don Giovanni,* for example, he evokes the Turkish mode in order to highlight aspects of the protagonist: "Don Giovanni creates a behavioral ethical code much closer to the 'Turkish,'" particularly with regard to themes of excessive sexuality, recklessness, but also "a utopian ideal, or a higher stage of humanity," thus making him "the lascivious Turk and the utopian Oriental at the same time."[114]

The new Turkish characters that were featured in German operas in the second half of the eighteenth century reflect the diminished Ottoman threat but also a generally more self-confident attitude of Germany (and Europe) toward cultural and religious difference. Ottomans were no longer demonized; indeed, Turks and Muslims were portrayed as individuals who inspire compassion and even respect. Yet the fact that Turkish or Muslim characters are no longer seen as threatening—as they were, for example, in Lohenstein's plays—does not necessarily indicate greater respect or understanding by German and other European composers and songwriters. The depiction of the sultan as adhering to German ethical ideals serves to highlight the superiority of those ideals, while the stubbornly negative characterization of Osmin marks the persistent impression of the Islamic/Turkish context as inferior. Nevertheless, the possibility of identification with these figures amounts to a marked departure from previous models in fiction, particularly in the German context.[115]

The new ideas expressed in Turkish operas, in conjunction with translations of popular French, British, and other plays, also brought changes to German dramatic works. As Balke states, from 1700 until 1810 more than 250 plays were written in Germany that use an Oriental setting.[116] A large number of these plays responded to the new trend to convey a transformed image of Turkish characters and popularized figures such as the enlightened sultan and the comical, but still dangerous, Osmin. *Adelheid in der Sclavery, oder Tugend und Unschuld bietet aller Verleumdung Trotz* (1760), for example, features a sultan (Meledin) who overcomes his sexual desires for a female slave (Adelheid).[117] The ethical position Meledin achieves is grounded in a new understanding of social and political norms.[118] Hans Carl Heinrich von Trautzsch's 1772 play *Temusin* also uses an Oriental setting to envision ideals of ethical behavior: the play centers on a Tatar couple, Temusin and Zaide, who are presented as a model of pure love. The couple's love, characterized in many ways by drawing on Christian imagery, is set off against a political order distinguished by violence and despotism. As Kleinlogel points out, the play does not dispense Ottoman ideas of marriage but, rather, conveys the new Enlightenment ideal of a just social and political order, exemplified here through the quest for marriage based on love.[119]

Wilhelm Johann Christian Gustav Casparson's *Osmann* (1767) also adheres to this model. Here the sultan's enlightened ideas about marriage and love are shaped by what he has seen in Europe and what he is learning through the female protagonist. August Wilhelm Iffland's *Achmet und Zenide* (1798) features a Turkish man (Bassa Achmet) who becomes enlightened through the education he receives from a German (Grolo), who, it turns out in the course of the play, is deceitful and disingenuous. The education of his wife, Zenide, however, transformed her into an emancipated Turkish woman who refuses to fulfill traditional female roles and insists on participating actively in society. Ultimately, her quest for education and independence is curbed, reflecting dominant late eighteenth-century ideals of female virtue. Finally, Joseph Franz Ratschky's play *Bekir und Gulroui* (1780) employs the Turkish setting as a stage to convey enlightened humanist views.[120]

Turkish and Islamic material was not always employed successfully. The central figure in Friedrich Maximilian Klinger's comedy *Der Derwisch* (1780) was clearly inspired by Lessing's Al-Hafi in *Nathan the Wise* (1779). Yet Klinger's play was not staged, and its reception was negligible. The comedy consists of a hodgepodge of popular themes and characters but does not present the material in captivating ways. Comical Turkish figures and magicians compete with more rational characters in a plot involving multiple tales of love.

Goethe's *Iphigenie auf Tauris* (1787), on the other hand, continues to engage audiences to this day. The play shares several features with operas and plays modeled after the abduction narrative. It draws on a tragedy by Euripides, *Iphigenia in Tauris,* which employs several central stories of Greek mythology. Goethe alters the narrative and the meaning of the story significantly. The conflict involves Greeks and Taurians, a people who belong to the Scythians, who are in turn associated with the Turks: the term *Scyths* was applied to the peoples living on the northern coast of the Black Sea but also more broadly to the peoples of Central Asia, the ancestors of Turkish societies. These multiple connections allow us to connect Goethe's play with Turkish operas and plays of the period. Whereas Euripides's play envisioned a stark contrast between Greeks and Barbarians, Goethe portrays the Greeks as conflicted and has the Taurian king Thoas emerge as the more enlightened and humane character.[121] Iphigenia functions as a vehicle for bringing about humanistic change in the men of societies thought to be diametrically opposed to each other but effectively caught up in similar cultures of violence.[122]

Only a few late eighteenth-century German plays, such as Johann Ulrich König's play *Zoroaster* (1717) and Christian Felix Weisse's *Mustapha und Zeangir* (1761), emulated the tradition of Baroque Turkish plays, casting Turkish characters as overwhelmingly negative. In *Oßmin und Fatime,* published anonymously in 1783, Sultan Bassa Ahmet is juxtaposed to the ideal couple, the Christian-born slave Osmin and his beloved, Fatime. Osmin's love for Fatime legitimates his conversion to Islam, which he undertakes for strategic purposes, only to convert back to Christianity in the end. Ideal ethical behavior and Christianity are paired in this tale, which clearly advocates the superiority of Christian-European culture. Kotzebue's *Sultan Wampum oder: Die Wünsche* (1794) features a sultan who, according to Kleinlogel, reflects an ironic attempt to "re-barbarize" the figure of the enlightened sultan. In Kotzebue's version the Turk announces his anti-Enlightenment stance: "I don't like the Enlightenment."[123]

Another example of the persistence of negative images is Christoph Martin Wieland's epic poem *Oberon* (1780).[124] Employing the abduction narrative in two separate scenarios, Wieland's narrative resonates with the rhetoric of crusading rather than the spirit of the Enlightenment, and clearly promotes the superiority of Christianity over Islam. Muslims are portrayed as reckless, violent, and sexually obsessed; absent are the enlightened Muslim characters featured in many operas and plays of the period. Wieland also wrote several tales after the model of *One Thousand and One Nights* and greatly contributed to shaping the Oriental fairy tale of German making, which was later perfected by Ludwig Tieck and Wilhelm Hauff.

Narrative texts, particularly novels, that used the Orient as a stage to present thought-provoking messages, tended to reflect upon society as a whole, with a focus on governance and social norms and often by referring to the Middle East within a larger picture of the world. European economic and political expansionism clearly drove much of what was being explored in these texts. *Die Türkische Helena* (1710) by Meleaton (Johann Leonhard Rost) follows the older model and begins by evoking the "Turkish murderous dog and cruel persecutor of Christianity."[125] Turkishness is associated with violence and excessive eroticism, although the novel contains internal contradictions and extends its critique of objectionable behavior to include European characters. When the novel was republished in 1733 (this time under the pseudonym Menander), the author had made significant changes, notably highlighting the contrast between Europe and the Orient.[126] In similar ways, *Tuerckische Asterie* (1720) by Joachim Meier von Perleberg (also known as "Imperialis") and *Der in den letzten Zügen liegende Cupido* (1747) by Murantes demonize Turkish men and characterize them as violent and sexually excessive. In Murantes's novel the female protagonist, Melodine, is transported by a violent flood to "an unchristian country whose language she did not understand."[127] The reader soon learns that the foreign barbaric country is clearly a Middle Eastern land.[128] Melodine finds empathetic allies in the pasha's wife, who is originally from England and had converted to Islam, and her son Mechmet. Mechmet's escape plan with Melodine is discovered, and the father has his son executed. In a dramatic resolution to the conflict, however, Melodine escapes the threatening sexual desire of the pasha. Clearly, this novel reflects basic elements of Lohenstein's Turkish plays.

Enlightenment thought influenced the novel *Die wunderbare* [*sic*] *Lebens- und Liebesbegebenheiten des Türcken Omers* (1754), which was published anonymously. The novel's Turkish characters abandon Islam and Turkish culture, flee Turkey, and convert to Christianity and a European lifestyle that is based on reason. As Kleinlogel shows, the novel follows an established pattern in that sexuality—specifically, the abstention from premarital sex—becomes the test case for the development of a new consciousness.[129]

Turkish motifs are also integral to a group of novels that were inspired by Daniel Defoe's *Robinson Crusoe* (1719), which was based on the true story of Alexander Selkirk, and other novels of exploration. This literature reflects European economic and political expansionism and often incorporated authentic stories: about forty narratives emulating Defoe's text were published in Germany between 1720 and 1760. The function of these motifs is comparable to that of the Oriental material in medieval *Spielmannsepen* in that these motifs speak to historical events of the time, do not engage with the non-European contexts in substantial ways, and fictionalize the non-European world while betraying underlying imperial ambitions. Wilhelm Retchir (also Richter) includes several Turkish episodes in *Der Sächsische Robinson* (1722), a novel resonating with the spirit of the Age of Discovery and featuring stories about pirates and converts to Islam.[130] The string of adventures ends with the narrator's expressed desire to return to traveling, to "make a journey to Turkey, and if possible, to Mecca and Egypt."[131]

Johann Gottfried Schnabel's *Die Insel Felsenburg* (1731–43) also exhibits elements that tie it to concrete historical developments. The narrator's father, for example, loses all of his money when his East Indian ship is plundered by pirates and his stocks plummet in value. In reaction to the loss, the father decides to leave Germany "in order to find in East or West India either my lost happiness or death."[132] After receiving a letter from the brother of his great-grandfather, the narrator embarks on a journey to find an island where people enjoy a social utopia. The novel features an episode of abduction and enslavement staged in Morocco in which cultural and religious difference is emphasized through a conflict over sexual mores, and once again, new ideas of proper behavior are articulated by juxtaposing German/Christian virtue to Oriental/Islamic degeneration.[133]

Several novels from the 1730s through the 1790s were structured by this paradigm, in which Turkishness and Islam served to highlight the virtues of European/German/Christian society and to shape new social and political norms.[134] Conversion to Christianity and the acceptance of European/German values underscored a sense of superiority and greater self-confidence in light of the decreasing threat from the Ottoman Empire. It was possible to envision Turks/Muslims as becoming like "us"; this gesture of appropriation, however, did not embrace cultural and religious difference; rather, it only highlighted apparent differences.

In *Geschichte Giafars des Barmeciden* (1792–94), intended by its author to elaborate on his Faust novels, Klinger used an Oriental setting for his tale about ethical behavior and freedom of the individual. French sources, in particular Voltaire's writings and Abbé de Marigny's *Histoires des Arabes sous le gouvernement des califes* (1750), provided information and impetus for the setting and characters, and the novel is entirely set in the Middle East.[135] Even though it was not received favorably in its time, the novel inspired for several early nineteenth-century plays.[136] In our context it falls within the group of narratives that explore Enlightenment thought in an Oriental context, without regard for the historical accuracy of images that evoke a clichéd Oriental milieu.

The writings reviewed in this section, often inspired by French and British models, used an Oriental setting to evaluate German society, in the spirit of new ideas about politics and religion but also in light of economic and political expansionism. If Turkish protagonists functioned as personifications of reckless violence and excessive sexuality in most seventeenth- and some eighteenth-century plays, they become vehicles for the articulation of new ethics in the majority of middle to late eighteenth-century German operas, dramatic works, and narratives. Ideas of love as the founding element of marriage, combined with the more general use of reason and the call for religious tolerance, are articulated in these plays, narratives, and operas, which feature new types of men and new forms of male-female relations. Turkish and other non-European characters stand in for outdated German behavior presented as being in dire need of reform; thus, cultural alterity serves to convey generational differences and the emergence of new norms. Turkish rulers are used as vehicles to criticize European aristocrats, whose claims to absolute political power are challenged. The critique of political power is articulated here through a focus on sex and violence. Whereas Turkish characters are conceptualized as being capable of transforming themselves to correspond to new ethical standards, their cultural context is identified with outdated and objectionable norms and ethics. Much like other European writings of this era, the German texts, in spite of their critical stance toward domestic issues, advanced a host of stereotypes about the Orient.

Engagement with Islam and the Middle East

Several German intellectuals and writers engaged with the Orient as a serious subject, especially as they attempted to conceptualize universal theories in various fields of knowledge. Whether their works were focused on literature, aesthetics, history, philosophy, or religion, these thinkers studied the new material about Islam and Middle Eastern cultures that was available through the works of Orientalist scholars and various travel accounts.

Johann Gottfried von Herder wrote a series of essays about language and poetry in which he focused on elements that facilitated an unprecedented level of appreciation for the literary production of non-European cultures, such as writings in Hebrew and Arabic. In its historical context his praise of Arab poetry (as part of his appreciation for the poetry of ancient peoples) in, for example, "Über die Wirkung der Dichtkunst auf die Sitten der Völker in alten und neuen Zeiten" (1778), reveals an open-minded attitude toward the achievements of Arab civilization, among others. Herder idealized Arab civilization and celebrated Arab courage and the quest for freedom, but he also characterized Arabs as vengeful, and his portrait is rife with clichés, however well-intended his praise may have been.[137] Nevertheless, Herder's appreciation for cross-cultural fertilization, brought about by the Crusades, revealed the importance he granted to Arab influence on European cultures.[138] Other thinkers, such as Johann Georg Hamann in his *Aesthetica in nuce* (1762), also turned to the Orient as a place of renewal and rebirth.[139] In this regard philorientalists were comparable to philhellenists of the first generation, who, as Suzanne Marchand writes, "exalted Greek art as the symbol and embodiment of humankind's true, free, uncorrupted nature."[140]

But the Sturm und Drang enthusiasm for non-European cultures (particularly from bygone periods) gradually gave way to ideas that stressed the superiority of Europe, elevating German culture particularly at a moment of political dissolution. In *Ideen zur Philosophie der Geschichte der Menschheit* (1784–91) Herder attempted to write a universal history of the development of life on the planet, including animals and plant life. Ideas of climate were central to his approach, in which he divided the earth into six regions whose climate determined the character of its inhabitants. The review of human civilization begins with the peoples of the Arctic region, whose physiognomy and culture are explained strictly as a result of extreme weather. The sections on Asian and African peoples express a deep-seated disdain for their physical appearance and associate physiognomy with level of civilization throughout, thus reflecting ideas that circulated at the time through writings such as Johann Caspar Lavater's *Physiognomische Fragmente zur Beförderung der Menschenkenntniss und Menschenliebe* (1775–78), a text already ridiculed in its time by Christoph Lichtenberg's *Über Physiognomik, wider die Physiognomen* (1778). Susanne Zantop, in her discussion of the emergence of racial theories in Germany, highlights the contradictions in Herder's account: Herder rejected slavery and "makes a clear attempt to disavow prejudice" but nevertheless resorts to racializing when he attempts to "explain the Africans' difference from the Europeans by resorting to anatomy," thus relating perceived character traits to physiological features.[141]

Residents of the "Region of beautifully formed peoples" (*Erdstrich schöngebildeter Völker*), those living on islands in hot regions, and those living in the American region, represent the other three groups that feature in Herder's global narrative. Development in all cultures follows organic principles, according to Herder's scheme, and entire cultures are associated with levels of development in ways that stress the influence of climate but also social influences and historical conflict, such as migration and conquest. Peoples of the Middle East belong to the "Region of beautifully formed peoples"; Persians, Hebrews, and Turks, for example, benefited from migrating into the region, yet their Asian origin remains visible in specific character and physical traits. Arabs, however, are featured in positive terms, and here Herder foreshadowed his more detailed acknowledgment of the achievements of Arab civilization in the ensuing sections of his study.

The third and fourth parts of *Ideen zur Philosophie der Geschichte der Menschheit* reviews cultural accomplishments of different civilizations. Generally, non-European cultures are relegated to an earlier stage of development; that is, geographical place and stage of civilization are associated in fundamental ways. Sections on the ancient Middle East and on Greek and Roman culture are followed by a review of European peoples, and within this section Herder speaks of Arabs, Turks, and Jews as "Foreign Peoples in Europe." As in his earlier writings, Herder praises the positive effect that Arabs had on the development of science in medieval Europe, and he acknowledges beneficial developments for Europeans resulting from the "acquaintance with their oriental brothers."[142] His assessment of Turks, however, is dismissive throughout; he represents them exclusively as having laid waste to European areas, and he clearly wants them out of Europe. Jews are compared to a "parasitic plant," but Herder envisions better days when "even the Jew will live according to European laws."[143]

Herder's discussion of Arab civilization in the nineteenth book of his study mirrors the sources available to him at the time, which conflict to some degree with Herder's own enthusiasm for Arab culture. On the one hand, he endorses notions about Arab societies as despotic and renders the history of Islamic empires as a quick succession of declining states, resulting from a lack of ethics, the effect of despotism, and tribalism. In his review of the achievements of Arab culture, however, Herder goes to great lengths to praise the benefits of Arab trade for the peoples on three continents: the civilizing aspects of Islam and of the Arabic language; the flourishing of the sciences; the tremendous achievements of Arab poetic traditions; and the development of a culture inspired by knighthood, which he suggests had a positive civilizing effect on European societies. Herder's ensuing critique of the Crusades on the final pages of the study, an insightful discussion of the detrimental repercussions of the Crusades which is more in line with what Sankar Muthu terms "Enlightenment anti-imperialist political thought," warrants a separate analysis.[144]

In Herder's discussion Arab civilization, like that of the Greeks and Romans, is clearly associated with the past; the relevant contemporary Middle Eastern power, the Ottoman Empire, is characterized by barbaric destruction. The respect paid to bygone Arab civilization contrasts with the ignorance about Ottoman civilization (regarding, for example, trade, government, and architecture) and also with those passages in the first part of the study that are distinguished by racializing classifications. Zantop succinctly characterizes the discordant gesture contained in Herder and other thinkers of the period: "While the works of individual thinkers, such as Herder's, are deeply inconsistent and contradictory, exhibiting both a tendency toward hierarchical classification and a desire for justice and cultural differentiation, an impersonal racist intertext emerges that 'permits' mixing observations in natural history with aesthetic judgment, and aesthetics with conjectures about the course of cultural-political history."[145]

In similar ways Kant's attempt to construct a universal history was characterized by classifications that served to exclude non-European groups. With Kant's "Von den verschiedenen Racen der Menschen" (1775), according to Zantop, "the term 'Race'—adopted from the English language and from the animal kingdom—is introduced into German discourse on humans."[146] In Kant's scheme the peoples of the Middle East are considered part of the white race.[147] Nevertheless, as Seyla Benhabib has shown, the categorization of human beings according to biologistic features structures notions of citizenship: "Women and slaves, servants, and propertyless white males, non-Christians and non-white races, were historically excluded from membership in the sovereign body and from the project of citizenship. They were, in Kant's famous words, 'mere auxiliaries to the commonwealth.'"[148] Even if Kant's 1775 categorization aligned peoples from the Middle East and Europe, his and other subsequent paradigms articulated exclusions described by Benhabib that also relegated peoples from the Middle East to a lower stage of development.[149] With regard to Kant's assessment of Islam, Silvia Horsch points out that for Kant it "serves as an example for fanaticism."[150] Thinkers such as Kant and Herder, beyond their individual intentions, thus laid the groundwork for models of exclusion. The tension between the desire for classification and ideas of progress, observable here in the writings of Kant and Herder, ultimately came to legitimate European and Christian superiority.

Only a few German authors of fiction approached Islam and the Middle East in a way that went beyond an uncritical reception of French or British works or the naive use of material from works that were translated from Arabic, Turkish, or Persian. In most cases German authors drew on elements from Middle Eastern tales and histories and perhaps on travel accounts but did not engage with Islam or the Middle East itself. Even if the views of Muslims and Turks and other Oriental characters were more benign in comparison to seventeenth-century fictional representations, the general attitude toward Islam remained dismissive. Two authors stand out whose efforts to learn about Islam and the Middle East occurred on an entirely different level, namely, Gotthold Ephraim Lessing and Johann Wolfgang von Goethe. Lessing and Goethe absorbed knowledge that was disseminated by Orientalist scholarship, written in French, English, and German. This scholarship broadened the horizon; no longer primarily interested in understanding the Ottoman Turks, it brought knowledge about Islam and about Arabic, Hebrew, and Persian culture to Germany.[151]

No other German intellectual and writer from the Enlightenment period interacted with Islam the way Lessing did. Silvia Horsch, who has generated the most detailed study of Lessing's engagement with Islam, points out that he can be credited with bringing Islam into the debate about tolerance that was conducted in the eighteenth century.[152] His views of Islam need of course to be understood in the context of his larger plea for religious tolerance. Beginning with his earliest publications, and in both his theoretical writings as well as his dramatic works, he consistently articulated this conviction. Much has been written about Lessing's views on Judaism and his friendship with the German Jewish thinker Moses Mendelssohn, which was crucial to Lessing's understanding of Judaism and the situation of Jews in Germany at the time. Lessing's debunking of stereotypes of Jews had already been articulated in his 1749 play *Die Juden,* and he continued his plea for religious tolerance in fiction and nonfiction writings throughout his career. His serious study of Islam and Middle Eastern cultures and his commentary on these topics in his writing, however, have not received much attention until recently, when the current debate over the legal, social, political, and cultural status of Islam in Germany and Europe also turned to Lessing's views of Islam.

Lessing's discussion of Islam occurred in the context of the author's critique of Christianity. His knowledge of Islam stemmed from careful study of Orientalist scholarship; he consulted French, British, and German sources and corresponded with distinguished scholars on specific questions.[153] The views of Islam put forth in these writings were diverse, ranging from condemnation of its perceived irrational aspects to acceptance of Islam as a rational religion. Lessing clearly sided with thinkers who promoted Deist views, which allowed them to include Islam in their understanding of religion. One of Lessing's earliest texts relevant in this regard is "Rettung des Hier. Cardanus" from 1754. In this essay he defends the scientist Hieronymus Cardanus (1501–76) against the charge of atheism by giving voice, among other rhetorical strategies, to the views of Jews, Muslims, and Christians. The Muslim voice stands out for arguing rational views. Critics have often pointed to the fact that a Muslim is given the stage for the first time to articulate views of Islam and a critique of Christianity. Yet, given the inclusion of such voices already in newspapers and pamphlets (see chap. 2), it is specifically the introduction of Islamic voices—in direct speech, as is often emphasized—into the discourse of the Enlightenment that is new.[154] Horsch has pointed out that Lessing's presentation of Islam in this essay emphasizes the ways in which Islam is compatible with Deism and that he selectively leaves out elements that align Islam more closely with other revealed religions (elements such as the role of angels and the revealed text). Horsch states that Lessing did not represent Islam according to an Islamic self-understanding, although given the diversity of Islamic views of itself, Lessing's version can be said to correspond to a minority view that does exist within Islam.[155] Ultimately, the use of rational arguments in the conversation by the Muslim participant functions to reveal inconsistencies and irrationality within Christianity, which was Lessing's ultimate target.

Another text crucial to understanding Lessing's view of Islam is "Von Adam Neusern. Einige authentische Nachrichten" (1774).[156] In this essay Lessing defends Adam Neuser, whose Unitarian views led to his arrest as a heretic. Neuser eventually escaped to Istanbul and converted to Islam (see chap. 2); this move irritated theologians, particularly in the sixteenth century. Lessing's defense of a conversion to Islam was a bold step in his struggle for religious tolerance.

Lessing's message was summed up in his 1779 play *Nathan der Weise.* The play is set in Jerusalem during the Crusades and brings together members of the three monotheistic religions. The plot evolves as a complicated web of family relations and ends with a reunion that reshuffles previous affiliations: Nathan's adopted daughter Recha, who thought she was Jewish, turns out to be the daughter of a Christian mother and a Muslim father; her brother, who thought he was Christian, finds out that he is partly of Muslim heritage; similarly, the sultan and his sister discover that they are related to Christians. Ultimately, however, the play's emphasis is not blood relations but human relations. Saladin's words "Ja wohl: das Blut, das Blut allein / Macht lange noch den Vater nicht! macht kaum / Den Vater eines Tieres!" (Yes, indeed: blood, blood alone does not nearly make a father! Makes barely the father of an animal! 5:7) sum up the central message: blood relations and religious affiliations do not determine the true essence of human relations; rather, the deeds of individuals bespeak their humanity.

Lessing goes farther than any other thinker or artist of the period in arguing for religious tolerance. He drew on historical sources, especially in creating a generous and respectable Sultan Saladin, but, as Navid Kermani rightly points out, Lessing did not intend to teach about Islam or the Arab world during the time of Saladin.[157] The play is unique in its attempt to debunk stereotypes and is highly critical of Christian intolerance. The most negatively portrayed character in the play is the Christian patriarch of Jerusalem, whose violent restrictions and cruel orders clash with the forgiveness and humanity of the sultan, Nathan, and even the templar, who acts more humanely than he thinks.[158] Lessing's critical writings may leave room for discussion about the inclusiveness or exclusiveness of his concept of tolerance.[159] The emphasis in *Nathan* on the significance of ethical behavior, however, clearly articulates a most inclusive gesture.[160]

Like Lessing, Goethe engaged with Islam and Middle Eastern material throughout his life. We already saw that in his play *Iphigenia in Tauris* Goethe presented his critique of outdated ethics in ways that showed both Greeks and Barbarians in need of reform. If the Scyths or Taurians of the play may be seen as standing in for Ottomans, or Muslims in general, Goethe incorporated characters and themes from Middle Eastern cultures and Islam in his works in extensive ways and for various reasons. Katharina Mommsen has provided the most detailed analysis of Goethe's engagement with Middle Eastern cultures and religions, documenting the sources of Goethe's knowledge and their influence on his writing. Goethe learned about the Middle East and Islam as a child, through fairy tales told by his mother and grandmother. The presence of elements from *One Thousand and One Nights,* for example, in Goethe's oeuvre is extensive. Goethe's very first dramatic work, *Die Laune des Verliebten*

(1767/68), is closely modeled on a story contained in Galland's collection *Mille et une nuit,* "Histoire d'Amine."[161] Mommsen states that references to stories from the collection were well understood by the educated readership and that Goethe and other authors appealed to this knowledge in light of the general fascination with the material.[162] *One Thousand and One Nights* is ubiquitous in Goethe's work, from the lesser-known texts such as *Die Laune des Verliebten* and *Lila* to key works such as *Wilhelm Meisters Lehrjahre* and *Faust.*

But Goethe's encounter with the Middle East went beyond a simple reception and use of material from *One Thousand and One Nights.* Again, Katharina Mommsen has provided the most comprehensive investigation chronicling the extent of Goethe's study of Orientalist knowledge and its resurfacing in his literary work. Goethe made several attempts to learn the Arabic language and script, and in fact, he wanted to study philology, for example, with Johann David Michaelis, the Göttingen professor.[163] Goethe's knowledge of the Middle East was based primarily on travel literature and writings of Orientalist scholars: He read accounts by Pietro della Valle, Jean Baptiste Tavernier, Jean Chevalier de Chardin, Carsten Niebuhr, and C. F. Volney, illustrating again that intercultural knowledge circulated across European state boundaries. Orientalist scholars introduced Goethe to Persian and Arab poets. His encounter with poets from the pre-Islamic period had a lasting impact and inspired much of his own writing.[164] Early on he engaged with Johann Jacob Reiske's translation of the work of the poet al-Mutanabbi (915–65). Reading the poetry of the Persian poet Hafiz (ca. 1325/26 to 1389/90) was central to his conception of the poems of the *West-östlicher Divan.* Goethe was also familiar with writers from the later period, such as Ibn 'Arabshah (1389–1450). It is worthwhile to note that, generally, Arabic-language scholarship on Goethe is appreciative, and many of Goethe's writings have been translated into Arabic, certainly a sign of respect for his work.[165]

Goethe studied the Koran throughout his life. Mommsen argues that Goethe developed a deep affinity for Islam because it corresponded to his own ideas about religion. She points out that monotheism, the idea of God's immanence in nature, the notion that God reveals himself through different prophets, the rejection of miracles, and the idea that religiosity is expressed through good deeds were central Islamic ideas that Goethe related to.[166] Goethe's appreciation of Islam is exemplified in his poem "Mahomets Gesang" (1773); here the writer uses the metaphor of a stream—gradually developing from its origin as a spring in the mountains to a powerful stream moving toward its creator—in order to describe the growth of the Islamic movement in positive terms. Goethe also planned to write a tragedy based on the life of Muhammad; only fragments of the play, which was begun in 1772, remain. However, as our discussion in the next chapter will show in more detail, in spite of Goethe's serious study of Middle Eastern cultures and religions, he clearly used the material for his own purposes and contributed to its persistent fictionalization.

Goethe was driven by a desire for comprehensive knowledge of the world's literatures, cultures, and religions, a quest that extended, as we know, also to the realm of natural science. He was dependent on translations and on commentary by Orientalists who often added dismissive judgment to the material they transmitted. Accordingly, Goethe's view of Middle Eastern cultures and Islam contains aspects of praise and criticism that can be related both to the knowledge he had access to and to his own and other contemporary views of religion and life in general. But his view of Islam did not include an understanding of the diversity within Islam and its historicity and geopolitical variations. His acceptance of Islam as an equal to Christianity, much like what Lessing expresses, was certainly an improvement over previous attitudes. Perhaps not surprisingly, Lessing's and Goethe's Islam was really more a reflection of their conception of religion than of Islam itself. It is also apparent that Goethe's image of Islam and the Middle East changed over time; whereas "Mahomet's Gesang" reflects the spirit of Sturm und Drang exuberance, and *Iphigenie* the idealism of the classical period, the poems of the *West-östlicher Divan* reveal the older poet's nuanced, perhaps somewhat resigned, and more pragmatic view of life. However, the appendix to the *Divan,* as well as his earlier translation of Voltaire's play about the prophet Muhammad, contains a host of clichés and negative images about the Middle East and its inhabitants; we will return to this dimension of Goethe's engagement with the Middle East and Islam in the next chapter.

The period from the Second Siege of Vienna to the end of the eighteenth century saw fundamental changes in the power relations between German countries and the Ottoman Empire. By the end of the century former enemies had become allies, with both Prussian and Habsburg powers in constant diplomatic exchange with the Ottoman court. The century lived through other upheavals as well: politically, claims for citizenship rights were voiced, and, economically, Great Britain and then France and other countries began to enter the industrial age. The Seven Years' War, Polish divisions, American independence, and the expansion of colonial empires all occurred during this time. By the end of the century these political, social, and economic developments had led to European imperial domination; within decades large parts of the Ottoman Empire would be snatched up by European powers.

The rise of the natural sciences and the quest for a secular approach to human history and culture was propelled by an emancipatory impetus but also brought about new hierarchies. While the struggle for citizenship rights, summarized in the famous motto "Egalité, Liberté, Fraternité," envisioned a new age of equality, the human being who was to profit from these new rights was defined as European, male, and—in most areas until the latter part of the nineteenth century—Christian. The inclusive gesture of religious tolerance was contradicted by ideas about civilization and race. The belief in progress relegated non-European societies to an earlier stage of development from which they had to be liberated—but that liberation came in the form of foreign rule and exploitation.

The time in which the quest for religious tolerance—which originated with sectarianism and conflicts within the Christian church—led to a vision of equality was short-lived. Not only was it a brief moment, but this vision was articulated by only a few individuals. The prejudice against and ignorance about Islam by Europeans remained deep-seated. The moment in which it was possible to write *Nathan the Wise* was soon lost and rendered unintelligible to those whose rediscovery of Christianity and belief in racial and civilizational superiority encouraged them to view Middle Eastern cultures and religion with contempt. The story of that deep-seated contempt for religious and cultural alterity will be at the center of the next chapter.

The comparative view across Europe of Islam and the Middle East reveals discursive similarities, a shared textual archive that was circulated in translations and original texts. But this archive of tropes and images signified in very specific ways. The British directed their attention toward India and the Far East; thus, British texts involving the Middle East did not contain the urgency that French and German texts display. France continued its close cooperation with the Ottomans but was challenged by German powers during the course of the century. In addition, colonial ideology and practice increasingly structured relationships between European and non-European countries.

By the end of the eighteenth century a tremendous amount of information was available to Europeans about Islam and the Middle East, but only a handful of authors and thinkers who made an attempt to engage with the Middle East were inspired to do so by ideas of equality and dialogue. Lessing and Goethe clearly stand out in the European context, particularly as their voices were actually heard. Like the similar views expressed by some of their lesser-known contemporaries across Europe, their vision of complementary and compatible religions and cultures was soon to be overshadowed by emerging ideologies of European superiority.

CHAPTER 4

Empire and Modernization (1792–1945)

The years from 1792 to 1945 were a time of complex and fast-paced developments that structured the relationship between Germany and the Middle East in novel ways. Economically, the period was propelled by industrialization, expanding world trade, and colonization. German states entered the industrial age later than France and Britain, but by the end of the nineteenth century industrialization had changed the German economy dramatically (less so with regard to the Austrian and Swiss economies). The German and Habsburg empires were important trading partners of Middle Eastern countries, and the Weimar Republic and Austria continued this close economic collaboration. The creation of new political structures facilitated trade across larger spaces. After the dissolution of the Holy Roman Empire and through a process lasting several decades, the myriad German states formed nation-states that pursued imperial politics, increasingly so—and thus catching up with France and England—toward the end of the nineteenth century. German states maintained close relations with the Ottoman Empire until its dissolution in 1918 and then with the Republic of Turkey. The Ottoman Empire/Turkey was allied with Germany in World War I and a "neutral collaborator" in World War II. Prussia/Germany and the Habsburg Empire/Austria, competing but also cooperating mainly with France and Britain, interfered in Middle Eastern affairs at various points. A host of changes in the social arena—including a population explosion, urbanization, and transformations in family structure—accompanied the economic and political developments.

Several ideological shifts occurred as well, affecting the ways in which Germans regarded the Middle East. Christianity, albeit challenged by the Enlightenment critique of religion, remained significant in determining policy and attitudes toward the Middle East. The new ideologies of racism and cultural superiority, based on paradigms developed in the natural, social, and human sciences, did not replace but, rather, supplemented earlier ideas of religious superiority as well as ideas of tolerance developed during the Enlightenment.

Modernization, too, became an ideological force, legitimating political, military, and economic action pursued by German and other European nations against those that were not seen as modern, including the Middle East.

As contact with the Middle East intensified, Germany's cultural production about the region grew on an unprecedented scale. Travel literature, scholarly writings, translations, newspapers, popular best sellers, and works in a variety of art forms disseminated ideas about the Middle East. German writers employed this arsenal of imagery to comment on domestic issues, express notions of German superiority, and articulate critical consciousness.

Modernization

German ideas of the Middle East must be evaluated against the background of events in the region itself. The colonization of northern Africa and other parts of the Middle East was preceded by developments that significantly transformed Middle Eastern societies. Ottoman rulers, faced with their declining influence and European competition, set out to reform society on a large scale. These reforms were carried out to differing degrees in specific areas and with differing levels of success. Modernization efforts by Egyptian leaders, for example, began long before the advent of the British colonizers in 1882.

Egypt entered the period of fundamental restructuring and economic and political expansion under Muhammad 'Ali (1805–48) and his successors. Muhammad 'Ali introduced sweeping changes to the economy. The focus on sugar and cotton production earned money in international markets but also made Egypt more dependent on those markets.[1] Irrigation projects were carried out that allowed for land cultivation during the entire year. For the first time Egyptian peasants were recruited into the new army. An educational system was devised that included a range of new institutions, from primary schools to universities. Muhammad 'Ali also set up a new tax system that shifted the economic power structure.

Under the reign of 'Abbas I (1848–54) many of the reforms were either halted or reversed. His successor Sa'id (1854–63), however, again embarked on the path of modernization and Westernization. In 1856 he granted the concession for the building of the Suez Canal to the Frenchman Ferdinand de Lesseps. The move had "disastrous" consequences, however, as the Suez Canal and other projects created "enormous financial obligations" for Egypt.[2]

Modernization efforts were pursued with renewed vigor under Isma'il, whose social, political, and economic reforms had an impact on the entire power structure of the country, creating new social groups of influence and destroying the old order at a breathtaking pace. He was said to be "a man ahead of his time, trying to achieve in the nineteenth century what Mustafa Kemal (Atatürk) in Turkey, and Reza Kahn in Iran, successfully achieved at the beginning of the twentieth."[3] The extent to which Egyptian aristocrats identified with European culture might be difficult to fathom today. In 1867 Isma'il announced that "Egypt is no longer part of Africa. It is part of Europe."[4] By 1872–73, however, mostly as a consequence of the harsh conditions under which international loans had been granted, 70 percent of the estimated revenue was needed to pay for the internal and external debt.[5] The Egyptian economy was completely dependent on foreign investors and governments.[6] This situation ultimately resulted in bankruptcy in April 1876 and then in the British occupation of the country through bondholders. Egypt's troubles arose from a complex set of factors that went beyond European economic and political policies, debt politics, and, later, the lack of protective tariffs. Resistance to change within the traditional sector, including in terms of social stratification and the uneven distribution of wealth, which limited buying power; physical obstacles; resource issues such as the absence of raw materials like iron and coal; as well as internal and external political obstacles also contributed to the situation.[7]

The dominance of foreign elements that began with Muhammad 'Ali lasted well into the twentieth century; indeed, the ruling elite in Egypt spoke Turkish or French until the 1930s. It was not until "1952 that rulers identifying themselves as ethnically Egyptian ruled the country. . . . This did not mean the end of foreign influence in the economic and political spheres, which continued to reflect the ideologies adopted by the Nasserists: nationalism, socialism, Arab unity, and non-alignment, which all stemmed from non-Egyptian concepts."[8] The women's movement in Egypt also dates back to the second half of the nineteenth century. Particularly supported by leaders of the *Nahda* (Awakening) movement, such as Muhammad 'Abduh (1849–1905), the *Al-Nahda al-Nisa'iyya* (Awakening of Woman) became a significant topic for discussion. The publication of *Tahrir al-Mar'a* (The Liberation of Woman, 1899) by Qasim Amin, for example, provoked a fierce debate, especially with regard to Amin's stand on abolishing the veil.[9]

Reforms carried out in Egypt corresponded to those instituted in other areas of the Ottoman Empire. The first phase of changes in the empire was introduced by Selim III (1789–1807) and involved military, administrative, and educational reforms. After setbacks, the innovative spirit was strengthened again under Mahmud II (1807–39), who followed modern Western models of government and economy. The *Tanzimat,* or Reorganization period (1839–1876), built on these changes, undertaking further economic, political, social, and religious reforms. As Ira Lapidus writes, "The Tanzimat amounted to a change in the very concept of Ottoman society. It repudiated the autonomous functioning of Islamic education and judicial institutions, and challenged the very concept of Muslim supremacy."[10] Over the next few decades power struggles shifted emphasis back and forth between pro-Western and conservative, even reactionary, models. The early phase of the modern Republic of Turkey was clearly dominated by pro-Western reforms (e.g., the change to the Latin alphabet and abolition of the Caliphate). With regard to economic and monetary developments, the Ottoman Empire became integrated into world markets. Şevket Pamuk offers the estimate "that the foreign trade of the core areas of the empire increased by more than tenfold between the 1840s and World War I."[11] Similar developments were also under way in Qajar Iran and in Morocco.

Many of the reforms taking place throughout the Middle East in the nineteenth century paralleled developments in Germany, which became a nation-state and colonial power only at the end of the century. The shift from the preindustrial to the industrial phase of the German economy is generally dated from 1795 to 1835, while the first phase of industrialization is said to have occurred between 1835 and 1873. Particularly in the early phase, Germany and the Middle East were not as far apart as is often assumed, but with colonization, differences in industrialization and modernization processes, and a range of additional factors stifling the development of Middle Eastern regions, the disparities grew.

Germany's involvement in restructuring Ottoman society occurred in four areas. The German military played a significant role in restructuring and training the Ottoman army. In 1798 the Prussian officer Oberst von Goetze was invited to inspect the Ottoman army, and Helmuth von Moltke led a small group of Prussian officers, who worked from 1835 to 1839 instructing the Ottoman army. In May 1882 another Prussian mission, under the leadership of General Kaehler, arrived in Istanbul to train the Turkish military.[12] In 1883 General von der Goltz began his twelve-year service reforming the Ottoman army. In addition, Prussians also trained Ottoman police: five years after Moltke's departure, Prussian Oberst Kuczkonski came to Istanbul to reform its police units.[13]

Connected to the training and restructuring of the Ottoman army was the trade with German arms dealers. The Krupp Company figures prominently in this regard: already in 1860 Alfred Krupp contacted Turkish diplomats, and after first shipments in the following years a significant contract was finalized in

1873. Because Krupp also sold weapons to Russia, the Russian-Ottoman war of 1877–78 was fought with weapons from Germany on both sides. As German military advising proliferated in the years after 1882, the deals for Krupp and other German arms dealers were also rising. As a result, Germany acquired a monopoly in the arms trade with the Ottoman Empire.[14]

Toward the end of the 1880s German financial institutions became involved in development projects in the Ottoman Empire, among them the Deutsche Bank, which in 1903 held 40 percent of the shares of the Baghdad Railway Company.[15] Germany ranked third as debtor to the Ottoman Empire.[16] In the 1890s economic relations between Germany, Austria, and the Ottoman Empire expanded. In the five years between 1888 and 1893 the volume of German exports into Turkey grew by about 350 percent, while imports from Turkey grew by more than 700 percent.[17] After France, Great Britain, and Austria, Germany ranked fourth since the end of the 1890s in exports to Turkey and North Africa. In its importance for the Austrian economy, trade with the Ottoman Empire and North Africa was comparable to that of Great Britain. In 1900, 4.2 percent of all Austrian imports came from the Ottoman Empire and North Africa (1910, 3.2 percent), and 4.7 percent of its exports went to those territories (1910, 6.9 percent).[18]

In 1888 a contract was finalized that guaranteed the Deutsche Bank a leadership role in the building of the Transanatolian Railway. In the following decades Germans were involved in the construction of several railways throughout the Ottoman Empire. These projects significantly enhanced the influence of German capital in European and Asian territories of the Ottoman Empire. Emperor Wilhelm II played an active role in spurring economic relations. His trip to the Middle East in 1898 aimed at both supporting Christian missions in the Middle East and promoting projects undertaken with German capital. He also paved the way for further German investment in the building of the Baghdad Railway, which was to provide access to the oilfields and ports in the Persian Gulf. In December 1899, a contract was signed granting preconcessions to Georg von Siemens. The construction lasted from 1903 until 1940 (although after 1919, as a result of the Treaty of Versailles, Germans no longer participated).[19] Departing from previous scholarship, Jonathan S. McMurray has shown that the Baghdad Railway was not merely "a symbol of German imperialism." The railway's construction was in fact a joint Turco-German enterprise, argues McMurray, "with the Turks clearly at the helm. By strictly controlling each stage of the construction process, the Turks manipulated the Great Powers to ensure the railway served Ottoman interests first."[20]

Colonization and Cooperation

At the end of the eighteenth century relations between Europe and the Middle East entered a new phase. As the Ottoman Empire grew weaker and the European powers continued their rise, Europe intervened more frequently in the area. After the brief interlude of French and British occupation between 1798 and 1802, Egypt remained under Middle Eastern rule until the end of the eighteenth century; the French occupation of Algiers in 1830, however, marked the beginning of a brutal chapter in the history of European colonialism. In 1839 the British seized Aden and made it a colony (including Hadramaut). It took several decades before the next northern African territory was colonized: the British took control of Bahrain in 1880, Tunisia became a French colony in 1881, Egypt was invaded by the British in 1882, and Libya was colonized by the Italians in 1911. Morocco, which never was part of the Ottoman Empire, became a French and Spanish protectorate in 1912. After World War I large areas of the Ottoman Empire, which had fought alongside Germany against the Allied powers, were divided into spheres of influence: Iraq was conquered by the British in 1917, Palestine and the newly created Transjordan became British mandates in 1920, and France gained control of Syria and Lebanon. In other areas, such as Iran, foreign control was short-lived or more indirect.

German interests and actions in the Middle East differed from those of other European powers and, as in earlier periods, were often shaped by internal European power struggles. At times Germany collaborated with Great Britain and France. In 1839–41, for example, Austrians and Prussians supported a joint Ottoman/European military undertaking that ended the Egyptian occupation of Palestine.[21] Prussian officers, including Helmuth von Moltke and Lieutenant Laue, advised the Ottoman army in the early stage; later the coalition forces were led by Hamburg-born general August G. Jochmus. A fleet consisting of British, Austrian, and Ottoman ships seized Beirut, Sidon, and Acre, among other places, in 1840. Acre was bombarded heavily and then occupied by troops; its defeat secured the coalition victory.[22] In the aftermath Germans came to Palestine in increasing numbers, as pilgrims, missionaries, and developers. They built roads, hospices, hospitals, and factories; the most reliable postal service in Palestine in the second half of the nineteenth century was provided by the Austrians. King Frederick Wilhelm IV of Prussia quickly took action to assert a Christian-Prussian presence in the area: in 1841 the Ottomans granted him permission to establish a Protestant diocese in Jerusalem. Christian activity in the area rose in the following years. In 1847, and for the first time since the Crusades, the Catholic Church appointed a patriarch to Jerusalem. Missionaries flooded into Palestine, supported by substantial financial aid from Christian countries. Pilgrimages to the Holy Land became popular again; according to some estimates, between ten thousand and twenty thousand pilgrims visited the Holy Land annually after the 1840s, including a large number of Western Europeans. Pilgrimages from German-speaking areas grew into mass events, involving up to five hundred pilgrims in specifically designed *Volkswallfahrten* (people's pilgrimages).[23]

The activities of the Templers from Württemberg, a Pietist Christian sect, had a significant impact on the history of Palestine "in spite of their limited numbers."[24] Based in Haifa, they developed trade, agriculture, and transportation.[25] In 1905 a contemporary traveler described this German presence:

> Haifa is practically a German town as far as its trade, agriculture, and property are concerned. Even the Russian, American, and till lately, the English consuls are Germans. . . . The hotels, shops, and banks are German. The Roman Catholic hospital and hospice are in the hands of a German sisterhood; the sanatorium on Mount Carmel with its luxurious accommodation and extensive grounds, *rendezvous* of English missionaries, is conducted by Germans.[26]

German and Prussian ambitions in the area were also affirmed through imperial visits. Austrian emperor Franz Joseph, who claimed the title "king of Jerusalem," a title that Habsburg emperors held until the end of their rule in 1918, visited in 1869. German emperor Wilhelm II followed in 1898, landing in Haifa "on a specially prepared landing-stage run out from the German colony there. He was thus able to announce that he had landed 'on German soil.'"[27] German settlements also existed in parts of Macedonia and Anatolia; Malte Fuhrmann's study on the issue highlights previously unacknowledged aspects regarding the persistence of German ambitions to establish colonies in the Orient.[28]

At other times Germany opposed specifically French and British interests. In the decade before World War I, for example, the German Empire tried to expand its influence in North Africa. France and Spain had already expressed interest in Morocco, which was formally independent and had never been part of the Ottoman Empire. In 1904 the European powers divided the Moroccan territory among each other. In 1905 Germany appointed itself for the first time as the guarantor of Moroccan independence. An agreement made following the First Moroccan Crisis (1905–6) secured French dominance in the area while guaranteeing rights to foreign economic interests. German economic powers, especially the Gebrüder Mannesmann, were interested particularly in the rich ore deposits of Morocco. French attempts to monopolize railway building in the area, together with a heightened military presence in reaction to uprisings against the French, led to the Second Moroccan Crisis. In July 1911 the German cannon boat SMS *Panther* reached the port of Agadir. The Germans planned to occupy the port cities Agadir and Mogador in order to gain leverage in negotiations with France. In November the crisis was settled; Germany accepted French domination of Morocco and in exchange received, among other provision, 275,000 square kilometers of French Congo, where about one million people lived. In the following year Spain and France formally founded protectorates in Morocco.[29]

German diplomatic relations with Middle Eastern powers changed almost invariably in response to conflicts between European powers, and, as Mustafa Aksakal has shown, the Ottoman alliance with Germany is also to be understood as part of this scenario.[30] During World War I and later World War II these actions and reactions reached unprecedented dimensions. Germany, for example, tried to instigate a "Holy War" against the British during World War I. The idea was concocted by archaeologist and diplomat Max Freiherr von Oppenheim; as Wolfgang G. Schwanitz has demonstrated, "The jihad developed as a concerted German-Ottoman campaign. . . . The kaiser . . . wanted the sultan to call for a jihad in Asia, India, Egypt, and Africa to get Muslims fighting for the Caliphate. Berlin and Istanbul cooperated closely in planning and realizing the jihad."[31] Tilman Lüdke explains the failure of the German plan by suggesting that both Germany and Britain (in its efforts to counter the German strategy) "were influenced by the mistaken perceptions of non-industrial, non-European societies."[32] One of the chapters in this messy history is the German attempt to convince Afghanistan to join the jihad against the British, which foreshadowed U.S. support of Islamic fighters against the Russians later in the century.[33] In spite of the fact that German endeavors did not prevail, German-Afghani relations continued to evolve, and indeed Germany was the first country to acknowledge independent Afghanistan: "By 1929 the Germans were the largest European group in the country, outnumbering the British ten to one."[34]

After World War I Germany continued a foreign policy geared toward supporting anticolonial movements in areas under British and French control. This strategy was largely abandoned under the Nazis, even though some diplomats, such as Fritz Grobba, continued to contrive plans involving Muslim populations for German political purposes.[35] An instance of German attempts to use local populations for German purposes are the activities of German spies in Iran.[36] Field Marshal Erwin Rommel's military campaigns in North Africa during World War II attested to Nazi Germany's territorial aspirations in the area. As Ralf Georg Reuth writes, "The colonial resonances of Africa allowed Rommel to appear in the eyes of many Germans as a new Colonel Paul von Lettow-Vorbeck, the famous commander of the Kaiser's army in German East Africa in World War I."[37] Rommel was idealized in Germany long beyond his lifetime. An additional dimension of German–Middle Eastern relations during the period involves Nazi support of Zionism, which is documented as early as 1933, and built on earlier collaborations between antisemites and Zionists.[38] Noteworthy in this regard is the treaty known as the "Transfer Agreement," which facilitated German Jewish emigration to Palestine.[39] Nizam 'Abbasi argues that Nazi Germany initially built on Germany's traditionally good relations with the Arab world but altered course and ultimately did not differ from other Western imperialist states in its attempt to rule over Arab territory.[40]

Nineteenth-century modern nationalism, with its emphasis on bloodlines and ethnic cohesion, found resonance across Arab, Turkish, Persian, and other contexts. The founders of modern Turkey, such as Ziya Gökalp and Mustafa Kemal Atatürk, propagated an imagined idea of Turkishness ("Turkism," "Pan-Turkism," or "Turanism"), thereby eliminating several hundred years of Ottoman multicultural and multireligious heritage. Ideas of a Greater Syria were crucial, for example, to the Parti Populaire Syrien, founded in the early 1930s by Antun Sa'ada, who was inspired to some extent by National Socialism.[41] Iranian nationalism took on different shapes over time, variously privileging linguistic, territorial, ethnic, and religious aspects as unifying factors.[42] National Socialism was also a model for radical politicians in Egypt.[43]

New Ideologies: Civilizationism, Racism, Nationalism, Modernizationism, and Philorientalism

In the nineteenth century, Germans no longer drew solely on Christianity, vague ideas about cultural alterity, or a belief in humanism, but increasingly turned to new scientific theories of presumed racial differences as well as notions of modernization and progress. The idea of European cultural and civilizational superiority was developed by eminent thinkers of German idealism. Building on the works of Immanuel Kant and Johann Gottfried Herder, for example, Georg Wilhelm Friedrich Hegel's understanding of world history as progressive relegated non-Western cultures and religions to a premodern, and thus implicitly inferior, status.[44] The fact that Hegel's ideas were clearly informed by contemporary colonialist discourses has been demonstrated by critics such as Susan Buck-Morss, who ties Hegel's idea of the master-slave relation to contemporary events in Haiti.[45] Whereas the worldview articulated by Hegel and others expressed a sense of entitlement based on a belief in Germany's/Europe's (and Christianity's) superior culture and civilization, medical and biological racism supported these claims on the basis of presumed biological differences. Susanne Zantop has studied the impact of writings by Christoph Meiners, Johann Friedrich Blumenbach, and Immanuel Kant, among others, on German ideas about other cultures and the emergence of scientific racism.[46] The role of science in constructing ideas of German superiority has also been demonstrated by scholars such as Andrew Zimmerman and H. Glenn Penny.[47]

Ideas about the uniqueness of the German nation were conceived from this nexus of different theories that assumed the superiority of Germans. Germans were particularly drawn to such paradigms in the aftermath of the dissolution of the Holy Roman Empire of the German Nation in 1806. The founding of the German nation-state in 1871 occurred in a climate of virulent nationalism across Europe, and ideas of German national superiority culminated in the vision of National Socialists. Another ideological framework that developed in response to the economic and political transformations of the nineteenth century was a belief in modernization as the panacea to a range of problems societies faced at the time. Modernizationism, to give a name to this ideology, is different from civilizationism in that it claims to overcome cultural, social, economic, and other differences between societies through the introduction of modern economic, political, and social institutions. Modernizers believing in the messianic powers of modernization covered the entire political spectrum, from communists to conservatives.

Along with the rise of biological racism, nationalism, and modernizationism, ideas from Christianity continued to play an important role not only in works of German fiction writers but also in speeches and writings of German politicians and other public figures, who evoked Christian symbolism to support their actions. The pilgrimages to Jerusalem by German aristocrats and political leaders, such as Emperor Wilhelm II's journey in 1898, epitomize the view held by many Germans that the Holy Land was, and should be again, a Christian land.

Germany's relationship to the Middle East was also colored by German perceptions of its internal others. From the late eighteenth and early nineteenth centuries onward, Jews living in German countries were no longer simply marginalized with regard to religious differences but were also increasingly set apart according to perceived cultural and then racial differences. German Jews developed various responses to this growing discrimination, which pegged Jews as Oriental others, notably Zionism and Jewish Philorientalism. Once Palestine was chosen by the Zionist movement as the site for a future state, German Jews pursued various strategies to achieve their goal. In lobbying for the Holy Land as the ancestral Jewish land to be recovered, political Zionists, such as Theodor Herzl, engaged contemporary colonialist rhetoric but particularly civilizationist and modernizationist arguments.[48] At the same time, cultural Zionist Martin Buber articulated a different approach by identifying with Oriental roots and creating a positive vision of the "Jew as Oriental." This movement turned antisemitic rhetoric on its head, embracing Oriental roots in a self-confident gesture that resembles the strategies of later identity politics movements.[49]

The Jewish affirmation of the Orient was part of a larger cultural trend. Along with a fascination with India, as expressed by the Romantic poets and thinkers, the followers of theosophy and anthroposophy, and later the writings of Hermann Hesse, interest in Middle Eastern culture was particularly high from about 1900 into the 1920s.

Travel Accounts, Orientalist Scholarship, Translations, Newspapers, Journals, and Popular Culture

Travel literature became more and more popular, and often appeared in the form of anthologies. Heinrich Eberhard Gottlob Paulus's seven-volume *Sammlung der merkwürdigsten reisen in den Orient. In übersetzung und auszügen mit ausgewälten kupfern und charten,* for instance, was published between 1792 and 1803 and included accounts, translated and in the original German, from the sixteenth to eighteenth centuries. Palestine became a preferred travel destination and was exposed during this time to more European traffic than it had seen since the Crusades.[50] In addition, scientists, merchants, pilgrims, and adventurous types trekked through areas of the Middle East that had been terra incognita to Europeans until then.

The list of Orientalist scholars, merchants, literary figures, and private individuals who wrote about their travels throughout the Ottoman Empire, the Arab Middle East, and North Africa is long, and a systematic study of this group of German travel writings would provide greater detail than possible in this overview. Clichés about Oriental decay, timelessness, and laziness appear repeatedly, but it is worth noting that many of the accounts are fact oriented and that their authors typically identify with the object of their studies. Among those who were enthusiastic in their admiration for the area and its inhabitants was the adventurous and politically liberal Fürst Hermann Ludwig Heinrich von Pückler-Muskau (1785–1871), who traveled widely in the Middle East and North Africa, writing popular accounts and providing firsthand information. He visited Egypt as the guest of Muhammad ʻAli and published a detailed account in *Aus Mehemed Ali's Reich* (3 vols., 1844), in which he reserves extensive praise for Muhammad ʻAli:

> With an admirable talent for organization, he has managed to introduce into one of the most neglected and disorganized countries in the world, the first conditions of a civilized state—*order and security*. . . . He has introduced . . . more equity and settled principle than at present exist in any other oriental state. He has endeavoured to put down fanaticism; has shown a greater tolerance in religious matters than is to be found in many Christian states. . . . He has not only encouraged commercial intercourse with Europe, but has, in a great measure, created it.[51]

The nineteenth century also witnessed an increasing number of female travelers. The accounts of Ida Hahn-Hahn (*Orientalische Briefe,* 1851) and Ida Pfeiffer (*Reise einer Wienerin in das Heilige Land,* 1844) shed light on aspects often neglected by their male counterparts, such as the way women in different countries lived. Whereas Lady Mary Wortley Montagu had offered favorable depictions of Turkish women's lives, Ida Hahn-Hahn mirrored views articulated by male European travelers by criticizing, for example, life in the harem.[52]

The most popular accounts from the mid-nineteenth century, however, were those authored by Friedrich Martin von Bodenstedt (1819–92), who published travel writings, poetry modeled after Persian sources, and translations of Persian poets, such as Hafiz. In 1849–50 he published *Tausend und ein Tag im Orient* (One Thousand and One Days in the Orient). Drawing on his travels and time lived in Russia and the multicultural areas of the Caucasus and Georgia, Bodenstedt sketched an image of Persians, Armenians, Georgians, and other groups living in the area that renders them as Arcadian, exotic, patriarchal, and premodern. Apart from information about the striking landscape, impressive architecture, the economy, social life, and government, Bodenstedt offers views on cultural and religious matters.[53] The role of women in the "Orient," for example, is described as "no better than the standing of a slave to her master."[54] Bodenstedt's autobiographical account conveyed a significant amount of factual information about an area largely unknown to German readers. Regardless of the accurateness of the information, Bodenstedt clearly saw himself in a superior position with respect to the people he encountered and described.[55]

Another group of writings was authored by individuals who served Ottoman or other Middle Eastern rulers and often converted to Islam. Representative here are the writings of Franz von Werner (1836–81), which document the life of a writer and diplomat who was born in Austria, converted to Islam, served the Ottomans as a diplomat, and was also known by his pseudonym Murad Efendi. He wrote tragedies (*Selim III,* 1872), comedies (*Bogadil,* 1874), and autobiographical narratives (*Türkische Skizzen,* 1877) that drew on his knowledge about the Ottoman Empire.

Travel accounts continued to gain in popularity in the first half of the twentieth century; for the period from 1914 to 1945 roughly twenty-five informative and analytically and ideologically divergent texts are reported on Morocco alone.[56] An analysis of accounts of Yemen in the period after 1930 suggests that texts about the Arabian peninsula are characterized by a matter-of-fact approach to the encountered foreignness.[57] Carl Reinhardt Raswan's *Im Land der schwarzen Zelte* (1934), for example, was based on the author's eleven stays with Bedouin over twenty-five years. The volume, illustrated with fascinating photographs, is not free of romanticization but strives to convey an accessible and historically grounded portrayal of the lives of Bedouin, who are introduced by Raswan as "his friends."[58]

Apart from pilgrimages, travel in the Middle East was, until the mid-nineteenth century, restricted to affluent individuals. Gradually, however, these journeys took on forms of tourism involving larger groups.[59] A travel account about a cruise to the Middle East, undertaken by a group of German tourists in 1891, suggests that the travelers had limited access to Egyptian society. The cliché-ridden account illustrates that the author's lack of knowledge about Egypt's encounter with modernization and colonization hampered his ability to make sense of what he saw.[60]

Germans also read travel accounts published in other languages and in translation. Among the popular texts during the first half of the nineteenth century were François-René Chateaubriand's *Itinéraire de Paris a Jérusalem et de Jérusalem a Paris en allant par la Grèce, et revenant par l'Égypte, la Barbarie et l'Espagne* (1811; *Reise von Paris nach Jerusalem durch Griechenland und Kleinasien, und Rückreise nach Paris durch Aegypten, Nordafrika und Spanien,* 1811), Alphonse de Lamartine's *Souvenirs, impressions, pensées et paysages pendant un Voyage en Orient 1832–1833* (1833; *Reise in den Orient in den Jahren 1832 und 1833: Erinnerungen, Empfindungen, Gedanken und*

Landschaftsgemälde, 1835), and Georg August Wallin's *Narrative of a Journey from Cairo to Medina and Mecca, by Suez, Arabá, Tawilá, al-Jauf, Jubbé, Háil, and Nejd, in 1845* (1854).

An in-depth comparative analysis of the rich material contained in accounts written by individuals as diverse as Friedrich Konrad Hornemann, Johann F. J. Borsum, Gerhard Rohlfs, Heinrich Karl Brugsch, Johann Ludwig Burckhardt, Maria Schuber, Richard Lepsius, Franz Grillparzer, Wilhelm Gentz, and Ármin Vámbéry is still wanting.[61] Nevertheless, it is reasonable to conclude that these writings conveyed a wealth of factual material and a range of approaches to the Middle East and its peoples. Whereas most texts can be linked to European imperialism and ideology in one way or another, individual travelers were able to encounter the Middle East on their own terms and they articulated views that were distinct from the dominant images circulated in literary writings and which were often in tension with political and economic developments. It is noteworthy, for example, that analyses by Arab-language scholars have at times been highly appreciative of the valuable contributions of German travelers to preserving knowledge about Arab culture and history.[62] In spite of the respect expressed for these contributions and also the hardships these Germans endured, scholars such as Abu al-'Id Dudu clearly identify the German travelers and scientists as accumulating knowledge that facilitated the colonization of the area.[63]

Many travel accounts were authored by Orientalist scholars. In spite of Germany's later start, German-based studies of Middle Eastern cultures and religions gained ascendancy by the middle of the nineteenth century. Silvestre de Sacy had trained an entire generation of French, German, and Russian scholars of Arabic, Hebrew, and other Middle Eastern languages, but now Germany acquired its own centers for the study of Middle Eastern languages and cultures and produced its own scholars.[64]

In Austria, the beginning of Oriental sciences was tied to the close contact with the Ottoman Empire; the need for translators and interpreters was a main factor in the 1754 founding of the Kaiserlich-königliche Akademie für Orientalische Sprachen (Imperial Royal Academy of Oriental Languages) in Vienna.[65] Further to the west and north, Göttingen, Tübingen, and Heidelberg were among the hubs of Middle Eastern studies, as was Gotha. The importance of Gotha was due to a journey undertaken in the early nineteenth century by Ulrich Jasper Seetzen and financed by Duke Ernst II of Sachsen-Gotha and Altenstein. Seetzen left Germany in 1802, traveled through Turkey, Syria, Palestine, and Egypt, and died during his travels in Yemen in 1811. The most notable result of this expedition are not only Seetzen's informative diaries and vocabulary lists but also the large number of manuscripts that were brought to Germany, which make up the core of the extensive collection at the Forschungs- und Landesbibliothek and the Schloßmuseum in Gotha, which has been a treasure trove for Orientalist scholars.[66]

The outstanding scholarship of Georg Wilhelm Freytag (1788–1861), Gustav Leberecht Flügel (1802–70), and Heinrich Leberecht Fleischer (1801–88), among others, moved Oriental studies to a leading position in Europe. Perhaps the most valuable contribution was the careful editing and publishing of primary sources. The beginning of German Islam studies dates back to the 1830s and 1840s, with the appearance of Gustav Weil's (1808–89) *Historisch-kritische Einleitung in den Koran* (1844). The founding of the Deutsche Morgenländische Gesellschaft in 1845 signaled the institutional advancement of Oriental studies in Germany.[67] The next generation of German Orientalists included Alfred von Kremer (1828–89), Theodor Nöldeke (1836–1930), Julius Wellhausen (1844–1918), Ignaz Goldziher (1850–1921), and Carl Brockelmann (1868–1956), all of whom compiled standard reference works and groundbreaking studies that are used to this day. Research on all aspects of the Middle East shed new light not only on linguistics, literary studies, and religion but also on geography, geology, anthropology, biology, and other areas of natural and social sciences.

Most relevant to understanding the role of German Orientalists is the question of ideology. To what extent were German Orientalists involved in political developments, and what positions did they take on contemporary events? To shed light on this question, let us consider two distinct features of German scholars' relationship to the Middle East, namely, the role of Jewish scholars and the imperial connection.

German Orientalist sciences were significantly shaped by German Jewish scholars and by the relationship of leading Orientalists to Jews and Judaism. One of the most significant figures of the early phase, Johann David Michaelis, was a rabid antisemite. Jonathan M. Hess demonstrates that research conducted by Michaelis prepared the ground for a biology-based antisemitism, decades before biological and medical sciences served to legitimate the persecution and killing of Jews.[68] Susannah Heschel shows that German Jewish Orientalists wrote against this kind of scholarship and against antisemitism in general. Her analysis of the work of Abraham Geiger (1810–74) argues that Geiger's scholarship exemplifies an early case of postcolonial scholarship, of writing back against dominant cultural views. Geiger published a study on the origins of Islam in Judaism; a later study followed the same approach and traced Christianity's origin in Judaism. While Geiger's work on Islam laid the foundation for a historical approach to Islam and was widely respected, his work on Christianity led to bitter attacks.[69] Michaelis and Geiger represented two ends of the spectrum, each scholar relating German Orientalist scholarship to internal German-Jewish affairs in different ways. The issue clearly highlights the ideological wars that shaped scholarship on Middle Eastern matters, even beyond or before the colonial question was raised. Said has written that antisemitism is Orientalism's "secret sharer."[70] But with Hess we might conclude that there was actually nothing "secret" about Orientalist antisemitism.[71]

By the middle of the nineteenth century colonial ideology clearly structured German Orientalist scholarship. Notwithstanding the fact that German states did not have colonies in the Middle East, some German scholars held views of Muslims and Islam that were tied to political and economic developments. A look at the central Orientalist journal, the *Zeitschrift der Deutschen Morgenländischen Gesellschaft,* provides a sense of the broad array of topics that were covered in this venue. The first volume of the journal appeared in 1847 and included articles on Ethiopian and Indian manuscripts, Arab writers, Sinology, and Arab ophthalmology. This array of topics reflects the fact that the idea of the Orient included nearly the entire non-Western world and that the journal was interdisciplinary. Two articles are particularly relevant with regard to colonial ideology. The first, authored by one Dr. Pruner and entitled "The Negro. An Aphoristic Study from the 'Medical Topography of Cairo,'" clearly reflects the influence of racializing theories, such as ideas expressed in Comte de Gobineau's *Essai sur inégalité des races* (1853–55).[72] While some Orientalist scholars may have distanced themselves from the racism explicit in Dr. Pruner's article, the fact that this contribution was published in the same journal that featured research on medieval Arab literature exemplifies the centrality of colonialist, Eurocentric, and modernizationist belief systems in Orientalist research of the time. Another article featured in the same volume directly established the link to colonial interest. Entitled "Ueber die Anlage eines Colonialhandel-Etablissements im ostindischen Archipel," the contribution amounts to a plea to establish a German colonial fleet. Germans, so the article's author Dr. E. Selberg asserts, "are excluded from those rich areas" with which "almost all civilized nations" are connected through "world trade"; establishing a German colony in the East Indies was thus advisable and feasible.[73]

German Orientalist scholars clearly participated in colonialist and Eurocentric discussions about the world, read the works of Orientalists that were written in various languages, and were familiar with debates as they occurred across Europe. While individual scholars pursued research that may have had no direct bearing upon contemporary events, none could ignore the political questions being raised during this period. Journals and introductions to scholarly works shed more direct light on contemporary beliefs than many scholarly editions and translations. Institutional histories also reflect the degree to which scholars were involved in Europe's expansion into the Middle East. The 1877 founding of the Deutscher Verein zur Erforschung Palästinas, an organization that was conceived to compete with the British Palestine Exploration Fund, exemplifies this nexus of scholarship and economic and political ambitions.[74]

Whereas the first generations of German Orientalists commented on political events of the day but were not directly involved in political developments, the situation changed in the last third of the century, particularly in the context of new institutional connections between state and science. The founding of the Seminar für Orientalische Sprachen in Berlin in 1887 created a link between scholarship and the state's foreign policy interests. The institute was financed in equal parts by the Prussian State and the German Empire and was clearly linked to interests of the state and economy at a moment when Germany was beginning to build its colonial empire. It trained translators and prepared diplomats for foreign service careers, specifically in the colonies.[75] Noteworthy also is the work of Carl Heinrich Becker (1876–1933), who is generally credited as the founder of modern Islamic studies.[76] In 1908 Becker accepted a professorship at the Kolonialinstitut in Hamburg and became its first director. Together with Martin Hartmann (1851–1918), and in spite of significant differences in outlook, Becker changed the field of German Oriental studies, making the *contemporary* Middle East a worthy object of study for the first time. As a consequence, the applicability of scholarly knowledge became a point of discussion.[77]

This latter issue became a matter of some urgency during World War I. Becker was involved in supporting the German attempt at instigating a jihad in the Middle East and other Muslim areas; in this misguided action, originally (as mentioned before) the idea of Max Freiherr von Oppenheim, Becker was joined by fellow Orientalists Enno Littmann (1875–1958), Eduard Sachau (1845–1930), and Eugen Mittwoch (1876–1942), among others.[78] Anticolonial propaganda was a key element in the leaflets and brochures produced by the Nachrichtenstelle für den Orient, which employed "a random mix of journalists, academics, and diplomats, and recruited additional collaborators for individual projects."[79] As Gottfried Hagen points out, however, "It is worth noting that texts with a mainly anticolonial thrust were mostly written by Muslim collaborators. . . . it is hard to avoid the impression that the Muslims had the better sense of their compatriots' real concerns."[80] The declaration of jihad had disastrous consequences for the religious minorities living within the Ottoman Empire, practically legitimating discriminatory Turkish policies and actions against the Armenians, for example.[81] Some Orientalists quickly realized the conundrum produced by the German initiative; as early as 1915, Ernst Herzfeld (1879–1948) emerged as an outspoken critic of the German plan and the war in general.[82] Herzfeld is notable for another reason: his excavations in Iran contributed greatly to bolstering nationalist discourse in the country. His findings enriched knowledge about the pre-Islamic period, which was used to elevate the country's image of that period versus that of its Islamic heritage.[83]

Several scholars continued to play a role as agents of the state throughout the Weimar Republic; Carl Heinrich Becker, for example, served as minister of sciences, arts, and public instruction in the 1920s. The following period made abstention from politics impossible. The Nazis quickly removed Jewish Orientalists, including converts, from German academia. Ludmila Hanisch suggests that 25 percent of professorships were affected, and an even larger percentage with regard to other academic positions.[84] Kader Konuk's study on German-Jewish émigrés to Turkey sheds light on the effect of this emigration on Turkish academia, but the United States, Israel, and other countries also absorbed the German brain drain.[85] The remaining Orientalists overwhelmingly collaborated with the repressive state. Hans Heinrich Schaeder (1896–1957), for example, was professor of Oriental Philology and Religious History at Berlin from 1931 to 1944 and, as Robert Irwin writes, "a leading spokesman of Nazi Orientalism": his "racism pervaded his thinking on Middle Eastern cultures" and omitted any reference to Jewish scholarship.[86] Other Orientalists in line with Nazi ideology were Curt Prüfer, Fritz Grobba, and Franz Taeschner. As Ekkehard Ellinger shows convincingly, collaboration was the norm, and not the exception.[87]

Let us return to the larger dissemination of knowledge about the Middle East in German-speaking societies, particularly as regards the role of translations and adaptations. During the early phase the translations from Turkish, Arabic, and Persian by Joseph von Hammer-Purgstall (1774–1856) were highly popular among German literati, such as Goethe, Friedrich Rückert, and August von Platen. Hammer-Purgstall's lack of knowledge and skills earned him adamant criticism from experts in various fields, which raises questions regarding a reception history based on insufficient translations and conveying inadequate notions about the style and content of Middle Eastern literatures.[88] And indeed, only few translators and writers attempted to understand the Middle East on its own terms. Here, Friedrich Rückert and August von Platen stand out for their level of engagement with source material. Rückert in fact was the first

German poet to learn Arabic, Persian, and Turkish, building on his knowledge of Hebrew and Syriac (he later learned Sanskrit and a number of other languages). His translations were often adaptations, *Nachdichtungen,* and Rückert also used Oriental forms to write his own poetry in German. In 1821 he published his first volume of adaptations of Rumi's poetry, *Ghaselen nach Dschelaleddin Rumi.* In 1826 he published his translation of *Makamen des Hariri,* which has been praised by Orientalists for its rhetorical features.[89] Numerous translations followed. Other writers, such as Friedrich Schlegel, J. W. von Goethe, and August von Platen, had engaged with the *ghazel,* but Rückert is credited with introducing this Arabic poetic form into the German language.[90] Rückert's and Platen's contributions to the dissemination of Oriental poetry, through translations and adaptations, derived from a sympathetic point of departure that engaged in dialogue and immersion. 'Awni Abd al-Ra'uf celebrates Rückert as an "admirer of Arabic poetry" and writes that "the nineteenth century was not ready to receive the genius of the Orientalist Friedrich Rückert."[91]

Like Rückert and Platen, other translators and poets added to a creative, but at times also imaginary, intercultural dialogue through their translations and adaptations. German writers and translators often took their cue from English and French translations, such as Edward Fitzgerald's *Rubaiyat of Omar Khayyam* (1859), which became extremely popular and was widely disseminated across Europe, despite its problematic relationship to the Persian source material.[92] Adolf Friedrich von Schack published a German translation of the *Rubaiyat* in 1878, and Friedrich von Bodenstedt delivered his version in 1881. Among the numerous German-language adaptations/translations of this text is a 1917 version composed by Klabund (*Das Sinngedicht des persischen Zeltmachers: Neue Vierzeiler nach Omar Khayyam*), who used translations of Persian (and also Chinese and Japanese) sources to create adaptations. Poetry by Hafiz, first introduced through Hammer-Purgstall and popularized by Goethe, appeared in variations throughout the period; Klabund's *Der Feueranbeter: Nachdichtung des Hafis,* for example, was published in 1919. The effect of translations and adaptations on literary German remains largely unexplored.

With the rise in literacy rates and the explosion of publications in the nineteenth century, information about the Middle East became accessible through a plethora of daily newspapers, specialized journals, and middlebrow publications targeted to nonacademic audiences. Systematic studies of these publishing venues are lacking, but a look at examples from the years 1878 to 1880, when events in the Balkans and in Turkey captured the attention of readers across Europe, sheds light on the vigor with which Middle Eastern topics were being debated in the German media.

Among the most widely circulated newspapers focusing on foreign affairs was *Das Ausland,* which was modeled after the *Foreign Quarterly Review.* It began as a daily newspaper in 1828, featuring articles about political developments, economies, and cultural and social aspects of peoples and countries across the globe. Articles consisted of original contributions as well as excerpts of recently published books, academic articles, and international papers, often in translation. Beginning in 1853, the paper appeared once a week, and the subtitle *Ueberschau der neuesten Foschungen auf dem Gebiete der Natur-, Erd- und Völkerkunde* was added in 1865. Among the articles published in 1878, to give a sense of its range, was a contribution on the al-Azhar Mosque in Cairo, a report about an expedition exploring the Eastern Sahara, a commentary on questions of faith in Islam, and a protracted discussion over several issues regarding the situation in the Middle East.[93] Another widely circulated journal, the *Deutsche Rundschau für Geographie und Statistik* (published from 1878/79 until 1914/15), regularly contained information about the Middle East. The journal's first volume featured articles about the finances and debt of Egypt, the size of the Ottoman army and fleet, the volume of trade between Austria and Turkey, and discussions about the war in the Balkans that had just ended.[94] Next to relatively neutral and primarily fact-centered articles, some contributions clearly convey ideological positions.

In spite of its relatively high price the *Illustrirte Zeitung,* which aimed to cover aspects of political, social, and cultural developments, also reached a large audience. This weekly newspaper, which appeared first in 1843, was also the first lavishly illustrated publication of its type in Germany. It included illustrations and advertisements from around the globe and thus added visual elements to political events in unprecedented ways. An analysis of these various nonacademic publications from around 1880 reveals that by and large the Middle East was seen as an area of political and cultural decline. Only few voices speak to the reform attempts undertaken by Ottoman leaders. At the same time, however, the economic and political infiltration of Ottoman territories was clearly under way; Middle Eastern locations and goods were advertised to German consumers and Middle Eastern cultural metaphors incorporated into commercial language.

As a result of the growing contact between Europe and the Middle East, artifacts were brought to Europe by individual travelers, scientists, colonial bureaucrats, imperial soldiers, and merchants. Gradually, they began to fill museums and private collections. These "trophies" came to symbolize European superiority over conquered cultures; at the same time, the symbolic value of possessing items from once great civilizations, be they Greek, Roman, Arab,

Persian, or Turkish, functioned to highlight the power of present-day European societies. Possessing Middle Eastern objects of art gave members of the German elite another means to express their economic power and social capital. The 1910 *Ausstellung Mohammedanischer Kunst* in Munich, which included items sent by the Ottoman sultan, reflects the appeal of such artifacts to members of the German and European aristocracy and upper-class bourgeoisie.

Archaeologists often brought monumental Middle Eastern structures to Germany. The archaeologist Carl Humann (1839–96), for example, excavated the ancient Greek Pergamon Altar, located in northwestern Anatolia. In the late 1800s and early 1900s the excavated pieces were sent to Germany, where the altar was reconstructed and remains on exhibit to this day in the Pergamon-Museum in Berlin. The same museum prides itself on displaying other Middle Eastern structures, such as the Ishtar Gate from Babylon in Iraq, which was excavated by Robert Koldewey (1855–1925). These monuments inspired German architects, such as the Nazi Albert Speer (1905–81), who modeled his Zeppelintribühne after the Pergamon Altar. Among the famous German archaeologists of the era is Heinrich Schliemann (1822–90), whose name has come to stand for the excavation of Troy.[95] The excavation of Pharaoh Tutankhamen in 1922 by British Egyptologist Howard Carter was covered widely in the media, and a German translation of Carter's account of the dig, cowritten with Arthur Cruttenden Mace, was first published in 1924 as *Tut-ench-Amun, ein ägyptisches Königsgrab, entdeckt von Earl of Carnarvon und Howard Carter.* Numerous best sellers about the famous excavation have appeared in German since the 1920s.

Enthusiasm for Middle Eastern artworks influenced the styles of art, architecture, and design across Europe. By the middle of the nineteenth century many non-Western forms and ornamental motifs had found their way into the vocabulary of European decorative arts. German, Austrian, and Swiss painters traveled to the Middle East and brought their impressions back home. Journeys to North Africa and the Middle East were popular with Austrian and German painters.[96] Wilhelm Gentz, for example, traveled to Morocco in 1847–48 and to Egypt and Nubia in 1850–51 and expressed his thoughts and observations in letters, drawings, and paintings.[97] Carl Leopold Müller is the most well-known representative of the school known as the Wiener Orientmalerei (Viennese Orientalist Painting), which also included painters such as Rudolf Swoboda and Franz Xaver Kosler. A group of painters, including Müller, Hans Makart, Carl Rudolf Huber, and Franz von Lenbach, traveled to Egypt in 1875–76 and immortalized their impressions in painting. Gustav Bauernfeind's extensive Orientalist work is also based on travels to the Middle East; in 1896 he settled in

Jerusalem, where he lived until his death.[98] Aesthetic styles changed and varied, and so did the images of the Middle East and North Africa, as, for instance, the visual records of the 1914 journey through Tunisia by the painters Paul Klee, August Macke, and Louis Moilliet demonstrate. The expressionist interpretations of the Tunisian environment inspire the viewer to reflect about the dialogical relationship between self and other.[99]

The presence of Oriental architecture in the southern regions of Europe is well documented, but Germans also incorporated Middle Eastern styles into their buildings. Oriental styles had become fashionable in late seventeenth- and eighteenth-century architecture (such as several buildings commissioned by Saxony's aristocracy); late nineteenth- and early twentieth-century Germany once again turned East for architectural inspiration. Synagogues in Speyer, Ingenheim, Hildesheim, Vienna, Berlin, Saarbrücken, Wiesbaden, Karlsruhe, Frankfurt, Cologne, Stuttgart, Leipzig, and other cities incorporated various Middle Eastern styles for buildings associated with the three monotheistic religions.[100] Oriental architecture also inspired the design of factories in Germany, supporting what Rosalind H. Williams has shown in *Dream Worlds,* namely, that Oriental themes facilitated the expression of tropes of abundance and consumption that were so central to the emerging consumer economy.[101] The "Dampfmaschinenhaus" in Potsdam, modeled after a mosque and designed by Ludwig Persius, was built in 1841–43; the Dresdner "Zigarettenfabrik Yenidze," designed by Martin Hammitzsch, followed in 1907–9. Its 63-meter-tall "minarett" served as the factory's chimney.[102] Actual mosques were built in Germany in conjunction with World War I, for example, in Wünsdorf outside of Berlin. In the 1920s another mosque was built in Berlin-Wilmersdorf.[103] We should not forget, however, that, while Germans were inspired by Middle Eastern architecture, Middle Eastern architects followed Western models in their attempts to shape a modern image of developing cities, as Zeynep Çelik has illustrated through insightful case studies of the Western influence on architectural development in Istanbul.[104]

Across Europe musical composers worked with Oriental themes. As Derek B. Scott suggests, however, "Orientalism does not simply take the music of the Other to represent the Other; it is used to represent our own thoughts *about* the Other."[105] Maurice Ravel's *Shéhérazade* overture (1899), for example, "illustrates the use of whole tones for exotic effect" but "some nineteenth-century songs concerning Arabs . . . are basically Western European in style."[106] That is, Orientalism in music may occur in content or in style and sometimes both. The works of composers who engaged with Oriental themes and topics, such as Félicien-César David, Georges Bizet, Léo Delibes,

Giuseppe Verdi, Nikolai Rimsky-Korsakov, and Alexander Borodin, were received widely in Germany. Yet, with the turn toward nationalistic themes (such as in the work of Richard Wagner and Johann Strauss I) and then atonal and twelve-tone music (Gustav Mahler, Arnold Schönberg), Oriental themes and styles inspired only a few German composers. In 1871 Johann Strauss II composed the operetta *Indigo und die vierzig Räuber* based on the tale "Ali Baba and the Forty Thieves" from *One Thousand and One Nights.* A failure in Vienna, it was more successful in France as *Queen Indigo* (1875) and as *A Night on the Bosphorus* (1876) in England. Richard Strauss also used Oriental material in his operas *Salome* (1905, including the famous "Tanz der sieben Schleier"), *Die Frau ohne Schatten* (1918), and *Die ägyptische Helena* (1927). Dance performances with Oriental themes were popular at the turn of the century, such as the rendition of *Scheherazade* by the Ballets Russes. This performance to the suite of Rimsky-Korsakov created an uproar in Europe during the troupe's tour in 1910. Costumes and decorations were designed by Leon Bakst and evoked an Oriental world of abundance and spectacular color combinations. In terms of its content the performance reproduced clichés of Oriental despotism, excessive sexuality, and cruel brutality.

But the Orient served multiple functions during this period. Oriental themes were also employed to express the very new and modern, a quality that emerges quite clearly with regard to early film. Egyptian motifs were particularly popular, and with Antonia Lant one may ask "what function the aura of Egypt served in cinema's beginnings that it took root there with such tenacity."[107] As Lant shows, "The alliance between optically novel and illusory forms of representation and ideas about Egypt precedes even the invention of cinema."[108] She traces that history of association through the nineteenth century by considering "lantern shows, panoramas, dioramas, photographs, and photographic criticism, and on into the emerging sphere of cinema itself."[109] Names of movie theaters (such as Alhambra, the Egyptian Hall), film production companies (such as the Kalem Film Company), and finally, the titles of films themselves highlight the association of Egypt with film—for example, *Boat on the Nile* (1905), *From Cairo to the Pyramids* (1905), *La Vie de Mise* (1906), *A Corner of Ancient Egypt* (1910), *Lord Kitchener in Egypt* (1910), and *Cleopatra* (five versions between 1908 and 1918). Films about mummies were particular popular, especially after the discovery of the grave of Tutankhamen.[110] The most well-known German film in this genre was Ernst Lubitsch's *Die Augen der Mumie Ma* (1918); lesser-known examples are *Die Tophar-Mumie* (1920, Johannes Guter); *Der Schädel der Pharaonentochter* (1920, Otz Tollen); and *Das Rätsel der Sphinx* (1921, Adolf Gärtner). While capturing Egypt in early modern film can be linked to imperialist appropriation, the creation of this nexus of the ancient and the modern begs further contemplation. Lant suggests that the association with Egypt was linked to "discourses on death, on preservation, on silence, and on light projection."[111] Perhaps film's (and photography's) unprecedented possibilities in creating a new memory culture, particularly at a moment when Western societies were changing at a phenomenal speed, explains its attraction to a civilization in which memory and death were central. Other films staged in an imaginary Middle East and communicating a wide range of social and political questions are, among others, *Sumurun* (1920, Ernst Lubitsch; the English version renders the title as *An Arabian Tale*); *Wüstenrausch* (1924, Geza von Bolvary), *Die Frauengasse von Algier* (1927, Wolfgang Hoffmann-Harnisch), and *Die Abenteurerin von Tunis* (1931, Willi Wolff).

Literature

Images of the Middle East attained new meanings and functioned in novel ways with the beginning of the French occupation of Germany in 1792 and the European invasion into North African territories a few years later. As we have seen, the nineteenth and early twentieth centuries witnessed a proliferation of images and themes related to the Middle East in virtually all areas of German culture, and literary writings drew on the available expressive vocabulary.

Negotiating Modernization

At the beginning of the nineteenth century the political changes brought on by the French Revolution and the French occupation of Germany generated literary responses that ranged from enthusiasm for a just political order to nostalgia for the lost paternal order, and often included a turning away from the social to the private, from the political to the religious. Several plays continued to convey eighteenth-century ideas about the successful conversion of an autocratic ruler to a just one, such as August Wilhelm Iffland's *Achmet und Zenide* (1799), Johann Heinrich Wilhelm Witschel's play *Balsora: Ein morgenländisches Schauspiel* (1799), and August von Kotzebue's play *Der Harem* (1810).[112] But the confidence in the prospective improvement of society was lost in postrevolutionary Europe, especially after the French occupation of Germany. The tension between a desire for social and political transformation and nostalgia for a lost cohesive order comes across in the writings of Karoline von Günderrode. Her "Geschichte eines Braminen," in contrast to some of her poems that articulate a vision of radical transformation, can be interpreted as a Romanticist critique of the Enlightenment's glorification of the social and of reason. The text, probably written in 1798, was first published in 1805.[113] Its protagonist, Almar, is the son of a French convert to Islam and a mother whose religion or ethnicity is not discussed and who dies too early for Almar to remember her. When he is sixteen years old, his father sends him from his birthplace, Smyrna, to be trained as a merchant in an unnamed big city in Europe. Much like Siddhartha in Hermann Hesse's eponymous novel (1922), Almar realizes how limited his life of material goods and sensual pleasures is and returns to his "fatherland," which, in a gesture typical of Orientalist writings, he calls both Asia and Orient, thus creating a vague landscape that is characterized by distinct qualities rather than geographical and historical specificity.[114] Insisting on the right of the individual to withdraw from society to pursue a path of personal enlightenment, Almar finds fulfillment in spiritual contemplation. His development displays a profound disillusionment with institutionalized religion, and his ideas resemble Spinoza's worldview.[115] As in other Romanticist writings of the time, the plea for radical individualism is paired here with a longing for security through religious devotion, illustrating the tension between a desire for social transformation (that allows individual freedom) and a return to stabilizing structures (religion). Resonating with, for example, linguistic theories of the period, the Orient emerges as the place of origin, which is, however, explicitly evoked as Europe's opposite, from which Europeans can learn.[116] Finding the solution to contemporary European issues in a timeless yet clearly premodern Orient conveys a nostalgia that is also a utopian vision, one that emerges from this fusion of temporal and spatial projection.

Novalis also imagined the Orient as a counterimage to Europe. In his novel *Heinrich von Ofterdingen* (1800) he attempts to humanize Oriental individuals and questions hostile antagonisms between East and West. Comparable to the tale by Günderrode, the Orient in Novalis's *Bildungsroman* emerges as a timeless and peaceful space. The narrator juxtaposes the violence of bloodthirsty crusaders with the sincerity and genuineness of a young Arab woman called Zulima. The Orient in this vision appears as a paradisiacal place and also a just order held together by compassionate religious values.[117] Other writings by Novalis, most notably his essay "Die Christenheit oder Europa" (1799), also express this "nostalgia for the good old days," ultimately aiming to present Germany as the cosmopolitan counterpart to imperial France.[118]

Goethe's *West-östlicher Divan* (1819) is clearly a document of Philorientalism in its enthusiasm for Arabic and Persian poetic forms, imagery, and stories.[119] At the same time, and especially so in the annotations he appended to his poetry, he articulates views that are dismissive of the Middle East and Islam. With regard to the poems, Anil Bhatti stresses that Goethe practices a "kind of cultural mimesis . . . in his appropriation of Hafiz and the Orient" but "does not surrender his Western identity."[120] Goethe's poem "Hegire" at the beginning of the *West-Östlicher Divan* illustrates the multiple function of the Orient in Goethe's work. Here the Orient is entirely associated with metaphors of patriarchal order, stability, sensuality, and pristine religiosity. A contrasting image to the threat of revolutionary upheaval brought about by the French Revolution and occupation of Germany, Goethe's Orient expresses a longing for a prerevolutionary and premodern paternal order that allows for male independence. The spirituality evoked is clearly not the conventional religiosity of institutionalized Christianity; in this regard Goethe's quarrel with Islam mirrors his quarrel with Christianity and, as Bernd Auerochs has argued, with any form of revealed religion.[121] The *Divan* touches upon a wide range of philosophical and social questions, but, regardless of these additional dimensions, the poems clearly convey a desire for patriarchal order and male freedom, and the Orient is the locus that allows for the articulation of this desire.

Although the reception of Goethe's collection was limited to educated circles and was never significant, *West-Östlicher Divan* contributed to the ongoing creation of a romantic and exoticized image of the Middle East in German highbrow culture. Often engaging irony and satire in his appropriating and performative narrative gestures, Goethe contributed to shaping an image of the Orient as the space in which paternal, aristocratic, sensual, and mystical desires could be articulated. Goethe's invocation of the dichotomy between East and West engages in acculturation and appropriation, in which West masquerades as East, is inspired by East, but clearly molds East for its own Western purposes.[122] Shafiq Shamel has pointed out, however, that, in spite of his masquerade and appropriation, Goethe did in fact capture aspects of Hafiz's poetry that are essential features of the Persian poet's work.[123] As mentioned before, it is noteworthy that Goethe's *Divan* has seen an overwhelmingly positive reception in the Middle East and in Asian countries.[124] As Anil Bhatti has shown with regard to Muhammad Iqbal's response to Goethe's writings, the *Divan*'s reception history is itself an example of appropriation.[125]

A variation on the themes of nostalgia and personal quest is articulated in poetry by Annette Elisabeth von Droste-Hülshoff. In her collection *Klänge aus dem Orient* (1838) the poet voices her desire for a just and compassionate world that is attentive to the needs of individuals by drawing on vocabulary associated with the Orient. In "Der Barmekiden Untergang" and "Bajazeth" she uses popular legends and images of violence and greed to raise issues concerning the transient nature of power. Other poems in the collection, such as "O Nacht!" "Herrlich," and "Herzlich," do not evoke the Orient explicitly.[126] Most of the short poems meditate on themes such as trust, care, and safety, revealing the poet's concern for the ethical realm and subjective emotions.

One of the most popular forms used to express the various changes associated with the political and social transformation in the postrevolutionary period was the fairy tale. This genre was well established in Germany after 1780. The Oriental fairy tale was part of the larger corpus of *Kunstmärchen* (literary fairy tale). From Wieland and Goethe to Wackenroder and later Hofmannsthal, German writers were inspired by Oriental tales, such as those included in the collection *One Thousand and One Nights,* and by, among others, British and French translations, adaptations, and new creations in this genre. In addition to negotiating changes generally associated with the early stage of modernization, the German fairy tale, as well as various forms of mythical writing, emerged as a genre facilitating the articulation of a German national consciousness.[127]

The Enlightenment fairy tale, such as those included in the collection *Dschinnistan oder auserlesene Feen- und Geistermärchen* (1786–89) by Christoph Martin Wieland, was committed to a didactic message about the improvement of political and social issues. The Romanticist Oriental fairy tale, however, reflected the multilayered ideals of another generation, which saw itself in opposition to the social goals of Enlightenment writers. Romanticist writers focused on the development of the individual and aimed at drawing a more complex image of the relation of the individual to society. As illustrated in the discussion of Günderrode and Goethe, Romanticist writers often expressed their desire for a stable order through a turn to the religious and/or a nostalgia for a patriarchal and aristocratic order. The Oriental fairy tale emerged as an ideal genre to articulate these visions: the possibilities provided by the movement between the realm of the real and that of the supernatural allowed for explorations of psychological development, and the clichéd Oriental setting conveyed premodern paternal and aristocratic structures.

Anke Bosse has shown that the Orientalist vocabulary in Ludwig Tieck's narratives *Almansur* (1790) and *Abdallah* (1792), for example, was limited, and that the descriptions of landscapes unite elements of European and Oriental vegetation, such as palms imagined next to birch trees.[128] Bosse argues, however, that this blending of landscapes was deliberate and occurred mostly in the supernatural world. Similar to Günderrode's tale "Geschichte eines Braminen," Almansur wants to escape the realm of the social, and, after several narrative shifts, the seeming message of the tale—namely, the responsibility of the individual to society—is reversed: the narrative ends with a vision of blissful hermitage. Tieck's stance in this tale thus mirrors Günderrode's plea for the primacy of subjectivity in "Geschichte eines Braminen." The tension between the desire to return to society, however, as articulated earlier in Tieck's short narrative, and the final vision of hermitage remains unresolved.

Tieck's narrative *Abdallah,* which is more aptly described as a gothic novel and might have been influenced by the novel *Vathek* by William Thomas Beckford, shares several structural elements with *Almansur.*[129] The protagonist's confusion articulates the loss of trust in the paternal, aristocratic order, and the inability to find solace in religion and love results in aporia. But this loss, or lack, is precisely what this narrative shares with other texts of the time that are staged in the Orient: namely, the dilemma of how to bring the ethical quest of the individual, who seeks stability and orientation, to a successful resolution. "Die Brüder" (1795), a brief narrative by Tieck that is also set in the Arab/Persian Middle East, ends on a more positive note. As Birgit Tautz has shown, Wilhelm Heinrich Wackenroder's fairy tale "Ein wunderbares morgenländisches Mährchen von einem nackten Heiligen" (1799) also draws on the trope of the Orient as a timeless place. Wackenroder's tale has elicited numerous interpretations,[130] but here what is noteworthy is that the tale identifies the Orient as a place of truth and insight about life, even—and in line with the Romanticist critique of Enlightenment's emphasis on reason—beyond that which can be understood by reason.[131]

A curious tale staged in the Ottoman Orient is contained in Johann Peter Hebel's *Schatzkästlein des Rheinischen Hausfreundes* (1811). The brief story, "Der kluge Sultan," examines the notion of the just ruler and the relationship between political power and religiously based notions of justice. Several narrative shifts allow for an easy transportation of the Oriental tale into a German context: the Turkish sultan is repeatedly called "Kaiser," and, even though reference is clearly made to the Koran and to Muslims, this sultan/kaiser does not worship in a mosque "on a Friday" but, rather, in a church. The genial tone of the story, which pits a generous ruler against an impoverished man, conveys a sense that all is well with state and religion: people are ruled by considerate leaders, and all are provided for by a framework that reconciles principles of justice and religion. Another variation of late Romanticist Orientalism is Franz Grillparzer's *Der Traum, ein Leben* (1834). The play, inspired by Pedro Calderón de la Barca's *La vida es sueño* and Voltaire's "Le blanc et le noir," and displaying Grillparzer's familiarity with Persian myth, creates a fairytale-like atmosphere set in a Persian environment in which dream and reality intermingle. Rustan, the play's hero, returns to his modest but peaceful existence after encountering the perils that accompany a politically and socially engaged life.

The literary writings discussed here use the Orient as a vehicle to express a longing for an order that is utopian in its desire for individual development yet also reactionary in its nostalgia for traditional normativity, whether primarily male, aristocratic, or religious. Most of the writings employing the Oriental setting in this way date from the beginning to the middle of the nineteenth century. Later in the century, similar concerns are raised in Hugo von Hofmannsthal's *Das Märchen der 672. Nacht,* first published in 1895. Other works by Hofmannsthal also engaged the Orient to meditate upon contemporary issues.[132]

The problematization of traditional gender roles and sexual normativity through Oriental tropes was widespread in German (and European) culture at the turn of the century. Paul Scheerbart's stylistically challenging novels (often labeled Expressionist but which also foreshadow Dadaist aesthetics) *Tarub, Bagdads berühmte Köchin: Arabischer Kulturroman* (1897) and *Der Tod der Barmekiden: Arabischer Haremsroman* (1897) and the narratives contained in *Machtspäße: Arabische Novellen* (1904) draw generously on clichés about Middle Eastern societies in order to articulate emotional, sexual, and power-related desires, views on emancipation, and a critique of Germany's political and social order.[133] More than three decades later, Joseph Roth's *Die Geschichte der 1002. Nacht* (1939) follows a similar approach by using a story frame involving Oriental characters in order to paint a satirical portrait of life in Vienna and Austria more generally.

For Hofmannsthal and Scheerbart the Orient was a means to express resistance to and critique of modern rationality and the multiple changes brought on by modernization, whether with regard to transforming gender relations, democratic aspirations, or conservative politics. In writings of this kind the Orient is not the other but is, rather, the problematic self and thus functions as the polar opposite to the image of the Orient as alternative, as ideal self (such as in Novalis and Goethe). With the radical changes brought to art by modernist aesthetics, Oriental metaphors again took on new meanings when primitivism, cubism, and expressionism changed the expressive vocabulary. Dada artists, for example, made use of Oriental metaphors to articulate their commentary on a dissociated world that no longer guaranteed easy access to meaning. Hugo Ball's poem "Karawane" (1917) consists of graphic and phonetic units that suggest associations with Oriental or African languages but—apart from the Spanish *habla,* which stresses the theme of speaking—do not convey any sort of coherent meaning. This gesture, which reflects upon contemporary developments, invokes the presumed inaccessibility of other cultures to make a statement about the incomprehensibility of the modern world.

In the 1920s and into the 1940s Oriental imagery was picked up primarily in films, travel accounts, operas, and popular fiction, but so-called highbrow literature generally did not draw on Oriental themes to comment on the changing political and social order. An exception is Thomas Mann's tetralogy *Joseph und seine Brüder* (1933–43). Based on intensive study of Middle Eastern myth and religion, Mann takes up the cultural material to remark on contemporary Western and even, more broadly, human history and to communicate his idea of humanism.[134]

One group of texts is located somewhere along the boundary that distinguishes works dealing primarily with domestic issues from those that comment more directly on actual relations with the Middle East. Wilhelm Hauff's collection, published as an annual *Märchen-Almanach* with the subtitles *Die Karawane, Der Scheik von Allessandria und seine Sklaven,* and *Das Wirtshaus im Spessart* in 1826–28, contains tales staged in the Orient that continue to be popular to this day. As Andrea Polaschegg points out, the tales share various epistemological shifts, all of which amount to an erasure of the boundaries between Orient and Occident. Several tales are located exclusively in the Orient, but others, told by both Western and Eastern narrators, relate to events occurring in both Orient and Occident ("Die Geschichte von der abgehauenen Hand") or exclusively in German areas ("Der Zwerg Nase," "Das kalte Herz"). These shifts and erasures of boundaries, like those in works by Tieck and Hebel, occur not only in terms of the geography of the texts but also with regard to aspects of landscape, specific cultural items and motifs, and the question of historical accuracy. According to Polaschegg, Hauff pursued an intercultural concept with his narratives.[135] Indeed, Hauff achieved a remarkable degree of alienation and an appropriation of the different and strange in his tales. But, as Polaschegg points out, this intercultural change of perspective does not entail a critique of the self, as Montesquieu's *Lettres Persanes* and texts written in this tradition attempt to achieve.[136] Polaschegg concludes that Hauff simply wanted to generate a disorienting effect that would draw in his readership, and this approach, she argues, is responsible for the continuing popularity of the tales.[137] Pushing the argument further, I suggest that Hauff's narrative constructions allow for appropriation and mastery of the Orient. Characters move in and out of the Oriental space precisely because that is how, as Polaschegg points out, the Orient becomes comprehensible and accessible.

The sense of normalcy that results from the tearing-down of boundaries between East and West speaks to the intensified actual interaction between Europe and the Middle East in the first few decades of the nineteenth century. Written only a few years before the French occupation of Algiers but during the decades after the growing political, economic, and cultural exchange between the spheres of influence following the French invasion of Egypt, Hauff's tales mark a historical moment that is defined by ambiguity but also reflects, or foreshadows, appropriation.

Articulating Ideologies of Superiority

Another group of German texts about the Middle East functioned both with regard to internal and external events. These texts are distinct in that they situate Germany in the position that Edward Said described as "positional superiority."[138] It is this group of texts that most closely resembles the type of Orientalist writings identified by Said as supporting imperialist actions (in spite of his own claim that Germans did not participate in this endeavor).

In the first decades of the nineteenth century, progress was regularly associated with political emancipation. European colonial intervention was thus celebrated as liberating transformation. Karoline von Günderrode, one of the earliest voices commenting on the French occupation of Egypt as a positive moment, heralds the French presence as the beginning of an age of freedom from servitude in "Buonaparte in Egypten" (1799). This poem reflects her enthusiasm for the French Revolution and associates Napoleon's troops with forces of light that liberate an enslaved people from the forces of darkness. The poem "Aegypten" (1806) conveys an image of the country as stuck in a state of lethargy. Another poem by Günderrode also associates dramatic social and political changes with the Middle East but in an entirely different way. "Mahomets Traum in der Wüste" (1802–4) evokes the moment in which Muhammad receives his calling to articulate a vision of dramatic change in the future ("Der Zukunft Geist will er beschwören"), which includes violent images of destruction through fire and light of all that is "impure."[139] Here Islam is associated with contemporary revolutionary forces and takes on a positive transformative energy. Whereas the poem "Aegypten" mirrors the image of lethargy painted in "Buonaparte in Egypten," Günderrode's poem "Der Nil" (1806), clearly inspired by Goethe's "Mahomets Gesang" (1774), emphasizes the transformative effect of the river on the soil of the country. Read together, these four poems endow the Middle East with contradictory qualities, from lethargy and enslavement to transformation and rejuvenation. In light of Günderrode's support of the French Revolution and given that Germany was occupied by France, in these poems Egypt/the Middle East stands as a placeholder for Germany. The confluence of images in support of revolutionary transformation, however, also works to support the colonial project.[140]

Antisemitism, nationalism, and religious zeal inform Achim von Arnim's narrative *Isabella von Ägypten* (1812). This tale is set in the sixteenth century and revolves around a love story between Archduke Charles, who is later appointed Holy Roman emperor as Charles V, and a beautiful Gypsy woman named Isabella. The complicated plot involving the supernatural, including the magical powers of an old Jew, culminates in Charles V liberating the Gypsies, who return to their ancestral homeland, Egypt. The message promotes the idea of cultural incompatibility ("but they do not belong to our European world"), in particular the return of Oriental peoples to their ancestral homeland, and a notion of proper Christianity (namely, Catholicism) and ethical behavior.[141] The incompatibility of European and Oriental peoples, in spite of an idealization of Gypsies, is highlighted in the narrative through the ominous role of Jews, who are presented as being responsible for the suffering of the noble Gypsies and generally characterized by drawing on stereotypical antisemitic rhetoric. As Wilhelm Solms has argued, von Arnim's idealizing distortion of Gypsies may be seen as "a model for 'the Final Solution to the Gypsy question.'"[142]

One tale included in Wilhelm Hauff's cycle "Der Scheich von Allessandria und seine Sklaven" (1827) also contains an antisemitic message in a plot associated with the Middle East. "Abner, der Jude, der nichts gesehen hat" is staged in Morocco, and its Jewish protagonist brings about his own downfall as he tries to outsmart the arbitrary and unjust rulings of the local "Emperor Muley Ismael." The story is introduced, however, as a parable, and the Jew's fate is presented as being deserved.[143] The antisemitic message resonates with another text by Hauff published in the same year, the novella *Jud Süß*. Hauff's story about Abner uses the Orient as a setting but not in order to discredit it; rather, the Orient is described with more sympathy than the Jewish character. Hauff's short narrative thus differs from other writings of the period. The "Orientalness" of Jews, particularly of Jewish women, was a familiar topos of nineteenth-century antisemitic writings; in Hauff's *Jud Süß,* for example, the protagonist's sister Lea is portrayed as an Oriental beauty.[144] This trope appears in Friedrich Hebbel's play *Judith* (1840) and Franz Grillparzer's play *Die Jüdin von Toledo* (1872) and later in Lion Feuchtwanger's novel *Die Jüdin von Toledo* (1955).[145]

Linking Jews with their Oriental origin was implicit in anti-Judaism of earlier centuries, but in the nineteenth century this direct association with Oriental cultural, ethnic, and then racial difference was the foundation on which racial antisemitism was built. In his 1803 pamphlet *Erklärung an das Publikum über meine Schrift "Wider die Juden,"* the Berlin lawyer C. W. F. Grattenauer declared Jews in Germany to be an "Oriental foreign people."[146] More than seventy years later, the notion of the Jews' Oriental origin became central to the debate over the question of whether German Jews could become an integral part of German society. Clearly, the association of Jews with an Oriental origin functioned to emphasize their radical difference in the German context, and the message was one of incompatibility and exclusion, in spite of the allure contained in the idea, for example, of the beautiful Jewess. Being Oriental thus implied negative symbolic capital, just like being Jewish symbolized negative symbolic capital, and both negative images worked together to convey an ideology of exclusion.

It might come as a surprise to some that Goethe, who is widely depicted as one of the proponents of tolerance toward Islam, produced one of the most problematic texts in this regard. In 1799, at the behest of Duke Carl August von Sachsen-Weimar, Goethe translated Voltaire's 1736 play *Le fanatisme ou Mahomet le Prophète.* The negative views contained in Goethe's adaptation can largely be accredited to Voltaire's original; the French author's play, however, was conceived as a critique of religious fanaticism of all kinds, which was well understood by his like-minded contemporaries. Goethe altered several passages of Voltaire's text to lessen the virulent depiction of the prophet; nevertheless, the changes Goethe made were rather insignificant, and the result was a German text that portrayed the prophet Muhammad as a questionable and lecherous character. Herder's indignant reaction to the premiere of the play in January of 1800 is telling: "I would have never believed Goethe capable of such sinning against history (he turned Mahomet into a rough simplistic fraud, murderer, and lecher) and against humanity."[147]

But Goethe's adaptation of Voltaire's play is not the only instance in which Goethe voices views that condemn aspects of Middle Eastern cultures in clichéd ways. Goethe's appendix to the *West-östlicher Divan* stands in stark contrast especially to those poems in the collection that express the affinity and compatibility of Eastern and Western thought. The appendix is proof that the poet himself considered the reality of the Middle East, as he understood it, relevant to a proper understanding of his poetry. Goethe explicitly seeks to establish a link between the ancient and the contemporary Middle East/Orient.[148] Overall, Islam is depicted as a force precluding any form of progress (130). Middle Eastern peoples, particularly Arabs, are associated with cruelty (130,

134) and hostility to intellectual thought and science (146). Persians, on the other hand, are depicted as "peaceful and civilized" (134). This positive view of Persians is in line with widespread views of the era associating Persians with Indo-European/Germanic cultures. Goethe describes Persian poetry as the true inspiration for his own writing (134). Negative aspects of Persians include feminization and a tendency to lie (136), and Arabs are described as prone to sensuality, idleness, and laziness (145). Goethe posits naïveté as another characteristic found throughout the Orient but especially in Persia (232). A crass contrast to Europeans is drawn when Goethe repeats dominant views linking Middle Eastern forms of government to despotism (169). Drawing on two unnamed English and German sources to solidify his argument, Goethe identifies the despotic mind-set of Orientals as the key impediment to cross-cultural understanding (171–75). Zafer Şenocak, in his essay "Literarische Übersetzung: Brücke oder Schwert," highlights the othering that Goethe practices in the *Noten und Abhandlungen.* According to Şenocak, Goethe articulated a set of characteristics that positions the Orient and the Oriental as diametrically opposed to Europe and the European.[149]

In disseminating these views, Goethe relied on the works of Orientalist scholars and translators, reflecting dominant opinions that were circulating across Europe and were shaped by the emerging Orientalist sciences. But it is noteworthy that he distances himself from new insights whenever he deems it necessary: Goethe declares that the writings of Orientalists confuse our thinking, and, in a refusal to rethink deep structures of key beliefs, he defends the "religious enthusiasm" of the Crusades, particularly their defense of civilized Europe, against the new knowledge that has come to Europe through familiarity with Oriental sources and also travel accounts (225–26). Goethe's defensive gesture seeks to elevate Europe's status in the world. By systematically relegating non-European cultures to an earlier time period, blocking out contemporary developments, and privileging a narrative of progress that culminates in enlightened Europe, Goethe's writings function to prop up Eurocentric claims to a superior position toward the Orient. Todd Kontje suggests that Goethe was displaying an "ironic awareness of the Western desire for Oriental origins," which "casts a kinder light on his imperial imagination."[150] While this assessment might be a useful way of looking at the *Divan*'s poetry, it certainly does not hold with regard to the *Noten und Abhandlungen.*

Until the founding of the first German nation-state, nationalist desire and resistance to foreign influence were pivotal topics in Germany. Germany's support of Greek and other nationalist movements mirrored its own aspirations for independence and statehood. In this regard a crucial chapter in German anti–Middle Eastern rhetoric was inspired by the Greek struggle for independence, which ended with Greek independence in 1832, when Greece became the first of the European Ottoman territories to achieve this goal. Philhellenism was a trans-European movement, born out of scholarly interest in antiquity but also in the context of Europe's economic and political expansionism, particularly into the territories of the Ottoman Empire. Europe's and Germany's enthusiasm for things Greek dates back to the last decades of the eighteenth century. Suzanne Marchand's eminent study on German Philhellenism begins its inquiry into the changing contours and functions of Philhellenism with the publications of Johann Joachim Winckelmann in the 1750s and 1760s.[151] The tradition of projecting German ideals of nationhood and nation-state onto the Greek foil was already well established by the time the Greek war for independence began; the anti-Ottoman revolts of the 1770s in particular had fueled German empathy for the Greek struggle. In the aftermath of the French Revolution and Germany's occupation by the French, the Greek struggle served as a vehicle to articulate Germany's ideas of nationhood and state. Friedrich Hölderlin's epistolary novel *Hyperion oder Der Eremit in Griechenland* (1797–99) exemplifies this desire for an ideal state. The narrative focuses on the Greek youth Hyperion, who, together with his friend Alabanda, joins the Greek struggle, only to be disappointed because of the violence he witnesses. The narrative ends with the protagonist withdrawing from the realm of the social, to spend a life in contemplative unity with nature. As such, Hölderlin works through his disappointment with the violence following the French Revolution by projecting the plot onto the Greek struggle for freedom.

Whereas Hölderlin ultimately rejects violent struggle, the support in Germany for armed resistance to Ottoman rule swelled in the nineteenth century. Anti-Ottoman propaganda was widespread throughout Europe. As Andrea Polaschegg points out, public discourse and political action were often at odds; the Habsburgs, for example, worried that the Greek struggle would inspire groups contained in its multicultural empire. In 1797, for example, Austrian officials arrested the Greek resistance fighter Rigas Feraios in Trieste, who was handed over to the Ottomans and killed shortly thereafter. Marchand argues that German authorities were apprehensive "that the Greek revolt would breathe new life into nationalist and democratic endeavors."[152] As a result, "the authorities issued prohibitions on the mustering of volunteers, on the formation of associations for the purpose of financing the cause, and even, in some states, on public expression of support for the Greeks."[153] Over time the German support of the Greeks lost its domestic dimension as an oppositional movement promoting democratic ideals and was integrated into foreign policy that operated in favor of Greek independence from the Ottomans.[154] The Greek struggle ended successfully with Greek independence and a German aristocrat as Greek king; European powers appointed Otto von Wittelsbach, the son of King Ludwig I of Bavaria, who had been particularly supportive of the Greek cause.

Regardless of the initially reluctant support of European state powers for the Greek struggle for independence, the Greek war against the Ottomans produced a flood of writings in Germany. Punitive measures taken by the Ottomans, in particular the massacre of Christians in Chios in 1822, received widespread attention and furthered literary output: "No fewer than 14 plays, 11 collections of poetry, 71 songs, poems, and ballads, as well as 22 novels" were, according to Andrea Polaschegg, the direct outcome of the philhellenic movement."[155] Many of these texts contained virulent anti-Turkish rhetoric. Wilhelm Müller, a popular poet of the period whose poems and songs celebrated, among other topics, patriotism, hiking, and wine drinking, was also known as "Griechenmüller" because of the large number of texts written in support of the Greek struggle for independence.[156] He published six cycles of "Griechenlieder" between 1821 and 1827, amounting to fifty-two poems. Müller repeatedly faced censorship when he attempted to publish these poems in support of a national liberation movement; the issue alarmed reactionary forces in Germany. The public, however, reacted enthusiastically, and the texts were widely circulated and translated into other languages, such as French.[157]

Whereas earlier poems celebrated Greek culture and spirit in a more general manner, the poems increasingly included concrete references to historical events. "Der Mainottin Unterricht" (1821) talks about "bloodied Turkish skulls" and accuses "Turks, who murdered your father."[158] One poem, "Byron" (1824), celebrates the British poet, who was the most famous Western European celebrity to die in the Greek struggle for independence.[159] Evoking crusading rhetoric, Turks are portrayed as "heathen" in several of the songs. The last of Müller's cycles dedicated to the Greek struggle is entitled "Missolunghi," an allusion to an especially gruesome chapter in the conflict between Greeks and Ottomans. The poem "Die Veste des Himmels," again evoking violent crusading rhetoric, envisions Greece as battling an onslaught from Asia and Africa.[160] As "city of the lord," Missolunghi stands metonymically for Jerusalem, thus reinforcing the crusading spirit of the battle. Müller was not the only poet of the Romantic period who took to the pen to fight for Greek independence. Jean Paul's short narrative "Gesichte einer Griechischen Mutter. Ein Traum in den letzten Tagen des Juli-Monats" (1821) and Adelbert von Chamisso's poetic cycle "Chios" (1829) also contributed to disseminating anti-

Turkish views, often imitating the spirit of the Crusades by foregrounding Christian motifs. The Greek situation allowed Germans to voice their own longing for a nation-state and a return to Christian religiosity.

In the novella *Die Judenbuche* (1842) by Annette von Droste-Hülshoff the evocation of Turkey functions to highlight the criminality and asocial character of the main culprit. After the murder of the Jew Aaron, Friedrich Mergel and his sidekick Johannes Niemand disappear from the scene of the crime; twenty-six years later Niemand returns to the village and is accepted back into the community. According to his account, he and Friedrich Mergel had spent years in captivity after being captured in a battle fighting for the Austrians against the Turks. Niemand claims that "the Turks keep us Christians just like dogs."[161] At the end of the novella Niemand is recognized as Mergel by a scar on his body but only after his dead body is found dangling from the same tree under which the murdered Aaron had been found. Friedrich Mergel's transgressions are thus underscored by associating him with Turkey, whereby Turkey symbolizes a space outside of the realm of acceptable ethics, religion, and social norms.

Racist and nationalist thought pervades Conrad Ferdinand Meyer's novella *Der Heilige* (The Saint, 1879). Here the problematic aspects of the main character, Thomas Becket, in particular his ambiguity, are explained through his partial Arab descent. Throughout the text references are made that associate Arabs with lying and deceit. "What [Meyer] endeavored to illuminate," Robert Holub has argued, "was why and how this figure was ambiguous."[162] In this regard "Becket's 'Oriental' background crops up frequently in the course of the novella, serving as a convenient explanation for motives and actions."[163] Meyer's rendering of the Arab falls into the tradition of medieval anti-Muslim rhetoric, according to which Muhammad is an impostor; this image of the Arab is a far cry from the heroic Bedouin familiar from Romantic writings. In fact, Meyer's portrayal of Arab characteristics resonates perhaps more directly with contemporary antisemitic rhetoric (cf. the lying and trickery of Abner in Hauff's tale). Cruelty, however, was a trope associated with Arabs that gained notoriety in the second half of the nineteenth century.

The work of Karl May, the most widely read German author, employs the full repertoire of Middle Eastern tropes available at the time. The *Orientzyklus* (1881–88), for example, is an extended detective story told in six volumes in which the protagonist, the German writer Kara Ben Nemsi Effendi, and several Middle Eastern friends track down a criminal organization spread throughout the entire Ottoman Empire. The hero's interventions into local Ottoman matters reflect Germany's imperialist aspirations, in particular German political involvement in the Balkan crisis of the 1870s, which ultimately resulted in further German economic expansion in the area. The novels' discussion of character traits and behavior of peoples living in the Ottoman Empire, such as Turks and Arabs, also helped to define the self-image of the newly founded German nation.[164] May consulted countless anthropological, geographical, sociological, and cultural sources about areas that he used as settings for his literary plots. He drew on both academic and popular writings and often altered only little in his adaptation of the material. Hauff and Bodenstedt, among others, clearly informed the style of May's novels. The views expressed by May (and C. F. Meyer) can also be found in the works of contemporary geographers and historians, such as Friedrich Christoph Schlosser (*Weltgeschichte in zusammenhängender Erzählung,* 1815–41), Friedrich von Hellwald (*Die Erde und ihre Völker. Ein Geographisches Hausbuch,* 1877), and Leopold von Ranke (*Weltgeschichte,* vol. 8, 1887). It should be noted that several works by Zionist German-Jewish authors also employed the Middle East as a foil to articulate notions about European and modern superiority. Theodor Herzl's novel *Altneuland* (1902), while envisioning peaceful coexistence between Arabs and Jews, promotes the creation of the Jewish state by drawing on ideas about the redemptive aspects of modern civilization.

Negative stereotypes of Oriental characters continued to be disseminated widely in popular culture and film at the turn of the century. Through his analysis of the repertoire of the *Bänkelsang,* Tom Cheesman has shown how negative images of Turks survived into the time of the Weimar Republic.[165] The images functioned as expressions of the problematic self and also as portrayals that legitimated European rule over the Orient. But, with regard to literature, the Islamic Middle East seems to have become less attractive as a foil for self-expression; Germany, the United States, and Europe were the preferred geographical loci chosen by writers associated with the literary movements—naturalism, expressionism, and symbolism—in vogue at the turn of the century. On the other hand, China, India, and the South Pacific became fashionable with authors such as Hermann Hesse, Bertolt Brecht, Anna Seghers, and Gottfried Benn.

One eminent writer who continued to make use of Middle Eastern imagery is Thomas Mann. Throughout his oeuvre Mann exploited notions of foreign physiognomy to express his ideas about ideal Germanness, ethical behavior, and social order.[166] Slavic features, Gypsy and Jewish characteristics, and the "southern" in general signal alarming developments and identify ethically inferior characters. His novella *Wälsungenblut* (1905) communicates the Jewishness of its main protagonists by associating their environment with Orientalness. The reader is asked to imagine the villa's interior as adorned by an "aged pale prayer rug," the entire space decorated with heavy carpets and the air "impregnated by sweet and exotic perfume."[167] Siegmund's foreignness is emphasized through the description of his thick, black curls, which are "violently" combed over to one side, and his overall hairiness (430). Sieglinde wears a golden ring with a pearl that lies on her forehead (430–31). To emphasize her foreignness, the narrator compares Sieglinde to an Egyptian statue (456). Without explicitly identifying them as Jewish, the narrator highlights the foreignness of the siblings by focusing on their physical features (462).[168] In the novella the Oriental (read Jewish) alterity of the siblings functions to explain their immoral behavior.

Another interesting case is Franz Werfel's novel *Die vierzig Tage des Musa Dagh* (1933), through which the author attempted to draw the German public's attention to the Ottoman pogroms against the Armenians while at the same time creating a prophetic text with regard to the fate of European Jewry. Werfel's outlook reveals an ambivalence regarding both East and West. As Donna K. Heizer points out, "Werfel constructs a hierarchy of Otherness" and "seems to advocate the assimilation of Oriental culture into Western culture by making the most positively depicted character an assimilated Oriental."[169] In this regard Werfel's own conversion from Judaism to Christianity reflects ideas expressed in the novel; he elevates Christian Armenians over "barbaric" Muslim Turks.[170] But Werfel also locates the seed of Eastern corruption in the adoption of "Western values: the secularism, materialism, and nationalism that the Young Turks championed," and implicates Armenians in the creation of "their own colonization and genocide."[171] As a result, the novel's message is primarily pro-Christian and pro-Western but also advocates a separation of East and West (perhaps an indication of Werfel's ambivalence regarding his conversion).

Critical Consciousness

Ludwig Tieck's play *Alla-Moddin* (1791) is staged in "Manilla, einer spanischen Besitzung in Ost-Indien" and is thus not immediately relevant to the exploration of texts that refer to the Middle East. The play's anticolonialist stance and critique of Christian missionaries, however, is noteworthy, as King Alla-Moddin is portrayed as a positive figure in contrast to the Spanish colonizers and missionaries. *Alla-Moddin* shows that a critique of colonialism and missionizing, particularly by the Jesuit order, was already articulated around 1800.

The play ends with one of its central characters, Valmont, renouncing life in Europe, with its "cruel tyranny," in order to live a paradisiacal agrarian utopia on "Suhlu."[172] A play by August von Kotzebue, *Die Kreuzfahrer* (1802), also displays positions that scrutinize European ideas of superiority; in this text Kotzebue is critical of the Crusades and paints a compassionate picture of Muslim characters. Tieck's and Kotzebue's texts indicate that critical consciousness regarding the relationship between European and non-European societies and a critique of colonial expansion already existed in late eighteenth- and early nineteenth-century Germany. While these writings did not reflect dominant opinions, they document that writers and other intellectuals of the period recognized the problematic aspects of European/German actions and representational practices.

Conceived in clear opposition to the image of Muhammad that was conveyed through Goethe's 1799 translation of Voltaire's play, Karoline von Günderrode's play *Mahomed, der Prophet von Mekka* (1805) communicates a positive view of the prophet. Muhammad is depicted as a revolutionary but also visionary and just peacemaker. Similar to her poems glorifying the French invasion of Egypt as an event bringing modernity to the country, the play considers Muhammad in the role of the revolutionary leader who introduces a new order to the Middle East. Resonating with her poem "Mahomets Traum in der Wüste" (ca. 1804), in *Mahomet* revolutionary change comes from within the Middle East. Both the poem and the play render a more positive image of Islam than Günderrode develops elsewhere. She voices criticism, however, concerning the social role of women, whom Günderrode depicts as victims of men's grander plans. Similarly, love emerges as a casualty of political development, to which it is subordinate.[173] Even in light of this critique, which is aimed at patriarchy in general, Günderrode's engagement with the Muhammad material takes a decisively more sympathetic approach toward the prophet of Islam than Goethe's did.

Translations and adaptations contributed widely to the growing knowledge about Middle Eastern literary forms and, in the case of Friedrich Rückert and August von Platen, clearly derived from positive identification with Middle Eastern cultures. That Rückert's enthusiasm and deep understanding of Persian and Arabic poetry coincided with a critical view of European superiority is confirmed by the fact that his play *Cristofero Colombo* (1845) contains a scathing critique of the unfortunate impact of Christianization on Native Americans. Similarly, Ferdinand Freiligrath, whose outspoken support of democratic and other liberation movements led him to idealize Native Americans ("Audubon," 1833), glorifies Bedouin Arabs by associating them with freedom and courage ("'Wär ich im Bann von Mekkas Toren,'" 1836; "Gesichte des Reisenden," 1836). Freiligrath comments critically on the French occupation of Algiers ("Der Scheik am Sinai," 1830), although the poem also eulogizes Napoleon, thereby undercutting any general condemnation of colonial occupation.[174]

One of the most exciting texts that used Islam to comment favorably on political circumstances in Germany is Bettina von Arnim's *Gespräche mit Dämonen* (Conversations with Demons, 1852). This publication resumes the radical political critique that von Arnim had voiced in *Dies Buch gehört dem König* (1843) and also in the fragment known as *Armenbuch* (1845), both of which pleaded for social justice and political emancipation. *Gespräche mit Dämonen* is exceptional in that it is dedicated to "The Spirit of Islam," which is specified in the subtitle as "vertreten durch den großmüthigen Abdul-Medschid-Khan, Kaiser der Osmanen." That is, Islam is represented here by the contemporary Ottoman sultan Abdülmecid I, who ruled from 1839 to 1861 and who drew on the expertise of a highly capable group of statesmen, including Mustafa Reşid Pasha. Abdülmecid I is generally credited with instituting the large-scale reforms of the Ottoman Empire that began the era of *Tanzimat* (Reorganization). He was also known for his humanitarian gestures to Europeans; in 1845 he granted support to the Irish afflicted by the Great Famine. He also offered political asylum to revolutionaries of the 1848 revolutions, particularly those from Poland and Hungary.[175] Clearly, his political stance impressed Bettina von Arnim.

The book amounts to a disputation involving various voices, such as the Sleeping King, a Demon, and several peoples, who debate the current state of affairs in Europe and particularly the notion of just government. At the end of the text the Spirit of Islam appears to express a final vision of peace and justice. In a key scene, the voice of "Völker" (Peoples) praises Islam as embodying a political utopia.[176] Other passages also contain implicit references to contemporary events, such as the political turmoil in post-1848 Europe and the asylum policies of the Ottoman sultan.

Throughout his life, but especially in the 1820s, Heinrich Heine engaged with fictional and nonfictional material from and about the Islamic Middle East.[177] Several critics have pointed out that Heine created Oriental masks in writings that focus on cultural and religious conflict.[178] The most prominent text in this regard is the play *Almansor* (1821), which depicts the suffering of the Spanish Muslim population under the Inquisition and glorifies the centuries of Muslim rule in Spain. The play contains the often-cited and prophetic words "Dort, wo man Bücher / Verbrennt, verbrennt man auch am Ende Menschen"

("Where they burn books, they will, at the end, also burn people").[179] Heine consulted a wide range of historical studies to educate himself about the situation of Muslims in Spain, and dedicated a couple of poems, "Ständchen eines Mauren" (1821) and "Almansor" (1825), to this topic.[180] The latter poem deplores the Christian transformation of Muslim cultural and religious heritage through the figure of Almansor, who may be understood as a "converso" and as such shares the fundamental dilemma of Heine, who converted to Protestantism in 1825 for strategic reasons. Other texts by Heine turn to Muslim Spain as a period distinguished by the relatively peaceful coexistence of the three monotheistic faiths (e.g., the poem "Jehuda ben Halevy" [1851]).

While the East emerges as a utopian, idealized space in Heine's writings, his romanticization gains a critical dimension through his focus on themes of tolerance and intercultural coexistence. It needs to be acknowledged, however, that this idealization occurs with regard to the medieval Orient and also that Heine's knowledge of Islam was limited and very much shaped by his personal approach to religion and by conventional views he adopted from scholarly works of the time. More important, however, Heine's interest in current affairs drew his attention to contemporary developments, such as the Greek struggle for independence, the occupation of Algiers, and the persecution of Syrian Jews during what has become known as the "Damascus affair." As Mounir Fendri points out, Heine's initial reluctance to join the chorus of Philhellenes was related to his suspicion of the crusading rhetoric that distinguished much of the anti-Turkish writings.[181] Yet Heine's later support of movements fighting for political emancipation also led him to support the Greek struggle. Regarding the occupation of Algeria, Heine remained, as Fendri has remarked, surprisingly silent, in spite of his familiarity with the events.[182] On the other hand, Heine reacted strongly to the news about the pogrom affecting the Jewish community in Damascus. The affair was initiated by an accusation of blood libel and ritual murder that was voiced by the French consul in Damascus. The charge that led to the torture and death of many Jews, and to pogroms beyond Syria, was clearly a case of imported European antisemitism, which in fact had major repercussions in Europe.[183] Heine wrote about the events in the newspaper *Allgemeine Zeitung,* devoting a significant portion of his analysis to a critique, and later rehabilitation, of the Egyptian governor Muhammad ʻAli, who ruled Syria at the time and who had indeed played an important role in fueling the disaster through his cooperation with French officials.[184]

Heine's personal situation as a Jew living in Germany and France shaped his relationship to Islam and the Middle East in general. In particular medieval Muslim Spain emerges in his work as a means through which Heine articulated a vision of multicultural/interfaith coexistence and a harsh critique of Christianity's intolerance. With regard to the contemporary context, however, Heine's belief in political and social progress, which he associated with Europe (and particularly with France), informed his critique of the Turks and may explain his silence with regard to French colonial violence.

A half century later Else Lasker-Schüler's written work and visual art engaged critically and playfully with constructions of ethnicity. Here the Orient serves as a stage for projecting ambivalent German-Jewish-Arab male-female figures that defy easy categorization. On the one hand, Lasker-Schüler participated in the attempt by German Jews to embrace their presumed Oriental alterity. But, whereas the movement around Martin Buber earnestly searched for Oriental roots, Lasker-Schüler's performance of Oriental alterity was strategic and at the same time more aggressively political.

In her prose texts *Die Nächte Tino von Bagdads* (1907) and *Der Prinz von Theben* (1914), for example, the Orient is imagined as a mythical, ahistorical, and constructed space, fabricated from elements associated with Arab, Persian, Greek, and Indian cultures. Her creation of a fictional "Ursprache," a mythical language she also refers to as "Old-Nazarean" or "Syrian"; the construction of the term *wild Jews,* which expresses opposition and energetic self-affirmation; her own performances as Tino and Prince Jussuf; and her drawings, especially the visual representations of Prince Jussuf, all share an aggressive gesture aimed at Christian European dominant culture.[185] The assertive, even violent images of opposition evoked in Lasker-Schüler's texts connect her work to the larger discussion of German Jewish identity; the identification and alliance with the Oriental context amount to a self-confident and playful provocation of those in power. Her figures' Orientalness is strategic but also allows them to express anger and to empower themselves.

Around the same time, Friedrich Wolf's play *Mohammed: Ein Oratorium* (1917), like the earlier work by Karoline von Günderrode and also Rainer Maria Rilke's poem "Mohammed's Berufung" (1907), revisits the material about the prophet's biography and the founding of Islam and presents a positive view of Islam's trajectory and Muhammad's ideals. Wolf had renounced his Jewish faith in 1913; nevertheless, his openness toward Islam can be understood in the context of the German Jewish turn toward the Orient and in light of his politics. In 1951 he revised the play "to strengthen some of its political implications and to weaken its mystical, religious ones."[186] But even the earlier version of the play contained a strong "political message . . . : a demand for social justice for the oppressed, an advocacy of nonviolent solutions to conflict, and a critique of the materialism which produces imperialistic behavior."[187]

Klabund's *Mohammed: Roman eines Propheten,* published in the same year as the play by Wolf, also belongs in the group of German-language texts that convey a friendly presentation of the prophet.[188]

German Jews continued to contemplate the Middle East, primarily as they discussed Zionism. Among the German Jews who displayed awareness of the plight of the Arab population was Franz Kafka, whose brief narrative "Schakale und Araber" (1917, the year of the Balfour Declaration) may be understood as an enigmatic parable about the conflict between Jews and Arabs over land and resources. Arnold Zweig's novel *De Vriendt kehrt heim* (1932) comments critically on Jewish-Arab relations by drawing on a true story of a Zionist turned anti-Zionist who allies himself with Arabs. In Anna Seghers's "Post ins gelobte Land" (1943/44), a eulogy on the fate of European Jewry, Arabs do not play any role at all. But the Jewish, Zionist, biblical, and Hebrew-speaking Middle East was clearly central to many German Jewish writers of the period. And some, such as Lion Feuchtwanger in several of his works and also in the 1930 essay "Der historische Prozeß der Juden," saw Jews as the mediator between East and West.[189]

German attitudes about the Middle East in the years from 1792 to 1945, as articulated in fiction, ranged from idealist identification with aspects of the region and notions of superiority to critical consciousness, and at times involved a critique of Christianity, colonialism, and Zionism. The fact that critical consciousness regarding imperialism, antisemitism, and colonialism was indeed articulated throughout this period counters claims by pundits who excuse racist and sexist prejudice as symptoms of the time. The writers targeting dominant ideologies were largely women and Jews; their experience with social and political marginality enabled the critique of oppressive mechanisms in other contexts.

The widespread use of Oriental imagery in German literature and in general cultural discourse during the nineteenth and into the twentieth century reflects the heightened contact with the region. Germany did not have colonies in the area, but its political and economic actions were geared at broadening its influence in the area: from the collaboration with European and Ottoman powers in stifling Muhammad 'Ali's expansive politics to the German call for a jihad against the British and the French, German powers were no silent bystanders. German political and economic interventions into the Middle East, participation in archaeological digs and scientific projects of all kinds, together with rising tourism and a renewed interest in the Holy Land, generated a large number of publications featuring Oriental imagery in German culture. Ideologically, German actions were supported by beliefs in cultural but also racial superiority, paired with beliefs in Christianity and the messianic nature of modernization.

As in previous periods, much of the Orientalist imagery was shared and circulated in Europe beyond national boundaries, regardless of the specific relations that distinct countries entertained with Middle Eastern states. One would perhaps expect a more extensive arsenal of texts that feature Turkish characters, but Germans were clearly influenced by larger events and absorbed the material about Arabs and Persians that was transmitted into German countries by way of various channels. Fiction and nonfiction writings by Lord Byron, William Beckford, Victor Hugo, Gustave Flaubert, and Howard Carter, among others, were eagerly embraced by the German public. One feature that distinguishes German relations to the Middle East during the period is identification, in the political realm and in discourses, with things and causes Middle Eastern. This identification was driven in part by anti-British and anti-French sentiment (i.e., the intra-European rivalry observable also in earlier periods) and by modernizationism. German Orientalists who propagated the call for jihad were largely inspired by a sympathetic view of the area and its peoples, rather than by colonialist aspirations, but they also resented British and French control over territories and hoped for fewer restrictions in conducting their scholarly work. Travelers such as Fürst Pückler-Muskau and engineers such as Max Eyth attempted to highlight the potential for development among Middle Eastern countries; modernizationism inspired the ease with which they interacted with the modernizing Middle Eastern elite. The identification with the Middle East also appears in the approach articulated by German Jews before World War I; here the identification with Oriental roots betrays a self-confident gesture directed against dominant Christian culture. It also reveals a solidarity with the Orient and its peoples that was not necessarily in line with the aspirations of political Zionists (such as Herzl). While resonating with earlier British and French writings (such as those by Lady Mary Wortley Montagu), the positive image of Islam and Turkey that appears in texts by progressive women writers, such as Bettina von Arnim, seems to have no equivalent in France or Britain.

In spite of the sympathetic and distinct features of this segment of German cultural discourse, German political and economic interventions mirrored those of France and Britain in that the ultimate goal was to broaden the political power base and economic influence in the area. In this regard the ideological purport of *dominant* German cultural discourse, from highbrow literary writings to popular best sellers, overlapped with dominant political and economic objectives.

CHAPTER 5

The Middle East Within (1945–89)

After World War II, large-scale migration profoundly changed European societies. The situation in German-speaking countries was shaped first by the arrival of refugees from eastern territories at the end of World War II and then by labor migration from the Middle East and the presence of a significant international student population, including a substantial number of students from the Middle East. In contrast, the growth of minority populations, in France and England particularly, resulted from the influx of individuals hailing from former colonies. Building on prewar relations, East and West Germany, Austria, and Switzerland renewed and strengthened diplomatic and economic ties with Middle Eastern countries. Most notable are the distinct diplomatic approaches pursued by the two German states: whereas the German Democratic Republic (GDR) established close alliances with socialist Arab countries, the Federal Republic of Germany (FRG) gradually emerged as an ally of Israel. While the debates of the public sphere incorporated the significant political, economic, and social events of the period, these topics are largely invisible in highbrow literature produced by writers without immigrant backgrounds. Alongside this mainstream disregard toward the transforming society, however, literary and other cultural works by authors and artists with immigrant roots shaped the German cultural landscape in innovative ways.

Cold War Politics, Trade, and Immigration

The fundamentally different approaches that East and West Germany took toward the Middle East were visible as early as 1952. That year West Germany concluded the *Wiedergutmachungsvertrag* with Israel, the treaty that detailed the restitution payments West Germany was to pay to direct survivors of the Shoah and to other victims of the Nazi system.[1] In hindsight one may ask why only West Germany and not both German states, and perhaps Austria, took responsibility for the Shoah.[2] The answer to this question lies, to some extent, in the complicated relationship between the two German states. Until the early 1970s and the establishment of West German chancellor Willy Brandt's policy of *Neue Ostpolitik,* the FRG did not recognize East Germany as an independent country. In fact, West Germany insisted on being the only legitimate state representing the German people, a doctrine known as the *Alleinvertretungsanspruch.*[3] This policy was formally cemented by the Hallstein Doctrine of 1955, which stated that West Germany would cut off diplomatic ties with any state that recognized East German statehood.

The Hallstein Doctrine not only defined German-German relations but also explains why, in spite of the treaty detailing restitution payments to survivors of the Shoah, West Germany did not entertain diplomatic relations with Israel until 1965.[4] West Germany was afraid that recognizing Israel would lead many countries who were opposed to the state of Israel, such as the Arab states, to acknowledge East Germany. West German politicians were wary of international recognition of East Germany as an independent state, as it was a direct challenge to the FRG's claim to be the sole legitimate German state and also to its pursuit of unification.[5] As Hannfried von Hindenburg writes, "the goal of German unification was far more important to government policy makers in the 1950s and early 1960s than full and open reconciliation with Israel in the aftermath of the Holocaust."[6] The later shift in West Germany's approach toward Israel, as von Hindenburg shows, did not come as a result of top-down policymaking but, rather, was a response to large-scale social pressures led by "domestic elites (such as students, professors, trade unions, religious groups, writers, the media, and others)."[7] But the conflicts between Middle Eastern states, and between Middle Eastern and the two German states, also contributed significantly to bringing about West Germany's new policy.

East Germany abandoned the goal of unification in the early 1950s, and its emergence as an independent state was largely facilitated by the solidarity expressed by other socialist and communist countries. The Soviet Union was the first country to recognize the GDR in 1954 (thus prompting the Hallstein Doctrine), followed by several Eastern bloc countries, China, North Korea, North Vietnam, and other states. Seeking solidarity with third world countries in the decolonization period, East Germany pursued diplomatic and economic relations with Arab countries. As Kai Hafez points out, East Germany, in order to gather support for recognition of its statehood, approached both socialist and nonsocialist countries.[8] Egypt and Syria were among the first states to welcome East German representatives and to engage the GDR politically, economically, and culturally.

In the course of the 1950s, East Germany established economic treaties with Egypt, Lebanon, Sudan, Syria, Yemen, and Iraq, but it did not develop diplomatic relations with them until the mid-1960s. In 1965, the East German president Walter Ulbricht made a highly publicized visit to Egypt. Public controversy over arms deals between West Germany and Israel had spurred Egyptian president Gamal Abdel Nasser to invite Ulbricht, among other steps taken to pressure West Germany. Nasser's efforts were successful in getting the FRG to suspend its weapons deals in conflict areas, but Ulbricht's visit to Egypt led to closer collaboration between the two states. In May 1965, the day after West Germany announced diplomatic relations with Israel, all Arab countries, with the exception of Morocco, Libya, and Tunisia, cut diplomatic ties to the FRG.[9] The year 1969 saw recognition of East Germany by Arab states (Iraq, Syria, Sudan, Egypt, and South Yemen), a process that emerged as a crucial step in the GDR's quest to win worldwide recognition. By the time of German unification, East Germany maintained diplomatic relations with thirteen Arab countries and the Palestine Liberation Organization but not with Israel.[10] Interestingly, in terms of their approach to Palestine and Israel, segments of West Germany's radical Left took the same course as East Germany.[11]

East Germany's refusal to acknowledge Israel was rooted in various aspects of socialist and communist ideology but also, and more pragmatically, in East Germany's integration into the Warsaw Pact and the Council for Mutual Economic Assistance (COMECON) and its general dependence on the Soviet Union. Communist ideology associated antisemitism with capitalism and feudalism, and did not acknowledge its broader pervasiveness. This assessment of antisemitism also facilitated the communist condemnation of Zionism, which was primarily seen as reactionary ideology and tied to imperialism. Joseph Stalin had supported the partition of Palestine with the goal of weakening British influence in the area and simultaneously expanding the Soviet presence there. It is largely forgotten today that the Soviet Union facilitated the immigration of 200,000 Jews to Palestine and even provided Israel with weapons in the 1948 war.[12] Over time, however, the Soviet Union's approach toward Israel changed fundamentally.

In addition, East Germany challenged West Germany's claim to being the sole legitimate representative of Germany. Framing itself as an antifascist state and refusing to take responsibility for National Socialism and the Shoah allowed East Germany to avoid confronting its relationship to Israel in terms of the National Socialist German past. As Angelika Timm shows, until the 1980s "the full magnitude of the Holocaust was not addressed [by East Germany]. The memorials in Buchenwald and Sachsenhausen did not mention Jewish inmates of the concentration camps."[13] Timm distinguishes several phases in East Germany's attitude toward Israel. In the immediate postwar period, which Timm dates from 1947 to the early 1950s, policy was pro-Israel. A shift occurred in 1952, when several antisemitic campaigns took place in East Germany and other communist states, and West Germany's reparation treaty was denounced as an agreement with agents of imperialism and capitalism. Over the next few years East Germany continued to cite its broad antifascist record to justify its refusal to pay reparations. Until the early 1980s East Germany's stance was hostile toward Israel and unequivocally supportive of Arab positions. In fact, as Timm shows, "sometimes East Germany adopted, both publicly and behind the scenes, an even more virulent line than that of the Soviets."[14] Only during the last five years of the GDR did the official stance shift once more.

By the end of the 1960s changes in West Germany's approach to both East Germany and Israel made the Hallstein Doctrine obsolete. Willy Brandt's *Neue Ostpolitik* was intended to improve the FRG's relationship with East Germany. The Basic Treaty of 1972 set the framework for establishing diplomatic relations between the two German states, and it created the preconditions for the two states to become members of the United Nations in 1973. Israel voted against GDR membership in the United Nations on account of East Germany's refusal to accept historical responsibility for its role in the Shoah. These shifts in German-German relations, combined with West Germany's increasingly critical attitude toward Israeli policies, also facilitated a renewal of ties with the Arab world: the FRG resumed diplomatic relations with Egypt in 1972, followed that year by Lebanon, Yemen, Jordan, Sudan, and Algeria.[15]

While the two German states redefined their relationship with each other, their respective policies toward the Middle East remained distinct. But here, too, regional developments made change inevitable. Until unification the two German states pursued very different policies in responding to pressing issues, such as Egypt's shifting attitude toward Israel, the Iraq-Iran War, and ongoing Israeli-Arab hostilities.[16]

Economic relations, however, did not necessarily match up with political developments, an aspect that has emerged consistently in this study. Both German states entertained economic relations even before diplomatic relations were established (e.g., between the GDR and Arab states in the 1950s and between the FRG and Arab states and Israel during the same period) or while diplomatic relations were suspended (e.g., between the FRG and Arab states in the late 1960s). Forming trade partnerships with the German states was a consequential move for Middle Eastern states but was less significant to the economies of the two German states, Austria, or Switzerland.[17] By the end of the 1950s only 5 percent of West German exports went to the Middle East.[18]

In 1960, both imports and exports amounted to about 6 percent of West Germany's trade volume with trading partners from the MENA region (6.17 percent for imports, and 5.50 percent for exports). Imports remained in this range, while exports dropped to 3.74 percent by 1970. The higher figure for imports in 1980 is primarily related to imports from oil producing countries, such as Algeria, Libya, and Saudi Arabia. Exports to the MENA region also increased by 1980, but the trade volume dropped again by 1988, to 3.34 percent (imports) and 4.11 percent (exports).

Overall, the figures in table 1 (see pp. 194–95) are relatively small in relation to the total trade volume, but they become more salient when considered from the perspective of Middle Eastern countries, an aspect that deserves closer attention here. By the end of the 1950s West Germany exported fewer goods to the Middle East than the United States, but more than Britain and France. In terms of imports Britain and France were ahead of West Germany, which is related solely to the high levels of oil imports.[19] From the perspective of Middle Eastern countries, West Germany's significance was obvious: already in 1949, 4.6 percent of Turkish imports came from and 16.1 percent of Turkish exports went to West Germany.[20] While imports from the FRG increased steadily, the percentage of exports in the period from 1974 to 1997 ranged roughly between 12 and 25 percent. In 1997 Turkey received 16.5 percent of its imports from unified Germany and sent 20 percent of its exports to that country.[21] In 1957 Syria received 10.7 percent of its imports, Egypt 9.9 percent, and Iraq 9.2 percent from West Germany.[22] In 1977 Turkey, Egypt, Algeria, Libya, Tunisia, Jordan, Syria, and Saudi Arabia imported more than 10 percent of their goods from West Germany, and Iran and Iraq close to 20 percent. With regard to exports in the same year, Turkey exported 22.3 percent to the FRG, Libya 19.6 percent, Tunisia 16.3, Algeria 14.7 percent, Morocco 10.5 percent, Israel 9 percent, Syria 7.9 percent, and Iran 7.7 percent. All other Middle Eastern countries ranged below these values.[23]

Regarding East Germany, its limited access to international currencies proved to be a roadblock to increasing the trade volume. The GDR traded with socialist and nonsocialist countries alike. In 1960 Egypt ranked third (12.4 percent) and Turkey seventh (2.1 percent) in trade with East Germany. By 1975 Iraq and Syria gained in importance, ranking second (11.6 percent) and ninth (3.2 percent), respectively. Egypt ranked third (9.7 percent). In 1980 five of East Germany's top ten trading partners were Middle Eastern states.[24]

In addition to distinct diplomatic and economic relations developed be-

TABLE 1. West Germany's Imports from and Exports to Middle Eastern and North African Countries

	1960				1970			
	Import		Export		Import		Export	
	Mill DM	%	Mill DM	%	Mill DM	%	Mill DM	%
West Germany (Total)	42,723	100	47,946	100	109,606	100	125,276	100
Algeria	107.6	0.25	57.6	0.12	549.4	0.50	362.7	0.29
Egypt	127.5	0.30	474.1	0.99	207.1	0.19	448.5	0.36
Iran	598.2	1.40	494.1	1.03	871.4	0.80	1,176.8	0.94
Iraq	382.8	0.90	136.4	0.28	213.5	0.19	70.5	0.06
Israel	101.3	0.24	277.9	0.58	304.6	0.28	638.2	0.51
Libya	3.4	0.01	86.2	0.18	2,431.5	2.22	168.5	0.13
Morocco	223.7	0.52	82.6	0.17	228.9	0.21	187.5	0.15
Saudi Arabia	528.2	1.24	68.5	0.14	732.8	0.67	238.4	0.19
Syria	22.5	0.05	107.3	0.22	32.1	0.03	86	0.07
Tunisia	15.6	0.04	37.8	0.08	77.8	0.07	102.2	0.08
Turkey	300.5	0.70	483.6	1.01	449.4	0.41	701.4	0.56
UAE	0	0.00	0	0.00	0	0.00	0	0.00
Other	222.6	0.52	332.3	0.69	692.7	0.63	502.8	0.40
MENA Trade Total (%)	2,633.9	6.17	2,638.4	5.50	6,791.2	6.20	4,683.5	3.74

Source: Compiled based on information provided in *Statistisches Jahrbuch für die Bundesrepublik Deutschland* (1961/1962), 316–17; *Statistisches Jahrbuch für die Bundesrepublik Deutschland* (1971/1972), 298–300; *Statistisches Jahrbuch für die Bundesrepublik Deutschland* (1981/1982), 263–65; *Statistisches Jahrbuch für die Bundesrepublik Deutschland* (1989/1990), 261–63.

Note: I am grateful to Sonja Amadae, John Brooke, Gene Mumy, and Vicente Nogueira for their input on this table.

tween German-speaking and Middle Eastern countries, West and East Germany, Austria, and Switzerland invited large numbers of migrant laborers from the Middle East to join its workforce. Comparatively, the largest number of Middle Eastern migrant workers went to West Germany. East Germany's much smaller number of migrant laborers hailed mostly from Angola, Mozambique, Cuba, North Vietnam, and China. While Switzerland is home to a large number of residents without a Swiss passport, namely, 21.6 percent of the Swiss population in 2002, the percentage of those with a Middle Eastern background is relatively small: only 5.2 percent of the foreign population are Turkish, and other groups from the Middle East are significantly smaller.[25] In Austria, on the other hand, as in West and later unified Germany, Turks are the largest immigrant group and also make up the majority of Muslims in Austria. But in comparison to Germany, Turks make up a smaller percentage of the overall Austrian population, constituting 1.5 percent in 2003.[26]

Labor migration to West Germany was facilitated by guest worker treaties that West Germany signed with Italy (1955), Spain and Greece (1960), Turkey (1961), Morocco (1963), Portugal (1964), Tunisia (1965), Yugoslavia (1968),

1980				1988			
Import		Export		Import		Export	
Mill DM	%	Mill DM	%	Mill DM	%	Mill DM	%
341,380	100	350,328	100	439,768	100	567,750	100
4,147.5	1.21	2,501.1	0.71	1,623.4	0.37	1,380.3	0.24
386.5	0.11	1,857.9	0.53	325.3	0.07	1,968.3	0.35
3,381.9	0.99	2,734.4	0.78	1,119	0.25	2,891.1	0.51
1,156.9	0.34	3,275.6	0.94	369.4	0.08	1,560.6	0.27
1,112.1	0.33	1,304.2	0.37	1,260.8	0.29	2,327.8	0.41
7,865.8	2.30	2,282.5	0.65	2,680	0.61	1,111	0.20
506.6	0.15	430.6	0.12	679	0.15	747.1	0.13
9,907	2.90	4,276	1.22	1,164.2	0.26	2,684.2	0.47
236.3	0.07	818.9	0.23	211.3	0.05	306.2	0.05
572.2	0.17	677.6	0.19	688.9	0.16	793.8	0.14
1,062.7	0.31	1,613.6	0.46	3,781.1	0.86	4,498.4	0.79
2,726.9	0.80	859.9	0.25	152.7	0.03	1,025.8	0.18
1,424.8	0.42	2,389.4	0.68	640.7	0.15	2,014.6	0.35
34,487.2	10.10	25,021.7	7.14	14,695.8	3.34	23,309.2	4.11

and, in the 1970s, various Asian countries. Turkish labor migration was numerically the largest and had the deepest impact on West German society. Karin Hunn, who provides the most extensive analysis of Turkish labor migration to the Federal Republic to date and draws on both Turkish and German sources in her analysis, structures her study according to interwoven major economic and political developments that were relevant to labor migration from 1961 until unification. The initial phase of Turkish labor migration during the period of underemployment in the Federal Republic ended with a brief recession (1961 to 1966–67). The changes occurring between 1968 and 1973, a period that began with a strong economy and massive recruitment of foreign labor, concluded with the oil crisis and the end of labor recruitment (*Anwerbestop*). The developments to the close of the 1970s and the period from 1981 to 1984 reflect measures that were introduced with the intention of "reintegrating" migrant workers into their countries of origin.[27]

Treaties regulating economic relations between the Federal Republic and Turkey were consistently connected to political interests and relations between the two countries. The convention to privilege labor migration treaties with

European nations (the *Europäergrundsatz*) was suspended with regard to Turkey (and to a lesser degree Morocco and Tunisia), which held a distinct status as a member of the North Atlantic Treaty Organization (NATO). Turkey was also favorably regarded in light of its long history of military, political, and economic cooperation with German states. In fact, as Hunn demonstrates, in the early phase Turkey was considered to be part of Europe, and differences in the treaties between Germany and Turkey, in comparison to those with other European nations, cannot be explained as resulting from cultural discrimination.[28] Hunn points out that the temporal restrictions—initially Turkish labor migrants were allowed to stay in West Germany for only two years—were also supported by the Turkish government, which hoped that labor migrants would return to Turkey quickly and apply the knowledge they had acquired during their stay in Germany to develop the Turkish economy.[29]

During the first phase of Turkish labor migration to the Federal Republic, cultural and religious differences received little attention, both in the media and in discussions directly related to political and economic dimensions of labor immigration. Turkish workers, for example, were typically seen as less demanding with regard to dietary restrictions than their Italian counterparts. Certain policies, such as the often demeaning physical examination, were not restricted to Turkish immigrants alone but, rather, according to Hunn, reflected a more deep-seated suspicion of "foreigners" and were also related to Third Reich–based negative notions of the *Fremdarbeiter*.[30]

What Turkish workers expected from their move to Germany and what their government wanted were, in reality, two different things. Turkey wanted unskilled workers to return as skilled workers; instead, it lost many skilled workers. Political motivations often weighed more heavily than economic objectives: in the early 1960s reducing unemployment was less important to the Turkish leadership than strengthening political and economic ties with Europe. In this regard the official objectives of the Turkish government and those of Turkish migrant workers often clashed significantly.[31] In addition, Turkish migrant workers held unrealistic expectations and were often unaware of what awaited them in Germany. The housing situations of Turkish-German workers and their families were often atrocious. Complaints about conditions at the workplace, high-risk and strenuous labor, and low pay were incessant and occasionally led to strikes.

Over the years the various Turkish governments often did not act as advocates for Turkish-born labor migrants. Facing unemployment at home, the Turkish government was not eager to facilitate these workers' return. In addition, and especially during periods in which Turkey was ruled by repressive regimes, actions by Turkish government officials that were, for example, related to anticommunist repression and support of fascist groups divided Turkish-German communities. As a result, West Germany ended up facing the entire range of Turkey's domestic conflicts. The divide between urban and rural communities, clashes between political groups, and internal ethnic conflicts, such as the struggle of the Kurdish population for political self-determination, all surfaced in Germany.

Recent studies have revised widely held beliefs about the social and regional origins of Turkish migrant workers in Germany. According to a 1963 survey, only 18.2 percent of workers hailed from villages with less than two thousand inhabitants; 41 percent came from Istanbul alone to Germany.[32] Indeed, many Turkish workers were accustomed to far more advanced sanitary facilities than those that awaited them in Germany and were shocked when confronted with the substandard sanitary and heating equipment in, for example, Berlin. The percentage of skilled workers was higher among immigrants from Turkey than those who came from Spain or Greece.[33] Discrimination against Turkish-German workers at the workplace escalated over time. Although in the early period German union members often fought side by side with their immigrant colleagues (mostly out of self-interest, to ensure that wages of the German workers would not fall), over the years solidarity grew weaker, especially once unemployment rates began to rise. Physical fights between German and Turkish-born workers were not unusual. In fact, during the 1960s immigrant workers pushed Germans out of certain jobs, but increasingly Turkish immigrants were forced to accept jobs that paid little and which Germans did not want to take.

German employers and the German state were initially responsive to the demands of immigrant workers on labor issues as well as to their cultural and religious needs. Indeed, at the beginning of 1963 the West German government agreed to pay monthly child support even for Turkish migrant workers' children who lived in Turkey.[34] Discriminatory views based in ethnocentric and racist beliefs were nevertheless pervasive, although it was not until the economic situation turned sour and the 1973 oil crisis aggravated the economic downturn that these views began to translate into widespread discriminatory practices. In addition, as workers' family members joined them in Germany, Turkish neighborhoods began to form. The emergence of a Turkish-German infrastructure, with shops and other business enterprises, schools, and cultural centers, created spaces of agency and self-determination for Turkish Germans but also contributed to the rising hostility of the German majority population toward the immigrants. Beginning in the early 1980s, amid an increasingly tough economic climate marked by rising unemployment, the German majority began to articulate a nationalist and ethnocentric discourse that reflected its growing animosity toward the immigrant population. This anger and unease led to acts of violence and further separated immigrants and their descendants from the German majority. These tensions, seen most explicitly in the mounting number of violent attacks, rose greatly after unification.[35]

The increasing ethnicization of Turkish-born workers in Germany must also be seen in the context of the changing political landscape in Turkey. As issues of religious and cultural identity gained importance in Turkey itself, resulting conflicts were once again imported to Germany, where they reinforced existing patterns of discrimination. A paucity of social workers and translators who could address the needs of Turkish-German workers as well as a lack of support from labor unions also contributed to their inadequate representation. Individual ministries in Germany often pursued opposing policies, and the general lack of coordination, both within Germany and between Germany and Turkey, negatively affected the situation of Turkish Germans, who, numbering around 1.6 million in 1989, lacked, and continue to lack, basic civil and political rights.

The impact of remittance flows on Middle Eastern economies, particularly Turkey, is also noteworthy in this context. After the decade of the 1960s, these foreign funds increased steadily, becoming

> the second major source of external financing (after foreign direct investment [FDI]) for developing countries. . . . For Lebanon, for example, official remittance receipts were as high as 38.8 percent of gross domestic product (GDP) during the 1990s. For Egypt and Morocco, this ratio was between 5 and 10 percent, and Greece, Portugal, and Tunisia fell into the same group with official remittance receipts to GDP ratios of 1 to 5 percent. . . . Likewise, remittances received by Turkey, one of the top remittance receivers in the world, corresponded to 2.3 percent of its GDP and 10.6 percent of its export revenues, and represented more than six times the amount this country received in FDI in 1999.[36]

As the German share of Turkish workers abroad ranged between 55 and 63 percent in the 1980s and 1990s, the economic impact of remittance flows stemming from Turkish-German workers was significant, their volatility notwithstanding, and highlights the growing economic interdependence between the two countries.[37] The same holds true for other Middle Eastern countries with significant immigrant communities in German-speaking countries.

Students seeking education in German-speaking countries constitute another key group of Middle Eastern immigrants. In 1960, there were 22,109 international students enrolled at West German universities and other secondary educational institutions (*Hochschulen*), representing more than 7 percent of the total student body.[38] The percentage of "colored students" (according to a 1962 study) among the international students was 68 percent.[39] Students from the Middle East formed a visible presence in the FRG. In the late 1950s and early 1960s Arabs alone made up more than one-fourth of the international student body and were mostly of economically and socially privileged backgrounds.[40] They chose West Germany to pursue their secondary education because of favorable conditions for admission and the reputation of German universities in their chosen field of study but also for political reasons; significantly, for example, they did not share a colonial history with Germany.[41] Often they went there with unrealistic expectations about the academic training they would receive and the social, political, and economic environment.[42]

By 1982–83, there were 6,994 students from Iran enrolled at West German universities (0.62 percent), a figure that increased to 10,723 by 1990–91 (0.71 percent). Figures are similar for students from Turkey (8,254/12,962 and 0.74/0.86 percent, respectively); those for other Middle Eastern countries range between 200 and 1,000 students. The proportion of students from the Middle East had thus reached between 2 and 3 percent in the last decade before unification in West Germany, with higher concentrations at specific universities, giving them a certain degree of visibility.[43]

The total number of students enrolled at East German universities was 143,163 in 1970 and 120,970 in 1980.[44] The available figures for foreign students indicate that 4,591 foreign students were enrolled in 1972, of whom 63 percent were identified as hailing from the "Third World" (including Africa, the Americas, and Asia). This number rose by 1979 to a total of 6,607 foreign students, though the proportion of so-called third world students dropped to 58 percent.[45] The number of Middle Eastern students in East Germany was thus small when compared to West Germany.

Although the number of foreign students in Switzerland has dropped in recent years, the country retains its strong tradition of recruiting foreign students. "With about one-fifth foreign students," wrote Roselyne Crausaz in 1979, "Switzerland heads the list of European countries."[46] Most of Switzerland's foreign students come from other European countries. Accordingly, the number of students from the Middle East is relatively low. In 1989 there were 1,379 students from Middle Eastern countries (208 from Turkey, 608 from North Africa, and 563 from West Asia; 1.66 percent), among a total of 83,277 students. In contrast, 11,002 (13.21 percent) students came from European countries.[47] With regard to Austria, 179,484 students were enrolled in 1988–89, of whom 16,580 were foreign (9.24 percent); most of these foreign students, however, were Europeans. Figures for students from the Middle East were not available with regard to Austria, but it is safe to assume that students from the Middle East did not represent more than 2 percent of the total student body. The influx of students from the Middle East was clearly most significant in West Germany.

In addition, the number of individuals seeking political asylum in West Germany, Switzerland, and Austria has increased steadily since the 1960s. While the total numbers of asylum seekers are higher for West Germany, the per capita percentage was at times higher for Switzerland and, beginning in the 1990s, also for Austria.[48] With regard to West Germany, the number of asylum seekers who came from the Middle East was relatively low until the late 1970s. In reaction to the Turkish military coup of 1980, their number in the FRG shot up: 57,913 Turks applied for political asylum, 53.7 percent of all asylum seekers.[49] In 1989 the number again reached 20,000 people, 16.5 percent of the total number of asylum seekers.[50]

West Germany's absorption of immigrants from Turkey was substantial, be they students, asylum seekers or legal or illegal immigrants. As their numbers grew, Turkey's political and social conflicts entered West Germany in increasingly visible ways, as evoked poignantly in the Turkish writer Orhan Pamuk's novel *Snow* (2004):

> Ka spoke about Hikmet, who had died under mysterious circumstances while working as a chauffeur in Berlin; Fadıl, who had married the elderly widow of a Nazi officer and now ran a small hotel with her; and Tarık, the theoretician, who had made a fortune working with the Turkish mafia in Hamburg. As for Sadık, who alongside Muhtar, Ka, Taner, and Ipek had once folded periodicals fresh off the press, he was now running a gang that smuggled illegal immigrants over the Alps and into Germany. . . . Of all the political exiles Ka had met in Germany, the happiest was Ferhat, who had joined the PKK and was now attacking various offices of Turkish Airlines with revolutionary fervor; he'd also been seen on CNN, throwing Molotov cocktails at Turkish consulates; apparently he was now learning Kurdish and dreaming of a second career as a Kurdish poet.[51]

Similar observations could be made with regard to immigrants from Iran and other areas. By the early 1990s the number of Iranian immigrants reached

100,000. Most came to Germany seeking political asylum, first from the regime of the Shah and, after 1979–80, the Islamist government. Twenty percent of Iranian asylum seekers are recognized as political refugees; the rest are tolerated as "de-facto refugees."[52]

Thus, during the postwar era individuals from the Middle East and North Africa immigrated to German-speaking societies as a result of, but also often in tension with, dominant political and economic developments, spurred by labor migration, the search for asylum, and educational opportunities. While East Germany did not foster these types of immigration, West Germany, Switzerland, and Austria experienced comparable immigration trends, resulting in significant changes to their societies' infrastructures.

Practices of Coexistence

With the rising number of foreign students in West Germany in the 1950s came a greater level of advocacy. Organizations and institutions founded by international students, including students from the Middle East, sought to address concerns related to their status in the West German context and to the question of how to apply Western knowledge usefully upon their return to their countries of origin, a topic that has been discussed since the nineteenth century.[53]

The Afrikanisch-Asiatische Studentenunion (AASU), for example, was founded in Göttingen in 1956–57 and included a substantial number of students from the Middle East. Over the years the organization developed several branches. In 1958, in an attempt to build a bridge to the larger German context, a German advisory council was founded. Also that year a proposal to build a dormitory for African, Asian, and German students was submitted to the president of the university.[54] This project was indeed realized in 1967, and to this day half of the dormitory's 120 rooms are rented out to students from Africa and Asia, the other half to German students. In order to create a legal body to facilitate the implementation of various projects, the Afrikanisch-Asiatische Studentenförderung e.V. (AASF) was founded in 1959. The AASU expanded into a national organization in the years that followed, and at a conference in Göttingen in 1963, with participants of twelve AASU chapters from different German universities, an umbrella organization was founded, the Föderation der Afrikanisch-Asiatischen Studentenunionen in der Bundesrepublik Deutschland, which itself ceased to exist after a few years. Another AASF was founded in Kassel in 1977 and was active for a few years, although it never attained sustainable momentum.

In 1974 the Arbeitskreis Afrikanisch-Asiatischer Akademiker und Akademikerinnen was established, reflecting the beginning of a new phase in the organization's work. While the AASF consists of Germans, Africans, and Asians, the members of the Arbeitskreis are exclusively African and Asian. The existence of the Arbeitskreis illustrates the project's spirit of independence from German institutions and dominant German discourses: concerns of Africans and Asians are the starting point. Over time the Arbeitskreis has developed a distinct institutional framework—with seminars, publications, and other initiatives—to address concepts such as *Reintegration* and *Selbsthilfe.* Seminars designed around specific Middle Eastern issues (such as water politics, infrastructure issues, and the status of women) were held on a regular basis. Publications in the yearbook series, in print since 1991, feature articles about ecological, economic, ethical, and cultural issues related to the Middle East.[55]

The AASU and AASF represent early forms of institutional practices that enabled students and academics from the Middle East, among others, to articulate their particular concerns in West Germany.[56] Intellectuals from the Middle East continue to organize locally and nationally and according to national and transnational criteria. The Verband Iranischer Hochschullehrer und Akademiker in Deutschland (VIHA) was founded in 1989, and, more recently, Verein Arabischer Studenten und Akademiker Tübingen was created in 2001. In Bremen the Türkisch, Iranisch, Kurdischer Studentenverein (TIK SV e.V.) unites students from various states of the region, and the University at Münster features a Türkischer Studentenverein Münster e. V. Similar organizations exist across Germany.

As students became academics and professionals, those who did not return to their countries of origin began to contribute to German societies in various ways. Among the Arab-German intellectuals who play a role in German academia and in the public sphere is the Syrian-born sociologist Bassam Tibi, who taught at the University of Göttingen and has an international reputation. Many of his publications are translated into English, among them titles that discuss political Islam. He is popular in the German media, but his views are controversial, and he is often perceived as assimilationist and insensitive toward the civil rights demands of Muslim immigrants. In a 1998 publication he introduced the term *Leitkultur* to outline what he presented as fundamentals of modern European culture.[57] The concept was quickly appropriated by conservatives to assert normative German cultural values. Tibi, regardless of how one might view his role in the German public sphere, stands out as one of the notable academics of Middle Eastern descent who have contributed to increasing political and cultural representation. These academics, along with others from Africa, Asia, and Latin/Central America, represent Germany's postcolonial voices, an aspect often overlooked in assessments of German-speaking countries as multicultural immigrant societies.

Outside of the academic realm individuals of Middle Eastern descent organize in ways that mirror the national, religious, and ethnic diversity of the Middle East. These organizations make use of German laws for *gemeinnützige Vereine* (non-profit organizations) and are in line with Germany's significant tradition of creating civil society through community-based organizations. Mirroring aspects of Germany's nineteenth-century political history in this regard, *Vereine* compensated for the lack of political, social, and cultural rights and at the same time provided frameworks that would generate increasing levels of political organization. These organizations are distinct from institutions that were established primarily by Germans, such as the Deutsch-Tunesische Gesellschaft e.V., founded in 1959.[58] Similarly, the Deutsch-Arabische Gesellschaft (DAG), established in 1966, was conceived along the lines of majority German concerns.[59]

Most organizations that were founded by immigrants themselves reflect the national origin of their members. One Web site lists twenty-seven "Deutsch-Ägyptische Vereine."[60] Similarly, "Tunesische Vereine" and "Marokkanische Vereine" exist across Germany, for example, in Hamm, Karlsruhe, Mainz, Munich, and Stuttgart. The "Verein Deutscher Frauen in Tunesien" documents the significant rate of intermarriage between Tunisians and Germans, both as a result of immigration and of German tourism in Tunisia.[61] Many of these organizations emerged in the 1970s and 1980s. The Deutsch-Palästinensische Gesellschaft e.V. (DPG) was founded in Cologne in 1986 and currently lists ten local chapters across Germany.[62] Reflecting the broad range of existing institutions, the Bundesverband Deutsch-Arabischer Vereine in Deutschland e.V. lists eighty-two member organizations.[63] The various Kurdish organizations existing in Austria in 1992 formed the Verband der Kurdischen Vereine in Österreich (FEYKOM).

Several organizations display distinct political orientations. The Föderation der Volksvereine türkischer Sozialdemokraten e.V. Sosyaldemokrat Halk Dernekleri Federasyonu was founded in late 1977 as an umbrella organization with strong ties to the German and Turkish social democratic parties. A left-leaning organization, the Föderation der Immigantenvereine aus der Türkei e.V. / Türkiyeli Göcmen Dernekleri Federasyonu, was created in 1988, while the Freiheitlich Türkisch-Deutscher Freundschaftsverein e.V. / Hürriyetçi Türk-Alman Dostluk Cemiyeti, founded in 1979, has ties to the Christian

Democratic Party in Germany and to conservative parties in Turkey, such as Anavatan Partisi. The Föderation der Türkisch-Demokratischen Idealistenvereine in Europa e.V. / Avrupa Demokratik Ülkücü Türk Dernekleri Federasyonu, founded in 1978, is associated with right-wing parties in Turkey, such as Milliyetçi Hareket Partisi, and are referred to in Germany as the *Graue Wölfe* (Grey Wolves).[64] Turkey's social and political landscape is reflected in these organizations, which sometimes creates tensions within the German context, especially as regards the activities of the Grey Wolves.[65] The links between various German parties and their Turkish equivalents, however, also highlight the transnational ties existing between the two countries.

In addition to societies that reflect a national or transnational Middle Eastern orientation, a wide range of schools, cultural centers, and organizations with specific foci allow individuals of Middle Eastern origin to pursue their interests.[66] One of the oldest organizations among them is the Vereinigung der Iranischen Ärzte und Zahnärzte in der Bundesrepublik Deutschland e.V., which was founded in 1961. Turkish-identified sports clubs exist throughout Germany. Many soccer clubs are organized along ethnic lines: Turkish soccer clubs exist in, for example, Bielefeld, Bremen Emmendingen, Neukölln, Pforzheim, Schwäbisch Hall, and Weilburg.[67] A Deutsch-Ägyptisch-Arabischer Sportverein e.V. exists in Bornheim, a Tunesischer Sportverein 83 Berlin e.V. in Berlin. Iranian sports organization, such as the Iranischer Sportverein in Berlin and the Sport Club Persia Hamburg 2004 e.V, are also popular.[68] Networks similar to those of the sport clubs exist in other areas, such as music (e.g., Firkat Klassisch-Türkischer Musikverein in Stuttgart e.V. and Förderkreis Iranischer Musik Hanau). It is also common for organizations to combine economic and cultural objectives.[69] In the postunification period social, economic, political, and cultural organizations and institutions mushroomed, a phenomenon yet to be adequately explored.

While the 1960s saw the creation of organizations in West Germany that mirrored the ethnic and national origin of immigrants, over the course of the following decade these and other new entities became increasingly concerned with issues related to Islam. Yasemin Karakaşoğlu suggests that this growing emphasis on religious orientation among Turkish immigrant communities resulted from the economic crisis of the 1970s and 1980s, during which "Islamic organizations acquired a new function as providers of social support and material assistance, for they were well placed to offer their members community networks and a trusted framework in which to reaffirm their traditional Turkish values."[70] Additionally, the global emergence of political Islam (and other religious fundamentalisms) in the late 1970s, in response to the challenges of secular modernization, failed initiatives in postindependence states, and new economic policies of the International Monetary Fund and the World Bank, contributed to the re-Islamization of Iranian, Turkish, and Arab individuals in Germany.

Islamic organizations proliferated on the national and local levels, reflecting the emergence of Islam in Europe in the German-speaking context.[71] Two umbrella organizations arose in the late 1980s.[72] The Islamrat für die Bundesrepublik Deutschland e.V.—whose largest member organization is the controversial Islamische Gemeinschaft Milli Görüş—was founded first, in 1986.[73] Then, in 1988, the Islamischer Arbeitskreis in Deutschland was formed with the hope of building a representational body that could act politically to address questions regarding the religious rights of the Islamic minority in Germany. Originally it included the largest Turkish organizations, some of which left the group in the early 1990s. The organization was renamed and reorganized in 1994 as Zentralrat der Muslime in Deutschland e.V. (ZMD). Today, the ZMD brings together nineteen Islamic organizations and includes mostly non-Turkish Muslims. The organization emphasizes its German character[74] and thus echoes views articulated by Tariq Ramadan, who promotes an integrated Islam for Europe.[75] In 2000 the ZMD lost another large member organization and, in spite of its ethnic diversity, can no longer claim to represent the majority of Muslims.

The lack of unity among Muslim organizations in Germany is mainly responsible for preventing Islam from being recognized as a *Körperschaft des öffentlichen Rechts* (corporation by public law). This legal status, which thus far has only been granted to Christianity and Judaism, "provides a number of far-reaching rights, such as the right to levy taxes from members of the community and to organize a parish, the right to employ people under a belief-oriented labour-law, the placement of property under public property law which grants tax-reductions and the exemption of other taxes and costs, the right to nominate members to broadcast-councils etc."[76] The lack of access to these rights remains a substantial grievance for Muslims in Germany, estimated to number about 3.5 million in 2009 (about 2.3 million in 1989).[77]

In Austria Muslims are in a better position in terms of their legal rights than those living in the Federal Republic because in Austria Islam is recognized as a corporation by public law. Islam has long been a historical presence in Vienna, and in Habsburg/Austrian society more generally, and was acknowledged legally as a religious community in 1912.[78] The original law restricted recognition to followers of the Hanafi rite, but it was modified in 1979 to include all Muslims. The Islamische Glaubensgemeinschaft in Österreich officially represents all Muslims in Austria, but, like the situation in Germany, there are numerous organizations reflecting the diversity of the Islamic community.[79] After Turks, Bosnians are the second largest group of Muslims in Austria. The country's 1981 census for the first time solicited information on Muslims and counted 76,939 individuals, a 300 percent increase compared to estimates from the early 1970s.[80] The number rose substantially over the next two decades: the 2001 census showed that Muslims make up 4.2 percent (338,988 individuals) of the population, 96,052 of them Austrian citizens.[81] In the 1990s mosques and Islamic organizations in Austria numbered around 80; today the number has grown to over 200.[82] Muslims in Austria have access to a wide range of social, cultural, religious, and political institutions.[83]

Switzerland's Islamic population reflects immigration patterns similar to the Federal Republic and Austria, its members arriving there for the most part as the result of labor migration, a growing international student population, or political conflicts in their countries of origin. According to census data, in 1990 the number of Muslim men was 96,783 (63.6 percent), and Muslim women numbered 55,434 individuals (36.4 percent). Ten years later the figures had doubled (169,726 men and 141,081 women), amounting to 4.3 percent of the overall population. Today 11.75 percent of Muslims in Switzerland are Swiss citizens.[84] The institutional landscape is even less unified than in the Federal Republic, in part because of the linguistic diversity of Switzerland.[85] No single organization represents Muslims in Switzerland. Comparable to Germany and unlike Austria, Islam does not have the legal status of a corporation by public law in Switzerland.[86] Nevertheless, according to a recent study, Muslims there are supported by well-established networks of mosques, cultural centers, and a wide range of Islamic organizations.[87] With regard to the religious affiliations of Middle Eastern immigrants it is also important to acknowledge that a large number of individuals of Arab origin who live in German-speaking countries are Christians and that a significant number of individuals of Turkish and Iranian origin are secular in orientation. In fact, German notions of secularism and Turkish notions of *laicité,* for example, often converge in a common agenda toward Islamism.[88]

Other practices of self-expression and self-representation by Middle Eastern immigrants were directed at the larger German-speaking public. A number of well-known storytellers with roots in the Middle East, such as Rafik Schami, Burhan Karkutli, Kemal Kurt, Jusuf Naoum, Salim Alafenisch, Idriss Al Jay, Saddek El Kebir, and Huda el-Hilali, have engaged the German public. Rafik Schami received as many as 150 invitations a year to present his oral art of storytelling; Salim Alafenisch accepted 200 or more invitations a year to perform for audiences ranging from children to adults.[89] These performers have succeeded in making the traditional *hakawati,* or *meddah* (storyteller), a figure that remains central in Arab and Turkish societies today, part of the German cultural sphere.

In the realm of music, artists with roots in the Middle East have made significant contributions to the German and the international scene. One of the original world music bands, the Dissidenten, was founded in Germany in 1982 and blends North African and Western traditions. Two of the North African members of the band also launched independent careers. Hamid Baroudi (born in Algeria) and Houssaine Kili (from Morocco) both address aspects of bicultural life in their Arabic lyrics. Syrian-born Fouad El-Auwad and Lebanese-born Rabih Abou Khalil, among others, create other blends of musical styles. Abou Khalil, who plays the *oud* and composes music, came to Germany to study political science and classical flute. Over the years he built an international reputation with his compositions, blending jazz and traditional Arabic musical styles.

Painters and other visual artists with roots in the Middle East have had a significant impact on the German art scene. The painters Marwan Kassab Bachi, Mehmet Güler, and Ibrahim Hazimeh, as well as other, lesser-known figures such as Adnan Shino, Shahid Alam, Zeki Arslan, Gehad Abonegelah, and Burhan Karkutli, have influenced German cultural life through their art. Among the notable exhibits with a special focus on the Middle East was *Al Fann—Die Kunst* (August 11–24, 1995, in Hann. Münden), curated by Egypt-born Hamdi el Attar, who taught at the Gesamthochschule Kassel and organized a number of exhibits featuring artists from the non-Western world.[90]

Critical to the emergence of an alternative public sphere were publishing houses and distribution centers specializing in translations of works by Middle Eastern writers, those by immigrant writers with roots in the Middle East, and other texts about the Middle East. Verlag Edition Orient was founded in 1980 in Berlin, followed by Palmyra Verlag (Heidelberg), and the distribution service Orient Buch Vertrieb (Aschaffenburg). Al-Kamel Verlag was established by Khalid al-Maaly in Cologne in 1983 and today is considered the leading "arabische Verlag."[91] The Perspol-Verlag in Hamburg has published works by authors from Iran and other areas of the Middle East since the early 1980s. Türkische Bibliothek: Verlag an der Ruhr and Literaturca Verlag are among the Turkish-German publishing houses. These publishing venues and local bookstores, such as Das Arabische Buch and Ufuk Kitabevi—Türkische Buchhandlung in Berlin, were crucial in raising awareness about the history and cultures of the Middle East, including the lives of immigrants in Germany.[92] Immigrant communities have also established their presence in the public sphere in the realm of broadcasting, though it is a relatively recent development, emerging over the past two decades in Germany.[93] In addition, Germany-based writers such as Fadhil al-Azzawi and Khalid al-Maaly are prominent in Middle Eastern intellectual circles. Al-Azzawi, for example, is a consulting editor for the respected literary journal *Banipal,* which regularly includes texts by Germany-based immigrant writers.

This brings us to another topic, namely, the presence of German-speaking individuals and German-related institutions in the Middle East. Practices that document the German–Middle Eastern exchange are extensive and deserve attention separately, but here it is important to acknowledge the degree to which these various institutions and individuals have influenced the image of the Middle East in Germany and the image of Germany in the Middle East. Educational institutions are one such area of interaction. Apart from the activities of the Goethe-Institute, the German Academic Exchange Service, and a range of political and cultural foundations, German-focused education has a long tradition in some parts of the Middle East. Several German schools exist in Middle Eastern countries, some of them since the end of the nineteenth century. The Deutsche Evangelische Oberschule Kairo, for example, was established in 1873 and grew into one of the most highly respected educational institutions in Cairo. Other confessional schools in Egypt include the Deutsche Schule der Borromäerinnen, founded in Alexandria in 1884 and in Cairo in 1904. Graduates from these schools often went to study in German-speaking countries. Both returning students who received their education in German-speaking countries and Germans who emigrated to the Middle East for various reasons significantly shaped the development of academia and other cultural institutions.[94]

Another area that is entirely understudied and related to the history and influence of educational institutions and cultural exchange is the image of German-speaking countries in literatures and autobiographies of the Middle East. Publications in Turkish about Germany are widely available, indicating that the subject of emigration to Germany preoccupies Turkish minds in profound ways.[95] Germany is the subject of numerous travel accounts and works of fiction. Several well-known Turkish writers drew on experiences they had in Germany during extended stays there. Sabahattin Ali, a leading modern Turkish author known particularly for his short stories, studied in Potsdam and Berlin from 1928 to 1930. Haldun Taner studied from 1935/36 to 1938 in Heidelberg, and Sevgi Soysal from 1957 to 1958 in Göttingen. Several short stories and novels by these authors, who are counted among the innovative modern Turkish writers, are staged in Germany.[96] Since the 1960s Turkish literature has explored the myriad repercussions of labor migration and continues to pick up other subjects related to Germany, such as National Socialism.[97]

Abdo Abboud has discussed the significant reception of German-language authors in the Arab Middle East, highlighting particularly the influence of Heinrich Mann, Thomas Mann, Hermann Hesse, and Franz Kafka.[98] A number of autobiographical writings by Arabs with roots in the Middle East were based on visits to East Germany and document the close relations between the Arab world and East Germany. Among these autobiographical texts are Mustafa Kamal's *Yawmiyyat Rihla min al-Ra'smaliyya ila al-Ishtirakiyya* (1976). This *Diary of a Journey from Capitalism to Socialism* recounts the author's observations on divided Berlin.[99] Fu'ad Badawi's *Warda min Birlin* (A Rose from Berlin [1974]) and Ahmad Musa Salim's *Sibaq al-Mustaqbal bayna al-Din wa-al-Shuyu'iyya: Min Mudhakkirat Muslim fi Mujtama' Shuyu'i* (Race for the Future between Religion and Communism: Thoughts of a Muslim in a Communist Society [1976]) focus on East Berlin and the East German political system.[100]

The impact of German, Austrian, and Swiss tourism on the Middle East is another important point of contact worth exploring. Apart from its direct economic effects, German travel to, for example, Tunisia, Egypt, Morocco, and Turkey has influenced intercultural relationships, including intermarriage (which is also a significant factor in Germany; in 1996, for example, 16.1 percent of Turkish nationals married Germans).[101] Other than select case studies, a comprehensive assessment of the ways in which German tourism to the Middle East has influenced dimensions of infrastructure, intercultural social relations, language contact, and acculturation has not yet been undertaken.

In spite of the considerable organizational, institutional, and cultural presence of Middle Eastern minorities in German-speaking societies, as well as a noteworthy history of interaction in the Middle East, minority and majority cultures continued to live largely separate lives in the period up to unification. According to a study by Hartmut Esser, in the late 1980s, 78 percent of first-generation and 65 percent of second-generation Turkish migrants indicated that they had only Turkish friends.[102] Whereas interaction at the workplace or in educational institutions vacillated between limited to significant levels, the private sphere remained largely segregated. As Esser's study demonstrates, however, second-generation immigrants interact with other ethnic groups at higher levels than first-generation immigrants, and this trend continues among members of subsequent generations to an even greater degree. Most astounding, however, is the persistent ignorance preserved by the German-speaking majority culture about the activities of minorities.

The Public Sphere: Majority Voices on the Middle East and Immigrants with Middle Eastern Background

As Middle Eastern minorities created their own educational, intellectual, cultural, and other social networks in German-speaking countries, large segments of the majority society remained unaffected by and unaware of the scope and scale of these developments.

In the realm of academia, for example, West Germany, Switzerland, and Austria continued to follow predominantly philological approaches to the study of the Middle East, focusing primarily on the premodern period. In light of the *Orientalism* debate of the 1980s and 1990s it is noteworthy that already in the early 1960s European Orientalists faced charges of ideological bias. In 1964 Rudi Paret defended the field against accusations that had been voiced by al-Azhar scholars by claiming that the goal of Oriental studies remained the attainment of "pure truth."[103]

East Germany, on the other hand, developed innovative models for the study of the Middle East that moved decidedly away from the paradigm that continued to define most West German, Swiss, and Austrian institutions. In his study of GDR scholarship on the Middle East, Kai Hafez provides ample evidence that the academic study of the Middle East was closely tied to the dominant ideological paradigm and to East German foreign policy. Interestingly, the East German model in many ways resembled the area studies approach pursued in the United States in the university-based centers supported by Title VI funds from the U.S. Department of Education.[104]

Several specialized institutes also contributed to disseminating knowledge about the Middle East. In 1982 the Institut für Geschichte der Arabisch-Islamischen Wissenschaften was established in Frankfurt and since that time has generated an impressive corpus of translations of and scholarship on scientific texts from the medieval period. In addition to university-based departments and institutes, several organizations and publications stress their role in "building bridges" or "improving dialogue" with the Middle East. The Deutsches Orient-Institut (DOI) in Hamburg, for example, was established in 1960, and has played a significant role in the public sphere, as it produces publications for newspapers, radio, and television. In addition, several high-profile publications, such as *Fikrun wa Fann,* a bilingual cultural magazine that is published by the Goethe Institut and devoted to "promoting the dialogue with the Islamic world," contribute to making scholarly knowledge about the Middle East available to a broader audience.[105] The Web-based magazine qantara.de pursues a similar trajectory:

> The Arabic word "qantara" means "bridge." The Internet portal Qantara.de represents the concerted effort of the Bundeszentrale für politische Bildung (Federal Center for Political Education), Deutsche Welle, the Goethe Institut and the Institut für Auslandsbeziehungen (Institute for Foreign Cultural Relations) to promote dialogue with the Islamic world. The project is funded by the German Foreign Office.[106]

To date there are no systematic studies of the role of these institutions and publications.

With West German academics largely abstaining from participation in political debates, the public sphere was open to self-appointed experts. These experts, however, often drew on the writings of established academics, and in this regard the discipline's biases, especially toward the modern period, are implicated in the shaping of widely circulated views.[107] Two figures stand out in this regard, namely, Gerhard Konzelmann and Peter Scholl-Latour, both of whom contributed significantly to defining German ideas about the Middle East. Konzelmann covered the Middle East for the broadcaster ARD (e.g., he contributed to the popular international issues show *Weltspiegel*) and published dozens of best-selling books on the Middle East (including *Die Araber und ihr Traum vom Großarabischen Reich* [1974]; and *Allahs neues Weltreich: Der Kampf um die arabische Einheit* [1986]). In the wake of the Iranian Revolution his publications focused on Islam and Islamism (*Die islamische Herausforderung* [1980]; and *Allahs Schwert: Der Aufbruch der Schiiten* [1989]). Konzelmann presented one-dimensional interpretations of current events by stressing a number of seemingly essential features of Islam, such as a presumed Islamic propensity to solve all conflict through violence and without respect for legal frameworks. In pursuing his reductive approach, Konzelmann did not pay attention to crucial factors such as colonial history, modernization, and regional and transregional power relations. In a detailed study from the early 1990s, Gernot Rotter, professor of Gegenwartsbezogene Orientwissenschaft at the Asien-Afrika-Institut of Hamburg University, unmasked the reductive nature of Konzelmann's questionable expertise.[108]

In comparison to Konzelmann, who studied literature and history but was never awarded an academic degree, Peter Scholl-Latour holds a doctorate from the Sorbonne and received a diploma in Arabic and Islamic studies from Lebanese University of Beirut. Before he turned to, among other topics, reporting and writing about the Middle East, he gained international fame through his coverage of the Vietnam War (*Der Tod im Reisfeld: Dreißig Jahre Krieg in Indochina* [1980]). Among his most popular titles are *Allah ist mit den Standhaften: Begegnungen mit der islamischen Revolution* (1983), *Das Schwert des Islam: Revolution im Namen Allahs* (1990), *Weltkrise Arabien: Allah, Blut und Öl: Hintergründe eines Konflikts* (1991), and *Kampf dem Terror—Kampf dem Islam? Chronik eines unbegrenzten Krieges* (2002). Just as Rotter took on Konzelmann for his biased reporting style, the Arabists Verena Klemm and Karin Hörner gathered a group of engaged and enraged academics and intellectuals to challenge the work of Scholl-Latour. *Das Schwert des "Experten": Peter Scholl-Latours verzerrtes Araber- und Islambild* is a scathing critique of the journalist's biased view of Islam and Arab civilization. Meticulous analyses of Scholl-Latour's writings reveal elements of a polarizing mindset that elevate anti-Islamic and anti-Arab sentiments and stoke xenophobia and racism.[109]

But are Konzelmann and Scholl-Latour representative of the prevailing coverage in German media? The image of the Middle East, Islam, Arabs, Turks, and Persians in the West German media has been the subject of numerous studies. The most comprehensive investigation was compiled by Kai Hafez. In his introduction to *Die politische Dimension der Auslandsberichterstattung* Hafez explains that the image of the Middle East was never static and was often extremely heterogeneous, with diametrically opposing views promoted by different media and ideological camps, sometimes even concurrently in the same report.

Hafez's systematic study, which confirms and greatly substantiates the findings of earlier studies by Kenneth M. Lewan, Sami Fayez Khalil Musallam, Richard Blank, Astrib Hub, and others, is based on an analysis of coverage presented in two prominent daily newspapers, the *Süddeutsche Zeitung* and the *Frankfurter Allgemeine Zeitung,* and two major weeklies, *Der Stern* and *Der Spiegel.*[110] The analysis focuses primarily on the years 1955 to 1994. The results of the study address topics such as the oil crisis of 1973 and the Iranian Revolution of 1978–79. Hafez also investigates the widespread perception that West Germany's view of the Israeli-Palestinian conflict, one of the central topics discussed in the media, is deeply structured by a culture of memory that is connected to the Shoah, albeit in often diametrically opposed ways. While one line of argument supposes that Germans identify with Israelis to compensate for the Shoah, another one insists that German identification with

Arab points of view reveals suppressed antisemitism and anti-Zionism in which Palestinians are viewed as "victims of Holocaust survivors."[111] German alliances, however, have continually shifted: analyses of the coverage of the 1967 war show that the West German public clearly identified with Israel, yet only a few years later the situation had changed. The war of 1973 shows a broader spectrum of views, including a questioning of stereotypes held about Arabs. This trend continued in the aftermath to the Egyptian-Israeli peace treaty of 1979, with more positive views of Arabs being articulated.

Hafez correlates the changing presentation of the Middle East to significant historical events, such as the secret weapon deals between Israel and the Federal Republic, the Israel visits of Walter Scheel in 1971 and Willy Brandt in 1973, and the Lebanon invasion of Israel in 1982. Hafez's analysis confirms the findings of earlier studies, which revealed an initial phase of indifference followed by a period of strong sympathies for Israel, which was gradually transformed by the inclusion of Arab points of view, leading (since the early 1980s) to much more balanced discussions. Hafez concludes that, with regard to the interrelatedness of Shoah-related memory culture and contemporary events of the Middle East, no predictable constellation is evident: views of the Middle East are varied and changeable.[112]

Throughout his detailed study Hafez convincingly illustrates his argument regarding the changeability of German images about the Middle East and Islam. In addition to debunking images regarding German attitudes toward Israel and Palestine, his work sheds light on the image of Islam in the German media. In contrast to widespread assumptions about the discursive prevalence of Islam, Hafez documents that, in the period from 1955 to 1994, the topic "Islam" was far less popular in comparison to other central topics associated with the Middle East, such as the Israeli-Palestinian conflict.[113] In the aftermath of the Iranian Revolution, however, Islam advanced to become one of the standard themes discussed in the German media. Hafez emphasizes the interplay of long-term and short-term factors in constructing Western views of Islam, whereby certain images and dynamics remain constant over time, and others are more directly related to contemporary events.[114] His analysis of German media thus largely confirms findings from our analysis of the continuities and variables observable in German literary and cultural discourses since the Middle Ages.

The coverage of Middle Eastern minorities *within* West Germany, while certainly connected to and influenced by the coverage of foreign affairs concerning the Middle East and Islam, shows additional areas of bias, reductive perception, and also change. The largest conceptual impediment to a differentiated understanding of the situation of Middle Eastern immigrant communities was the identification of Middle Eastern immigrants with "guest workers" from Turkey. By reducing the social and ethnic diversity of immigrants to one dominant paradigm, the significant student population from the Middle East and the social diversity of immigrants, including Christian Arabs, secular Turks, and educated individuals, were largely overlooked. Instead, the Turkish *Gastarbeiter* became the central subject of ethnographic studies, popular best sellers, and media reports. Rita Chin's insightful study, *The Guest Worker Question in Postwar Germany,* shows just how pervasive the discussion of the *Gastarbeiter* was, and how it "was inextricably bound up with the central issues of German social, political, and cultural history after 1945."[115] These issues varied over time, as did the foci of the discussions and the dominant views.

Among the studies investigating the image of the Turkish minority in the German press, Orhan Gökçe's analysis focuses on media coverage of the visit to West Germany of the Turkish president Turgut Özal in 1984 and reveals that, at the time, Turks were largely seen by members of the German majority as a nuisance and in need of charity.[116] This approach to immigrant populations is also evident in popular writings that aimed at presenting immigrant life "from the perspective of the Turks themselves."[117] Arlene Teraoka's analysis of three examples of documentary reportage on Turkish lives in West Germany—namely, Max von der Grün's *Leben im gelobten Land: Gastarbeiterporträts* (1975), Paul Geiersbach's *Bruder, muss zusammen Zwiebel und Wasser essen!* (1982), and Günter Wallraff's *Ganz unten* (1985)—reveals "differing politics of approach, understanding, and control" in their attempts to represent Turkish individuals.[118] Geiersbach, in Teraoka's view, does not engage in the manipulative strategies employed by Wallraff and von der Grün but, rather, lets "the Other speak."[119] Unfortunately, the most differentiated approach to the representation of Turkish life in Germany was also the least circulated. Wallraff's *Ganz unten,* on the other hand, which draws attention to the plight of the dismal working and living conditions of illegal immigrants, was tremendously successful. The text, which contributed greatly to shaping the overdetermined image of the helpless and voiceless Turkish immigrant worker, sold three million copies in the first three years and has been translated into thirty languages.[120]

In the aftermath of the Islamic Revolution in Iran there has been a marked shift in focus, from studies of Turks and Turkish culture to discussions of Islam as the primary marker of difference between members of the German majority culture and members of Middle Eastern immigrant communities more broadly. A flood of publications on every aspect of Islam, inside and outside of Germany, has persisted since the early 1980s. With regard to the image of Islam in the media, Detlef Thofern's study of the Islam coverage presented by the weekly magazine *Der Spiegel,* focusing on the period from 1950 to 1989, highlights typical discursive patterns and identifies dominant topoi. Thofern documents, for example, that close to half of the documents he analyzed feature images of "fanatical" and "extremist" Muslims. Only rarely and less frequently after 1979 is Islam presented as being *relatively* important in the lives of Muslims.[121] His analysis also shows a tendency to emphasize Islam as a political movement; the idea of an Islamic state began to receive specific attention after 1979. The notion of Islam as a backward ideology structures about three-quarters of the texts analyzed by Thofern.[122] Other studies confirm this reductive view of Islam and particularly the emergence of political Islam as a topic in the German media, schoolbooks, and other publications.[123]

Among the key sources structuring the image of the Middle East and Islam in West Germany, Austria, and Switzerland are autobiographies and travel accounts, both in translations and the original German. The German translation of Betty Mahmoody's controversial memoir *Not without My Daughter* (1987), for example, sold two million copies. Mahmoody had visited Iran in 1984 for what she thought would be a two-week stay, but she was prevented from leaving by her husband. Her description of her eighteen months in Islamist Iran and her escape via Turkey contributed greatly to popularizing negative views of Islam, which became emblematic for the oppression of women in Islamic societies.

In sum, during the first two decades of postwar immigration the dominant discussion focused on social, economic, and select cultural issues associated mainly with Turkish labor migration, but the discourse turned decidedly more negative against Middle Eastern immigrants more generally in the aftermath of the Iranian Revolution and the emergence of political Islam as a global and, in the context of re-Islamization, also local phenomenon. This shift, observable in views articulated about Middle Eastern immigrants, steered attention away from questions of cultural difference and social status, emphasizing religious difference instead as the primary impediment to a successful coexistence of German majority populations and Middle Eastern minorities.

Majority German Writers and Filmmakers on the Middle East and Immigrants with a Middle Eastern Background

In examining the differing representational strategies of writers and filmmakers belonging to the German majority and minority populations, it is useful (in some respects) to distinguish self-representations of immigrants with roots in the Middle East from those texts and films that were produced by Germans with no personal connection to the Middle East through immigration. The German term *Mehrheitsdeutsche* highlights issues of domination that are related to the sheer size of the majority population but also to questions of political representation and access to social and economic resources. As our analysis shows, when divided into majority and minority writings, one can discern distinct tendencies related to the positionalities of the authors. While West Germans, Austrians, and Swiss gradually took notice of the growing minority with Middle Eastern roots, East Germans were not confronted with large-scale labor immigration from the Middle East, and as a result East German literature and film did not address the issue in any substantial way.

It is noteworthy to add that, after World War II, Jews lost their status as "Orientals" in Germany. The absence of a sizable German Jewish minority after the Shoah resulted in a lack of contact with that minority, which numbered around 30,000 in West Germany after the dissolution of the transitional camps in 1947–48. For most of the period up to 1989, with few exceptions, German majority writers engaged with Jews who had died in the Holocaust, not those living. Even when the number of Jews living in German- speaking countries increased as a result of the end of the Cold War, the older rhetorical strategies that associated Jews with the Orient did not resurface. New migrants with roots in the Middle East by then occupied that space.

German majority writers wrote narratives staged in the Middle East itself and narratives related to the new phenomenon of immigration from the Middle East to German-speaking countries.

The Middle East Without: A Space of Abjection

Ishrak Kamaluldin identifies several main themes in his analysis of post-1945 German-language narratives about the Middle East. In these texts the Middle East emerges as a place of barbarism, despotism, and cruelty (e.g., in Wolfgang Koeppen's novel *Der Tod in Rom* [1954]) but also serves as a vehicle to articulate a host of diverse ideas about life. The desert, for example, is portrayed both as a locus of existential desperation and as a counter-image to the decadence of modern life.[124] In most cases the engagement with Middle Eastern history is directly motivated by a quest to understand German history. Edgar Hilsenrath's novel *Das Märchen vom letzten Gedanken* (1989) is a case in point: it comments on the Armenian genocide but relates the events, directly and indirectly, to the Shoah. What most of these texts share, however, is a tendency to portray the Middle East as a space of abjection.

Among the most prominent of these narratives is Ingeborg Bachmann's fragment *Der Fall Franza* (posthumous, 1978; Xaver Schwarzenberger directed the 1986 film version of the novel). About half of the text's events are set in Egypt. The country's intrinsic qualities and cultural signifiers—the desert, the culture of death associated with the pyramids, the hieroglyphs—serve to illustrate central struggles the protagonist is facing. Franza's psychic illness, a result of an abusive relationship and misguided medical treatment, but also related to endemic violent social structures, manifests as a profound sense of alienation, personal disintegration, and a lingering death wish. The narrative brings the colonial and National Socialist past into dialogue and identifies fascist and patriarchal oppression as causal factors of Franza's illness. In the scene that leads to her death she is raped at a pyramid and hits her head in agony against the rocks, after which she loses consciousness and dies. References to contemporary Egypt are secondary in this somber narrative; the country remains an abstract foil for Bachmann's narrator, who engages the country's symbolic power primarily to flesh out Franza's painful demise.

Wolfgang Hildesheimer's novel *Masante* (1973) employs the Middle Eastern setting in similar ways. Essential qualities of the Arabian desert form the backdrop for the existentialist monologue of the unnamed first-person narrator. As Kamaluldin points out, *Masante* features not a single Middle Eastern protagonist; rather, the novel's characters are European or North American. The Middle East emerges as a place "that symbolizes the psychological state of the narrator and the mental state of his culture."[125] This emptying of the Middle East of its people and cultural specificity also structures Erhart Kästner's narrative *Zeltbuch von Tumilat* (1949), which is based on the author's captivity in the Egyptian desert at the end of World War II. Friedrich Dürrenmatt's detective novel *Der Richter und sein Henker* (1952) includes an episode staged in Istanbul (identified by its older name, Constantinople, which ties it to Christian history). While the scene features several Middle Eastern characters, they remain flat and clichéd, and function as "exotic extras."[126] Irmtraud Morgner's *Hochzeit in Konstantinopel* (1968) similarly does not engage with the Turkish setting but, rather, focuses on the relationships between the German characters of the novel.

In contrast, Elias Canetti's *Die Stimmen von Marrakesch* (1967) and Hubert Fichte's *Der Platz der Gehenkten* (1985, published posthumously in 1989) strive to engage with the Middle Eastern environment. Both texts focus on the central square in Marrakesh, the famous Djemaa el Fna. Canetti's text contains two distinct tales: on the one hand, Canetti's first-person narrator describes the milieu in Marrakesh by focusing on the city's poverty, illness, death, and instances of cruelty, and thus engages established views of the Middle East as a diseased and abject locus. The middle part of the narrative, however, recounts his exploration of the *mellah,* the Jewish quarter. Here we follow the narrator on his quest for his Sephardic roots, and he does indeed find a universe that is at once Jewish and a mirror of universal humanity.[127] The text is noteworthy as a personal documentary that chronicles the author's 1954 journey to Morocco but also as a historical document of once-flourishing Jewish life in North Africa. Regardless of these dimensions, however, Canetti's narrative engages a host of clichés about the Middle East. Ultimately, the negative images function to highlight the notion of an idealized Jewish community and simultaneously entertain another cliché, namely, the Orient as a place of origin.

Hubert Fichte's overall work is a testament to his relentless attempt at interrogating the politics of cross-cultural representation. His novel *Der Platz der Gehenkten* amounts to an aesthetic experiment in which he innovatively uses specific poetic forms in his approach and ideas about cultural difference. For example, the text's structure mirrors the Koran in that it reverses the Koranic structural principle of proceeding from longer to shorter units. After an introductory section Fichte's text begins with the letter *A,* followed by the word *Aliph* on the next page. The next page reads "Djemma el Fna," the Arabic name for the public square that is at the center of Fichte's text. The text gradually moves from words, phrases, and complete sentences to passages, but even these passages lack linear narrativity. In his refusal to offer an easily accessible text, Fichte's narrator communicates snapshots, moments, images, and sensations. The body and affect are central to Fichte's approach to representation, as are his concerns for the marginalized, the oppressed, and the violated. Fichte refuses to exoticize Djemaa el Fna, which has been the subject of folkloristic narratives for centuries, and offers a narrative that forces the reader to engage in serious interpretive work. David Simo explains that Fichte's "aesthetics of the fragmentary, of discontinuity, ambiguity, and destruction of the secured auctorial narrative perspective . . . were inspired from the beginning by the ethnographic material and ethnographic practices."[128] But what is the result of Fichte's approach? The reader is faced with an agglomeration of images that ultimately resonate with established tropes of writing about the Orient. The focus on disease and poverty, on the weird and strange, leaves the reader struggling; the absence of interpretive commentary, in fact, constructs Morocco as an inaccessible and abject space.

Another attempt at a consciously self-reflexive text is Nicolas Born's novel *Die Fälschung* (1979; made into a movie in 1981 by Volker Schlöndorff), which is staged in Lebanon during its Civil War. On his journey through the destroyed country, the journalist Georg Laschen experiences a fundamental crisis as he struggles with how to relate the "facts" of the horrendous war to the German reading audience. The crisis of the journalist exemplifies the crisis of the human being in the face of suffering. The novel ends with his resignation as a journalist and thus resonates strongly with the political frustrations and disillusionment of the West German political Left at the end of the 1970s. Similar to Bachmann's use of Egypt and Canetti's portrayal of Morocco, Lebanon serves primarily as a symbolic locus to meditate on existential questions of life and politics that are clearly related to Germany's history. The historical specificity of the countries used as a backdrop is not explored. In Born's novel, however, the question of representation is directly addressed. As Ishrak Kamaluldin argues, *Die Fälschung* debunks the Western media focus on Arab violence as reflective of the West's thirst for violence.[129]

The Austrian author Barbara Frischmuth has engaged with relations between Germans and Middle Eastern individuals and cultures extensively since the early 1970s. Frischmuth studied Turkish and approaches her subject with substantial knowledge about Turkey, Islam, and the Middle East in general. Among her Middle East–related publications are novels (*Das Verschwinden des Schattens in der Sonne* [1973]; *Die Schrift des Freundes* [1998]; *Vergiss Ägypten* [2008]), poems (*Schamanenbaum* [2001]), and radio plays (*Eine Liebe in Erzurum* [1994]; *Vier Verse für einen Mantel oder die Verwandlung des Abu Seid von Serug* [1997]). In addition, Frischmuth has published countless shorter prose pieces and essays on Middle Eastern topics. Her novel *Das Verschwinden des Schattens in der Sonne* explores Turkish-German relations by following the experiences of a first-person female narrator during her travels in Turkey, where she does research on the Bektashi Sufi order. By assuming the role of an outsider, Frischmuth's narrator exposes herself to the social situation of the migrants. Frischmuth displays knowledge of the challenges confronting 1970s Turkish society and addresses the struggles of intellectuals in a politically oppressive environment. Nevertheless, the novel perpetuates a host of essentializing clichés; ultimately, Turkey and its people remain inaccessible and alien. As Dagmar C. G. Lorenz points out, "Frischmuth's novels neither provide new insights, nor do they provide vistas for change. Instead, they reassure the majority of her readership of the validity of their time-honored clichés: In Frischmuth's novels, East remains East and West, West."[130] Other critics applaud precisely this feature of Frischmuth's engagement with the Middle East by praising her for representing "the strange and the other in its unmistakable specificity and independence."[131] Whereas Frischmuth seems bound by centuries of representations of the Orient in her earlier work, she has certainly developed a more nuanced understanding over time. Her most recent work, *Vergiss Ägypten,* for example, attempts to pursue a nonessentialist examination of Middle Eastern and European contexts by focusing on the dynamic lives of individuals.

Overall, post-1945 narratives about the Middle East draw on established clichés but also project new topics onto the Middle Eastern setting. As Kamaluldin points out, most of the texts feature a new type of traveler to the Middle East, one who, in contrast to the self-confident traveler of, for example, Karl May's novels, is ontologically insecure. But the journey to the Middle East does not, in most cases, bring resolution; on the contrary, the crisis intensifies. While the Middle East emerges as the place that highlights "the evil of the Western individual," it remains associated with that evil.[132] In this regard post-1945 narratives do not represent a radical break with literary traditions of the past. In spite of a turn toward self-reflexivity, the Middle East, for the most part, remains enigmatic, devoid of individuality and cultural specificity, and associated with Western fears and desires: a space of abjection.

The Middle East Within: Questions of Perspective and Communication

The majority of German-language texts staged in the Middle East were written before 1980. After the 1970s the focus of German-language writers turned to the Middle East at home. What kind of issues and representational strategies might one expect to be addressed in literature and films, especially when considering the wealth of new issues confronting German-speaking countries as a result of labor migration? First of all, in contrast to the omnipresence of migration-related issues in the popular press, popular literature, and the everyday reality of majority populations in German-speaking countries, these issues only rarely became the main focus of literature and film. By the mid-1960s several works of fiction featured immigrants from Italy, Greece, and other southern European states. But even in these works immigration came into view only as a minor aspect, or the engagement with the topic resulted in a generalization that deprived the migration experience of its specificity. Among the representations featuring Middle Eastern immigrants one type of text and film focuses on the topic of "foreignness" as a more general ontological question, and often this foreignness entails issues of communication and intercultural romantic relations. A second cluster of texts and films gives attention to the situation of immigrant women.

One of the first, and certainly groundbreaking and definitive, works foregrounding communication is Rainer Werner Fassbinder's 1974 movie *Angst essen Seele auf.* The plot revolves around a relationship between a young Moroccan immigrant and a much older German woman who works as a cleaner. To the surprise of their friends and relatives, they move in together and get married. As the couple faces a wide range of challenges regarding the social acceptability of their relationship, the film highlights questions of perspective and power. Issues of inclusion and exclusion are brought to the fore by the camera continuously zooming in and out of doors and windows, thus emphasizing themes of framing and gazing. In addition, Fassbinder's film addresses communication and the relationship between minority and majority cultures by juxtaposing the limited command of the German language typically associated with immigrants to the formulaic and empty speech of German characters who draw heavily on passive constructions and enunciate normative phrases. With his aesthetically and thematically sophisticated film, Fassbinder, who had already addressed German hostility toward immigrant workers in his 1969 feature *Katzelmacher,* laid the groundwork for subsequent works exploring the social place of immigrants in Germany.

Groß und Klein: Szenen, a play by Botho Strauss from 1978 that was turned into a movie directed by Peter Stein in 1980, features a character called "The Turk," whose linguistic agonies symbolize the collapse of interpersonal communication.[133] While Strauss's play integrates communication problems between Turks and Germans in the larger complex of social relations in capitalist consumer society, Franz Xaver Kroetz relates the issue of communication in his play *Furcht und Hoffnung der BRD* (1984) more directly to immigration. The Turkish character in the scene "Ausländerdeutsch" is at the center of a German woman's monologue about intercultural relations between Turks and Germans during which she makes up her mind to have sexual intercourse with the Turk. Throughout the scene the Turk gestures but does not utter a single word.[134] Heinrich Böll, in the earlier novel *Gruppenbild mit Dame* (1971), used a similar strategy to draw attention to the powerlessness of Turkish immigrants regarding their self-representation. His Turkish character Mehmet does not speak for himself; rather, the views of others about him reveal their discriminatory and dehumanizing nature.

Communication and intercultural understanding are also at the core of Sten Nadolny's novel *Selim oder Die Gabe der Rede* (1990). Next to Fassbinder's movie *Angst essen Seele auf,* this novel is one of the few works of fiction that engages centrally with a Turkish immigrant character. As opposed to the silent or speech-impaired figures in the works by Böll, Strauss, Kroetz, and Fassbinder, the novel's Turkish protagonist, Selim, is endowed with the gift of speech. His German counterpart, Alexander, is lacking exactly this ability to communicate successfully. Leslie A. Adelson has pointed out that Nadolny's novel poses "a radical break with the trope of 'Turkish' speechlessness."[135] But in the view of some critics the fact that Selim is speaking does not imply a noncliched portrayal of Turks or Turkey.[136] Adelson, on the other hand, emphasizes the novel's potential to question binary oppositions and to invite the reader to reflect critically on established representational conventions.[137] Ülker Gökberk celebrates the novel as successfully envisioning a model of interculturality.[138]

In their explorations of communication between majority and minority groups in Germany, some of these filmmakers and authors encourage us to reflect upon dominant views and stereotypes, while others draw on clichés and reify representational conventions that preclude an understanding of immigrants as human beings with distinct histories. More often than not, the question of cross-cultural communication is removed from its concrete historical and geopolitical context and presented as an ontological problem.

The status of women emerged as another vehicle to voice majority German views on Turks and other immigrants, a phenomenon not unique to the German situation; on the contrary, images of "white men [and women] saving brown women from brown men" are a prominent trope in Western texts about non-Western societies. In addition, the status of women is an ideological battleground for political agendas throughout the world. Turkish immigrant women are at the center of a number of controversial films from the 1970s and 1980s. Helma Sanders-Brahms's 1975 film *Shirins Hochzeit* is a case in point. The made-for-television black-and-white feature tells the story of Shirin, who refuses to enter into an arranged marriage with a rich man, flees to Germany to find her boyfriend, and, failing in her quest to locate him, begins a life as a factory worker. She loses her work, becomes a prostitute in guest worker circles, and, after a tragic encounter in which she sees her boyfriend but he does not recognize her, gets shot in a dispute between pimps. Aras Ören, one of the most prolific and respected Turkish-German writers, appears in the film as an actor and was credited by Sanders-Brahms for contributing considerably to the script. Nevertheless, the film was sharply criticized and led to protests by right-wing Turkish groups. Hark Bohm's 1988 *Yasemin* drew even more controversy.

Yasemin symbolizes the conflicts of second-generation Turkish Germans who were born in the Federal Republic and find themselves stuck between two worlds. Even though "Yasemin's assorted family members embody different levels of assimilation and acceptance of West German culture," the film ultimately condemns Turkish patriarchal immigrant culture, while, according to Susan C. Anderson, "Germans . . . seem the superior social group owing to their apparent openness to gender roles."[139]

The focus on the situation of Turkish women is also picked up in Hanne Mede-Flock's *Im Schatten der Mondsichel* (1985). This novel, like Frischmuth's *Das Verschwinden des Schattens,* is primarily staged in Turkey but relates German and Turkish histories in multiple ways. Female solidarity is explored in a plot that brings together a German, a Turkish German, and several Turkish women. Against the background of the 1980 military coup, the novel aims to highlight the interconnections between fascist violence and systemic violence against women.[140] In contrast to the films by Sanders-Brahms and Bohm and the novel by Mede-Flock, *Die Kümmeltürkin geht* (1984–85) by Jeanine Meerapfel takes a different approach. The film blends documentary and fictional elements to tell the story of a young woman who is not oppressed by her extensive patriarchal family but, rather, fails in her quest to build a life in Germany, in spite of her attempt to confront daily humiliation with humor. After fourteen years in Germany she returns to Turkey.

A few outliers among German works depicting immigrants from the Middle East do not focus primarily on communication or the situation of women. *Metin,* a 1979 made-for-television film by Thomas Draeger, centers on the life of a six-year-old Turkish boy who lives in Kreuzberg in Berlin, which is said to be the home of the largest concentration of Turks living outside of Turkey. The film turns to the world of children to explore the ways in which stereotypes structure cross-cultural relationships among children but also attempts to show spaces in which children can move beyond the models passed on to them by their parents. Jan Schuette's 1987 feature *Drachenfutter* ties the situation of Middle Eastern immigrants more generally to the influx of global migrants, from asylum seekers to labor migrants, who are challenged to form relations of solidarity in order to survive in a hostile world.

Jakob Arjouni's detective novels embody another type of fiction genre that is markedly different from other majority representations of immigrants. The protagonist of the four novels is Kemal Kayankaya, who engages German stereotypes about Turks in creative ways. Arlene A. Teraoka has argued that Kayankaya's main qualities are all in tension with mainstream stereotypes about Turks: making an immigrant worker the key protagonist of a German-language detective story was unprecedented; he is a Turk but holds a German passport; his Turkishness defies notions of "Orientals as illogical, thus as ill-suited for the role of detective"; and, finally, the Turkish man, most often associated with criminality, as "an agent of justice flies in the face of German belief."[141] These factors explain why the question of the author's identity occupied the minds of critics intensely. For years critics speculated about the identity of the author and wrongly suspected that he himself, like his protagonist, was of Turkish origin.[142]

In 1991 Doris Dörrie made Arjouni's most well-known Kayankaya novel an eponymous film, *Happy birthday, Türke.* Whereas Arjouni defied German stereotypes about Turks creatively, Dörrie seems to have thought that a reethnicization and greater use of clichés would make the film more attractive. As Teraoka points out, "presumably in order to make Kayankaya more 'authentically' Turkish, Dörrie put dark contact lenses on her lead actor, inserted an affair between Kayankaya and a Turkish widow, and replaced Arjouni's depiction of economic pressures and police corruption with an emphasis on Turks' 'culture shock.'"[143] Dörrie's interpretation of Arjouni's novel thus places her closer to films that reinforce rather than challenge cultural stereotypes about Turkishness.

Documenting the process of acculturation are also the Turkish characters that populate the popular television series *Liebling-Kreuzberg* (1986–98), created by Jurek Becker. As Nazire Akbulut points out in her discussion of several episodes that were produced between 1985 and 1987, the relevant episodes highlight differences and conflicts between first- and second-generation Turkish immigrants and succeed in debunking clichéd representations; references to religion, however, are often treated with cynicism.[144] As Sander Gilman suggests, "there is neither liberal romanticizing of Turkish life nor general condemnation of a 'foreign' way of life. The 'Turkish' figures run the gamut from the secularized daughter to the older man who holds to the traditional order of things. No easy answers are given to the problems raised, and the plot does not actually resolve, but the problems are defined by brilliant dialogue and striking situations."[145]

In conclusion we can discern a trend away from an approach that shows majority Germans almost completely unable to imagine the individuality of German–Middle Eastern immigrants to a gradual turning toward engaging with concrete instances of lived reality. Whereas most representations that focus on questions of communication or the situation of women perceive Turkish-German relations in binaries and categories of exclusion and inclusion, Arjouni's novels and Becker's *Liebling-Kreuzberg* picture Turkish Germans as an integral part of German life. With few exceptions, texts that engage with the Middle East itself remain largely stuck in established representational clichés, such as ideas of the Orient as a space of abjection, and do not touch upon the range of issues German society faced as a result of labor immigration.

Minor Literature and Film

One of the outcomes of post–World War II large-scale immigration to Europe was the creation of minor literatures, in the sense that Gilles Deleuze and Félix Guattari describe as "that which a minority constructs within a major language."[146] The considerable corpus of German-language minor texts and films was produced mostly in West Germany, with fewer artists actively contributing in East Germany, Austria, and Switzerland. Two related areas of interest will not be discussed here: First, works by authors and artists who create in Middle Eastern languages, unless their translated works had considerable impact on the German public sphere; and, second, the place that Israel has in the writings of German-Jewish authors such as Rafael Seligmann and Stefan Heym, a topic that has gained prominence only recently, during the postunification period.

As a result of the scale and scope of immigration from Turkey, investigations of works by German-language minority artists in the post–World War II period were closely tied to aspects of labor immigration. At first the impetus of critics was to categorize the emerging literatures in ways that seemed to reflect historical stages of integration, from *Gastarbeiterliteratur* and *Ausländerliteratur* to migrant literature and German literature. Over time, common themes such as inbetweenness and particular ways of engaging with inter-/cross-/trans-/multiculturalism emerged as distinctive elements of minor literature. Tom Cheesman's review of the critical literature in this regard highlights the close connection between studies of Turkish-German cultural production and German minority culture in general.[147] Recently, critics have introduced the idea of cosmopolitanism and the notion of a "literature of settlement" to the discussion, acknowledging the cultural output of second and third generations of artists, many of whom have a German passport.[148] These approaches to categorizing the works of minority artists are to some degree complementary: historical developments affect changes in the nature and content of German minor literature, and new topics arise as migrants become citizens.

Because of the significant scope of labor migration from Turkey, much of the scholarly discussion of German minor literature and film has focused on German-language writers and artists of Turkish origin; indeed, the list of authors has grown tremendously over time. As of the writing of this book, the list of "Turkish-German Writers" published by Wikipedia shows 233 names of novelists, poets, translators, screenwriters, satirists, nonfiction authors, and other writers.[149] In addition, 29 Turkish-German authors are identified as publishing primarily in Turkish.

Yet, because of its focus on the Turkish-German community, the critical discussion often misses central aspects of the larger phenomenon of germanophone minor literature. While labor migration is certainly the primary factor behind the growing minority populations in Germany, criticism that privileges this phenomenon is conceptually unable to address the contribution of other minor artists whose biographies and cultural output are not tied to labor migration. The existence of a noteworthy Arab and, to a lesser extent, Iranian contribution to the German cultural sphere, for example, has barely been acknowledged. This omission is evidenced by the lack of scholarship on these groups of authors; in addition to several articles, book chapters, and unpublished master's theses, only two book-length studies by Uta Aifan and Manar Omar are devoted exclusively to Arab-German authors.[150] Omar's study was published in Egypt and has not received the scholarly appreciation it deserves. In addition, a Web site maintained by Mohamed Esa provides information on Arab-German writers and other artists.[151] While an anthology has acknowledged Iranian-German writers as a group, literary criticism has thus far not addressed the subject.[152]

In comparison to the two and a half million people of Turkish origin, German residents or citizens of Arab descent account for a smaller minority, currently consisting of approximately 500,000 people. The group of Iranian Germans probably exceeds 150,000 individuals.[153] Over the last four decades, however, writers, artists, and intellectuals belonging to these groups have achieved considerable visibility as writers, academics, musicians, storytellers, and painters.[154] Because of the focus on Turkish-German writers, dominant themes central to the works of artists of Arab and Iranian origin have not been sufficiently considered by scholars. Several high-profile writers, such as Said, Torkan, and Adel Karasholi, came to Germany as political exiles escaping oppression in Iran and Syria. Salim Alafenisch, whose roots are in the Negev Desert in Israel, foregrounds political history in the cloak of fairy tales. Rafik Schami, the only Arab-German writer about whom a biography was published, and Burhan Karkutli also played a significant role as messengers relating the plight of Middle Eastern conflicts to German audiences. In addition, like the artists of Turkish descent, authors with connections to Arab countries or Iran brought with them aesthetic traditions rooted in their respective cultures of origin. The interplay of German and non-German aesthetic dimensions in the works of these artists, however, did not catch the attention of literary critics, who, for the most part, were not prepared to engage with the bi- or multicultural dimensions of these texts.

For the period up until 1989 minor literature (and a few films) by artists with roots in the Middle East can be divided into two main groups. The first consists of works that employ narrative strategies of social realism and symbolism, are secular and cosmopolitan in outlook, thematize the experience of exile, and deemphasize questions of ethnic and religious belonging. The second group of works draws on Middle Eastern aesthetic traditions and engages the Middle East thematically to a greater extent than the works of the first group. Beginning in the early 1990s (and not considered here), a third cluster emerges, which includes works that engage satire, self-reflexive aesthetics, and often nonlinear narrative strategies to question essentializing notions about Middle Eastern (and German) peoples and cultures. Emine Sevgi Özdamar, Feridun Zaimoğlu, Sinasi Dikmen, Osman Engin, Zafer Şenocak, Wadi Soudah, and Jamal Tuschick, among others, belong to this group of authors. In the late 1990s minority filmmakers also turned to innovative representational strategies and departed from the "pictures of victimisation and closure [which] continued to circulate" in the 1980s.[155] Several path-breaking anthologies—such as those by Cathy S. Gelbin, Kader Konuk, and Peggy Piesche; Jamal Tuschick; and Hito Steyerl and Encarnación Rodríguez—paid tribute to these developments, and generated a substantial broadening of the discussion, including a questioning of basic categories related to questions of cultural identity.[156]

Social Realism, Cosmopolitanism, and Exile

In 1981 the term *Gastarbeiterliteratur* was used strategically by a group of immigrant writers to draw attention to the emergence of a minor literature.[157] Rafik Schami, who is from Syria, and Franco Biondi, who was born in Italy, in collaboration with the Lebanese Jusuf Naoum and Suleman Taufiq (who was born in Beirut and grew up in Syria), envisioned a literature that would raise consciousness and allow for political solidarity across different nationalities and ethnicities. Their focus on the economic roots of different forms of oppression resonated strongly with Leftist agendas, and also deliberately evoked historical models of exile and emigrant literature.[158] Both the idea of a "literature of the affected" (*Literatur der Betroffenheit*) and "Gastarbeiterliteratur" were thus conceptualized strategically as forms of resistance. In 1980 the founding of the first literary series dedicated to publishing *Gastarbeiterliteratur, Südwind Gastarbeiterdeutsch* (renamed *Südwind Literatur* in 1983), and the organization PoLi-Kunstverein (Polynationaler Literatur- und Kunstverein) reflected these aspirations. The political ambitions, however, generated division rather than unity; the renaming of the literary series reflects "a definite move from political issues to a more literary program."[159] The literary series was discontinued in 1986, PoLi-Kunstverein dissolved in 1987.[160]

While most writers and artists of Middle Eastern origin did not come to German-speaking countries as labor migrants, the legal, political, and social challenges they faced mirrored the experience of their working-class compatriots.[161] Political refugees identified with the fate of those who had emigrated for economic reasons. Immigrant students joined the workforce to support themselves and were thus able to relate to the experiences of working-class migrants. Several key actors who were crucial to founding the early initiatives were of Arab origin, and the conceptual tendencies visible in these first attempts at organizing can be attributed to the political biographies of their founders. Rafiq Schami and Adel Karasholi, for example, left Syria for political reasons. In fact, writers and artists from the Arab Middle East were intellectually inspired by decolonization and the nonalignment and related Afro-Asian movements, which emerged in the aftermath of the Bandung Conference of 1955. These movements and the experience of decolonization shaped the first generation of immigrants from the Arab and Iranian Middle East, but for historical reasons affected those who arrived from Turkey less.

The plight of immigrant workers is at the center of an early short story by Rafik Schami, "Zwischen Traum und Straßenbahn" (1980), which depicts the dismal working and living conditions of immigrants from Turkey, Greece, Yugoslavia, Syria, Spain, and Italy, and who overcome their internal divisions in light of the relentless insults from their German employers.[162] The anguish related to living between two cultures is the theme of Fahri Kaya's short story "Gedanken zu Deutschland," Zehra Çırak's poem "tatsächlich," and Alev Tekinay's "Du machst dich, Mädchen!"[163] The emotional and physical effects that loneliness, deprivation, and alienation have on immigrants are the subject of stories and poems by Habib Bektaş ("krank in deutschland"), Aras Ören ("Bahnhöfe"), Semra Ertan ("ich habe gesehen," "wofür lebe ich"), Şiir Eroğlu ("Abschied"), Sabriye Cemboluk ("Nacht in einem fremden Land"), Alev Tekinay ("Das Kind am Anlegeplatz," "Ali Stern"), and Özgür Savaşçı ("Unsere Lage").[164] The challenges of cross-cultural communication pervade poems and narratives by Suleman Taufiq ("warum") and Şiir Eroğlu ("Gespräche").[165] Countering stereotypes is the subject of stories by Hülya Özkan ("Beziehungen") and Alev Tekinay ("Biergarten-Impressionen").[166] These texts are united in focusing on economic and sociocultural realities, and engage traditions of social realism in both style and pedagogical trajectory. Poetry may at times use symbolist and other forms but nevertheless shares the political goals evident in the narratives.[167]

In the 1980s several women writers set out to educate the German reading public about the situation of women in Middle Eastern countries and of immigrant women in Germany. The most prominent among them were of Turkish origin, and most of them employed social realist narrative techniques to tell stories that at times drew on their own autobiographies. Melek Baklan's short story "Das Korsett" relates the memories of a first-person narrator who remembers an accident that left her younger sister crippled for life and for which her family held her responsible. The sober tone conveys the emotional hardship of a young Turkish girl growing up in an environment hostile to girls and women.[168] Saliha Scheinhardt's narratives are also devoted to drawing attention to the situation of Turkish women. The titles of her narratives—*Frauen, die sterben, ohne dass sie gelebt hätten* (1983), *Und die Frauen weinten Blut* (1985), and *Träne für Träne werde ich heimzahlen: Kindheit in Anatolien* (1987)—clearly reveal the agenda of an author whose depiction of female oppression resonates strongly with mainstream German ideas about Turks and Muslims. Other female authors, such as Aysel Özakin, Alev Tekinay, and later Renan Demirkan and Emine Sevgi Özdamar countered Scheinhardt's approach and created multidimensional narratives aimed at debunking German clichés about Turkey and particularly gender relations in Turkey.

40 m² Deutschland (1986) by Tevfik Başer in Germany also comments on the situation of Turkish immigrant women in Germany. The film depicts the plight of a young Turkish woman who is locked up and virtually kept prisoner by her husband, who cannot fathom a life for her within Germany and outside of his control. Başer's film *Abschied vom falschen Paradies* (1988) again focuses on the oppression of Turkish immigrant women. The film's female protagonist, who has killed her abusive husband, prefers prison to the life awaiting her outside. According to Hamid Naficy, "The film posits that for Turkish immigrants, particularly women, confinement to a prison in Germany and protection by German laws are preferable to life outside the prison in either Germany or Turkey."[169] In their representation of female oppression these films resonate with perspectives offered in the narratives of Scheinhardt. As Rita Chin has pointed out, however, both artists link the actions of their female protagonists to their socialization in the women's networks of Turkey's rural communities. This aspect adds a layer of complexity to the works of Scheinhardt and Başer; it complicates the cultural binary Germany-Turkey by pointing to additional underlying social factors, such as the urban-rural divide.[170]

Whereas this group of writers highlighted the economic and social hardships of immigrants, several mostly Turkish-born writers took a decidedly different stance with their appeals to embrace cross-cultural experiences. Yüksel Pazarkaya came to Germany in 1958 to study chemistry, completing his degree in 1966, then taking up a new course of study in German literature and philosophy. He received his doctoral degree in 1972. Pazarkaya began writing and translating in 1959, and his fiction and nonfiction oeuvre in both Turkish and German is substantial. In one of his early poems Pazarkaya describes the positive experience of having discovered a "second homeland" in the German language, and he articulates these affirmative feelings in opposition to those who see in the German language a tool of oppression.[171] Pazarkaya also plays a significant role as a translator and writer of nonfiction texts designed to educate German readers about Turkish culture. In *Rosen im Frost: Einblicke in die türkische Kultur* (1982), for example, Pazarkaya emphasizes Turkey's multiethnic and multireligious history and stresses that Turkish culture is a result of the cross-cultural interaction that occurred over several centuries. By highlighting this multicultural history, Pazarkaya also provides the blueprint for a productive Turkish-German symbiosis.

In similar ways the early work of Aras Ören, who came to Germany as an already established writer and who writes mainly in Turkish, envisioned, according to Heidrun Suhr, "a multicultural community that develops out of the coexistence of discrete cultural groups."[172] As Rita Chin points out, in the first installment of his Berlin trilogy (*Was will Niyazi in der Naunynstraße* [1973]) Ören "explored the life of a Turkish laborer" and "established a particular subject (Niyazi) within a specific neighborhood (Berlin's Kreuzberg) and drew public attention to his individual concerns (*wollen*). Thus, from his very first literary gesture in German, Ören offered a challenge to the mostly atemporal, rootless, and faceless guest worker that had dominated public discussions of the recruitment over the previous two decades."[173] The 1981 novel *Bitte nix Polizei* (which was first written in Turkish and quickly translated into German) also promotes building bridges between different cultural groups by emphasizing their shared socioeconomic struggles but no longer exudes an optimistic air and thus shares more with the first group of writers. Optimism reigns supreme, however, in the somewhat naive short story "Frau Duman" by Fakir Baykurt. The story sketches the life of a Turkish couple that supports each other and lovingly masters the challenges of immigrant life.[174] Another optimistic stance is articulated in Mehmet Ünal's poem "Neue Freunde."[175]

Adel Karasholi shares the approach pursued by Pazarkaya. Karasholi was born in Damascus in 1936 and had already published poetry in Arabic before emigrating to Germany in 1960, in response to the outlawing of the Syrian writers' association. Karasholi is the most prominent (to the best of my knowledge the only) published author of Middle Eastern origin who had a significant impact on the East German cultural scene. In contrast, the well-known poet Fadhil al-Azzawi, who came to the GDR in 1977 and lives in Berlin today, publishes almost exclusively in Arabic. In a conversation with me in July 2008 Karasholi explained that before 1989 he was considered first and foremost a writer and that his ethnic origin did not play a significant role when he performed along with other East German writers, such as Sarah Kirsch and Volker Braun. After unification, however, he saw himself categorized as a minority writer and was no longer invited to cultural events, unless the event specifically focused on the situation of Germany's ethnic minorities.[176]

In contrast to the recent ethnicization to which he finds himself subjected, Karasholi's work emphasizes individual aspects of belonging; in that he situates himself locally rather than within larger collectivities, such as nations, religions, or ethnic groups. As Uta Aifan reports, he claims a "Karasholiidentität" for himself and declares that he is a "Syro-Sachse."[177] Accordingly, Karasholi's poetry engages with philosophical and existentialist themes without avoiding the topic of biculturality. Indeed, much of his poetic work—he speaks of a "Poetik einer Zweisprachigkeit"—explores the effect of writing with and between two languages and cultures.[178] But Karasholi refuses to be reduced to a sociological phenomenon; he denounces the marginalization of the minority writers who receive "Sonderpreise" for their work and continue to be discussed outside of the dominant cultural sphere. In spite of his rejection of this reductive reading of the works of immigrant writers, he grants that immigrant writers share a unique perspective.[179] The perspective of the immigrant writer, according to Karasholi, contributes to the overcoming of divisions and the challenging of stereotypes, topics poignantly articulated in the poem "Der alte Turban."[180] In his desire to highlight the shared aspects of humanity, Karasholi's views are less confrontational than other Arab-German writers who published in the West German context of the 1980s. The East German cultural context, with its emphasis on international solidarity, surely contributed to facilitating this attitude. West German writers of Middle Eastern origin faced a significantly more hostile cultural climate.

Aysel Özakin belongs to the group of writers who emphasize commonalities between Turkish, German, and other cultures and envision a transnational synthesis. Her views question notions of national and cultural belonging.[181]

Her poem "Poetry International," for example, meditates on the lives of immigrants and exiles who eke out an existence between Poland, the Netherlands, Germany, Turkey, and France.[182] A cosmopolitan trajectory is also central to Kemal Kurt's satirical novel *Ja, sagt Molly* (1998).[183] Cosmopolitanism is clearly a defining feature more often articulated by Turkish-German writers: Tom Cheesman's *Novels of Turkish German Settlement* discusses Turkish-German writers whose work is inspired by a cosmopolitan vision, particularly the ways in which this vision emerges in distinct ways in the writings of Akif Pirinçci, Renan Demirkan, and Saliha Scheinhardt as well as authors who began publishing in the 1990s, including Emine Sevgi Özdamar, Feridun Zaimoğlu, Zafer Şenocak, and Selim Özdogan. B. Venkat Mani's *Cosmopolitical Claims* pursues the topics in the works of Özdamar and Zaimoğlu, among others.

Another group of texts is best understood as exile literature and includes a significant number of Iranian writers. Foremost in this regard is the novel *Tufan: Brief an einen islamischen Bruder* by Torkan, who has lived in West Germany since 1964. This text, published in 1983, covers the time under the regime of the shah, the Iranian Revolution and its oppressive aftermath, and the narrator's exile in Germany. Told from a female perspective, the narrative conveys aspects of the oppression of women spanning the period before and after the Iranian Revolution and decries deeply misogynist structures of Iranian patriarchy. Torkan's second narrative, *Kaltland: Wah'schate Ssard* (1984), centers on life in Germany, recording the often humiliating experiences of an exile immigrant woman. Her third narrative shifts the focus from a reflection upon lived reality to the realm of dreams and desires. *Allnacht: Roya und Alp-Traum* (1987), told in a nonlinear style and drawing increasingly on the language of symbolism, expresses a vision of love and humanity that most powerfully defies the painful experiences chronicled in Torkan's first two works. Another Iranian woman author who elicits comparison with Torkan in terms of biography and the content and style of the narratives is Fahime Farsaie. Farsaie, who was born in 1952 and persecuted under the shah, returned to Iran from exile in England in 1979. She fled Iran in 1983 and has lived in Germany since.[184]

The most prominent Iranian-German writer is Said who came to Germany as an exile in 1965. He briefly returned to Iran after the Revolution in 1979 but left the country once the oppressiveness of the new regime became obvious. He began publishing poetry, radio plays, translations, and prose in the 1980s and gained significant popularity. Reflecting his high visibility in the German literary sphere are the prestigious awards he received and the fact that he served as vice president (1995–96) and then president of the German PEN (2000–2002). Said's work evokes broad aspects of human existence (*Sei Nacht zu mir. Liebesgedichte* [1998]), and also gives voice to the experience of exile (such as his radio plays *Ich und der Schah* and *Die Beichte des Ayatollah* [both 1987] and the collection of poems entitled *Wo ich sterbe ist meine Fremde* [1983]). The nightmare of political persecution haunts the poet in exile: "Still / my voice / whispers / when freedom is talked about."[185]

Iranian-German literature by first-generation immigrants is thus deeply structured by the trauma of two consecutive oppressive regimes, that of the shah and the new Islamist regime. This literature is a testament to the international emigration of countless Iranian intellectuals, artists, and skilled professionals. But political exiles from other regions of the Middle East also found a voice in the German language with which to comment upon exile. In "Wir werden zurückkehren," for example, the Kurdish writer Yêhat powerfully expresses the desire to return to a liberated Kurdistan.[186] Rafik Schami's short story "Ein Kassiber" is designed as a letter that he asks the mother of an incarcerated Syrian friend to relate to the prisoner. The gist of the narrative is an attempt to create an image of solidarity uniting those who suffer from political oppression in Syria and the oppressed immigrant workers of Germany.[187] Other authors who came to Germany as exiles do not foreground the political dimension of their exile in their works, but those like Adel Karasholi, who describes himself as a writer in exile, consistently comment on the experience as an exile in Germany.[188] As a new phenomenon, exile literature written in German by authors of non-German background contributes a multidimensional chapter of transnational history in the German language.

Drawing on Middle Eastern Aesthetic Traditions: Fairy Tales, Fables, Parables, and Poetry

German-language authors with Middle Eastern origins are often published within what I will call the *fairy tale niche.* This term points to particular expectations of the German reading public, which, I suggest, encourages authors to tailor their literary endeavors accordingly. While only a few authors of Turkish origin write fairy tales—Kemal Kurt and Habib Bektaş are notable examples—writers of Arab background seem to be especially drawn to this niche, which offers creative opportunities, but is also restrictive.

Arab performance artists who made a name for themselves as *hakawatis* took to writing fairy tales, parables, and fables. Following his social realist activism of the early 1980s, Rafik Schami began composing narratives that evoke European ideas about *One Thousand and One Nights. Das Schaf im Wolfspelz:*

Märchen und Fabeln was published in 1982, and other collections of tales followed in quick succession (*Der Fliegenmelker: Geschichten aus Damaskus* [1985]; *Weshalb darf Babs wieder lachen?* [1985]; *Eine Hand voller Sterne* [1987]; *Erzähler der Nacht* [1989]). Jusuf Naoum, Suleman Taufiq, and Salim Alafenisch also authored narrative texts in this tradition. Naoum published *Der rote Hahn. Erzählungen des Fischers Sidaoui* (1979), *Karakus und andere orientalische Märchen* (1986), and *Die Kaffeehausgeschichten des Abu al Abed* (1987). Taufiq, who had written in the social realist genre and also publishes poetry, turned to fairy tales with his novel *Oh, wie schön ist Fliegen oder Wie die Ente den Mond sucht: Ein Märchen für deutsche und arabische Kinder* (1988). Salim Alafenisch's tales from the 1980s include *Der Weihrauchhändler: Märchen und Geschichten aus dem Zeltlager der Beduinen* (1988) and *Die acht Frauen des Großvaters* (1989).

While some of these tales are written for children, the bulk of the stories are meant for an adult audience. The tales are often explicitly pedagogical; they include lessons about different aspects of life and serve as parables and fables, often ending with moral advice. For the most part the tales are located in geographically identifiable Middle Eastern locations: Naoum's texts are staged in Lebanon, Schami's in Syria, and Alafenisch writes about the Negev Desert. Germany is also a locus of action, as, for example, in Rafik Schami's radio play *Der Kameltreiber von Heidelberg* (1986). The tales staged in Germany foreground questions of cultural contact, attempt to debunk clichés about Arab culture, and strive to convey a sense of the everyday experiences of Arab immigrants. Texts that focus predominantly on the Middle East comment on the political and social struggles of the region.

While many German-language authors of Arabic origin have decided to write their narratives by drawing on the fairy tale and the fable/parable tradition, twentieth-century literature from the Arabic-speaking Middle East only rarely builds on these genres. Social realism, symbolism, and, since the 1980s, postmodern aesthetics clearly dominate the literary landscape. The reluctance of Arab literati and critics to express their ideas in the form of fairy tales, parables, and fables stems from the long-standing association of these genres with popular culture, and thus lowbrow literary aesthetics. Some Arab authors, such as Taha Hussein (*The Dreams of Scheherazade* [1943]) and Naguib Mahfouz (*Arabian Nights and Days* [1982]), attempted to rehabilitate the genres and built particularly on their political dimensions. German-language authors of Arab origin who create fairy tales, fables, and parables write in that tradition. The frame story and many of the individual tales of *One Thousand and One Nights,* for example, raise questions about political justice, particularly regarding how to educate a despotic ruler.[189] Another model that inspires Arab-German writers is *Kalila wa Dimna,* the great collection of fables that draws heavily on the Indian *Panchatantra* and was used in the education of civil servants. In addition, Bedouin oral literature, evoked by, for example, Salim Alafenisch, has often taken up political subjects, especially during the period of British colonialism.[190] In addition, Rafik Schami and Jusuf Naoum, among others, feature oral narrators in their writings.[191] Another Arab-language literary genre that dates back to medieval times is the prose version of *hija',* a form of satire, which inspires the works of Salim Alafenisch and Wadi Soudah, among others. As Uta Aifan has shown, Rafik Schami often draws on the genre of the *maqama,* a genre of rhymed prose featuring trickster figures.[192]

Such connections are for the most part lost on German audiences, who do not have the background to comprehend the specific political and other references inherent to these genres. While German readers will expect fairy tales, parables, and fables to convey ethical lessons, they are less prone to pick up on the explicitly political messages of these narratives. Stories that comment on oppressive regimes of, for example, Syria, Jordan, or Israel are bound to deliver their critical message to only a limited degree.[193] Marketing and book covers of works contribute greatly to erasing their political content. The illustrations and blurbs on the covers of Schami's and Alafenisch's books, for example, give these texts the appearance of children's literature or fairy tales for an adult audience, even if the content of the individual tales relates a sociopolitical message.

Arab-German writers address diverse topics in their tales but in terms of the political trajectory of the stories they have a lot in common. Jusuf Naoum's short story "Großmutters Auto," for example, tells the story of the narrator's grandmother, who had been forced to migrate for economic reasons within Lebanon, away from her birthplace, and is disturbed to learn that her grandson plans to migrate to Germany. The story, clearly autobiographical in nature, conveys a snapshot of the complexity of Lebanese social history.[194] Salim Alafenisch, a Bedouin from the Negev Desert, highlights the history of his people, who are often overlooked in the turmoil of the Arab-Israeli conflict. With the tales collected in *Der Fliegenmelker: Geschichten aus Damaskus* (1985) and *Erzähler der Nacht* (1989), Rafik Schami creates a testament to the vanishing cultural diversity of the Damascus of his childhood. His accounts of the lives of Syrian Aramaic Christians address an aspect of Middle Eastern history that has been greatly diminished over the past fifty years. References to political conflicts are interspersed throughout the narrative, but their depth is lost on an uninitiated audience.[195] The tale "Als der Angstmacher Angst bekam," for example, recounts the case of a secret service agent who disrupts the peace of a neighborhood but is fooled by a brave citizen who parodies the state's power structures through an ingenious trick.[196] While this dream of successful subversion would presumably have a considerable effect on a Syrian audience, its meaning in the German context is less certain.

Another innovation brought to German-language literature is found in poetry that is inspired by Middle Eastern aesthetic forms and uses Middle Eastern themes and motifs. One of the earliest and most outstanding poets is Cyrus Atabay (1929–96), who spent part of his childhood in Germany, returned to Iran in 1945, but then decided to continue his education in Switzerland. Until the late 1970s he moved back and forth between Germany, London, and Tehran. As a nephew of Shah Reza Pahlavi, he was unable to return to Iran after the Islamic Revolution. He was granted asylum in London in 1978 and five years later was given permission to return to Munich. His poetry and short prose feature a wide range of styles, German and non-German, and make use of Iranian poetic traditions associated with mysticism and Sufism. His first publications in German date from 1956 (*Einige Schatten*), and he published an impressive eighteen anthologies of poems and short prose. In addition, he translated Iranian poetry into German, including works by Hafiz, al-Ma'arri, and Rumi.

Two accomplished poets who have published extensively in Arabic and are widely known in the Arabic-speaking world are Khalid al-Maaly and Fadhil al-Azzawi. Both authors have translated their own poetry from the Arabic into German.[197] To the best of my knowledge, they have not published collections of works that were originally composed in German, but their contributions as translators from Arabic and as public intellectuals in Germany are considerable.

German-language poetry that draws on languages, aesthetic traditions, and cultural knowledge of the Middle East is largely inaccessible without mediating exegesis by critics. An excellent example in this regard is provided by Mustafa Al-Slaiman, who shows that the understanding of a poem by Adel Karasholi, "Die Fremde ist mir nicht fremd," requires considerable cultural knowledge about the Middle East. As Al-Slaiman explains, the form of the poem is inspired by Islamic poetry of the tenth century. He interprets the phrase "Hinter die sieben Berge," which the German reader will be prone to associate with the fairy tale "Schneewittchen," as a reference to the seven stages of Sufi development. Al-Slaiman further shows that the Arabic letters interspersed in Karasholi's volume of poetry that includes this particular poem convey a message about love by forming the phrase "bridge of love." Readers unfamiliar with these cultural references will not be able fully to appreciate the knowledge and skills that went into these poetic creations, not to mention their resonant meanings.[198]

The corpus of minor texts and films by artists with roots in the Middle East has grown tremendously since the 1980s. Along with other German-language minor literature and film, it continues to redefine the notion of German culture. The main impediment to a full appreciation of German minor literature is the challenge inherent to the complexity of writings by bicultural authors. The linguistic intricacies of Emine Sevgi Özdamar's prose, for example, escapes most uninitiated readers and critics, who are unable to enjoy the playful bilinguality of the narratives. As Jarrod Shepherd demonstrated in a meticulous analysis of *Das Leben ist eine Karawanserei,* Özdamar incorporates Turkish syntax, proverbs, idioms, songs, and poetry into her German.[199] Azade Seyhan also points to instances of code mixing, code switching, and bilingualism in Özdamar's work.[200] A broader acknowledgment of such complex dimensions of German minor literature would facilitate their reception as innovative and sophisticated contributions to the German-language canon.

On more than one level the postwar story of immigrants from the Middle East and their descendants who live in German-speaking countries is comparable to developments in other European countries and beyond. Iranians in Germany, Arabs in France, Pakistanis in Britain, or Mexicans in the United States face similar social, political, and economic challenges but also very different legal frameworks and cultural environments. The distinctness of the situation in German-speaking countries is tied to specific citizenship laws but also to the long history of Ottoman/Turkish–German/Austrian cooperation; Germany's complex relationship to Israel and the Arab states; to the particular laws surrounding the recognition of non-Christian religions; and to the persistent suspicion with which the changes that are under way as a result of demographic, social, and cultural developments are viewed by members of the majority cultures. The emergence of Islam as an aspect of discrimination but also self-ethnicization in recent years is clearly a transnational phenomenon. Similarly, the decreasing economic capital of unskilled workers, which directly affects legal and illegal immigrants from the Middle East, is also a global issue. Germany's relationship to the Middle East has been conditioned by internal and external developments, many of them tied to processes beyond the control of the German state or the German economy alone. German states have felt the repercussions of political coups in Turkey and Iran, and have learned to accommodate the actual long-term results of a labor migration that was first initiated as a short-term policy in the history of German employment.

Once again, we observe a tension between different discourses, and between textual and various other practices. Whereas minority artists who give voice to the experiences of migrants and debates in the public sphere interact with the transforming social, political, and economic landscapes, fiction writings and films produced by majority Germans have been slow to recognize and acknowledge the changing fabric of German-speaking societies. Majority representations of aspects of the Middle East abroad and at home are distinguished for the most part by a startling lack of engagement with sociocultural, material, and other historical developments. It seems that the archive of images gathered over centuries in the German collective memory actively impedes the absorption of new material and the emergence of alternate views.

Conclusion

Relating German-language literary and other texts on the Middle East to social, economic, and political practices allows us to recognize the complex interaction between various forces that define the particular face of distinct historical moments as well as historical change. In the process of evaluating this vast pool of information, comparative work makes its invaluable contribution: considering, for instance, the wide range of practices that make up intercultural contact, evaluating various representations of the same social practice, comparing German and other European to Ottoman historical accounts, correlating autobiographies written from different perspectives, and assessing the realm of fiction across linguistic and cultural boundaries brings us closer to drawing a nuanced picture of historical events.[1]

Do literary and other textual discourses have an effect on social, political, or economic action? Our study about the German literary discourse on the Middle East showed that no predictable pattern exists in this regard. At certain moments, ideas and beliefs can be credited with significantly propelling social action, action that is nevertheless grounded in materiality (the Crusades, colonialism); at other times individuals decide the outcome of significant events (Frederick II's strategy toward executing a crusade he wanted to avoid, which allowed him to subvert the pope's confrontational approach); and often, material developments set into motion large-scale changes (the invention of porcelain in Saxony in the early eighteenth century, which fostered trade with the Ottoman Empire). Textual practices may be in tension with social, economic, and political practices, and different groups of texts may also oppose each other in their distinct trajectories. In the ever-changing sea of historical change, highbrow writings may be the mouthpiece of dominant power (von Lohenstein in the seventeenth century), the voice of the elite opposition (Wolfram in the early thirteenth century), or testimony to intellectual movements and social changes (Lessing in the eighteenth century). Popular culture documents may be fact-oriented (as many of the early modern broadsheets and newspapers were) or they may be partial and reflective of particular ideological orientations (such as segments of twentieth-century mainstream news reporting). Minority views of yesterday may align with the dominant discourse of today, only to be revised again in light of new circumstances. The literary archive may be shared across linguistic boundaries, but the actions of individual European powers are not linked to this discourse in any predictable fashion.

Kai Hafez's study on the German media landscape in the second half of the twentieth century provides ample evidence for the connection between social, political, and economic action and the shifts observable in the news coverage of selected newspapers and magazines. His analysis is one of many that led me to acknowledge the complex relationship of textual discourses to historical events. What remains at the end of this journey through the centuries is a picture made up of continuities and discontinuities: significant modifications notwithstanding, certain discursive tropes seem to have been constant in literature and the public sphere, and to have remained readily available over the centuries, in spite of noteworthy political, social, and economic changes (such as the notion that Christian culture needs to defend itself against the Muslim onslaught, the association of violence and sexuality with the Middle East, and the romantic fascination with the wisdom and splendor of the Middle East).

Thus *German Literature on the Middle East* shows how literary and other cultural discourses may be in tension or in unison with social, political, and economic action and materiality. Only careful consideration of the complex interaction between these various components allows us to comprehend the dynamics of historical processes, especially from today's vantage point. As Walter Benjamin writes, "The materialist presentation of history leads the past to bring the present into a critical state."[2]

When I set out to write this study I expected that it would put closure to two decades of researching and teaching on Germany's relationship to the Middle East. At the end of my endeavor, I find myself with a new research agenda, particularly with regard to the study of materials that circulated in Europe in translation and to comparative analyses on almost any level. It would be most rewarding if my study were to inspire further inquiries into the complex history of German—and, more broadly, European—Middle Eastern relations.

For instance, the processes of cross-cultural transfer and sharing of knowledge, experience, and artistic expressions within Europe are crucial to every time period investigated here and have recently received increased attention.[3] Acknowledging the extent of these cross-cultural and transnational processes certainly affects our understanding of national literatures. Perhaps the idea of "European literature" is useful after all—a literary archive with local variations that deserve to be studied in their particularity, but one that recognizes the fact that much of the content and aesthetics of the European literary heritage is shared across linguistic boundaries. The same holds true with regard to the cross-cultural transfer of knowledge between Europe and the Middle East. The example of the late sixteenth-century text by Hans Lewenklaw that was based on the author's familiarity with an Ottoman source, but then circulated in Europe as a text thought to be originally conceived by a European author, exemplifies the complexity of cross-cultural exchange. Multilingual research is the bedrock of the kind of comparative work that is needed here, and often essential material is preserved in languages that researchers tend to neglect, such as Croatian or Polish.

Another aspect that deserves to be explored further is the relationship between competing public discourses, as articulated in print and electronic media. We also lack studies that explore the relationship between religious and secular discourses. While such studies exist for some periods, such as the eighteenth century, our comprehension of these issues regarding, for example, the nineteenth and twentieth centuries is still insufficient.

Finally, my study raises questions about the functioning of memory, questions that I was able to trace but not answer sufficiently. How is it possible that images, such as those of "the Crusades" or "the violent Arab," can be readily invoked in public discourse after decades and even centuries during which these images played only minor roles? It seems that earlier models of identification are stored in the collective memory of cultures in a way that allows for such models to be activated whenever needed, for instance, during times of extensive conflict and change. The theories of Maurice Halbwachs and Jan Assmann, which literary and cultural studies scholars draw on frequently, only partially explain these issues. David A. Sousa's *How the Brain Learns,* his brilliant overview of recent neuroscience scholarship, offers valuable insights in this regard. It seems that certain ideas and images are passed on through generations and end up stored in the long-term memory section of the brain, a process that occurs overwhelmingly at a subconscious level. In this regard, these ideas and images are part of people's "nondeclarative memory . . . that is, memories that can be used for things that cannot be declared or explained in any straightforward manner."[4] In our context it is particularly relevant that "nondeclarative memories do not require the intentional recall of experiences"; that is, they may consist of passed-down information of the kind we encounter in the study of German notions of the Middle East.[5] Along the same lines, the notion of "transfer" is utterly important: "Whenever new learning moves into working memory, long-term memory . . . simultaneously searches the long-term storage sites for any past learnings that are similar to, or associated with, the new learning."[6] This brain function explains the solidification of certain stereotypes, and it also explains why new knowledge is so difficult to integrate after a certain point. The inability to integrate new learning is called "negative transfer" and accounts for why individuals who have not been exposed to diverse experiences are prone to reject new learning.[7] We also know from brain research that, even though humans are able to learn throughout their lives, critical learning periods ("windows of opportunity") occur early in life.[8] The ability to question bequeathed knowledge depends on exposure to learning patterns that foster the ability to form one's own judgment and the pursuit of the unknown.

I conclude this study by turning to a recent artwork that comments on the idea of cultural and religious interaction, namely, the *Kaaba—Das eckige Haus* (Kaaba—The Square House) by Sudanese-born visual artist Zaki Al-Maboren.[9] Al-Maboren, who resides in Kassel, is known for blending different techniques taught at art schools in Europe and in Sudan; more important, he has developed a unique style, using radiant inks and applying gold leaf to his paintings. Al-Maboren engages with a broad range of topics, such as Islam (*Der Aufstieg*/Ascension [1995]), African mythology (*Die Flußgötter*/Gods of the River [1995]), and his German context (*Agrikultur*/Agriculture [2006]). He paints both figuratively (*Freundliche Geste 1 und 2 und 3*/Friendly Gesture 1 and 2 and 3 [2000]) and abstractly (*Erinnerung an die Erde*/Memories of Earth [1999]), and his international visibility is acknowledged by a long list of solo exhibitions and by scholarly articles about his work published in periodicals such as *Fikrun wa Fann,* an eminent journal on Middle Eastern art and intellectual thought.

The building, which Al-Maboren transformed into the *Kaaba,* is a small classicist structure known in Kassel as "The Temple," more exactly, the "Temple of Art." During the twelfth *Documenta,* Al-Maboren covered the building with wind-permeable and fire-resistant black cloth, which was draped over rectangular scaffolding, so that the building resembled the Kaaba, the central sanctuary of Islam. Already during pre-Islamic times the Kaaba was the center of pilgrimages, and the notion of "pilgrimage" is ultimately more important to understanding the artwork than its connection to Islam. The association with religious pilgrimages, which the work implicitly relates to *Documenta XII,* raises the question whether modern art has taken over the role of religion, and whether today's major art exhibits fulfill the function of the pilgrimage ritual. One may argue that the ethical and social dimensions of religious pilgrimages

Fig. 1. Kaaba—Das eckige Haus

are indeed easily transferred onto the secular pilgrimages to sites of art. Through its immanent connection to the pre-Islamic period, Al-Maboren's *Kaaba* also embodies a central aspect of cultural memory, particularly the transhistorical signifying power of rituals and symbols.

This topic, especially the relationship between present and past, is also evoked by one of the leitmotifs of *Documenta XII,* namely, the phrase "Is our modernity our antiquity?" Al-Maboren's artwork displays this sentence in Arabic repeatedly around the veiled building. "Hal hadaratuna al-muʻasiratu hiya asalatuna?" is printed in Arabic script on thick, hard plastic (42 meters long, 90 centimeters tall).

The Arabic phrase, however, is not a direct translation of the *Documenta XII* leitmotif; rather, the word *asala* evokes ideas of "origin," "descent," "ge-

هل حضارتنا المعاصرة هي أصالتنا

Fig. 2. Is our modern civilization our origin?

nealogy," and "authenticity." One possible translation of the sentence reads, "Is our modern civilization our origin?" Al-Maboren's phrase thus gives emphasis to an interpretation that connects the actual Kaaba in Mecca, the Temple of Art in Kassel (with its inherent tie to ancient Greek civilization), and the *Kaaba*-project, namely, the question of the interconnectedness of cultures and the transmission of cultural symbols across time.

Al-Maboren transformed Kassel's Temple of Art and simultaneously deepened the building's inherent meaning. His work raises questions about the function of art in modern society, the historical and transcultural continuity of ritual, and the affinity between art and religion. It does not pit one culture or religion against another; rather, it evokes the deep structures of intercultural exchange and transformation over time. *Kaaba—Das eckige Haus* invites us to consider cultures, our own as well as those of others, as participating in change and exchange over time and across space. In this regard, Al-Maboren's artwork addresses key questions explored in this study.

Notes

INTRODUCTION

1. Salman Rushdie, *The Enchantress of Florence* (New York: Random House, 2008), 78.

2. Karl Marx, *Theses on Feuerbach,* in Karl Marx and Frederick Engels, *The German Ideology* (Moscow: Progress Publishers, 1964), 647.

3. Regarding levels of consumption see Richard W. Unger's chapter on the topic in *Beer in the Middle Ages and the Renaissance* (Philadelphia: University of Pennsylvania Press, 2004), 126–42.

4. This concept was originally coined by the philosopher of language Gustav Bergmann in the early 1960s. In 1967, Richard Rorty published the anthology *The Linguistic Turn: Recent Essays in Philosophical Method* (Chicago: University of Chicago Press, 1967); in his "Introduction: Metaphilosophical Difficulties of Linguistic Philosophy," he acknowledged the early twentieth-century roots of the approach, and credits Bergmann with coining the term *linguistic turn* (9 n. 10).

5. Sherry B. Ortner, *High Religion: A Cultural and Political History of Sherpa Buddhism* (Princeton: Princeton University Press, 1989), 198–99.

6. William H. Sewell Jr., *Logics of History: Social Theory and Social Transformation* (Chicago: University of Chicago Press, 2005), 162–64.

7. Sewell, *Logics of History,* 164.

8. Sewell, *Logics of History,* 165.

9. Andreas Reckwitz, "Toward a Theory of Social Practices: A Development in Culturalist Theorizing," *European Journal of Social Theory* 5, no. 2 (2002): 245–46.

10. Ludwig Wittgenstein outlines his view of language most comprehensively in *Philosophical Investigations* (*Philosophische Untersuchungen,* 1953). A German-English edition was edited by G. E. M. Anscombe, who also translated the text ([1953, 1958] Oxford: Blackwell, 2001).

11. Reckwitz, "Toward a Theory," 259.

12. Reckwitz, "Toward a Theory," 254.

13. Reckwitz, "Toward a Theory," 254–55.

14. Reckwitz, "Toward a Theory," 259.

15. Teun A. van Dijk, "Editor's Introduction: The Study of Discourse: An Introduction," in *Discourse Studies,* ed. Teun A. van Dijk, vol. 1 (Los Angeles: Sage Publications, 2007), xxv.

16. Achille Mbembe, *On the Postcolony* (Berkeley: University of California Press, 2001), 5.

17. William H. Sewell Jr., "AHR Forum: Crooked Lines," *American Historical Review* 113 (April 2008): 401.

18. For an overview of debates in Latin American Cultural Studies, see *The Latin American Cultural Studies Reader,* ed. Ana Del Sarto, Alicia Ríos, and Abril Trigo (Durham: Duke University Press, 2004); for an introduction to the work of South Asian Subaltern scholars, see *Selected Subaltern Studies,* ed. Ranajit Guha and Gayatri Chakravorty Spivak (Oxford: Oxford University Press, 1988).

19. Eric Paras outlines the distinct reception of Foucault in the U.S. and French contexts. Eric Paras, *Foucault 2.0: Beyond Power and Knowledge* (New York: Other Press, 2006), 150–53.

20. Michel Foucault, *The Archaeology of Knowledge,* trans. A. M. Sheridan Smith (New York: Pantheon Books, 1972), 211.

21. Paras, *Foucault 2.0,* 46.

22. Michel Foucault, "Politics and the Study of Discourse," in *The Foucault Effect: Studies in Governmentality,* ed. Graham Burchell, Colin Gordon, and Peter Miller (Chicago: University of Chicago Press, 1991), 54. The article originally appeared in the French journal *Esprit,* no. 371 (May 1968): 850–74; the quote is on 853.

23. Sara Mills, *Michel Foucault* (London: Routledge, 2003), 55–56.

24. David Howarth and Yannis Stavrakakis, "Introducing Discourse Theory and Political Analysis," in *Discourse Theory and Political Analysis: Identities, Hegemonies, and Social Change,* ed. David Howarth, Aletta J. Norval, and Yannis Stavrakakis (Manchester: Manchester University Press, 2000), 3–4.

25. Edward W. Said, *Orientalism* (New York: Vintage Books, 1979), 15.

26. Regarding Said's use of the term *positional superiority* see *Orientalism,* 7.

27. See my chapter on the role of the engineer Max Eyth in 1860s Egypt in Nina Berman, *Impossible Missions? German Economic, Military, and Humanitarian Efforts in Africa* (Lincoln: University of Nebraska Press, 2004), 25–59.

28. See, for example, "The End of Postcolonial Theory? A Roundtable with Sunil Agnani, Fernando Coronil, Gaurav Desai, Mamadou Diouf, Simon Gikandi, Susie Tharu, and Jennifer Wenzel," *PMLA* 122, no. 3 (2007): 633–51; *Relocating Postcolonialism,* ed. David Theo Goldberg and Ato Quayson (Oxford: Blackwell Publishers, 2002).

29. Edward W. Said, *Culture and Imperialism* (New York: Knopf, 1993). See also the afterword in the 1994 edition of *Orientalism* (New York: Vintage Books), 329–52; "East Isn't East: The Impending End of the Age of Orientalism," *Times Literary Supplement* (February 3, 1995), 3–6. Various aspects of the debate regarding Said's paradigm are documented in *Orientalism: A Reader,* ed. Alexander Lyon Macfie (New York: New York University Press, 2000); perhaps the most controversial contribution to the debate from a Marxist perspective was presented by Aijaz Ahmad with *In Theory: Classes, Nations, Literatures* (London: Verso, 1992); a special issue of the journal *Public Culture* was devoted to a discussion of Ahmad's theses (6, no. 1, Fall 1993). See also Zachary Lockman's excellent summary of the *Orientalism* debate in *Contending Visions of the Middle East: The History and Politics of Orientalism* (Cambridge: Cambridge University Press, 2004), 182–214.

30. Edward Said, "In Conversation with Neeldari Bhattacharya, Suvir Kaul, and Ania Loomba." See the edited version of the interview in *Relocating Postcolonialism,* ed. Goldberg and Quayson, 1–14.

31. Said, *Orientalism,* 9, 21.

32. Max Weber, *Economy and Society: An Outline of Interpretive Sociology,* ed. Guenther Roth and Claus Wittich, trans. Ephraim Fischoff et al. (Berkeley: University of California Press, 1978).

33. Theo van Leeuwen, *Discourse and Practice: New Tools for Critical Discourse Analysis* (New York: Oxford University Press, 2008), 6.

34. William M. Reddy draws on findings of cognitive and affective neuroscience to bolster the concept of the "loosely structured actor" that is central to practice theory. "Saying Something New: Practice Theory and Cognitive Neuroscience," *arcadia* 44, no. 1 (2009): 8–23.

35. Pierre Bourdieu, *Outline of a Theory of Practice,* trans. Richard Nice (Cambridge: Cambridge University Press, 1995; the French original appeared in 1972), 1.

36. John J. Gumperz and Stephen C. Levinson, "Introduction: Linguistic Relativity Re-Examined," in *Rethinking Linguistic Relativity,* ed. John J. Gumperz and Stephen C. Levinson (Cambridge: Cambridge University Press, 1996), 8.

37. Clifford Geertz, "Thick Description: Toward an Interpretive Theory of Culture," *The Interpretation of Cultures* (New York: Basic Books, 1973), 18.

38. Thomas P. Kasulis, "Philosophy as Metapraxis," in *Discourse and Practice,* ed. Frank Reynolds and David Tracy (Albany: State University of New York Press, 1992), 169–95.

39. Brian Rotman, *Becoming Beside Ourselves: The Alphabet, Ghosts, and Distributed Human Being* (Durham: Duke University Press, 2008), 1.

40. Tom Lutz, *American Nervousness, 1903: An Anecdotal History* (Ithaca: Cornell University Press, 1991); Daniel T. Reff, *Plagues, Priests, and Demons: Sacred Narratives and the Rise of Christianity in the Old World and the New* (New York: Cambridge University Press, 2005).

41. Gayatri Chakravorty Spivak, *Death of a Discipline* (New York: Columbus University Press, 2003), 6.

42. Geoff Eley, *A Crooked Line: From Cultural History to the History of Society* (Ann Arbor: University of Michigan Press, 2005), 181. Sewell urges that "it is necessary to work out *in theoretical terms* some means of combining, on the same epistemological terrain, the materialism of 'social history' and the idealism of 'cultural history.'" "AHR Forum," 403–4. Practice theory seems to offer direction in this regard.

43. Gabrielle M. Spiegel, "AHR Forum: Comment on *A Crooked Line,*" *American Historical Review* 113 (April 2008): 416.

44. This overview does not include works written before the publication of Edward Said's *Orientalism,* such as Fawzy D. Guirgis's *Bild und Funktion des Orients in Werken der deutschen Literatur des 17. und 18. Jahrhunderts* (PhD diss., Free University Berlin, 1972).

45. Regarding Said's assessment of German Orientalism, see *Orientalism,* 18–19.

46. Tilman Nagel, *Die islamische Welt bis 1500* (Munich: Oldenbourg, 1998), 223. Rudi Paret, *Arabistik und Islamkunde an deutschen Universitäten: Deutsche Orientalisten seit Theodor Nöldeke* (Wiesbaden: Steiner, 1966), 3.

47. Robert Irwin, *For Lust of Knowing: The Orientalists and Their Enemies* (London: Allen Lane, 2006).

48. Holger Preissler, "Die Anfänge der Deutschen Morgenländischen Gesellschaft," *Zeitschrift der Deutschen Morgenländischen Gesellschaft* 145, no. 2 (1995): 241–327; Holger Preissler, "Orientalische Studien in Leipzig vor Reiske," in *Johann Jacob Reiske: Leben und Wirkung,* ed. Hans-Georg Ebert and Thoralf Hanstein (Leipzig: Evangelische Verlagsanstalt, 2005), 19–43; *Deutsche Orientalistik am Beispiel Tübingens: Arabistische und islamkundliche Studien,* ed. Gernot Rotter (Tübingen: H. Erdmann, 1974); Ludmila Hanisch, *Die Nachfolger der Exegeten: Deutschsprachige Erforschung des Vorderen Orients in der ersten Hälfte des 20. Jahrhunderts* (Wiesbaden: Harrassowitz, 2003).

49. Suzanne L. Marchand, *German Orientalism in the Age of Empire* (Cambridge: Cambridge University Press, 2009); Ursula Wokoeck, *German Orientalism: The Study of the Middle East and Islam from 1800 to 1945* (New York: Routledge, 2009); Sabine Mangold, *Eine "weltbürgerliche Wissenschaft": Die deutsche Orientalistik im 19. Jahrhundert* (Stuttgart: F. Steiner, 2004); Tuska Benes, "Comparative Linguistics as Ethnology: In Search of Indo-Germans in Central Asia, 1770–1830," *Comparative Studies of South Asia, Africa, and the Middle East* 24, no. 2 (2004): 117–32; Alexander Haridi, *Das Paradigma der "islamischen Zivilisation" oder die Begründung der deutschen Islamwissenschaft durch Carl Heinrich Becker (1876–1933)* (Würzburg: Ergon, 2005); Ekkehard Ellinger, *Deutsche Orientalistik zur Zeit des Nationalsozialismus 1933–45* (Edingen-Neckarhausen: Deux Mondes, 2006).

50. Kai Hafez, *Orientwissenschaft in der DDR: Zwischen Dogma und Anspassung, 1969–1989* (Hamburg: Deutsches Orient-Institut, 1995).

51. Arnold Reisman, *Turkey's Modernization: Refugees from Nazism and Atatürk's Vision* (Washington, DC: New Academia Publishing, 2006); Kader Konuk, *East West Mimesis: Auerbach in Turkey* (Stanford: Stanford University Press, 2010).

52. See, for example, 'Awni 'Abd al-Ra'uf and Iman al-Sa'id Jalal, *Juhud al-Mustashriqin fi al-Turath al-'Arabi bayna al-Tahqiq wa-al-Tarjama,* 2 vols. (Cairo: al-Majlis al-A'la li-al-Thaqafa, 2004–2006); Adnan Rashid, *Ta'thir Alf Layla wa-Layla wa-al-Mu'allaqat 'ala Adab Sha'ir Almaniyya Kuta* (al-Riyadh: Mu'assasa al-Yamama, 1996).

53. Andrea Fuchs-Sumiyoshi, *Orientalismus in der deutschen Literatur: Untersuchungen zu Werken des 19. und 20. Jahrhunderts, von Goethes West-östlichem Divan bis Thomas Manns Joseph-Tetralogie* (Hildesheim: Olms, 1984); W. Daniel Wilson, *Humanität und Kreuzzugsideologie um 1780: Die "Türkenoper" im 18. Jahrhunderts und das Rettungsmotiv in Wielands "Oberon," Lessings "Nathan," und Goethes "Iphigenie"* (New York: Lang, 1984); Nina Berman, *Orientalismus, Kolonialismus und Moderne: Zum Bild des Orients in der deutschsprachigen Kultur um 1900* (Stuttgart: Metzler, 1997); Reika D. Ebert, "Vom Barbaren zum aufgeklärten Herrscher: Zur Entwicklung des Türkenbildes im deutschsprachigen Drama des 17. Jahrhunderts" (PhD diss., University of Washington, 2000).

54. Andrea Polaschegg, *Der andere Orientalismus: Regeln deutsch-morgenländischer Imagination im 19. Jahrhundert* (Berlin: de Gruyter, 2005), 531.

55. Mirjam Weber, *Der 'wahre Poesie-Orient': Eine Untersuchung zur Orientalis-*

mus-Theorie Edward Saids am Beispiel von Goethes West-östlichem Divan *und der Lyrik Heines* (Wiesbaden: Harrassowitz, 2001).

56. Todd Kontje, *German Orientalisms* (Ann Arbor: University of Michigan Press, 2004); Robert C. Holub, "The Narrator of Realism: Orientalism in C. F. Meyer's *Der Heilige*," in Robert C. Holub, *Reflections of Realism: Paradox, Norm, and Ideology in Nineteenth-Century German Prose* (Detroit: Wayne State University Press, 1991), 152–73; Cornelia Kleinlogel, *Exotik-Erotik: Zur Geschichte des Türkenbildes in der deutschen Literatur der frühen Neuzeit (1453–1800)* (Frankfurt am Main: Lang, 1989).

57. Arlene Teraoka, "Talking 'Turk': On Narrative Strategies and Cultural Stereotypes," *New German Critique* 46, special issue on "Minorities in German Culture" (Winter 1989): 104–28; Leslie A. Adelson, "Opposing Oppositions: Turkish-German Questions in Contemporary German Studies," *German Studies Review* 17, no. 2 (May 1994): 305–30; Nazire Akbulut, *Das Türkenbild in der neueren deutschen Literatur 1970–1990* (Berlin: Köster, 1993); Ishrak Kamaluldin, *Das Bild des Nahen Ostens in der deutschen Prosa seit 1945: Untersuchungen zum Charakter und der Funktion von Orientalismuskonzepten bei modernen deutschsprachigen Autorinnen und Autoren* (Frankfurt am Main: Lang, 1997); Azade Seyhan, *Writing Outside the Nation* (Princeton: Princeton University Press, 2001); Uta Aifan, *Araberbilder: Zum Werk deutsch-arabischer Grenzgängerautoren der Gegenwart* (Aachen: Shaker, 2003); Manar Mahmoud Omar, *Exotisches und Ästhetisches in ausgewählten Werken der 90er Jahre von deutschschreibenden Autoren arabischer Herkunft* (PhD diss., Cairo University, 2006); Tom Cheesman, *Novels of Turkish German Settlement: Cosmopolite Fictions* (Rochester, NY: Camden House, 2007); B. Venkat Mani, *Cosmopolitical Claims: Turkish-German Literatures from Nadolny to Pamuk* (Iowa City: University of Iowa Press, 2007).

58. Mounir Fendri, *Halbmond, Kreuz und Schibboleth: Heinrich Heine und der islamische Orient* (Hamburg: Hoffmann und Campe, 1980); Donna K. Heizer, *Jewish-German Identity in the Orientalist Literature of Else Lasker-Schüler, Friedrich Wolf, and Franz Werfel* (Columbia, SC: Camden, 1996); Nina Berman, "Else Lasker-Schüler: Die Nächte Tino von Bagdads, Der Prinz von Theben," in Berman, *Orientalismus, Kolonialismus und Moderne,* 260–345; Noah Isenberg, "To Pray Like a Dervish: Orientalist Discourse in Arnold Zweig's *The Face of East European Jewry,*" in *Orientalism and the Jews,* ed. Ivan Davidson Kalmar and Derek J. Penslar (Waltham, MA: Brandeis University Press; Hanover: University Press of New England, 2005), 94–108.

59. *Reassessing Orientalism in German Studies, Seminar* 41, no. 3, special issue, ed. Friederike Eigler (Summer 2005); *Orient- und IslamBilder,* ed. Iman Attia (Münster: Unrast, 2007); *'Istanbul'—Geistige Migrationen aus der 'Welt in Scherben,'* ed. Georg Stauth and Faruk Birtek (Bielefeld: transcript, March 2007); *Orientdiskurse in der deutschen Literatur,* ed. Klaus-Michael Bodgal (Bielefeld: Aisthesis Verlag, 2007); *Der Deutschen Morgenland: Bilder des Orients in der deutschen Literatur und Kultur von 1770–1850,* ed. Charis Goer and Michael Hofmann (Munich: Fink, 2008).

60. Exemplary analyses include Maria Elisabeth Pape, "Turquerie im 18. Jahrhundert und der 'Recueil Ferriol,'" *Europa und der Orient: 800–1900,* ed. Gereon Sievernich and Hendrik Budde (Gütersloh: Bertelsmann, 1989), 305–23; Deniz Göktürk, "Turkish Women on German Streets: Closure and Exposure in Transnational Cinema,"

in *Spaces in European Cinema,* ed. Myrto Konstantarakos (Exeter: Intellect Books, 2000), 64–76; Almut Höfert, *Den Feind beschreiben: 'Türkengefahr' und europäisches Wissen über das Osmanische Reich 1450–1600* (Frankfurt am Main: Campus, 2003); Eugene Sensening-Dabbous, "Will the Real Almásy Please Stand Up! Transporting Central European Orientalism via *The English Patient,*" *Comparative Studies of South Asia, Africa, and the Middle East* 24, no. 2 (2004): 163–80; Susan R. Boettcher, "German Orientalism in the Age of Confessional Consolidation: Jacob Andreae's *Thirteen Sermons on the Turk,* 1568," *Comparative Studies of South Asia, Africa, and the Middle East* 24, no. 2 (2004): 101–15.

61. Sonja Schultheiß-Heinz, *Politik in der europäischen Publizistik: Eine historische Inhaltsanalyse von Zeitungen des 17. Jahrhunderts* (Stuttgart: Steiner, 2004); Astrib Hub, *Das Image Israels in deutschen Medien: Zwischen 1956 und 1982* (Frankfurt am Main: P. Lang, 1998); Samir Aly, *Das Bild der islamischen Welt in der westdeutschen Presse in den 70er Jahren: Eine Inhaltsanalyse am Beispiel ausgewählter überregionaler Tageszeitungen* (Frankfurt am Main: Dr. Hänsel-Hohenhausen, 2002); Kai Hafez, *Die politische Dimension der Auslandsberichterstattung,* vol. 2: *Das Nahost- und Islambild der deutschen überregionalen Presse* (Baden-Baden: Nomos, 2002).

62. Francis R. Nicosia, *The Third Reich and the Palestine Question* (Austin: University of Texas Press, 1985); Jonathan S. McMurray, *Distant Ties: Germany, the Ottoman Empire, and the Construction of the Baghdad Railway* (Westport, CT: Praeger, 2001); Jennifer Jenkins, "German Orientalism: Introduction," *Comparative Studies of South Asia, Africa, and the Middle East* 24, no. 2 (2004): 97–100; Gottfried Hagen, "German Heralds of Holy War: Orientalists and Applied Oriental Studies," *Comparative Studies of South Asia, Africa, and the Middle East* 24, no. 2 (2004): 145–62; Wolfgang G. Schwanitz, "The German Middle Eastern Policy, 1871–1945," in *Germany and the Middle East, 1871–1945,* ed. Wolfgang G. Schwanitz (Princeton: Markus Wiener, 2004), 1–23; Thomas L. Hughes, "The German Mission to Afghanistan, 1915–1916," in *Germany and the Middle East, 1871–1945,* ed. Schwanitz, 25–63; Tilman Lüdke, *Jihad Made in Germany: Ottoman and German Propaganda and Intelligence Operations in the First World War,* Studien zur Zeitgeschichte des Nahen Ostens und Nordafrikas (Münster: Lit, 2005); Malte Fuhrmann, *Der deutsche Traum vom Orient: Zwei deutsche Kolonien im Osmanischen Reich 1851–1918* (Frankfurt am Main: Campus, 2006); Margaret Lavinia Anderson, "'Down in Turkey, Far Away': Human Rights, the Armenian Massacres, and Orientalism in Wilhelmine Germany," *Journal of Modern History* 79, no. 1 (2007): 80–111; 'Abd al-Ra'uf Sinnu, *Almaniyya wa-al-Islam fi al-Qarnayn al-Tasi' 'Ashar wa-al-'Ishrin* (Beirut: al-Furat li-al-Nashr wa-al-Tawzi', 2007); Paula Sutter Fichtner, *Terror and Toleration: The Habsburg Empire Confronts Islam, 1526–1850* (London: Reaction Books, 2008); Carole Fink, "*Ostpolitik* and West German-Israeli Relations," in *Ostpolitik, 1969–1974: European and Global Responses,* ed. Carole Fink and Bernd Schaefer (Cambridge: Cambridge University Press, 2009), 182–205.

63. Taner Akçam, *A Shameful Act: The Armenian Genocide and The Question of Turkish Responsibility* (New York: Metropolitan Books, 2006); Marc David Baer, *Honored by the Glory of Islam* (Oxford: Oxford University Press, 2007); Mustafa Aksakal, *The Ottoman Road to War in 1914: The Ottoman Empire and the First World War* (Cam-

bridge: Cambridge University Press, 2008); M. Şükrü Hanioğlu, *A Brief History of the Late Ottoman Empire* (Oxford: Princeton University Press, 2008).

64. *Der Islam in den Schulbüchern der Bundesrepublik Deutschland,* vols. 1–7, ed. Abdoldjavad Falaturi (Braunschweig: Georg-Eckert-Institut, 1986–90); Detlef Thofern, *Darstellungen des Islams in* Der Spiegel*: Eine inhaltsanalytische Untersuchung über Themen und Bilder der Berichterstattung von 1950 bis 1989* (Hamburg: Kovac, 1998); *Islam and the West: Judgments, Prejudices, Political Perspectives,* ed. Werner Ruf (Münster: agenda-Verlag, 2002); Boettcher, "German Orientalism in the Age of Confessional Consolidation"; Silvia Horsch, *Rationalität und Toleranz: Lessings Auseinandersetzung mit dem Islam* (Würzburg: Ergon, 2004); Nina Berman, "Ottoman Shock-and-Awe and the Rise of Protestantism: Luther's Reactions to the Ottoman Invasions of the Early Sixteenth Century," *Reassessing Orientalism in German Studies,* special issue on Edward Said, ed. Friederike Eigler, *Seminar* 41, no. 3 (Summer 2005): 226–45; *Orient- und IslamBilder,* ed. Attia.

65. Said, *Orientalism,* 27.

66. Susannah Heschel, *Abraham Geiger and the Jewish Jesus* (Chicago: University of Chicago Press, 1998); Jonathan M. Hess, *Germans, Jews, and the Claims of Modernity* (New Haven: Yale University Press, 2002).

67. *"Im vollen Licht der Geschichte": Die Wissenschaft des Judentums und die Anfänge der kritischen Koranforschung,* ed. Dirk Hartwig, Walter Homolka, Michael J. Marx, and Angelika Neuwirth (Würzburg: Ergon, 2008).

68. Ian Almond, *Two Faiths, One Banner: When Muslims Marched with Christians across Europe's Battlegrounds* (Cambridge: Harvard University Press, 2009).

69. See, for example, *The First World War as Remembered in the Countries of the Eastern Mediterranean,* ed. Olaf Farschid, Manfred Kropp, and Stephan Dähne (Beirut: Orient-Institut; Würzburg: Ergon Verlag, 2006); Stuart B. Schwartz, *All Can Be Saved: Religious Tolerance and Salvation in the Iberian Atlantic World* (New Haven: Yale University Press, 2008); see also contributions in *Orientalism's Interlocutors: Painting, Architecture, Photography,* ed. Jill Beaulieu and Mary Roberts (Durham: Duke, 2002).

70. George Steinmetz, *The Devil's Handwriting: Precoloniality and the German Colonial State in Qingdao, Samoa, and Southwest Africa* (Chicago: University of Chicago Press, 2007).

71. Ute Frevert, "Europeanizing German History," *Bulletin of the German Historical Institute* 36 (Spring 2005): 9–24.

72. Emily Apter, *The Translation Zone: A New Comparative Literature* (Princeton: Princeton University Press, 2006), 10.

73. Spivak, *Death of a Discipline,* 10.

74. Jan Assmann, *Thomas Mann und Ägypten: Mythos und Monotheismus in den Josephsromanen* (Munich: Beck, 2006), 69–70.

75. Maurice Halbwachs, *On Collective Memory,* ed. and trans. Lewis A. Coser (Chicago: University of Chicago Press, 1992), 47.

76. Said, *Orientalism,* 1.

77. To mention just a few studies on Occidentalism, see Sadik Jalal al-'Azm, "Orientalism and Orientalism in Reverse," *Khamsin* 8 (1981): 5–27; Laura Nader, "Orientalism, Occidentalism, and the Control of Women," *Cultural Dynamics* 2, no. 3 (1989):

323–55; Xiaomei Chen, *Occidentalism: A Theory of Counter-Discourse in Post-Mao China* (New York: Oxford University Press, 1995); *Occidentalism: Images of the West*, ed. James G. Carrier (New York: Oxford University Press, 1995); Ian Buruma and Avishai Margalit, *Occidentalism: The West in the Eyes of Its Enemies* (New York: Penguin Press, 2004); Rasheed El-Enany, *Arab Representations of the Occident: East-West Encounters in Arabic Fiction* (New York: Routledge, 2006).

78. For a detailed discussion of terminology, see Aksakal, *The Ottoman Road to War*, x–xi.

79. Ibn Khaldun, *The Muqaddimah: An Introduction to History*, trans. Franz Rosenthal (Princeton: Princeton University Press, 1967), 11.

80. Geertz, "Thick Description," 20, 29.

CHAPTER 1

1. Roswitha Wisniewski cites the higher number. See *Kreuzzugsdichtung: Idealität in der Wirklichkeit* (Darmstadt: Wissenschaftliche Buchgesellschaft, 1984), 51.

2. Wisniewski, *Kreuzzugsdichtung*, 50–51.

3. F. E. Peters, *Jerusalem: The Holy City in the Eyes of Chroniclers, Visitors, Pilgrims, and Prophets from the Days of Abraham to the Beginnings of Modern Times* (Princeton: Princeton University Press, 1985), 145.

4. See accounts collected by John Wilkinson in *Jerusalem Pilgrims before the Crusades* (Warminster: Aris and Phillips, 2002).

5. Louis Carlen, *Wallfahrt und Recht im Abendland* (Freiburg, Switzerland: Universitätsverlag, 1987), 140.

6. Ludwig Schmugge, "Zu den Anfängen des organisierten Pilgerverkehrs und zur Unterbringung und Verpflegung von Pilgern im Mittelalter," in *Gastfreundschaft, Taverne und Gasthaus im Mittelalter*, ed. Hans Conrad Peyer (Munich: R. Oldenbourg, 1983), 37–60.

7. Hans Conrad Peyer, *Von der Gastfreundschaft zum Gasthaus: Studien zur Gastlichkeit im Mittelalter* (Hannover: Hahnsche Buchhandlung, 1987), 57.

8. Augustine develops this theory in his *City of God*, book 22, chap. 30.

9. For a detailed discussion of eschatological thought during the era, see Christoph Auffarth, *Irdische Wege und himmlischer Lohn: Kreuzzug, Jerusalem und Fegefeuer in religionswissenschaftlicher Perspektive* (Göttingen: Vandenhoeck und Ruprecht, 2002).

10. Jacques Le Goff, *Medieval Civilization, 400–1500*, trans. Julia Barrow (1964, French; New York: Barnes and Noble, 2000), 180–94.

11. For basic concepts and case studies regarding travel in Islam, see *Muslim Travellers: Pilgrimage, Migration, and the Religious Imagination*, ed. Dale F. Eickelman and James Piscatori (London: Routledge, 1990).

12. A. J. Gurevich, *Categories of Medieval Culture*, trans. G. L. Campbell (London: Routledge, 1985), 74.

13. Manfred W. Wenner, "The Arab/Muslim Presence in Medieval Central Europe," *International Journal of Middle East Studies* 12, no. 1 (1980): 59.

14. "Pelagius," *Kindlers Literaturlexikon*, vol. 5 (Zurich: Kindler, 1965), 1631. See also Linda A. McMillin's account of the story's oral and textual migration in "'Weighed

down with a thousand evils': Images of Muslims in Hrotsvit's *Pelagius,*" in *Hrotsvit of Gandersheim: Contexts, Identities, Affinities, and Performances,* ed. Phyllis R. Brown, Linda A. McMillin, and Katharina M. Wilson (Toronto: University of Toronto Press, 2004), 41–42.

15. Angel Fábrega-Grau, "Pelagius," *Lexikon für Theologie und Kirche,* vol. 8 (Freiburg: Herder, 1999), 9–10. McMillin suggests that Hrotsvit, by including humiliating references to a contemporary Muslim ruler, "adds an additional layer of political satire to her work." "'Weighed down with a thousand evils,'" 54.

16. Martin Erbstösser, *Die Kreuzzüge: Eine Kulturgeschichte* (Leipzig: Kunst und Wissenschaft, 1977), 71.

17. David Abulafia, "The Role of Trade in Muslim-Christian Contact during the Middle Ages," in *The Arab Influence in Medieval Europe,* ed. Dionisius A. Agius and Richard Hitchcock (Reading, PA: Ithaca Press, 1994), 1–24.

18. Norbert Ohler, *The Medieval Traveller,* trans. Caroline Hillier (Woodbridge, Suffolk: Boydell Press, 1989), 59.

19. David Jacoby, "The Migration of Merchants and Craftsmen: A Mediterranean Perspective (12th–15th Century)," in David Jacoby, *Trade, Commodities, and Shipping in the Medieval Mediterranean* (1994; Aldershot: Variorum Reprints, 1997), I:540–41.

20. Jacoby, "The Migration of Merchants and Craftsmen," 549.

21. See articles by John H. Pryor on *commenda* contracts in *Commerce, Shipping, and Naval Warfare in the Medieval Mediterranean* (London: Variorum Reprints, 1987).

22. Jacoby, "The Migration of Merchants and Craftsmen," 542.

23. Janet L. Abu-Lughod, *Before European Hegemony: The World System, A.D. 1250–1350* (New York: Oxford University Press, 1989), 12, 186.

24. David Abulafia, "The Impact of the Orient: Economic Interactions between East and West in the Medieval Mediterranean," in *Across the Mediterranean Frontiers: Trade, Politics and Religion, 650–1450,* Dionisius A. Agius and Ian Richard Netton (Turnhout, Belgium: Brepols, 1997), 40.

25. *Arabische Berichte von Gesandten an germanische Fürstenhöfe aus dem 9. und 10. Jahrhundert,* trans. and ed. Georg Jacob, in *Quellen zur Deutschen Volkskunde,* ed. V. v. Geramb and L. Mackensen (Berlin: de Gruyter, 1927). I would like to thank Wolfgang Schwanitz for providing me with this text.

26. See references to Isaac who accompanied Charlemagne's embassy to Harun al-Rashid in Einhard, Annales a. 801. Mon. Script. I, p. 190. Quoted in *Arabische Berichte von Gesandten,* trans. and ed. Jacob, 6.

27. S. D. Goitein, ed. and trans., *Letters of Medieval Jewish Traders* (Princeton: Princeton University Press, 1973).

28. The term goes back to Carl Erdmann's discussion of the Crusades in *Die Entstehung des Kreuzzugsgedankens* (Stuttgart: Kohlhammer, 1935), 306.

29. See Norman Housley, "Crusades Against Christians: Their Origins and Early Development, c. 1000–1216," in Norman Housley, *Crusading and Warfare in Medieval and Renaissance Europe* (1985; reprint, Aldershot: Ashgate, 2001), I:17–36.

30. Dieter Kartschoke, *Geschichte der deutschen Literatur im frühen Mittelalter* (Munich: dtv, 1990), 202.

31. Joachim Bumke, *Höfische Kultur: Literatur und Gesellschaft im hohen Mittelalter,* vol. 1 (Munich: dtv, 1986), 11–12.

32. For a summary of economic and political factors, see Hans Eberhard Mayer, *Geschichte der Kreuzzüge* (Stuttgart: Kohlhammer, 1980), 29–30; see also Jonathan Riley-Smith who reviews some of the same aspects and points out knowledge gaps due to the lack of conclusive data. *The First Crusaders, 1095–1131* (Cambridge: Cambridge University Press, 1997), 15–22, 83–84. In this study Riley-Smith emphasizes the importance of kinship networks for recruiting crusaders.

33. Medieval theologians made a difference between "the sinner's guilt before God (*culpa*) and the punishment due for the sin (*pena*). The former was addressed by contrition and confession, followed by absolution, the latter by the performance of penance. Indulgences remitted penance either in terms of time or of a certain proportion of the total due." The difference between *culpa* and *pena,* even though defined more clearly after the Second Crusade, was often not clear to ordinary people. Diana Webb, *Pilgrims and Pilgrimage in the Medieval West* (London: I. B. Tauris, 1999), 15.

34. Christopher Tyerman, "What the Crusades Meant to Europe," Peter Linehan and Janet L. Nelson, eds., *The Medieval World* (London: Routledge, 2001), 134.

35. See Hunt Janin, *Four Paths to Jerusalem: Jewish, Christian, Muslim, and Secular Pilgrimages, 1000 BCE to 2001 CE* (Jefferson, NC: McFarland, 2002), 84–85.

36. Ralph-Johannes Lilie, *Byzanz und die Kreuzzüge* (Stuttgart: Kohlhammer, 2004), 15–16, 34–35.

37. For an account of the founding of the kingdom under Roger II, see Hubert Houben, *Roger II of Sicily: A Ruler between East and West,* trans. Graham A. Loud and Diane Milburn (Cambridge: Cambridge University Press, 2002; 1997, German). Evaluating European, Arab, and Byzantine sources, Houben assesses Roger II's legal, fiscal, and political policies that enabled him to build his multicultural kingdom.

38. Tyerman, "What the Crusades Meant to Europe," 139.

39. Erbstösser, *Die Kreuzzüge,* 86. Tyerman suggests an army of twenty thousand, including noncombatants. *God's War: A New History of the Crusades* (Cambridge: Belknap Press of Harvard University Press, 2006), 97.

40. Amin Maalouf, *The Crusades through Arab Eyes,* trans. Jon Rothschild (New York: Schocken, 1984), 8.

41. Mayer, *Geschichte der Kreuzzüge,* 50.

42. Clearly the status and actual living conditions of Jews and Christians under Islamic rule differed across time and space, and the scholarly literature in this regard is substantial. For a recent study that approaches the subject from a human rights perspective, see Ann Elizabeth Mayer, *Islam and Human Rights: Tradition and Politics* (Boulder: Westview Press, 2007). See also Martin Tamcke, *Christen in der islamischen Welt: Von Mohammed bis zur Gegenwart* (Munich: Beck, 2008).

43. See, for example, Wolfram von Eschenbach, *Willehalm,* trans. and ed. Dieter Kartschoke (Berlin: de Gruyter, 1968), 10.

44. For examples, see Minou Reeves, *Muhammad in Europe* (New York: New York University Press, 2000), 88–89. See also John V. Tolan, *Sons of Ishmael: Muslims through European Eyes in the Middle Ages* (Gainesville: University Press of Florida, 2008).

45. Irwin, *For Lust of Knowing,* 24. See also Thomas E. Burman, *Reading the Qur'an in Latin Christendom, 1140–1560* (Philadelphia: University of Pennsylvania Press, 2007); John Victor Tolan, *Saracens: Islam in the Medieval European Imagina-*

tion (New York: Columbia University Press, 2002); Norman Daniel, *Islam and the West: The Making of an Image* (Edinburgh: Edinburgh University Press, 1962).

46. See sources compiled in Robert G. Hoyland's anthology *Seeing Islam as Others Saw It* (Princeton: Darwin Press, 1997).

47. See case studies discussed in *Christian Arabic Apologetics during the Abbasid Period, 750–1258,* ed. Samir Khalil Samir and Jørgen S. Nielsen (Leiden: Brill, 1994).

48. See, for example, articles in *Christians, Muslims, and Jews in Medieval and Early Modern Spain: Interaction and Cultural Change,* ed. Mark D. Meyerson and Edward D. English (Notre Dame: University of Notre Dame Press, 2000).

49. Irwin, *For Lust of Knowing,* 26.

50. Irwin, *For Lust of Knowing,* 37.

51. An example of such an exchange between Muslims and Christians is "The Letter from the People of Cyprus" which emphasizes the Christian roots of Islam to a degree that amounts to an attempt to "Christianise the Qur'an," which "provoked two of the longest refutations by Muslims against Christianity that have survived." Rifaat Y. Ebied and David Thomas, eds., *Muslim-Christian Polemics during the Crusades: The Letter from the People of Cyprus and Ibn Abi Talib al-Dimashqi's Response* (Leiden: Brill, 2005), 35, 5.

52. Christoph T. Maier, *Preaching the Crusades: Mendicant Friars and the Cross in the Thirteenth Century* (Cambridge: Cambridge University Press, 1994), 116.

53. Mayer, *Geschichte der Kreuzzüge,* 48–49.

54. James A. Brundage, "Crusades, Clerics, and Violence: Reflections on a Canonical Theme," Marcus Bull and Norman Housley, eds., *The Experience of Crusading,* vol. 1, *Western Approaches* (Cambridge: Cambridge University Press, 2003), 149.

55. Maier, *Preaching the Crusades,* 1.

56. Maier, *Preaching the Crusades,* 3.

57. Tyerman, "What the Crusades Meant to Europe," 140.

58. Bettina Heinrich, *Frühmittelalterliche Bibeldichtung und die Bibel: Ein Vergleich zwischen den altenglischen, althochdeutschen und altsächsischen Bibelparaphrasen und ihren Vorlagen in der Vulgata* (Frankfurt am Main: Lang, 2000), 344–45.

59. Heinrich, *Frühmittelalterliche Bibeldichtung und die Bibel,* 2.

60. Elisabeth Peters, *Paradiesvorstellungen in der deutschen Dichtung vom 9. bis 12. Jahrhundert* (Quellen und Charakter der, 1915; reprint, Hildesheim: Olms, 1977).

61. Regarding examples of such melodies, see Goswin Spreckelmeyer, ed., *Mittellateinische Kreuzzugslieder: Texte und Melodien* (Göppingen: Kümmerle, 1987), 65–86.

62. Regarding the linguistic heterogeneity of the text, see Olive Sayce, *Plurilingualism in the Carmina Burana: A Study of the Linguistic and Literary Influences on the Codex* (Göppingen: Kümmerle, 1992).

63. For a detailed discussion, see Goswin Spreckelmeyer, *Das Kreuzzugslied des lateinischen Mittelalters* (Munich: Fink, 1974), 119–31.

64. Michael Routledge, "Songs," in *The Oxford History of the Crusades,* ed. Jonathan Riley-Smith (Oxford: Oxford University Press, 1999), 90–110.

65. Dieter Kartschoke, ed., *Das Rolandslied des Pfaffen Konrad* (Munich: Reclam, 1996), 798.

66. Kartschoke, *Rolandslied,* 791.

67. Wolfgang Spiewok, "Karl und Roland—Funktionswandel bei Adaptation und Rezeption," in *Das "Rolandslied" des Konrad,* ed. Danielle Buschinger and Wolfgang Spiewok (Greifswald: Reineke, 1996), 36–37.

68. In Ulrich Müller, ed., *Kreuzzugsdichtung* (Tübingen: Niemeyer, 1979), 57. To make the poetry cited here more accessible, I refer to this anthology, rather than to individual critical editions.

69. See "Mîn herze und mîn lîp diu wellent scheiden," in Müller, *Kreuzzugsdichtung,* 40.

70. See "Si waenent sich dem tôde verzîn," in Müller, *Kreuzzugsdichtung,* 41–42.

71. Müller, *Kreuzzugsdichtung,* 42–47.

72. Müller, *Kreuzzugsdichtung,* 49–50.

73. See, for example, Stephen G. Nichols, "Urgent Voices: The Vengeance of Images in Medieval Poetry," *France and the Holy Land: Frankish Culture at the End of the Crusades,* ed. Daniel H. Weiss and Lisa Mahoney (Baltimore: Johns Hopkins University Press, 2004), 22–42.

74. See Wisniewski, *Kreuzzugsdichtung,* 107–26, for a detailed discussion; Müller, *Kreuzzugsdichtung,* 82–89, for a selection of the poems.

75. See Richard Stoneman, *Alexander the Great: A Life in Legend* (New Haven: Yale University Press, 2008); *Memory as History: The Legacy of Alexander in Asia,* ed. Himanshu Prabha Ray and Daniel T. Potts (New Delhi: Aryan Books International, 2007).

76. See, for example, Buzurg ibn Shahriyar of Ramhormuz, *The Book of the Wonders of India,* ed. and trans. G. S. P. Freeman-Grenville (London: East-West Publications, 1981).

77. *Dichtung des europäischen Mittelalters: Ein Führer durch die erzählende Literatur,* ed. Rolf Bräuer (Munich: Beck, 1990), 257–85.

78. Elisabeth Lienert, *Deutsche Antikenromane des Mittelalters* (Berlin: Erich Schmidt, 2001), 10.

79. Walter Kofler's study, *Der Held im Heidenkrieg und Exil: Zwei Beiträge zur deutschen Spielmanns- und Heldendichtung* (Göppingen: Kümmerle, 1996), supports this view.

80. The perception of India as a Christian country is tied to legends involving St. Thomas the Apostle and a figure known as Prester John, a presumably Christian king who was perceived to be a ruler in India and other regions of Asia, the Middle East, and Africa. See Manuel João Ramos, *Essays in Christian Mythology: The Metamorphosis of Prester John* (Lanham, MD: University Press of America, 2006).

81. H. T. Norris, *The Adventures of Antar* (Warminster: Aris and Phillips, 1980).

82. For a detailed discussion of the epic's sources see Bernhard Heller, *Die Bedeutung des arabischen 'Antar-Romans für die vergleichende Litteraturkunde* (Leipizig: Eichblatt, 1931).

83. Jacques Le Goff, *The Medieval Imagination,* trans. Arthur Goldhammer (Chicago: University of Chicago Press, 1988), 29. Le Goff draws on the work of Erich Köhler in formulating this thesis.

84. For a general introduction, see Walter Johannes Schröder, *Spielmannsepik* (Darmstadt: Wissenschaftliche Buchgesellschaft, 1977); see also Claudia Bornholdt,

Engaging Moments: The Origins of Medieval Bridal-Quest Narrative (Berlin: de Gruyter, 2005).

85. Horst Wenzel, *Höfische Geschichte: Literarische Tradition und Gegenwartsdeutung in den volkssprachigen Chroniken des hohen und späten Mittelalters* (Bern: Lang, 1980), 87–103.

86. Ingrid von Tippelskirch, *Die "Weltchronik" des Rudolf vom Ems: Studien zur Geschichtsauffassung und politischer Intention* (Göppingen: Kümmerle, 1979).

87. Wenzel, *Höfische Geschichte,* 346.

88. Norman Housley, "Politics and Heresy in Italy: Anti-Heretical Crusades, Orders and Confraternities, 1200–1500," in Norman Housley, *Crusading and Warfare in Medieval and Renaissance Europe* (1982), II:194.

89. Michael Costen, *The Cathars and the Albigensian Crusade* (Manchester: Manchester University Press, 1997), 170–79. See also Mark Gregory Pegg, *A Most Holy War: The Albigensian Crusade and the Battle for Christendom* (New York: Oxford University Press, 2009).

90. Norman Housley, "Crusades Against Christians: Their Origins and Early Development, c. 1000–1216," in Norman Housley, *Crusading and Warfare in Medieval and Renaissance Europe,* I:17–36.

91. Tyerman, *God's War,* 282–86.

92. For an overview of German expansion into eastern Europe, see Wolfgang Wippermann, *Der "deutsche Drang nach Osten": Ideologie und Wirklichkeit eines politischen Schlagwortes* (Darmstadt: Wissenschaftliche Buchgesellschaft, 1981). Also relevant are essays in *The Germans and the East,* ed. Charles Ingrao and Franz A. J. Szabo (West Lafayette: Purdue University Press, 2008).

93. Mayer, *Geschichte der Kreuzzüge,* 106. See also Maalouf, *The Crusades through Arab Eyes,* 147–49; Tyerman, *God's War,* 329–38; and Jonathan Phillips, *The Second Crusade: Extending the Frontiers of Christendom* (New Haven: Yale University Press, 2007).

94. Maalouf, *The Crusades through Arab Eyes,* 195. Regarding negotiations during the reconquest of Jerusalem, see Malcolm Cameron Lyons and D. E. P. Jackson, *Saladin: The Politics of Holy War* (Cambridge: Cambridge University Press, 1982), 274–77.

95. See excerpts from Arab historians discussing Saladin and the Third Crusade in Francesco Gabrielli, ed. and trans., *Arab Historians of the Crusades,* trans. from the Italian by E. J. Costello (Berkeley: University of California Press, 1984), 87–252. Also Salih J. al-Ta'ma, *Salah al-Din fi al-Shi'r al-'Arabi* (Riyadh: al-Nadi al-Adabi, 1979).

96. Tyerman, *God's War,* 372.

97. The accompanying publication explores a wide range of issues connected to contact, practices, material history, representation, and ideology. *Saladin und die Kreuzfahrer,* ed. Alfried Wieczorek, Mamoun Fansa, and Harald Meller (Mainz: Philipp von Zabern, 2005).

98. The Latin text begins: "Heu, voce flebili cogor enarrare facinus, quod accidit nuper ultra mare." *Carmina Burana: Die Lieder der Bendiktbeurer Handschrift,* bilingual edition, ed. and trans. Carl Fischer, Hugo Kuhn, and Günter Bernt (Munich: dtv, 1979), 138, see also notes on 896.

99. Gabrielli, *Arab Historians of the Crusades,* 9.

100. Gabrielli, *Arab Historians of the Crusades,* 11.

101. Hans Wollschläger, *Die bewaffneten Wallfahrten gen Jerusalem: Geschichte der Kreuzzüge* (Zurich: Diogenes, 1973), 40 n. 133.

102. Regarding the charge of cannibalism, see Maalouf, *The Crusades through Arab Eyes,* 38–40.

103. Usama Ibn Munqid, *Die Erlebnisse des syrische Ritters Usama ibn Munqid: Unterhaltsames und Belehrendes aus der Zeit der Kreuzzüge* (Leipzig: Kiepenheuer, 1981), 148–50.

104. Maalouf, *The Crusades through Arab Eyes,* 20.

105. Umberto Eco gives a gripping fictionalized account of the events in his novel *Baudolino* (2000).

106. Lilie, *Byzanz und die Kreuzzüge,* 173.

107. Lilie, *Byzanz und die Kreuzzüge,* 175.

108. Peter Lock, *The Franks in the Aegean, 1204–1500* (London: Longman, 1995).

109. Norman Daniel, *The Arabs and Mediaeval Europe* (London: Longman, 1975), 153.

110. Klaus von Eickels and Tania Brüsch, *Kaiser Friedrich II: Leben und Persönlichkeit in Quellen des Mittelalters* (Düsseldorf: Artemis und Winkler, 2000), 118.

111. Rudolf Hiestand, "Friedrich II. und der Kreuzzug," in *Friedrich II: Tagung des Deutschen Historischen Instituts in Rom im Gedenkjahr 1994,* ed. Arnold Esch and Norbert Kamp (Tübingen: Niemeyer, 1996), 143–49.

112. Maalouf, *The Crusades through Arab Eyes,* 229.

113. For Arab historians, see Gabrielli, *Arab Historians of the Crusades,* 267–83. For recent Arab-language scholarship, see 'Abd Al-Latif Hamza, *Adab al-Hurub al-Salibiyya* (Cairo: Dar Fikr al-'Arabi, 1984), 151–53; Hamid Zayyan Ghanim, *Al-Ambaratur Fridirik Barbarusa wa-al-Hamla al-Salibiyya al-Thalitha* (Cairo: Dar al-Thaqafa li-al-Tiba'a wa-al-Nashr, 1977). Carole Hillenbrand reviews Arab admiration for Frederick II in her section "Frankish Leaders Who Are Praised by Medieval Muslim Writers"; next to Frederick II, she discusses his son Manfred, Baldwin the Little, King Louis IX, and Richard the Lionheart. *The Crusades: Islamic Perspectives* (Chicago: Fitzroy Dearborn, 1999), 336–41.

114. Peter F. Ganz, ed., *Graf Rudolf* (Berlin: Erich Schmidt, 1964), 31.

115. "Alda wart der vride gegeben. / doch hete manic man da[z leben] virlorn inbeiden siten." Ganz, *Graf Rudolf,* 39.

116. Ganz, *Graf Rudolf,* 72.

117. William E. Jackson has shown that of the twenty-nine poems published in Goswin Spreckelmeyer's study, only nine poems "exude positive tone," and all of these were written before the Battle of Hattin. William E. Jackson, *Ardent Complaints and Equivocal Piety: The Portrayal of the Crusader in Medieval German Poetry* (Lanham, MD: University Press of America, 2003), 11.

118. Wolfram von Eschenbach, *Parzival,* trans. Wolfgang Spiewok (Stuttgart: Reclam, 1981), 2:656.

119. Kathryn Starkey, *Reading the Medieval Book: Word, Image, and Performance in Wolfram von Eschenbach's "Willehalm"* (Notre Dame: University of Notre Dame Press, 2004), 3.

120. See Wolfram von Eschenbach, *Willehalm,* 168–71.

121. See, for example, Paul Kunitzsch, "Die Arabica im *Parzival* Wolframs von Eschenbach," in *Wolfram Studien II,* ed. Werner Schröder (Berlin: Erich Schmidt, 1974), 9–35. With regard to the question of Wolfram's sources, Arthur Groos writes that "one hundred and fifty years of philological hunter-gathering have led nowhere." "Orientalizing the Medieval Orient," *Kulturen des Manuskriptzeitalters,* ed. Arthur Groos and Hans-Jochen Schiewer (Göttingen: V&R unipress, 2004), 63.

122. Groos, "Orientalizing the Medieval Orient," 86.

123. See William E. Jackson, "Das Kreuzzugmotiv in Reinmars Lyrik," *Germanisch-Romanische Monatsschrift* 43, no. 2 (1993): 144–66.

124. Müller, *Kreuzzugsdichtung,* 60. Regarding von Botenlauben's fascinating biography, see *Otto von Botenlauben: Minnesänger, Kreuzfahrer, Klostergründer,* ed. Peter Weidisch (Würzburg: Schöningh, 1994).

125. Jackson, *Ardent Complaints,* 2.

126. Jackson, *Ardent Complaints,* 91.

127. Müller, *Kreuzzugsdichtung,* 109.

128. Neidhart von Reuenthal, "Ez guonet wol diue heide" and "Komen sint uns die liehten tage lange," in Müller, 96–100. Jackson questions that "Komen sint uns die liehten tage lange" is related to the Crusades. *Ardent Complaints,* 103.

129. Müller, *Kreuzzugsdichtung,* 102.

130. I would like to thank Susanne Hafner for pointing out this connection.

131. Müller, *Kreuzzugsdichtung,* 103.

132. Müller, *Kreuzzugsdichtung,* 109.

133. Mayer uses this term, in apparent analogy to seasonal workers (*Geschichte der Kreuzzüge,* 204).

134. R. J. C. Broadhurst, trans. and ed., *The Travels of Ibn Jubayr* (London: J. Cape, 1952), 313–25.

135. Ibn al-Athir in Gabrielli, *Arab Historians of the Crusades,* 20–23.

136. Jonathan Phillips, "The Latin East, 1098–1291," in Jonathan Riley-Smith, ed., *The Oxford History of the Crusades* (Oxford: Oxford University Press, 1999), 113–14.

137. Daniel, *Arabs,* 167–72.

138. Gabrielli, *Arab Historians of the Crusades,* 78.

139. Gabrielli, *Arab Historians of the Crusades,* 79.

140. Daniel, *Arabs,* 199.

141. Siobhain Bly Calkin, *Saracens and the Making of English Identity: The Auchinleck Manuscript* (New York: Routledge, 2005), 55.

142. Daniel, *The Arabs,* 195.

143. The text survived in manuscripts from the first half of the fourteenth and the end of the fifteenth century. Xenja von Ertzdorff, *Rudolf von Ems: Untersuchungen zum höfischen Roman im 13. Jahrhundert* (Munich: Wilhelm Fink, 1967).

144. The story is at least in part based on a Jewish legend. See von Ertzdorff, *Rudolf von Ems,* 167.

145. "Reinfried von Braunschweig," in Müller, *Kreuzzugsdichtung,* 121. Otto Neudeck, *Continuum historiale: Zur Synthese von tradierter Geschichtsauffassung und Gegenwartserfahrung im "Reinfried von Braunschweig"* (Frankfurt am Main: Lang, 1989), 11.

146. Neudeck, 147. See also Klaus Ridder's discussion of the scene in *Mittelhochdeutsche Minne- und Aventiureromane: Fiktion, Geschichte und literarische Tradition im späthöfischen Roman* (Berlin: de Gruyter, 1998), 84–85.

147. This material was often reworked over the next three centuries. See Karin Cieslik, "Orientabenteuerepik," in *Dichtung des europäischen Mittelalters: Ein Führer durch die erzählende Literatur,* ed. Rolf Bräuer, 310.

148. Daniel, *Arabs,* 202–6. See also Elizabeth Siberry, *Criticism of Crusading, 1095–1274* (Oxford: Clarendon Press, 1985). Palmer A. Throop, whose study precedes those by Daniel and Siberry by several decades, also draws on material from across Europe in *Criticism of the Crusade: A Study of Public Opinion and Crusade Propaganda* (Amsterdam: N. V. Swets & Zeitlinger, 1940).

149. D. A. Trotter, *Medieval French Literature and the Crusades (1100–1300)* (Geneva: Librairie Droz, 1988), 210–11.

150. Jaye Puckett, "'Reconmenciez novele estoire': The Troubadours and the Rhetoric of the Later Crusades," *Modern Language Notes* 116 (2001): 844–89.

151. See, for example, Brenda Deen Schildgen, *Dante and the Orient* (Urbana: University of Illinois Press, 2002).

152. Geraldine Heng, "Beauty and the East, a Modern Love Story," in *Empire of Magic: Medieval Romance and the Politics of Cultural Fantasy,* (New York: Columbia University Press, 2003), 180–237. Calkin suggests that the English version of the *Floris and Blauncheflur* tale presents an alternate vision of interfaith relations by presenting "Saracen-Christian integration in theologically unifying marriage" (Calkin, *Saracens and the Making of English Identity,* 131).

153. Antony Leopold, *How to Recover the Holy Land: The Crusade Proposals of the Late Thirteenth and Early Fourteenth Centuries* (Aldershot: Ashgate, 2000), 203.

154. Klaus Ridder, *Mittelhochdeutsche Minne- und Aventiureromane: Fiktion, Geschichte und literarische Tradition im späthöfischen Roman: "Reinfried von Braunschweig," "Wilhelm von Österreich," "Friedrich von Schwaben"* (Berlin: de Gruyter, 1998), 376–91.

155. See, for example, Benjamin Z. Kedar, *Franks, Muslims, and Oriental Christians in the Latin Levant: Studies in Frontier Acculturation* (Aldershot: Ashgate Variorum, 2006).

156. Michael A. Köhler, *Allianzen und Verträge zwischen fränkischen und islamischen Herrschern im Vorderen Orient: Eine Studie über das zwischenstaatliche Zusammenleben vom 12. bis ins 13. Jahrhundert* (Berlin: de Gruyter, 1991).

157. Michael Lower, "Tunis in 1270: A Case Study of Interfaith Relations in the Late Thirteenth Century," *International Historical Review* 28, no. 3 (2006): 505.

158. On Middle Eastern women in literature, see, for example, Jacqueline de Weever, *Sheba's Daughters: Whitening and Demonizing the Saracen Woman in Medieval French Epic* (New York: Garland, 1998).

159. There is no agreement on the total numbers, but several million people died in the course of the two centuries of warfare.

160. Daniel, *Arabs,* 219–29.

161. Yvonne Friedman, "Captivity and Ransom: The Experience of Women," in *Gendering the Crusades,* ed. Susan B. Edgington and Sarah Lambert (New York: Columbia University Press, 2002), 126.

162. Friedman, "Captivity and Ransom," 127–28.

163. Qasim 'Abdu Qasim evaluates Arabic historical sources and literary texts (such as *One Thousand and One Nights*) and sketches a complex image of the crusaders, which is distinguished by admiration for their courage and religious piety, but also by criticism of their caution, cruelty, and treachery. *Bayna al-Adab wa al-Tarikh* (Cairo: Dar al-Fikr, 1986).

164. See H. T. Norris, "From Asia to Africa: The *tuhfat al-albab* by Abu Hamid al-Gharnati (473/1080-565/1169) as a Source for the Chronology and Content of the *Sirat 'Antar B. Shaddad*," *Bulletin of the School of Oriental and African Studies* 57, no. 1 (1994): 174–83; Peter Heath, *The Thirsty Sword: Sirat 'Antar and the Arabic Popular Epic* (Salt Lake City: University of Utah Press, 1996).

165. M. C. Lyons, "The Land of War: Europe in the Arab Hero Cycles," in *The Crusades from the Perspective of Byzantium and the Muslim World*, ed. Angeliki E. Laiou and Roy Parviz Mottahedeh (Washington, DC: Dumbarton Oaks, 2001), 41–51.

166. Mahmud 'Abd Allah Abu al-Khayr reviews this poetry in its historical context in the two-volume *Al-Shi'r al-Shami fi Muwajahat al-Salibiyyin* (Amman: Dar al-Isra' li-al-Nashr wa al-Tawzi', 2003).

167. Carol F. Heffernan, among other scholars, discusses the influence of Oriental tales, such as stories from *One Thousand and One Nights*, and Arab scientific knowledge in *The Orient in Chaucer and Medieval Romance* (Cambridge: D. S. Brewer, 2003). The issue of Dante's familiarity with Arabic sources has stirred passionate debate among Italianists for decades. An influential contribution is María Rosa Menocal, "Italy, Dante, and the Anxieties of Influence," *The Arabic Role in Medieval Literary History: A Forgotten Heritage* (Philadelphia: University of Pennsylvania Press, 1987), 115–35.

168. See, for example, Calkin's discussion of the function of the figure of Saracen knights in medieval English literature in *Saracens and the Making of English Identity*, esp. 13–60. Calkin terms the reworking of French sources the "'Englishing' of French literary inheritances" (20). Also, in contrast to Wolfram's conception of Belakane and Feirefiz, Heng's discussion of an early fourteenth-century English romance highlights a different attitude toward interfaith and interracial relations. Here the offspring of the Christian princess and her Muslim husband in *King of Tars* is not viable—rather, it is a "hideous lump of bodily matter"—until the "senseless lump is baptized by a priest . . . and instantly transforms into a little infant." Following the miracle of the infant's rescue, the sultan also converts, whereupon his skin color turns white. "Beauty and the East, a Modern Love Story," in *Empire of Magic* (228–29).

169. Starkey, *Reading the Medieval Book*, 3.

170. Studies by Benjamin Z. Kedar shed light on the intercultural contact in Palestine during the Crusades. *Franks, Muslims, and Oriental Christians in the Latin Levant.*

171. See Ramos, *Essays in Christian Mythology.*

172. Carol Falvo Heffernan, *The Melancholy Muse: Chaucer, Shakespeare, and Early Medicine* (Pittsburgh: Duquesne University Press, 1995), 38–94.

173. See Hugh Kennedy, *Crusader Castles* (Cambridge: Cambridge University Press, 1994).

174. Jaroslav Folda, *The Art of the Crusaders in the Holy Land, 1098–1187* (Cambridge: Cambridge University Press, 1995).

175. See, for example, M. Herwig Wolfram, ed., *Kommunikation zwischen Orient und Okzident: Alltag und Sachkultur* (Vienna: Verlag der österreichischen Akademie der Wissenschaften, 1994); *The Arab Influence in Medieval Europe,* ed. Agius and Hitchcock; *Occident et Proche-Orient: Contact scientifiques au temps des Croisades,* ed. Isabelle Draelants, Anne Tihon, and Baudouin van den Abeele (Turnhout, Belgium: Brepols, 2000); Piers D. Mitchell, *Medicine in the Crusades: Warfare, Wounds and the Medieval Surgeon* (Cambridge: Cambridge University Press, 2004).

CHAPTER 2

1. Robert C. Davis details the high numbers of white slaves taken as a result of the raids of North African corsairs. See *Christian Slaves, Muslim Masters: White Slavery in the Mediterranean, the Barbary Coast, and Italy, 1500–1800* (Houndmills: Palgrave Macmillan, 2003).

2. Jean Schillinger, "Le Saint-Empire face à la menace ottomane (1526–1568)," in *Luther et la Réforme, 1525–1555: Le temps de la consolidation religieuse et politique,* ed. Jean-Paul Cahn and Gérard Schneilin (Paris: Éditions du Temps, 2001), 34.

3. Walter Sturminger, *Die Türken vor Wien in Augenzeugenberichten* (Düsseldorf: Rauch, 1968), 11.

4. Norman Housley, "Frontier Societies and Crusading in the Late Middle Ages," *Crusading and Warfare in Medieval and Renaissance Europe* (Aldershot: Ashgate Variorum, 2001), V:107. First published in *Mediterranean Historical Review* 10, no. 1 (1995): 104–19.

5. Norman Housley, "Cyprus and the Crusades, 1291–1571," *Crusading and Warfare in Medieval and Renaissance Europe* VI:189.

6. Leopold, *How to Recover the Holy Land,* 1.

7. John Kelly, *The Great Mortality: An Intimate History of the Black Death, the Most Devastating Plague of All Time* (New York: HarperCollins, 2005), 11–12.

8. Şevket Pamuk, "The Black Death and the Origins of the 'Great Divergence' across Europe, 1300–1600," *European Review of Economic History* 11, no. 3 (2007): 292.

9. For a discussion of Sachs's rewriting of *Wilhelm von Österreich* in light of changing social norms, see Michael Schilling, "Zur Dramatisierung des *Wilhelm von Österreich* durch Hans Sachs," in *Zur deutschen Literatur und Sprache des 14. Jahrhunderts: Dubliner Colloquium 1981,* ed. Walter Haug, Timothy R. Jackson, and Johannes Janota (Heidelberg: Carl Winter, 1983), 262–77. Regarding adaptations of medieval texts, see Karin Cieslik, "Orientabenteuerepik," in *Dichtung des europäischen Mittelalters,* ed. Bräuer, 310, 313.

10. "Ein niederrheinischer Bericht über den Orient," ed. Reinhold Röhricht and Heinrich Meisner *Zeitschrift für deutsche Philologie* 19 (1887): 34.

11. *Ludolfs von Sudheim Reise ins Heilige Land,* ed. Ivar von Stapelmohr (Lund: Hakan Ohlsson, 1937). Loss of the Holy Land is also mentioned on 94, Acre on 102.

12. *Ludolfs von Sudheim Reise,* 103.

13. Bernhard von Breydenbach, *Die Reise ins Heilige Land: Ein Reisebericht aus dem Jahre 1483,* ed. Elisabeth Geck (Wiesbaden: Pressler, 1977), 31.

14. Breydenbach, *Die Reise ins Heilige Land,* 24, 27.

15. Breydenbach, *Die Reise ins Heilige Land,* 43.

16. See Aleya Khattab, *Das Ägyptenbild in den deutschsprachigen Reisebeschreibungen der Zeit von 1285–1500* (Frankfurt am Main: Lang, 1982).

17. Gerhard Wolf, "Die deutschsprachigen Reiseberichte des Spätmittelalters," *Der Reisebericht,* ed. Peter J. Brenner (Frankfurt am Main: Suhrkamp, 1989), 86.

18. Ursula Ganz-Blättler, *Andacht und Abenteuer: Berichte europäischer Jerusalem- und Santiago-Pilger (1320–1520)* (Tübingen: Gunter Narr, 1990), 40. Ganz-Blättler stresses that authors often copied and adapted their accounts from other texts.

19. *Europäische Reiseberichte des späten Mittelalters: Eine analytische Bibliographie,* ed. Werner Paravicini and Christian Halm, Kieler Werkstücke Reihe D, vol. 5 (2nd ed.; Frankfurt am Main: Peter Lang, 2001).

20. Paravicini and Halm, *Europäische Reiseberichte des späten Mittelalters,* 31–33, 36–40. Wolf lists twenty-three and forty for the respective authors ("Die deutschsprachigen Reiseberichte des Spätmittelalters," 91). According to Hartmut Becker, twenty-two manuscripts of Boldensele's account are extant. "Der Orientreisebericht Wilhelms von Boldensele in einer ripuarischen Überlieferung des 14. Jahrhunderts," *Rheinische Vierteljahrsblätter* 44 (1980): 149.

21. Paravicini and Halm, *Europäische Reiseberichte des späten Mittelalters,* 203–6.

22. Georgios Sphrantzes, *Die letzten Tage von Konstantinopel,* ed. and trans. Endre von Ivánka (Graz: Styria, 1954), 81.

23. *Mehmet II. erobert Konstantinopel: Das Geschichtswerk des Kritobulos von Imbros,* trans. and ed. Diether Roderich Reinsch (Graz: Styria, 1986), 77. Another detailed contemporary account of the fall of Constantinople is given by Laonikos Chalkokondyles in *Apodeixeis Historion,* Book VIII. He proposes that the size of the army was forty myriads, that is, 400,000 soldiers. Laonikos Chalkokondyles, *Laonici Chalcocondylae Atheniensis Historiarum libri decem,* ed. Immanuel Bekker and Konrad Clauser (Bonnae: Weber, 1843), 383. (I would like to thank Anthony Kaldellis for translating for me the relevant passages from Laonikos's text.) Steven Runciman estimates the size of the Ottoman army to have consisted of "some eighty thousand men and . . . hordes of irregulars." *The Fall of Constantinople, 1453* (Cambridge: Cambridge University Press, 1965), 85.

24. *Mehmet II. erobert Konstantinopel,* 119–29. See also Doukas's detailed description of the siege in *Decline and Fall of Byzantium to the Ottoman Turks,* trans. Harry J. Magoulias (Detroit: Wayne State University Press, 1975).

25. Nancy Bisaha, *Creating East and West: Renaissance Humanists and the Ottoman Turks* (Philadelphia: University of Pennsylvania Press, 2004), 133.

26. Ian Manners, "Constructing the Image of a City: The Representation of Constantinople in Christopher Buondelmonti's *Liber Insularum Archipelagi,*" *Annals of the Association of American Geographers* 87, no. 1 (1997): 87.

27. Manners, "Constructing the Image of a City," 96.

28. Albrecht Berger and Jonathan Bardill, "The Representations of Constantinople in Hartmann Schedel's *World Chronicle,* and Related Pictures," *Byzantine and Modern Greek Studies* 22 (1998): 3.

29. Movable-type printing had been already known in China since the tenth century.

30. The original print is kept at the Bavarian State Library; a facsimile print was

edited by Ferdinand Geldner, *Der Türkenkalender: "eyn manung der cristenheit widder die durken,"* Mainz 1454 (Wiesbaden: Reichert, 1975).

31. For a discussion of the contemporary spectrum of views, see Matthias Thumser, "Türkenfrage und öffentliche Meinung: Zeitgenössische Zeugnisse nach dem Fall von Konstantinopel (1453)," in *Europa und die osmanische Expansion im ausgehenden Mittelalter,* ed. Franz-Reiner Erkens (Berlin: Duncker und Humblot, 1997), 59–78.

32. In a similar way the dynastic alliance between Habsburg and Bohemian rulers had also stabilized the region. Karl Gutkas, *Geschichte Niederösterreichs* (Munich: Oldenbourg, 1984), 100.

33. One of the most eminent Ottoman sources covering the events of the period is Mustafa Celalzade's *Tabakat ül-Memalik.* See facsimile edition, with introduction, German-language summary, and notes, *Geschichte Sultan Süleyman Kanunis von 1520 bis 1557,* ed. Petra Kappert (Wiesbaden: Franz Steiner, 1981).

34. Ferenc Szakály, "Der Wandel Ungarns in der Türkenzeit," in *Habsburgisch-osmanische Beziehungen. Beihefte zur Wiener Zeitschrift für die Kunde des Morgenlandes,* ed. Andreas Tietze, vol. 13 (Vienna: Verlag des Verbandes der wissenschaftlichen Gesellschaften Österreichs, 1985), 40. Regarding the treaties between Transylvania, Hungary, and the Ottomans, see Sándor Papp, *Die Verleihungs-, Bekräftigungs- und Vertragsurkunden der Osmanen für Ungarn und Siebenbürgen: Eine quellenkritische Untersuchung* (Vienna: Verlag der Österreichischen Akademie der Wissenschaften, 2003).

35. Hans Joachim Kissling, "Türkenfurcht und Türkenhoffnung im 15./16. Jahrhundert: Zur Geschichte eines 'Komplexes,'" *Südost-Forschungen* 23 (1964): 1–18.

36. Bisaha, *Creating East and West,* 75.

37. Bisaha, *Creating East and West,* 144.

38. Carl Göllner, *Turcica III: Die Türkenfrage in der öffentlichen Meinung Europas im 16. Jahrhundert* (Bucharest: Editura Academiei, 1978), 26. See also Dieter Mertens, "'Europa, id est patria, domus propria, sedes nostra . . .': Zu Funktionen und Überlieferung lateinischer Türkenreden im 15. Jahrhundert,"in Erkens, *Europa,* 39–57.

39. See the extensive discussions and anthology of songs in Şenol Özyurt, *Die Türkenlieder und das Türkenbild in der deutschen Volksüberlieferung vom 16. bis zum 20. Jahrhundert* (Munich: Fink, 1972); Bertrand Michael Buchmann, *Türkenlieder zu den Türkenkriegen und besonders zur zweiten Wiener Türkenbelagerung* (Vienna: Böhlau, 1983).

40. See Özyurt, *Die Türkenlieder und das Türkenbild,* 27–34.

41. Helen Watanabe-O'Kelly, "Lohenstein, Haugwitz und das Türkenmotiv in deutschen Turnieren des Barock," *Internationaler Germanisten-Kongreß in Tokyo,* vol. 7, ed. Yoshinori Shichiji (Munich: iudicium, 1991), 350–51.

42. See the excellent analysis of *Türkensteuer* records in Fulda in *Das Türkensteuerregister der Fürstabtei Fulda von 1605,* ed. Thomas Heiler et al. (Fulda: Parzeller, 2004).

43. Susan R. Boettcher, "German Orientalism in the Age of Confessional Consolidation," 102.

44. Boettcher provides an excellent case study on the various ideological functions of Ottoman-related sermons. She shows that Andreae's sermons on the Ottomans

served different goals—namely, to express Lutheran superiority over Islam but also to comment "upon the contemporary religious scene" in Germany. "German Orientalism in the Age of Confessional Consolidation," 110.

45. Göllner, *Turcica III,* 216–26.

46. Suraiya Faroqhi, *Approaching Ottoman History: An Introduction to the Sources* (Cambridge: Cambridge University Press, 1999), 120–21.

47. Göllner, *Turcica III,* 201–3.

48. Bisaha, *Creating East and West,* 161–66.

49. Rudolf Mau, "Luthers Stellung zu den Türken," in *Leben und Werk Martin Luthers von 1526 bis 1546: Festgabe zu seinem 500. Geburtstag,* ed. Helmar Junghans, vol. 2 (Göttingen: Vandenhoeck und Ruprecht, 1983), 647–48.

50. The humanist Johann Cuspinian wrote: "Laßt euch nicht wankend machen durch die nichtige Versuchung eines gewissen jemand, der behauptet, gegen die Türken zu kämpfen heiße gegen Gott zu kämpfen." Mau, "Luthers Stellung zu den Türken," in Junghans, *Leben und Werk Martin Luthers von 1526 bis 1546,* 649. See also Schillinger, "Le Saint-Empire face à la menace ottomane," 41–42.

51. Georg Schmidt, *Geschichte des Alten Reiches: Staat und Nation in der Frühen Neuzeit, 1495–1806* (Munich: Beck, 1999), 100–111.

52. Regarding the genesis of Luther's essay and the history of reprints, see F. Cohrs and A. Goetze, introduction to "Vom Kriege wider die Türken," in *D. Martin Luthers Werke. Kritische Gesamtausgabe,* vol. 30.2 (Weimar: Hermann Böhlaus Nachfolger, 1909), 81–106.

53. Heinrich Kábdebo's *Bibliographie zur Geschichte der beiden Türkenbelagerungen Wien's* (Vienna: Faesy und Frick, 1876) lists 135 textual and visual representations of the first Siege and 341 such sources for the second Siege of Vienna. The references include material composed in various European languages; the bibliography is followed by an appendix listing seventy-one coins referring to the sieges.

54. Martin Luther, "Vom Kriege wider die Türken," *D. Martin Luthers Werke. Kritische Gesamtausgabe,* vol. 30.2 (Weimar: Hermann Böhlaus Nachfolger, 1909), 108–9. References to this text are given in parentheses.

55. Pál Fodor, "Making a Living on the Frontiers: Volunteers in the Sixteenth-Century Ottoman Army," in *Ottomans, Hungarians, and Habsburgs in Central Europe: The Military Confines in the Era of Ottoman Conquest,* ed. Géza Dávid and Pál Fodor (Leiden: Brill, 2000), 262–63. Even as late as 1844, two-fifths of the inhabitants of the Ottoman Empire were Christians and other non-Muslims, with higher figures for earlier periods, especially in European areas. Yunus Koç, "The Structure of the Population of the Ottoman Empire (1300–1900)," in *The Great Ottoman-Turkish Civilization,* ed. Kemal Çiçek, Ercüment Kuran, Nejat Güyünç, and İlber Ortaylı, vol. 2 (Ankara: Semih Ofset, 2000), 545.

56. Other Protestant pamphlets of the period pick up Luther's metaphors and rhetorical devices to set off pope and Turk, arguing, for example, that if the Turks knew how bad they were, they would have a change of heart, while followers of the papacy consciously conceal their evil nature, thereby proving that they are inspired directly by the devil.

57. For the textual history of the essay, see F. Cohrs and A. Goetze, introduction to "Heerpredigt wider den Türken," in *D. Martin Luthers Werke. Kritische Gesamtausgabe,* vol. 30.2 (Weimar: Hermann Böhlaus Nachfolger, 1909), 149–59.

58. "Heerpredigt wider den Türken," in *D. Martin Luthers Werke. Kritische Gesamtausgabe,* vol. 30.2 (Weimar: Hermann Böhlaus Nachfolger, 1909), 143–44, 148. References to this text are given in parentheses.

59. In this regard my discussion challenges Bernard Lewis's argument that "Islamic religion was no longer feared as a serious rival" in the sixteenth and seventeenth centuries. "The Question of Orientalism," *Islam and the West* (New York: Oxford University Press, 1993), 73. A version of the article was previously published in the *New York Review of Books,* June 24, 1982.

60. Ottoman sources often present the war by resorting to religious terminology; that is, the attempt to erase the internal complexities is also a trait of Ottoman commentators.

61. Stephen A. Fischer-Galati, *Ottoman Imperialism and German Protestantism, 1521–1555* (Cambridge: Harvard University Press, 1959), 117. See also Fischer-Galati, "Ottoman Imperialism and the Religious Peace of Nürnberg," *Archiv für Reformationsgeschichte* 47, no. 2 (1956): 160–80.

62. Mark U. Edwards, *Printing, Propaganda, and Martin Luther* (Berkeley: University of California Press, 1994), 21.

63. Bisaha, *Creating East and West,* 174.

64. Bisaha, *Creating East and West,* 175.

65. For a broader discussion of religious arguments voiced in pamphlets, broadsheets, single-leaf woodcuts, and book sections, see Thomas Kaufmann, *"Türckenbüchlein": Zur christlichen Wahrnehmung "türkischer Religion" in Spätmittelalter und Reformation* (Göttingen: Vandenhoeck und Ruprecht, 2008).

66. For a more detailed discussion of Luther's writings, see my article "Ottoman Shock-and-Awe and the Rise of Protestantism." See also Adam S. Francisco's *Martin Luther and Islam: A Study in Sixteenth-Century Polemics and Apologetics* (Leiden: Brill, 2007), which approaches Luther's writings on Islam primarily from a theological perspective.

67. Göllner, *Turcica III,* 18.

68. Göllner, *Turcica III,* 18.

69. See also Stephane (Stefanos) Yerasimos, *Les voyageurs dans l'Empire Ottoman, XIVe–XVIe siècles: bibliografie, itinéraires et inventaire des lieux habités* (Ankara: Société turque d'histoire, 1991). For a comparison of the sources evaluated by Göllner and Yerasimos, see Almut Höfert, *Den Feind beschreiben,* 163–65.

70. Höfert's detailed study, *Den Feind beschreiben,* emphasizes the increase in ethnographic knowledge during the period and its relevance for diplomatic relations. She compares primarily Venetian, French, and German sources. Based on an analysis of select texts, an appendix lists frequently mentioned specific topics (326–53).

71. *Johann Schiltbergers Irrfahrt durch den Orient,* adapted from the Middle High German, ed. Markus Tremmel (Taufkirchen: via verbis bavarica, 2000), 22–24, 42, 49, 54–55, 98–99.

72. Albrecht Classen argues that Georgius's "open admiration of Ottoman culture is undeniable, and his sharp criticism of Islam ultimately proves to be the writer's self-de-

fense against a deep-seated fear of having transgressed traditional European norms." "The World of the Turks Described by an Eye-Witness: Georgius de Hungaria's Dialectical Discourse on the Foreign World of the Ottoman Empire," *Journal of Early Modern History* 7, no. 3–4 (2003): 257.

73. I would like to thank Annett Krause for our inspiring discussions of these accounts.

74. John Larner emphasizes the novel character of Polo's account. *Marco Polo and the Discovery of the World* (New Haven: Yale University Press, 1999).

75. *Die Pilgerfahrt des Ritters Arnold von Harff,* ed. E. von Groote (Cologne: Heberle, 1860), 204–5.

76. *Die Pilgerfahrt,* ed. Groote, 99–101.

77. Margaret T. Hodgen's study *Early Anthropology in the Sixteenth and Seventeenth Centuries* (Philadelphia: University of Philadelphia Press, 1964) describes the emergence of interest in ethnographic knowledge in Europe; she focuses mainly on French, Italian, and British textual traditions, but the evidence confirms developments I have described for the German case. I would like to thank Dan Reff for pointing me to Hodgen's study.

78. Aleya Khattab discusses stylistic aspects of these early autobiographies. *Das Ägyptenbild in den deutschsprachigen Reisebeschreibungen der Zeit von 1285–1500,* esp. 326–40.

79. Charles Beckingham, "The Arabian Travels of Johann Wild," *New Arabian Studies* 3 (1996): 9.

80. The following discussion draws on prints kept at the Georgia-Augusta library in Göttingen.

81. For a summary of the events of 1529, see Günter Düriegl, "Die erste Türkenbelagerung," *Wien 1529: Die erste Türkenbelagerung,* ed. Günter Düriegl (Vienna: Böhlau, 1979), 7–33.

82. See "Warhafftige handlung / wie vnd welcher massen der Tuerck die Stat Ofen vnd Wien belegert / Erstlich durch Koen. Mayt. zu Hungern und Behem / u. Kriegs Secretari / Herrn Peter Stern von Labach kuertzlich begriffen vnd beschrieben / Nachfolgend durch Nicolaum Meldeman / Bürger zu Nuernberg / mit merer anzeigung / was von tag zu tag sich zugetragen hat / aus angeben deren / so von anfang mit vnd dabei gewesen sind / gemehrt vnd erlengert / im Jahr 1530." No. 1 in 4 Hist. Turc. 712, Göttingen. This volume of *Turcica* includes fifty-six broadsheets in quarto format. The first print dates from 1530, the last from 1717. Cf. no. 396 in Carl Göllner, *Turcica: Die europäischen Türkendrucke des XVI. Jahrhunderts,* vol. 1 (Bucharest: Editura Academiei, 1961), *Turcica I.*

83. See Sutter Fichtner, *Terror and Toleration,* for additional examples of gruesome Ottoman warfare practices (especially pages 42–58).

84. Colin Imber, *The Ottoman Empire, 1300–1650* (New York: Palgrave, 2002), 265.

85. Fodor, "Making a Living on the Frontiers, 263.

86. Imber, *Ottoman Empire,* 261; David Nicolle, *Armies of the Ottoman Turks, 1300–1774* (Oxford: Osprey, 1983), 14.

87. Rhoads Murphey, *Ottoman Warfare, 1500–1700* (New Brunswick: Rutgers University Press, 1999), 160–63.

88. Walter Sturminger juxtaposes both German-language and Ottoman sources in *Die Türken vor Wien in Augenzeugenberichten* (Düsseldorf: Rauch, 1968). See also Joseph von Hammer (*Geschichte des Osmanischen Reiches,* vol. 2 [Pest: Hartleben, 1834]), who wrote the earliest history of the Ottomans in the German language by drawing on Turkish sources. Sutter Fichtner also states that European imagery of the Ottomans was "confirmed by contemporary Ottoman publicists themselves." *Terror and Toleration,* 41.

89. *Der fromme Sultan Bayezid: Die Geschichte seiner Herrschaft (1481–1512) nach den altosmanischen Chroniken des Oruç und des Anonymus Hanivaldanus,* trans. and ed. Richard F. Kreutel (Graz: Styria, 1978), 70. Details regarding the treatment of captives and enemies are also provided by Aşıkpaşazade. For a German translation, see *Vom Hirtenzelt zur hohen Pforte: Frühzeit und Aufstieg des Osmanenreiches nach der Chronik ›Denkwürdigkeiten und Zeitläufe des Hauses 'Osman‹ vom Derwisch Ahmed, genannt 'Aşik-Paşa-Sohn,* ed. and trans. Richard F. Kreutel (Graz: Styria, 1959).

90. Cited in Helen Watanabe-O'Kelly, "Lohenstein, Haugwitz und das Türkenmotiv in deutschen Turnieren des Barock," 354 n. 24.

91. Göllner, *Turcica III,* 24.

92. Franz Christoph Graf von Khevenhiller, *Annalium Ferdinandeorum,* vol. 5 (Leipzig: Moritz Georg Weidmann, 1722), 2256–57.

93. Gutkas, *Geschichte Niederösterreichs,* 106.

94. Bertrand Michael Buchmann, *Österreich und das Osmanische Reich: Eine bilaterale Geschichte* (Vienna: WUV-Universitätsverlag, 1999), 87–89; Richard F. Kreutel, ed. and trans., *Kara Mustafa vor Wien: 1683 aus der Sicht türkischer Quellen,* rev. ed., ed. Karl Teply (Graz: Styria, 1982), 242–43.

95. Kreutel, *Kara Mustafa vor Wien,* 224.

96. Imber, *Ottoman Empire,* 267–75; Gábor Ágoston, "Ottoman Warfare in Europe, 1453–1826," in *European Warfare, 1453–1815,* ed. Jeremy Black (New York: St. Martin's Press, 1999), 125–26.

97. *An Economic and Social History of the Ottoman Empire, 1300–1914,* vol. 1, ed. Halil Inalcik (Cambridge: Cambridge University Press, 1994), 14. On military strategies and weapons of the Ottomans, see Ünsal Yücel, "Türkische Kriegführung und Waffen," *Wien 1529: Die erste Türkenbelagerung,* ed. Düriegl, 107–21.

98. Inalcik, *An Economic and Social History of the Ottoman Empire,* 21.

99. "Von zweien Turcken newlich gefangen was Sie gefraget worden / vnnd geantwort habenn. Auch nawe zeytung wie der Turck das Stetlein Guenns gesturmbt hatt. Einem guten freundt schrieben ist." H. Turc 1067, Göttingen; cf. nos. 478 and 479 in Göllner, *Turcica I.*

100. "Der Landfarer mit eym Franckfurter Meßkrom. / Newe zeitung nach gestalt der welt aller nation durch die Christenheyt vnd Turckey für eyn Franckfurter meßkrom / diser gegenwürtigen zeyt Anno 1533." 8 Hist. un. IV 360 RARA, Göttingen; cf. no. 501 in Göllner, *Turcica I.*

101. "Ware New zeitung vom Türcken / Durch einen Glaubwirdigen Man / der damit vnd da bey gewest / Aus Ungern einem guten Freund zugeschrieben. Item andere New zeitung / aus Venedig geschrieben / vom Türcken und Frantzosen / den dritten Jenner im XLii. Mehr noch andere zeitung / vom Babst aus Rom geschrieben. Anno MDXLii"; H. Turc. 1069, Göttingen; cf. no. 786 in Göllner, *Turcica I.*

102. "Türkische Beschneidung. / Warhaffte kurtze Beschrei- / bung wie Amurath, der jetzt regierende Türkische Keiser / seinen Son Mahmeten, so er von Circassa, einer Natolianerin, sei- / nem Kebsweib erzeuget, und nu mehr bey fünffzehen Jaren alt, im / vergangenen Monat Junio, dises lauffenden Jares, mit / grossem Pomp und Herrlichkeit, zu / Constantinople beschneiden lassen." No. 17, 4 Hist. Turc. 712, Göttingen; cf. Carl Göllner, *Turcica: Die europäischen Türkendrucke des XVI. Jahrhunderts,* vol. 2 (Bucharest: Editura Academiei, 1968), Nos. 1750, 1757, 1758, 1759.

103. "Türkische Beschneidung. Warhaffte kurtze Beschreibung / wie Amurath / der jetzt regierende Tuerkische Keiser / seinen Sohn Mahometen / so er von Cricassa / einer Natolianerin / seinem Kebsweib erzeuget / vnd nu mehr by funffzehen Jaren alt / im vergangenenm Monat Junio / dieses lauffenden Jares / mit grossem Pomp und Herrlichkeit / zu Constantinople beschneiden lassen." No. 37, 4 Hist. Turc. 712, Göttingen. Not contained in Göllner.

104. Dieter Metzler, "Johannes Löwenklau," *Westfälische Lebenbilder* 13 (1985): 39.

105. *Der fromme Sultan Bayezid,* trans. and ed. Richard F. Kreutel, 187–285. Reference to Hans Lewenklaw is on 182–83.

106. Metzler, "Johannes Löwenklau," 39.

107. For an assessment of sources available on Ottoman history, see Faroqhi, *Approaching Ottoman History.*

108. "Vom Türkischen Reich. Bericht / was es fuer ein zustand vnd gelegenheit in der Tuerkey jtziger zeit habe. Aus einer vorrede Joannis Lewenklaw von Amelbeurn / die er vber seine Lateinische Tuercken Chronick gestellet / dem Christlichen Leser zu gute verdeutscht / daraus zu befinden / wie starck das Tuerckische Reich noch heute bey Tage sey / darob man sich zu fuerchten vnd nicht so sicher Ruchlos vnnd nachlessig Jm gebet wache vnd Gegenwehr / wie leider Jtziger zeit geschieht / als wenn der Tuercke bereit gar todt vnnd uberwuenden were." No. 47, 4 Hist. Turc. 712, Göttingen; cf. no. 2046 in Carl Göllner, *Turcica: Die europäischen Türkendrucke des XVI. Jahrhunderts,* vol. 2 (Bucharest: Editura Academiei, 1968).

109. I was unable to establish whether this particular text quotes Lewenklaw directly, as is implied in the broadsheet's title; none of the editions of Lewenklaw's texts that I had a chance to review contains a summary of the kind presented here.

110. Sutter Fichtner also acknowledges the significant amount of factual information in a large number of sources. *Terror and Toleration,* 82.

111. Schultheiß-Heinz, *Politik in der europäischen Publizistik,* 99.

112. Schultheiß-Heinz, *Politik in der europäischen Publizistik,* 179.

113. Hermann Kellenbenz, "Südosteuropa im Rahmen der europäischen Gesamtwirschaft," in *Die wirtschaflichen Auswirkungen der Türkenkriege: Die Vorträge des 1. internationalen Grazer Symposiums zur Wirtschafts- und Sozialgeschichte Südosteuropas (5. bis 10. Oktober 1970),* ed. Othmar Pickl (Graz: Lehrkanzel für Wirschafts- und Sozialgeschichte der Universität Graz, 1971), 52.

114. Gutkas, *Geschichte Niederösterreichs,* 108–15.

115. Milan Vasić, "Der Einfluß der Türkenkriege auf die Wirtschaft des osmanischen Grenzgebietes in Serbien und Bosnien (1480–1536)," in *Die wirtschaftlichen Auswirkungen der Türkenkriege,* ed. Pickl, 314–18.

116. Inalcik, *An Economic and Social History of the Ottoman Empire,* 188.

117. Murat Çizakça, *A Comparative Evolution of Business Partnerships: The Islamic World and Europe, with Specific Reference to the Ottoman Archives* (Leiden: Brill, 1996).

118. For a case study on the effect of capitulations, see Mehmet Bulut, "The Ottoman Approach to the Western Europeans in the Levant during the Early Modern Period," *Middle Eastern Studies* 44, no. 2 (March 2008): 259–74.

119. Göllner, *Turcica III,* 24; see also Kissling, "Türkenfurcht und Türkenhoffnung im 15./16. Jahrhundert."

120. Jean Delumeau, *La Peur en Occident (XIVe–XVIIIe siècles): Une cité assiégée* (Paris: Fayard, 1978), 263.

121. Dominique de Courcelles, "Un lieu pour la raison des 'Lumières': La conversion à l'islam d'Adam Neuser au xvie siècle," in *Conversions islamiques: identités religieuses en Islam méditerranéen,* ed. Mercedes García-Arenal (Paris: Maisonneuve et Larose, 2002), 141–49.

122. Regarding the factors that inspired conversion to Islam, see Claire Norton, "Conversion to Islam in the Ottoman Empire," *Wiener Zeitschrift zur Geschichte der Neuzeit* 7, no. 2 (2007): 25–39. An invaluable resource that I was unable to integrate in this study and that sheds light on travel and migration to the Ottoman Empire is Ralf C. Müller's ten-volume *Prosopographie der Reisenden und Migranten ins Osmanische Reich (1396–1611): Berichterstatter aus dem Heiligen Römischen Reich, außer burgundische Gebiete und Reichsromania* (Leipzig: Eudora-Verlag, 2006). Also, by the same author, *Franken im Osten: Art, Umfang, Struktur und Dynamik der Migration aus dem lateinischen Westen in das Osmanische Reich des 15. / 16. Jahrhunderts auf der Grundlage von Reiseberichten* (Leipzig: Eudora-Verlag, 2005).

123. C. F. Finkel, "French Mercenaries in the Habsburg-Ottoman War of 1593–1606: The Desertion of the Papa Garrison to the Ottomans in 1600," *Bulletin of the School of Oriental and African Studies* 55, no. 3 (1992): 451.

124. Finkel, "French Mercenaries," 460.

125. See Hermann Wiegand, "Neulateinische Türkenkriegsepik des deutschen Kulturraums im Reformationsjahrhundert," in *Europa und die Türken in der Renaissance,* ed. Bodo Guthmüller and Wilhelm Kühlmann (Tübingen: Max Niemeyer, 2000), 177–92; see also, in the same volume, Wilhelm Kühlmann, "Der Poet und sein Reich: Politische, kontextuelle und ästhetische Dimensionen der humanistischen Türkenlyrik in Deutschland," 193–227.

126. Ebert stresses this dual focus and function of German plays about the Turks written during this period ("Vom Barbaren zum aufgeklärten Herrscher").

127. See Peter N. Skrine, "Turks, Moors, and Mariners," *The Baroque: Literature and Culture in Seventeenth-Century Europe* (London: Methuen, 1978), 67–89.

128. Glenn Ehrstine, "Fastnachtsrhetorik: Adelskritik und Alterität in *Des Turken Vasnachtspil,*" *WerkstattGeschichte* 37 (2004): 22. Eckehard Simon explains the positive aspects of the Turkish sultan in light of the carnival's license to turn the social and political order upside down. "Der Türke in Nürnberg: Zur Türkenpolemik nach 1453 und 'Des Turcken vasnachtspil,'" in *Internationaler Germanisten-Kongreß in Tokyo,* ed. Yoshinori Shichiji, vol. 7 (Munich: iudicium, 1991), 322–28.

129. See Kleinlogel, *Exotik-Erotik,* 55–70.

130. See Kleinlogel, *Exotik-Erotik,* 57; Sarah Colvin, *The Rhetorical Feminine: Gender and Orient on the German Stage, 1647–1742* (Oxford: Clarendon, 1999), 37.

131. Kleinlogel, *Exotik-Erotik,* 81.

132. Kleinlogel, *Exotik-Erotik,* 128.

133. Robert Waissenberger, "Orientierung im Zeitalter: Österreich und Europa vom Westfälischen Frieden bis zum Frieden von Karlowitz," *Die Türken vor Wien: Europa und die Entscheidung an der Donau 1683* (Vienna: Residenz, 1982), 18.

134. Hasan Aga mentions that forty to fifty piaster were paid for a prisoner, twenty to thirty piaster for a head. *Krieg und Sieg in Ungarn: Die Ungarnfeldzüge des Großwesirs Köprülüzade Fazil Ahmed Pascha 1663 and 1664 nach den 'Kleinodien der Historien' seines Siegelbewahrers Hasan Aga,* trans. and ed. Erich Prokosch (Graz: Styria, 1976), 56.

135. *Krieg und Sieg,* ed. Prokosch, 55, 56, 146.

136. Colvin, *Rhetorical Feminine,* 29.

137. Skrine, "Turks, Moors, and Mariners," 86.

138. Lohenstein used a considerable number of historical sources about Ottoman society. See Ebert, "Vom Barbaren zum aufgeklärten Herrscher," 8.

139. Colvin has pointed out, however, that "throughout the drama we see the eventually virtuous Sultan against a background of 'real' Turkishness: hence we must perceive him as an exception, not as the rule" (*Rhetorical Feminine,* 54). This aspect—namely, to set off against each other positive and negative Turkish characters—becomes a feature of operas and plays in the eighteenth century and is discussed in chap. 3. Ebert ties Haugwitz's play to the defeat of the Ottomans in 1683 ("Vom Barbaren zum aufgeklärten Herrscher," 223, 261).

140. Skrine, "Turks, Moors, and Mariners," 86.

141. Kleinlogel, *Exotik-Erotik,* 249.

142. See Kleinlogel, *Exotik-Erotik,* 253–63.

143. Hans Jakob Christoffel von Grimmelshausen, *Der Abenteuerliche Simplicissimus Teutsch* (Munich: dtv, 1975), 473–74.

144. Grimmelshausen, *Simplicissimus,* 562.

145. *Im Reiche des Goldenen Apfels: Des türkischen Weltenbummlers Evliya Çelebi denkwürdige Reise in das Giaurenland und in die Stadt und Festung Wien anno 1665,* ed. and trans. Richard F. Kreutel (Graz: Styria, 1963), 48, 196.

146. *Im Reiche des Goldenen Apfels,* ed. Kreutel, 160–64.

147. The desirability of Vienna is documented by the existence of numerous Turkish tales and legends about the city. See *Türkische Sagen und Legenden um die Kaiserstadt Wien,* ed. Karl Teply (Vienna: Böhlau, 1980).

148. Waissenberger, "Orientierung im Zeitalter," 26.

149. Figures for the size of the army vary, especially with regard to the number of actual combatants; I settled for figures that represent a consensus among scholars.

150. For a detailed summary of the events, see Günter Düriegl, *Wien 1683: Die zweite Türkenbelagerung* (Vienna: Böhlau, 1981).

151. For a German eyewitness account, see *Tagebuch eines Augenzeugen 1683: Aufzeichnungen des Freiherrn von P.,* ed. Kurt Eigl (Vienna: Tusch, 1983).

152. See, for example, the following passage: "Den zur Hölle verdammten Giauren

wurden gleich einundzwanzig Köpfe abgenommen; sie wurden dem Großwesir . . . vor die Füße gelegt, und dafür wurden allen diesen Glaubensstreitern mit den Geschenken des erhabenen Großwesirs die Geldbeutel gefüllt und die Herzen erfreut." Richard F. Kreutel, ed. and trans., *Kara Mustafa vor Wien: 1683 aus der Sicht türkischer Quellen,* rev. ed. by Karl Teply (Graz: Styria, 1982), 179–80. Other passages mentioning severed heads are on 173, 174, 175, 180, and 183.

153. Pál Ács, "Tarjumans Mahmud and Murad: Austrian and Hungarian Renegades as Sultan's Interpreters," *Europa und die Türken in der Renaissance,* ed. Guthmüller and Kühlmann, 307–16.

154. See Józef Jankovics, "The Image of the Turks in Hungarian Renaissance Literature," *Europa und die Türken in der Renaissance,* ed. Guthmüller and Kühlmann, 267–73; see also, in the same volume, András Szabó, "Die Türkenfrage in der Geschichtsauffassung der ungarischen Reformation," 275–81.

155. For select analyses of Italian writings, see Bodo Guthmüller, "'Se tu non piangi, di che pianger suoli?' Der *Lamento di Constantinopoli* in *ottava rima,*" *Europa und die Türken in der Renaissance,* ed. Guthmüller and Kühlmann, 317–32; see also, in the same volume, Wolfgang Friedrichs, "Das Türkenbild in Lodovico Dolces Übersetzung der *Epistolae magni Turci* des italienischen Humanisten Laudivio Vezzanense," 333–44. Mustafa Soykut's *Image of the "Turk" in Italy: A History of the "Other" in Early Modern Europe, 1453–1683* (Berlin: Schwarz, 2001) focuses predominantly on the negative image of Turks and explores the varying functions of this image.

156. Klaus Malettke, "Die Vorstöße der Osmanen im 16. Jahrhundert aus französischer Sicht," *Europa und die Türken in der Renaissance,* ed. Guthmüller and Kühlmann, 388.

157. Skrine points to distinct French attitudes toward the Ottomans. "Turks, Moors, and Mariners," 84.

158. Luc Deitz, "Das Türkenbild in der englischen Literatur des 16. Jahrhunderts," *Europa und die Türken in der Renaissance,* ed. Guthmüller and Kühlmann, 395–407.

159. Daniel Vitkus, *Turning Turk: English Theater and the Multicultural Mediterranean, 1570–1630* (New York: Palgrave, 2003), 79.

160. Bisaha, *Creating East and West,* 175.

161. Daniel J. Vitkus, "Introduction," *Three Turk Plays from Early Modern England: Selimus, A Christian turned Turk, and The Renegado,* ed. Daniel J. Vitkus (New York: Columbia University Press, 2000), 3. See also Nabil Matar, *Turks, Moors, and Englishmen in the Age of Discovery* (New York: Columbia University Press, 1999), 9.

162. Vitkus, *Three Turk Plays,* 3. For historical background on the slave raids, see Davis, *Christian Slaves, Muslim Masters.*

163. Vitkus, *Three Turk Plays,* 4.

164. Matar, *Turks, Moors, and Englishmen in the Age of Discovery,* 7, 13.

165. Matar, *Turks, Moors, and Englishmen in the Age of Discovery,* 5, 43.

166. A nineteenth-century analysis of the relationship is given by Leopold von Ranke in *Die Osmanen und die Spanische Monarchie im 16. und 17. Jahrhundert* (Leipzig: Duncker und Humblot, 1877).

167. Kate Fleet, *European and Islamic Trade in the Early Ottoman State: The Merchants of Genoa and Turkey* (Cambridge: Cambridge University Press, 1999), 140.

CHAPTER 3

1. Holger Schuckelt, "Zwischen den Kriegen: Kultureller Austausch in der Zeit der Entspannung (1566–1593)," *Im Lichte des Halbmonds: Das Abendland und der türkische Orient,* ed. Staatliche Kunstsammlungen Dresden (Leipzig: Edition Leipzig: 1995), 93.

2. Matthias Pfaffenbichler, "Orientalische und orientalisierende Waffen," *Im Lichte des Halbmonds,* 97.

3. Sutter Fichtner, *Terror and Toleration,* 94.

4. Mike Dash, *Tulipomania: The Story of the World's Most Coveted Flower and the Extraordinary Passions It Aroused* (New York: Three Rivers Press, 1999), 32.

5. Dash provides figures on prices during the boom (*Tulipomania,* 108–9); see also Anne Goldgar, *Tulipmania: Money, Honor, and Knowledge in the Dutch Golden Age* (Chicago: University of Chicago Press, 2007).

6. John Kenneth Galbraith, *A Short History of Financial Euphoria* (Knoxville: Whittle Direct Books, 1990), 22.

7. Galbraith, *Short History of Financial Euphoria,* 27.

8. Claudia Schnitzer, "Zwischen Kampf und Spiel: Orientrezeption im höfischen Fest," *Im Lichte des Halbmonds,* 227.

9. Ralf Martin Jäger, "Türkische Musik und Musiker in Mitteleuropa im 17. und 18. Jahrhundert," in *Fremde Erfahrungen: Asiaten und Afrikaner in Deutschland, Österreich und in der Schweiz bis 1945,* ed. Gerhard Höpp (Berlin: Das Arabische Buch, 1996), 423.

10. Elisabeth Mikosch, "Ein Serail für die Hochzeit des Prinzen: Turquerien bei den Hochzeitsfeierlichkeiten in Dresden im Jahre 1719," *Im Lichte des Halbmonds,* 235.

11. Mikosch, "Ein Serail für die Hochzeit," 236.

12. Gunther Joppig comments on this development in "Alla Turca: Orientalismen in der europäischen Kunstmusik vom 17. bis zum 19. Jahrhundert," *Europa und der Orient,* ed. Sievernich and Budde, 295–304.

13. Jäger, "Türkische Musik und Musiker in Mitteleuropa," 425.

14. Rudolf Klein, "*Alla turca* in der europäischen Musik," *Die Türken vor Wien: Europa und die Entscheidung an der Donau 1683* (Vienna: Residenz, 1982), 321.

15. Jäger, "Türkische Musik und Musiker in Mitteleuropa," 422.

16. Quoted in Jäger, "Türkische Musik und Musiker in Mitteleuropa," 425 n. 17.

17. See the description of a 1731 ceremony at the court in Warsaw; the Saxon king played a significant role as king of Poland after 1697, and adjustments in protocol reflect the growing importance of diplomatic relations. Anni Miksch, "Außenpolitik im Spiegel des sächsisch/polnischen Zeremoniells," *Im Lichte des Halbmonds,* 184–91.

18. Mikosch, "Ein Serail für die Hochzeit," 243.

19. Friedrich Reichel, "Die Türkenmode und ihr Einfluß auf die sächische Kunst," *Im Lichte des Halbmonds,* 265–66.

20. Elisabeth Mikosch and Holger Schuckelt, "Das sächische Janitscharenbataillon beim Zeithainer Lager 1730," *Im Lichte des Halbmonds,* 289–90.

21. Mikosch and Schuckelt, "Das sächische Janitscharenbataillon," 291.

22. Reichel, "Die Türkenmode und ihr Einfluß auf die sächische Kunst," 268.

23. Anette Loesch, "Zum Einfluß der Türkenmode auf das Meißner Porzellan," *Im Lichte des Halbmonds,* 273.

24. Kurt Erdmann, *Europa und der Orientteppich* (Berlin: Kupferberg, 1962), 60–77.

25. Volkmar Enderlein, "Das Berliner Kostümbuch von 1763," *Im Lichte des Halbmonds,* 275–78.

26. Maria Elisabeth Pape, "Turquerie im 18. Jahrhundert und der 'Recueil Ferriol,'" *Europa und der Orient,* ed. Sievernich and Budde, 307.

27. Pape, "Turquerie im 18. Jahrhundert," 309–12. See "Bildnis der Herzogin Louisa von Schleswig-Holstein-Sonderburg-Augustenburg in türkischer Tracht" (1780–90) by J. Juel, 314.

28. Günther Schiedlausky, *Tee, Kaffee, Schokolade: Ihr Eintritt in die Europäische Gesellschaft* (Munich: Prestel, 1961), 15.

29. Wolfgang Schivelbusch, *Tastes of Paradise: A Social History of Spices, Stimulants, and Intoxicants,* trans. David Jacobson (New York: Pantheon, 1992), 81.

30. Schivelbusch, *Tastes of Paradise,* 59.

31. David Spurr, *The Rhetoric of Empire: Colonial Discourse in Journalism, Travel Writing, and Imperial Administration* (Durham: Duke University Press, 1993), 32.

32. On the role of consumption in the late eighteenth/early nineteenth centuries, see Karin Wurst, *Fabricating Pleasure: Fashion, Entertainment, and Cultural Consumption in Germany, 1780–1830* (Detroit: Wayne State University, 2005); Daniel L. Purdy, *The Tyranny of Elegance: Consumer Cosmopolitanism in the Era of Goethe* (Baltimore: Johns Hopkins University Press, 1998).

33. Hartmut Heller, "Beutetürken: Deportation und Assimilation im Zuge der Türkenkriege des 16. und 17. Jahrhunderts," in *Fremde Erfahrungen,* ed. Höpp, 160.

34. Heller, "Beutetürken," 162.

35. Erwin A. Schmidl, "Türken, Grenzer, Bosniaken: 'Orientalen' in Österreich(-Ungarn)," *Fremde Erfahrungen,* ed. Höpp, 320.

36. Heller, "Beutetürken," 164.

37. The details of this summary come from "Einleitung," *Der Gefangene der Giauren: Die abenteuerlichen Schicksale des Dolmetschers 'Osman Aga aus Temeschwar, von ihm selbst erzählt,* ed. and trans. Richard F. Kreutel and Otto Spies (Graz: Styria, 1962), 9–16.

38. Richard F. Kreutel and Karl Teply, ed. and trans., *Der Löwe von Temeschwar: Erinnerungen an Ca'fer Pascha den Älteren, aufgezeichnet von seinem Siegelbewahrer 'Ali* (Graz: Styria, 1981).

39. On the subject of the proliferation of sultan portraits in Europe, see Hans Georg Majer, "Giovio, Veronese und die Osmanen: Zum Sultansbild der Renaissance," in *Europa und die Türken,* ed. Guthmüller and Kühlmann, 345–71.

40. Joachim Schardin, "Uhren und Automatenwerke im Rahmen der kaiserlichen 'Türkenverehrung,'" *Im Lichte des Halbmonds,* 134.

41. See, for example, Filiz Yenişehirlioğlu, "Western Influences on Ottoman Architecture in the 18th Century," in *Das Osmanische Reich und Europa 1683 bis 1789: Konflikt, Entspannung und Austausch,* ed. Gernot Heiss and Grete Klingenstein (Munich: Oldenbourg, 1983), 153–78.

42. Virginia H. Aksan, "Ottoman Sources of Information on Europe in the Eighteenth Century," *Archivum Ottomanicum* 11 (1986): 5–16.

43. "Science in the Ottoman World," *Imperialism and Science: Social Impact and Interaction,* ed. George N. Vlahakis et al. (Santa Barbara: ABC-CLIO, 2006), 84–87.

44. Wilson, *Humanität und Kreuzzugsideologie um 1780,* 18.

45. Donald Quataert, *The Ottoman Empire, 1700–1922* (Cambridge: Cambridge University Press, 2000), 38.

46. On diplomatic relations during the period, see Ivan Parvev, "Habsburg-Ottoman Coexistence, 1718–1736," in *Habsburgs and Ottomans between Vienna and Belgrade (1683–1739)* (New York: Columbia University Press, 1995), 193–209.

47. Klaus Schwarz, "Vom Krieg zum Frieden: Berlin, das Kurfürstentum Brandenburg, das Reich und die Türken," *Europa und der Orient,* 275–77.

48. The Ottoman ambassador Ahmed Resmi Efendi described Frederick the Great and Berlin in a report that he wrote during his stay in the city in 1763/64. According to Virginia H. Aksan, "Ahmed Resmi's observations on the European balance of power are evident" in this account, which also includes "an analysis of Frederick's character and his military expertise." "An Ottoman Portrait of Frederick the Great," *Oriente Moderno* 18, no. 1 (1999): 210–11.

49. The second Ottoman embassy was sent to Berlin in 1791; the third Ottoman ambassador died in Berlin in 1798 and was buried there. Schwarz, "Vom Krieg zum Frieden," 278.

50. For a brief introduction and translation of the text, see Anton C. Schaedlinger, "Die Entdeckung des Abendlandes als Vorbild: Ein Vorschlag zur Umgestaltung des Heerwesens und der Außenpolitik des Osmanischen Reiches zu Beginn des 18. Jahrhunderts," *Das Osmanische Reich und Europa 1683–1789: Konflikt, Entspannung und Austausch* (Munich: R. Oldenbourg, 1983), 89–112.

51. Klaus Kreiser, *Der Osmanische Staat 1300–1922* (Munich: R. Oldenbourg, 2001), 32.

52. Heinrich Benedikt, *Der Pascha-Graf Alexander von Bonneval 1675–1747* (Graz: Böhlau, 1959), 8.

53. Quataert, *Ottoman Empire,* 42.

54. For a case study exploring European encroachment on Middle Eastern economies, see Bruce Masters, *The Origins of Western Economic Dominance in the Middle East: Mercantilism and the Islamic Economy in Aleppo, 1600–1750* (New York: New York University Press, 1988).

55. Edhem Eldem, "French Trade and Commercial Policy in the Levant in the Eighteenth-Century," *Oriente Moderno* 18, no. 1 (1999): 27. See also the detailed case study by the same author, *French Trade in Istanbul in the Eighteenth Century* (Leiden: Brill, 1999).

56. Şevket Pamuk, *A Monetary History of the Ottoman Empire* (Cambridge: Cambridge University Press, 2000), 161.

57. Figures quoted in Fatma Müge Göçek, *Rise of the Bourgeoisie, Demise of Empire: Ottoman Westernization and Social Change* (New York: Oxford University Press, 1996), 88.

58. Donald Quataert, "An Essay on Economic Relations between the Ottoman and

Habsburg Empires, 1800–1914," in *Habsburgisch-osmanische Beziehungen,* ed. Andreas Tietze (Vienna: Verlag des Verbandes der wissenschaftlichen Gesellschaften Österreichs, 1985), 244.

59. Walter B. Denny, "Images of Turks and the European Imagination," in *Court and Conquest: Ottoman Origins and the Design for Handel's 'Tamerlano' at the Glimmerglass Opera,* ed. Walter B. Denny et al. (Kent, OH: Kent State University Museum, 1998), 15.

60. Walter Preibisch, "Quellenstudien zu Mozart's *Entführung aus dem Serail:* Ein Beitrag zu der Geschichte der Türkenoper," *Sammelbände der Internationalen Musikgesellschaft* 10, no. 3 (1909): 432.

61. Preibisch, "Quellenstudien," 434.

62. J. Merrill Knapp, "Handel's *Tamerlano:* The Creation of an Opera," *Musical Quarterly* 56, no. 3 (1970): 406.

63. Knapp, "Handel's *Tamerlano,*" 407.

64. See Knapp's discussion of the relationship between libretto and score in "Handel's *Tamerlano.*"

65. See Kent M. Smith, "Three Eighteenth-Century 'Turkish' Operas: A Comparative Study of Gluck's *La Rencontre Imprévue,* Haydn's *L'Incontro Improviso,* and Mozart's *Die Entführung aus dem Serail*" (Master's thesis, University of Wisconsin, 1971), 15–22; Preibisch, "Quellenstudien," 438–42.

66. For a discussion of the novel's commentary on subjectivity and representation, see Harriet Stone, "Scudéry's Theater of Disguise: The Orient in *Ibrahim,*" *L'Esprit Créateur* 32, no. 3 (1992): 51–61.

67. Ali Behdad, "The Oriental(ist) Encounter: The Politics of *turquerie* in Molière," *L'Esprit Créateur* 32, no. 3 (1992): 39.

68. See Ali Behdad's discussion of events leading up to the writing of the comedy. Apparently, the French public was disappointed with the lack of exotic appearance and behavior of the Ottoman ambassador Soliman Aga, who visited France in 1669. Nevertheless, the visit sparked desire for Orientalist representations, and in this context the play was commissioned by the king. "Oriental(ist) Encounter," 37–49.

69. Behdad, "Oriental(ist) Encounter," 42. Michèle Longino, "Acculturating the Audience: *Le Bourgeois gentilhomme,*" *Orientalism in French Classical Drama* (Cambridge: Cambridge University Press, 2002), 109–46. Behdad also relates Molière's comedy to French overseas expansionism and the "power of colonialist consciousness in mid-seventeenth-century representations of France's others." "Oriental(ist) Encounter," 48.

70. On the circulation and adaptation of the text in Europe, see Winfried Weißhaupt, *Europa sieht sich mit fremdem Blick: Werke nach dem Schema der "Lettres persanes" in der europäischen, insbesondere der deutschen Literatur des 18. Jahrhunderts* (Frankfurt am Main: Lang, 1979).

71. Regarding basic principles of despotic government, see Montesquieu, *The Spirit of the Laws,* ed. and trans. Anne M. Cohler, Basia Carolyn Miller, and Harold Samuel Stone (Cambridge: Cambridge University Press, 1989), 28–30.

72. See the extended passage on China in Montesquieu, *Spirit of the Laws,* 126–28.

73. For a case study exploring the interaction of international and domestic dimensions of the debate on despotism, see Thomas Kaiser, "The Evil Empire? The Debate on

Turkish Despotism in Eighteenth-Century French Political Culture," *Journal of Modern History* 72, no. 1 (March 2000): 6–34.

74. Minou Reeves, *Muhammad in Europe* (New York: New York University Press, 2000), 155.

75. Voltaire, *Candide; or, Optimism: A Fresh Translation, Backgrounds, Criticism,* ed. and trans. Robert M. Adams (1966; rpt., New York: W. W. Norton, 1991), 75.

76. Voltaire, *A Treatise on Toleration and Other Essays,* trans. Joseph McCabe (Amherst: Prometheus Books, 1994), 162–63.

77. See, for example, Rebecca Joubin, "Islam and Arabs through the Eyes of the *Encyclopédie:* The 'Other' as a Case of French Cultural Self-Criticism," *International Journal of Middle East Studies* 32 (2000): 197–217.

78. For a discussion of the novel's Orientalist themes, see Julia V. Douthwaite, "Embattled Eros: The Cultural Politics of Prévost's *Grecque moderne,*" *L'Esprit Créateur* 32, no. 3 (1992): 87–97.

79. Ros Ballaster, *Fabulous Orients: Fictions of the East in England, 1662–1785* (Oxford: Oxford University Press, 2005), 55.

80. See Ballaster's chapters on "Shape-Shifting: Oriental Tales" and "Tales of the Seraglio: Turkey and Persia," in *Fabulous Orients,* 25–58, 59–192.

81. Ballaster, *Fabulous Orients,* 136.

82. Ballaster, *Fabulous Orients,* 145–71.

83. See also Sir William Jones's *Palace of Fortune* (1769) and *Hymn to Narayena* (1785); Clara Reeve's *History of Charoba, Queen of AEgypt* (1785), Walter Savage Landor's *Gebir* (1798), Robert Southey's *Curse of Kehama* (1810); and Thomas Moore's *Lalla Rookh, and Oriental Romance* (1817).

84. Irwin, *For Lust of Knowing,* 66.

85. Irwin, *For Lust of Knowing,* 87.

86. Irwin, *For Lust of Knowing,* 121.

87. For a case study, see Alastair Hamilton, *Arab Culture and Ottoman Magnificence in Antwerp's Golden Age* (Oxford: Oxford University Press, 2001).

88. Marchand, *German Orientalism in the Age of Empire.*

89. For a review of the period before Reiske, see Holger Preissler, "Orientalische Studien in Leipzig vor Reiske," 19–43.

90. Raymond Schwab, *The Oriental Renaissance: Europe's Rediscovery of India and the East, 1680–1880,* trans. Gene Patterson-Black and Victor Reinking (1950; rpt., New York: Columbia University Press, 1984), 17.

91. Marchand, *German Orientalism,* 38–42, focuses on Michaelis; Hess, *Germans, Jews, and the Claims of Modernity,* 50–89.

92. A. Hinckelmann, *Al-Coranus s. lex islamitica Muhammedis, filii Abdallae, Pseudoprophetae, ad optimorum Codicum fidem edita ex Museo Abrahami Hinckelmanni* (Hamburg: Schultze und Schiller, 1694).

93. Mahmud Muhammad Haggag, "Deutsche Koran-Übersetzungen und ihr Islambild," in *Religiöser Text und soziale Struktur,* ed. Walter Beltz and Jürgen Tubach (Halle: Martin-Luther-Universität, 2001), 180.

94. Ian Almond, "Leibniz, Historicism, and the 'Plague of Islam,'" *Eighteenth-Century Studies* 39, no. 4 (2006): 473.

95. Behdad, "Oriental(ist) Encounter," 38.

96. Carsten Prange, *Die Zeitungen und Zeitschriften des 17. Jahrhunderts in Hamburg und Altona: Ein Beitrag zur Publizistik der Frühaufklärung* (Hamburg: Hans Christians, 1978), 193–202.

97. Helga Fischer bases her discussion of travel accounts on texts reviewed in this journal. The accounts discussed in her essay include texts by French (J. C. Flachat, Peyssonel, K. F. Volney), British (M. Montagu, F. C. Baltimore, J. Porter, E. Habesci, E. Craven, J. Dallaway, W. Eton), Italian (P. Businello, G. Toderini), and German authors (Ch. Lüdeke, F. v. Tott, v. Riedesel). "Das Osmanische Reich in Reisebeschreibungen und Berichten des 18. Jahrhunderts," *Das Osmanische Reich und Europa,* 113–42.

98. Ronald W. Ferrier, ed. and trans., *A Journey to Persia: Jean Chardin's Portrait of a Seventeenth-Century Empire* (London: Tauris, 1996), 11.

99. Fischer, "Das Osmanische Reich," 117.

100. Lisa Lowe, *Critical Terrains: French and British Orientalisms* (Ithaca: Cornell University Press, 1991), 44.

101. Lowe, *Critical Terrains,* 51.

102. For a detailed study of the considerable power exerted by women at the imperial court, see Leslie P. Peirce, *The Imperial Harem: Women and Sovereignty in the Ottoman Empire* (New York: Oxford University Press, 1993).

103. A fourth volume was published in 1837, edited by Niebuhr's daughter.

104. See entries in David H. K. Amiran's revised editions of Reinhold Röhricht's *Bibliotheca Geographica Palaestinae: Chronologisches Verzeichnis der von 333 bis 1878 verfassten Literatur über das Heilige Land, mit dem Versuch einer Kartographie* (Jerusalem: Universitas Booksellers, 1963), 279–328. These entries cover the years 1683 to 1780 and include publications in European languages, Arabic, and Hebrew.

105. See Ulrich van der Heyden, *Rote Adler an Afrikas Küste: Die brandenburgisch-preussische Kolonie Grossfriedrichsburg an der westafrikanischen Küste* (Berlin: Brandenburgisches Verlagshaus, 1993).

106. Lloyd Spencer, "Adorno, Theodor Wiesengrund (1903–1969)," in *The Routledge Companion to Postmodernism,* ed. Stuart Sim (New York: Routledge, 1999), 158.

107. See my discussion of the ideological framework of modernization in the introduction to *Impossible Missions,* 1–17.

108. Preibisch, "Quellenstudien," 435, 451.

109. See list in Wilson, *Humanität und Kreuzzugsideologie,* 13–14.

110. See Wilson's summary of the plot in *Humanität und Kreuzzugsideologie,* 14.

111. Wilson, *Humanität und Kreuzzugsideologie,* 31.

112. Helmut Wirth, "Gluck, Haydn und Mozart: Drei Entführungs-Opern," in *Opernstudien: Anna Amalie Abert zum 65. Geburtstag,* ed. Klaus Hortschansky (Tutzing: Hans Schneider, 1975), 34.

113. On Mozart's relationship to Enlightenment thought, see Nicholas Till, *Mozart and the Enlightenment: Truth, Virtue, and Beauty in Mozart's Operas* (New York: W. W. Norton, 1992). *Die Entführung aus dem Serail* is discussed on 102–16.

114. Benjamin Perl, "Mozart in Turkey," *Cambridge Opera Journal* 12, no. 3 (2000): 230, 233, 235. For an additional exploration of Turkish elements in instrumental music, see David Korevaar, "Exoticism Assimilated: 'Turkish' Elements in Mozart's Sonata, K. 331 and Beethoven's 'Waldstein' Sonata, op. 53," *Journal of Musicological Research* 20 (2002): 197–232.

115. For a discussion of Turkish operas after Mozart, see Margaret Ross Griffel, "'Turkish' Operas from Mozart to Cornelius" (PhD diss., Columbus University, 1975).

116. Diethelm Balke, "Orient und orientalische Literaturen," 838.

117. The full title of the play reveals the continuing claim to Jerusalem by Habsburg rulers; in *Reallexikon der deutschen Literaturgeschichte,* ed. Werner Kohlschmidt and Wolfgang Mohr, vol. 2 (Berlin: de Gruyter, 1965): "Adelheid in der Sclaverey, oder, Tugend und Unschuld bietet aller Verleumdung Trotz: Ein Trauerspiel von fünf Aufzügen; aufgeführet an dem glorreichen allerhöchsten Geburtsfeste Sr. Römisch-Kaiserlichen Majestät Francisci in Germanien, und zu Jerusalem Königs, etc."

118. Kleinlogel, *Exotik-Erotik,* 333–37. The following discussion of novels relies in several instances on Kleinlogel's plot summaries, as I was unable to obtain copies of some of the texts.

119. Kleinlogel, *Exotik-Erotik,* 342–43.

120. See also Sutter Fichtner's discussion of Austrian plays and operas with Turkish themes, *Terror and Toleration,* 96–110.

121. In contrast, Gluck's 1779 opera *Iphigénie en Tauride* conceived Scythians as "frightening representations of primitive, savage unreason." Till, *Mozart,* 105.

122. Wilson elaborates on aspects that link Goethe's play to the tradition of operas and plays following the abduction model. *Humanität und Kreuzzugsideologie,* 87–111.

123. Quoted in Kleinlogel, *Exotik-Erotik,* 370.

124. See Wilson's detailed discussion in *Humanität und Kreuzzugsideologie,* 39–57.

125. Meleaton (Johann Leonhard Rost), *Die Türkische Helena* (N.p.: n.p., 1710), x.

126. Kleinlogel, *Exotik-Erotik,* 386–88.

127. Murantes, *Der in den letzten Zügen liegende Cupido, oder das fatal- und unglückliche Lieben* (Frankfurt am Main: n.p., 1747), 208.

128. Murantes, *Der in den letzten Zügen liegende Cupido,* 209.

129. Kleinlogel, *Exotik-Erotik,* 390–92.

130. Wilhelm Retchir, *Der Sächsische Robinson* (Leipzig: Friedrich Lanckischens Erben, 1722), 216–35.

131. Retchir, *Sächsischer Robinson,* 423.

132. Johann Gottfried Schnabel, *Die Insel Felsenburg* (Stuttgart: Reclam, 1959), 9.

133. Kleinlogel, *Exotik-Erotik,* 396–98; Schnabel, 106–11.

134. For a discussion of these novels, see Kleinlogel, *Exotik-Erotik,* 398–411.

135. Sander L. Gilman, Karl-Heinz Hartmann, and Thomas Salumets, "Einleitung," in Friedrich Maximilian Klinger, *Geschichte Giafars des Barmeciden: Ein Seitenstück zu "Faust's Leben, Thaten und Höllenfahrt,"* ed. Sander L. Gilman, Karl-Heinz Hartmann, and Thomas Salumets (Tübingen: Max Niemeyer, 2004), xii–xiii.

136. Alois Weissenbach, *Die Barmekiden oder die Egyptier in Bagdad* (1801), Josef von Hammer, *Dschafer, oder der Sturz der Barmegiden* (1813), and Franz Grillparzer, *Der Traum ein Leben* (1817–34). Gilman, Hartmann, and Salumets, "Einleitung," xxii.

137. Johann Gottfried Herder, "Über die Würkung der Dichtkunst auf die Sitten der Völker in alten und neuen Zeiten: Eine Preisschrift," *Über Literatur und Gesellschaft: Ausgewählte Schriften* (Leipzig: Reclam, 1988), 40.

138. Herder, "Über die Würkung der Dichtkunst," 42.

139. "Wodurch sollen wir aber die ausgestorbene Sprache der Natur von den Todten

wieder auferwecken?—Durch Wallfahrten nach dem glücklichen Arabien, durch Kreuzzüge nach den Morgenländern, und durch die Wiederherstellung ihrer Magie, die wir durch alte Weiberlist, weil sie die beste ist, zu unserer Beute machen müssen." Johann Georg Hamann, *Sokratische Denkwürdigkeiten; Aesthetica in Nuce* (Stuttgart: Reclam, 1968), 129.

140. Suzanne L. Marchand, *Down from Olympus: Archaeology and Philhellenism in Germany, 1750–1970* (Princeton: Princeton University Press, 1996), 15–16.

141. Susanne Zantop, *Colonial Fantasies: Conquest, Family, and Nation in Precolonial Germany, 1770–1870* (Durham: Duke University Press, 1997), 75.

142. Johann Gottfried Herder, *Ideen zur Philosophie der Geschichte der Menschheit,* in *Johann Gottfried Herder, Werke* vol. 3.1, ed. Wolfgang Pross (Munich: Hanser, 2002), 645.

143. Herder, *Ideen,* 645–46.

144. Sankar Muthu, *Enlightenment Against Empire* (Princeton: Princeton University Press, 2003), 3. See also the chapter "Pluralism, Humanity, and Empire in Herder's Political Thought," 210–58.

145. Zantop, *Colonial Fantasies,* 79.

146. Zantop, *Colonial Fantasies,* 68.

147. Immanuel Kant, "Von den verschiedenen Rassen der Menschen," *Werke in 12 Bänden* (Frankfurt am Main: Insel, 1964), 11:14.

148. Seyla Benhabib, *The Rights of Others: Aliens, Residents, and Citizens* (Cambridge: Cambridge University Press, 2004), 45–46.

149. Regarding Kant's use of the figure of an "Asiatic Turk," see Peter Melville, "Staging the Nation: Hospitable Performances in Kant's *Anthropology,*" *European Romantic Review* 17, no. 1 (2006): 39–53.

150. Horsch, *Rationalität und Toleranz,* 25.

151. A lesser-known author who exemplifies this engagement with the new knowledge is Johann Carl Wezel. His novel *Belphegor oder die wahrscheinlichste Geschichte unter der Sonne* (1776) conveys a considerable amount of detail about foreign countries, and his view of non-European societies, particularly Islam, reveals an open mind and curiosity comparable perhaps to that of Lessing and Goethe.

152. Horsch, *Rationalität und Toleranz,* 3.

153. Regarding a list of sources, see Horsch, *Rationalität und Toleranz,* 13–24.

154. Horsch, *Rationalität und Toleranz,* 30. For a detailed discussion, see Helmut Göbel, "Lessing und Cardano: Ein Beitrag zu Lessings Renaissance-Rezeption," in *Aufklärung und Humanismus,* ed. Richard Toellner (Heidelberg: Lambert, 1980), 167–86.

155. Horsch, *Rationalität und Toleranz,* 33.

156. Horsch raises an important question by asking why Lessing did not address Islam in his treatise "Erziehung des Menschengeschlechts" (1780), which was largely conceptualized in 1777, before Lessing wrote *Nathan the Wise. Rationalität und Toleranz,* 49–51.

157. Navid Kermani, *Toleranz: Drei Lesarten zu Lessings Märchen vom Ring im Jahre 2003,* with contributions by Angelika Overath, Navid Kermani, and Robert Schindel (Göttingen: Wallstein, 2003), 34.

158. Fred O. Nolte has argued that the patriarch is modeled after Voltaire's Ma-

homet, as rendered in his 1741 play. "Voltaire's Mahomet as a Source of Lessing's *Nathan der Weise* and *Emilia Galotti*," *Modern Language Notes* 48, no. 3 (1933): 153.

159. Karl S. Guthke points to contradictions and limitations of Lessing's notion of tolerance. *Lessings Horizonte: Grenzen und Grenzenlosigkeit der Toleranz* (Göttingen: Wallstein, 2003).

160. For an in-depth investigation of theological questions, see Horsch, who discusses the question of whether the play argues for a view of Islam as a religion of reason compatible with Deism or for the equality of revealed religions. According to Horsch, Lessing suggests with his play that in all religions, humanity is achieved through ethical behavior. *Rationalität und Toleranz,* 71–97.

161. Katharina Mommsen, *Goethe und 1001 Nacht* (1960; rpt., Frankfurt am Main: Suhrkamp, 1981), 24–30.

162. "Anspielungen aller Art wurden also mit Sicherheit verstanden." *Goethe und 1001 Nacht,* 35.

163. Katharina Mommsen, *Goethe und die arabische Welt* (Frankfurt am Main: Insel, 1988), 25.

164. Mommsen, "Vorislamische Beduinendichtung," *Goethe und die arabische Welt,* 51–156.

165. See, for example, ʻAbd al-Rahman Sidqi, *Al-Sharq wa-al-Islam fi Adab Juta* (Cairo: Dar al-Hilal, 1967); Adnan Rashid, *Taʾthir Alf Layla wa-Layla wa-al-Muʻallaqat.*

166. Mommsen, *Goethe und die arabische Welt,* 171.

CHAPTER 4

1. On agricultural reforms, see Afaf Lutfi Al-Sayyid Marsot, *Egypt in the Reign of Muhammad Ali* (Cambridge: Cambridge University Press, 1984), 137–61.

2. Roger Owen, *The Middle East in the World Economy, 1800–1914* (London: Methuen, 1981), 122; see also 123–26.

3. Trevor Mostyn, *Egypt's Belle Epoque: Cairo, 1869–1952* (London: Quartet Books, 1989), 43.

4. Mostyn, *Egypt's Belle Epoque,* 44.

5. Egypt's loans were generally obtained on "harsher terms" than comparable loans that went, for example, to Turkey. See Owen, *Middle East in the World Economy,* 122.

6. Owen, *Middle East in the World Economy,* 127. On the buildup of the debt, see F. Robert Hunter, *Egypt under the Khedives, 1805–1879* (Pittsburgh: University of Pittsburgh Press, 1984), 38–40. See also Abdel-Maksud Hamza, *The Public Debt of Egypt, 1854–1876* (Cairo: Government Press, 1944).

7. See E. R. J. Owen's conclusion to *Cotton and the Egyptian Economy, 1820–1914: A Study in Trade and Development* (Oxford: Clarendon, 1969), 352–75, in which he reviews the development of the Egyptian economy and attempts to explain the lack of sustained modernization.

8. Amira El-Azhary Sonbol, *The New Mamluks: Egyptian Society and Modern Feudalism* (Syracuse: Syracuse University Press, 2000), 216–17.

9. For a study of early Egyptian feminists, see Susanne Bräckelmann, *"Wir sind die Hälfte der Welt!" Zaynab Fawwaz (1860–1914) und Malak Hifni Nasif (1886–1918), zwei Publizistinnen der frühen ägyptischen Frauenbewegung* (Beirut: Ergon, 2004).

10. Ira M. Lapidus, *A History of Islamic Societies* (Cambridge: Cambridge University Press, 1988), 599–600.

11. Şevket Pamuk, "Money in the Ottoman Empire," in *An Economic and Social History of the Ottoman Empire,* vol. 2, *1600–1914,* ed. Suraiya Faroqhi, Bruce McGowan, Donald Quataert, and Şevket Pamuk (Cambridge: Cambridge University Press, 1994), 970–71.

12. On the role of Prussian officers in reforming the Ottoman army, see Jehuda L. Wallach, *Anatomie einer Militärhilfe. Die preußisch-deutschen Militärmissionen in der Türkei 1835–1919* (Düsseldorf: Droste, 1976); Ulrich Trumpener, "German Officers in the Ottoman Empire, 1880–1918," in *Germany and the Middle East, 1835–1939,* ed. Jehuda L. Wallach (Tel Aviv: Institut für Deutsche Geschichte, Universität Tel-Aviv, 1975), 30–44.

13. Lothar Rathmann, *Berlin-Bagdad: Die imperialistische Nahostpolitik des kaiserlichen Deutschlands* (Berlin: Dietz, 1962), 14.

14. Armin Kössler, *Aktionsfeld Osmanisches Reich: Die Wirtschaftsinteressen des Deutschen Kaiserreiches in der Türkei 1871–1908* (New York: Arno, 1981), 107–25. For a comprehensive discussion, see Fahri Türk, *Die deutsche Rüstungsindustrie in ihren Türkeigeschäften zwischen 1871 und 1914* (Frankfurt am Main: Lang, 2007).

15. Lothar Gall, Gerald D. Feldman, Harold James, Carl-Ludwig Holtfrerich, and Hans E. Büschgen, eds., *The Deutsche Bank, 1870–1995* (London: Weidenfeld and Nicolson, 1995), 73.

16. Rathmann, *Berlin-Bagdad,* 42.

17. Gregor Schöllgen, *Imperialismus und Gleichgewicht: Deutschland, England und die orientalische Frage 1871–1914* (Munich: Oldenbourg, 1984), 80.

18. Andreas Birken, *Die Wirtschaftsbeziehungen zwischen Europa und dem Vorderen Orient im ausgehenden 19. Jahrhundert* (Wiesbaden: Reichert, 1980), 171–231.

19. Kössler, *Aktionsfeld Osmanisches Reich,* 125–48, 195–216, 290–375; Pinhas W. Pick, "German Railway Construction in the Middle East," in *Germany and the Middle East, 1835–1939,* ed. Wallach, 72–85.

20. McMurray, *Distant Ties,* 1, 137.

21. For an overview of Egypt's expansionism, see William L. Cleveland, *A History of the Modern Middle* East, 3rd ed. (Boulder: Westview, 2004), 71–74.

22. On the bombardment of Acre, see Letita W. Ufford, *The Pasha: How Mehemet Ali Defied the West, 1839–1841* (Jefferson, NC: McFarland, 2007), 174–81.

23. On the works of missionaries, development of infrastructure, and scholars and travelers in the area, see contributions in Bernhard A. Böhler, ed., *Mit Szepter und Pilgerstab: Österreichische Präsenz im Heiligen Land seit den Tagen Kaiser Franz Josephs* (Vienna: Österreichischer Wirtschaftsverlag, 2000).

24. Nathan Schur, *Twenty Centuries of Christian Pilgrimage to the Holy Land* (Tel Aviv: Dvir Publishing House, 1992), 192.

25. For a detailed study, see Alex Carmel, *Die Siedlungen der württembergischen Templer in Palästina 1868–1918,* trans. Perez Leshem (Stuttgart: Kohlhammer, 1973).

26. A. Goodrich-Freer, *In a Syrian Saddle* (London: Methuen, 1905), 248–49.

27. Estelle Blyth, *When We Lived in Jerusalem* (London: John Murray, 1927), 120. See also *Des Kaisers Reise in den Orient 1898,* ed. Klaus Jaschinski and Julius Waldschmidt (Berlin: trafo-Verlag Weist, 2002).

28. Fuhrmann, *Der deutsche Traum vom Orient.*

29. Emily Oncken, *Panthersprung nach Agadir: Die deutsche Politik während der Zweiten Marokkokrise 1911* (Düsseldorf: Droste, 1981).

30. Aksakal, *The Ottoman Road to War in 1914.* On Turkish-German collaboration during World War I, see also Isabel V. Hull, *Absolute Destruction: Military Culture and the Practices of War in Imperial Germany* (Ithaca: Cornell University Press, 2005), esp. "The Armenian Genocide," 263–90.

31. Schwanitz, "The German Middle Eastern Policy," 6–7.

32. Lüdke, *Jihad Made in Germany,* 12:1.

33. Hughes, "German Mission to Afghanistan," 24–63.

34. Hughes, "German Mission to Afghanistan," 60.

35. Wolfgang G. Schwanitz, "'The Jinnee and the Magic Bottle': Fritz Grobba and the German Middle Eastern Policy, 1900–1945," *Germany and the Middle East, 1871–1945,* ed. Schwanitz, 86–117.

36. *Ata Taheri: Deutsche Agenten bei iranischen Stämmen 1942–1944. Ein Augenzeugenbericht,* ed. and trans. Burkhard Ganzer (Berlin: Klaus Schwarz-Verlag, 2008).

37. Ralf Georg Reuth, *Rommel: The End of a Legend,* trans. Debra S. Marmor and Herbert A. Danner (London: Haus, 2005), 130.

38. Nicosia, *The Third Reich and the Palestine Question;* Francis R. Nicosia, *Zionism and Anti-Semitism in Nazi Germany* (Cambridge: Cambridge University Press, 2008). The topic has inspired much Arabic-language scholarship on the issue. See, for example, 'Abd al-Rahman 'Abd al-Ghani, *Almaniyya al-Naziyya wa Filastin, 1933–1945* (Beirut: Mu'assasa al-Dirasat al-Filastinyya, 1995).

39. Saul Friedländer, *Nazi Germany and the Jews* (New York: HarperCollins, 1997).

40. Nizam 'Abbasi, *Al-'Alaqat al-Sihyuniyya al-Naziyya wa-Atharuha 'ala Filastin wa-Harakat al-Taharrur al-'Arabi, 1933–1945* (Kuwait: Sharika Kazima, 1984), 7.

41. Contributions collected in *Antun Sa'adeh: The Man, His Thought,* ed. Adel Beshara, highlight various aspects of Sa'ada's ideas (Reading, PA: Ithaca Press, 2007). See also Francis Nicosia, "Arab Nationalism and National Socialist Germany, 1933–1939: Ideological and Strategic Incompatibility," *International Journal of Middle East Studies* 12 (1980): 351–72.

42. Firzoozeh Kashani-Sabet, "Cultures of Iranianness: The Evolving Polemic of Iranian Nationalism," in *Iran and the Surrounding World: Interactions in Culture and Cultural Politics,* ed. Nikki R. Keddie and Rudi Matthee (Seattle: University of Washington Press, 2002), 162–81.

43. Shimon Shamir, "The Influence of German National-Socialism on Radical Movements in Egypt," in *Germany and the Middle East, 1835–1939,* ed. Jehuda L. Wallach, 200–209.

44. On the use of conceptions of time in science, see Johannes Fabian, *Time and the Other: How Anthropology Makes Its Object* (New York: Columbia University Press, 1983).

45. Susan Buck-Morss, "Hegel and Haiti," *Critical Inquiry* 26, no. 4 (2000):

821–65. In *Hegel, Haiti, and Universal History,* Buck-Morss builds on this article and provides further illuminating contextual material and analysis of Hegel's writings (Pittsburgh: University of Pittsburgh Press, 2009).

46. Zantop, *Colonial Fantasies.*

47. Andrew Zimmerman, *Anthropology and Antihumanism in Imperial Germany* (Chicago: University of Chicago Press, 2001); H. Glenn Penny, *Objects of Culture: Ethnology and Ethnographic Museums in Imperial Germany* (Chapel Hill: University of North Carolina Press, 2002); see also contributions in *Worldly Provincialism: German Anthropology in the Age of Empire,* ed. H. Glenn Penny and Matti Bunzl (Ann Arbor: University of Michigan Press, 2003).

48. See, for example, Herzl's memorandum to Count Eulenburg from September 1898, in *Theodor Herzls Tagebücher, 1895–1904,* vol. 2 (Berlin: Jüdischer Verlag, 1923), 125–26.

49. See my discussion in *Orientalismus, Kolonialismus und Moderne,* 264–91.

50. Klaus Polkehn, *Damals im Heiligen Land: Reisen in das alte Palästina* (Berlin: Kai Homlius, 2005).

51. Prince Puckler Muskau, *Egypt, and Mehemet Ali* (London: T. C. Newby, 1845), 8–9. An Arabic translation of excerpts from Pückler-Muskaus's *Semilasso in Afrika* was published in 1989.

52. Annette Deeken and Monika Bösel, "Vers l'Orient: Reisejournale von Frauen des 19. Jahrhunderts," in *"Und tät das Reisen wählen!" Frauenreisen—Reisefrauen,* ed. Doris Jedamski, Hiltgund Jehle, and Ulla Siebert (Zurich: eFeF, 1994), 59–77.

53. Bodenstedt also published "Die Völker des Kauskasus und ihre Freiheitskämpfe gegen die Russen" (1848). It would be worthwhile to compare his image of Russia to that of the Orient.

54. Friedrich Bodenstedt, *Tausend und Ein Tag im Orient,* 5th ed. (Berlin: R.v. Decker, 1891), 155.

55. In 1851 Bodenstedt published the collection *Die Lieder des Mirza-Schaffy* (The Songs of Mirza Schaffy); to this day scholars are undecided on the question of the poetry's authorship—that is, whether Bodenstedt composed it himself, following Persian models, or whether the poems are in fact translations. The collection of poems was extremely successful; in fact, one could probably attribute the dissemination of Persian poetry and images of the Orient in the second half of the nineteenth century to Bodenstedt's writings more than to Goethe's. *Die Lieder des Mirza Schaffy* saw 142 printings by the time Bodenstedt died in 1892 and has been translated into countless languages. William H. McClain, "Friedrich von Bodenstedt," *Nineteenth-Century German Writers, 1841–1900. Dictionary of Literary Biography,* ed. James Hardin and Siegfried Mews (Detroit: Gale Research, 1993), 129:20.

56. Hanspeter Mattes, "L'Image du Maroc à travers la tradition littéraire allemande du récit de voyage pendant les années 1914–1945," in *Le Maroc et l'Allemagne: Actes de la première rencontre universitaire* (Rabat: Publications de la Faculté des Lettres et des Sciences Humaines, 1991), 16.

57. Jens Willhardt, *Kulturbegegnung mit dem Orient: Eine Untersuchung historischer Reiseberichte sowie der Berichte von Touristen und Auslandsentsandten am Beispiel des Jemen* (Berlin: Klaus Schwarz, 2004).

58. Carl R. Raswan, *Im Land der schwarzen Zelte: Mein Leben unter den Beduinen* (Berlin: Ullstein, 1934), 9.

59. See, for example, F. Robert Hunter, "Tourism and Empire: The Thomas Cook & Son Enterprise on the Nile, 1868–1914," *Middle Eastern Studies* 40, no. 5 (2004): 28–54.

60. Hans Weth, *Die Orient-Reise der 'Augusta Victoria' vom Januar bis März 1891* (Hamburg: Gustav Diedrich, 1891).

61. For excerpts from a variety of accounts, see Ulrich Erker-Sonnabend, *Orientalische Fremde: Berichte deutscher Türkeireisender des späten 19. Jahrhunderts* (Bochum: Brockmeyer, 1987).

62. Isma'il Al-'Arabi, *Tarikh al-Rihla wa al-Istikshaf fi al-Barr wa al-Bahr* (Algiers: Al-Mu'assasa al-Wataniyya li-al-Kitab, 1986), 291, 302–3, 315–17.

63. Abu al-'Id Dudu, *Al-Jaza'ir fi Mu'allafat al-Rahhalin al-Alman, 1830–1855* (Algiers: Al-Mu'assasa al-Wataniyya li-al-Kitab, 1989 [1975]), 8.

64. For a list of scholars trained by de Sacy, see Irwin, *For Lust of Knowing,* 153.

65. For an overview of the development of Oriental sciences in Austria, see Sutter Fichtner, *Terror and Toleration,* 117–61.

66. See contributions to the anthology *Ulrich Jasper Seetzen (1767–1811): Leben und Werk. Die arabischen Länder und die Nahostforschung im napoleonischen Zeitalter,* ed. Hans Stein (Gotha: Forschungs- und Landesbibliothek, 1995).

67. See Mangold, "Die Deutsche Morgenländische Gesellschaft" in *Eine "weltbürgerliche Wissenschaft,"* 176–225. See also Preissler, "Die Anfänge der Deutschen Morgenländischen Gesellschaft," 241–327.

68. Hess, *Germans, Jews, and the Claims of Modernity,* 50–89.

69. Heschel, *Abraham Geiger and the Jewish Jesus.*

70. Said, *Orientalism,* 27.

71. Hess, *Germans, Jews, and the Claims of Modernity,* 89. See also *"Im vollen Licht der Geschichte,"* ed. Hartwig et al.

72. Dr. Pruner, "Der Neger. Eine aphoristische Skizze aus der 'Medizinischen Topographie von Cairo,'" *Zeitschrift der Deutschen Morgenländischen Gesellschaft* (Leipzig: Brockhaus, 1847), 1:129–36.

73. Dr. E. Selberg, "Ueber die Anlage eines Colonialhandel-Etablissements im ostindischen Archipel," *Zeitschrift der Deutschen Morgenländischen Gesellschaft* (Leipzig: Brockhaus, 1847), 1:138.

74. Mangold, *Eine "weltbürgerliche Wissenschaft,"* 217–25. For a study of the British organization, see John James Moscrop, *Measuring Jerusalem: The Palestine Exploration Fund and British Interests in the Holy Land* (London: Leicester University Press, 2000).

75. Mangold, *Eine "weltbürgerliche Wissenschaft,"* 229–36.

76. Alexander Haridi has delivered an excellent study of Becker's work and approach with *Das Paradigma der "islamischen Zivilisation."*

77. See also Marchand's detailed discussion of Becker and Hartmann in *German Orientalism in the Age of Empire,* 348–67.

78. See Marchand, *German Orientalism in the Age of Empire,* 438–54.

79. Hagen, "German Heralds of Holy War," 150.

80. Hagen, "German Heralds of Holy War," 152.

81. On the debate of the Armenian question in Germany, see Anderson, "'Down in Turkey, Far Away.'"

82. Marchand, *German Orientalism in the Age of Empire,* 462.

83. See contributions in *Ernst Herzfeld and the Development of Near Eastern Studies, 1900–1950,* ed. Ann C. Gunter and Stefan R. Hauser (Leiden: Brill, 2005); Kamyar Abdi, "Nationalism, Politics, and the Development of Archaeology in Iran," *American Journal of Archaeology* 105, no. 1 (2001): 51–76.

84. Ludmila Hanisch, "Akzentverschiebung: Zur Geschichte der Semitistik und Islamwissenschaft während des 'Dritten Reiches,'" *Berichte zur Wissenschafts-geschichte* 18 (1995): 218.

85. Konuk, *East West Mimesis.*

86. Irwin, *For Lust of Knowing,* 235.

87. See also Ellinger, *Deutsche Orientalistik zur Zeit des Nationalsozialismus;* Marchand, *German Orientalism in the Age of Empire,* 487–95.

88. Irwin, *For Lust of Knowing,* 151.

89. Annemarie Schimmel, *Friedrich Rückert: Lebensbild und Einführung in sein Werk* (Freiburg: Herder, 1987), 30.

90. Platen's claim to be the first German poet of the *ghazel* led to a dispute with Rückert. Mahmoud Alali-Huseinat, *Rückert und der Orient: Untersuchungen zu Friedrich Rückerts Beschäftigung mit arabischer und persischer Literatur* (Frankfurt am Main: Lang, 1993), 177–79. See also Muhammad Zouheir Sharaf, *August von Platen und die arabische Welt: Grundzüge und Kontext seiner Rezeption arabischer Literatur* (Berlin: dissertation.de, 2003).

91. 'Awni 'Abd al-Ra'uf, *Friedrich Rückert: 'Ashiq al-Adab al-'Arabi* (Cairo: Dar al-'Arab li-al-Bustani, 1974), 7.

92. See Ali Dashti, *In Search of Omar Khayyam,* trans. L. P. Elwell-Sutton (New York: Columbia University Press, 1971).

93. *Das Ausland. Ueberschau der neuesten Forschungen auf dem Gebiete der Natur-, Erd-, und Völkerkunde,* ed. Friedrich von Hellwald (Stuttgart: Cotta, 1878), 51:1–5, 81–85, 534–35.

94. *Deutsche Rundschau für Geographie und Statistik* (Vienna: A. Hartleben's, 1879), 1:32–33, 239, 256, 477, 529.

95. Susan Heuck Allen, *Finding the Walls of Troy: Frank Calvert and Heinrich Schliemann at Hisarlık* (Berkeley: University of California Press, 1999).

96. See Gerbert Frodt, "Wiener Orientmalerei im 19. Jahrhundert," *alte und moderne kunst* 26, no. 178–79 (1981): 19–25.

97. See Irina Rockel, ed., *Wilhelm Gentz: Briefe einer Reise nach Ägypten und Nubien 1850–1851* (Berlin: trafo, 2004).

98. Hugo Schmid, *Der Maler Gustav Bauernfeind (1848–1904) und der Orient* (Stuttgart: Hauswedell, 2004).

99. Ernst-Gerhard Güse, *Die Tunisreise: Klee, Macke, Moilliet* (Stuttgart: Hatje, 1982).

100. Harold Hammer-Schenk, *Synagogen in Deutschland: Geschichte einer Baugattung im 19. und 20. Jahrhundert (1780–1933),* 2 vols. (Hamburg: Hans Christians, 1981); Pierre Genée, *Synagogen in Österreich* (Vienna: Löcker, 1992).

101. Rosalind H. Williams, *Dream Worlds: Mass Consumption in Late Nineteenth-Century France* (Berkeley: University of California Press, 1982).

102. Thomas Schmitt, *Moscheen in Deutschland: Konflikte um ihre Errichtung und Nutzung* (Flensburg: Deutsche Akademie für Landeskunde, Selbstverlag, 2003), 49.

103. Schmitt, *Moscheen in Deutschland,* 49–50.

104. Zeynep Çelik, *The Remaking of Istanbul: Portrait of an Ottoman City in the Nineteenth Century* (Seattle: University of Washington Press, 1986); see also Mark Crinson's chapters on British architecture in Istanbul and Egypt and on evangelical architecture in Jerusalem in *Empire Building: Orientalism and Victorian Architecture* (London: Routledge, 1996), 124–66, 167–97, 198–226.

105. Derek B. Scott, "Orientalism and Musical Style," *Critical Musicology Journal: A Virtual Journal on the Internet,* http://www.leeds.ac.uk/music/Info/CMJ/Articles/1997/02/01.html.

106. Scott, "Orientalism and Musical Style."

107. Antonia Lant, "The Curse of the Pharaoh, or How Cinema Contracted Egyptomania," *October* 59 (Winter 1992): 90.

108. Lant, "Curse of the Pharaoh," 89.

109. Lant, "Curse of the Pharaoh," 89.

110. Nick Browne, "Orientalism as an Ideological Form: American Film Theory in the Silent Period," *wide angle* 11, no. 4: 23–31. On Orientalism in U.S. film, see also Jack G. Shaheen's comprehensive study *Reel Bad Arabs: How Hollywood Vilifies a People* (New York: Olive Branch Press, 2001).

111. Lant, "Curse of the Pharaoh," 98.

112. See, for example, the following dialogue: "Mustapha: 'Ein Europäer seyd Ihr geworden.'—Achmet: 'Immerhin.'—Mustapha: 'Ein Franke.'—Achmet: 'Sey es! Ich erschrecke nicht davor.'" August Wilhelm Iffland, *Achmet und Zenide* (Leipzig: Georg Joachim Göschen, 1799), 13.

113. Ingeborg H. Solbrig, "Die Orientalische Muse Meletes: Zu den Mohammed-Dichtungen Karoline von Günderrodes," *Jahrbuch der Deutschen Schillergesellschaft* 33 (1989): 301 n. 14.

114. Karoline von Günderrode, "Geschichte eines Braminen," in *Karoline von Günderrode. Sämtliche Werke und ausgewählte Studien,* ed. Walter Morgenthaler (Frankfurt am Main: Stroemfeld, 2006), 1:306.

115. Solbrig, "Die orientalische Muse Meletes," 310.

116. Karoline von Günderrode, *Sämtliche Werke und ausgewählte Studien,* 1:311–12.

117. Novalis, *Heinrich von Ofterdingen,* in *Novalis Werke,* ed. Gerhard Schulz (Munich: Beck, 1981), 174.

118. Kontje, *German Orientalisms,* 87.

119. Anne Bohnenkamp provides an excellent overview of the creation, reception, and composition of the *Divan* in "West-östlicher Divan," *Goethe-Handbuch* (1996): 1:306–23.

120. Anil Bhatti, "Iqbal and Goethe: A Note," *Goethezeitportal,* http://ourbeacon.com/wp-content/uploads/admin2/2007/08/iqbal-and-goethe-by-abhatti.pdf, p. 9. First published in *Yearbook of the Goethe Society of India* (1999–2000): 184–201.

121. Bernd Auerochs states: "Indem er Glaubensartikel in Poesie verwandelt und

behutsam die absolute Autorität heiliger Texts dementiert, nimmt er den Offenbarungsreligionen ihren ausschließenden Charakter." "Goethe als Muslim: Zum Spiel mit den positiven Offenbarungsreligionen im *West-oestlichen Divan*," in *Goethe und die Weltkultur*, ed. Klaus Manger (Heidelberg: Winter, 2003), 288.

122. Regarding the performance of acculturation, see Polaschegg, "*Der Orient bin ich:* Goethe's Poetologie des Ostens," *Der andere Orientalismus*, 293–397.

123. See Shafiq M. Shamel, "Goethe and Hafiz: Poetry and History in the *West-oestlicher Divan*" (PhD diss., Stanford University, 2007).

124. In addition to titles mentioned before, see, for example, 'Abd al-Ghaffar Makkawi's *Al-Nur wa-al-Farashah: Zahrat min Bustan al-Diwan al-Sharqi li-Juta ma'a Ru'yatihi li-al-Adab al-'Arabi wa-Adab al-Fars* (Cairo: Dar al-Ma'arif, 1979), which relies heavily on Katharina Mommsen's studies. A biography of Goethe was composed by 'Abbas Mahmud 'Aqqad, *Tidhkar Jiti* (Cairo: Matba'at al-Ma'ahid, 1932); 'Abd al-Rahman Badawi translated the *Divan* into Arabic as *Al-Diwan al-Sharqi li-al-Mu'allif al-Gharbi* (Beirut: Al-Mu'assasa al-'Arabiyya li-al-Dirasat wa-al-Nashr, 1980 [Cairo 1944]). 'Adnan 'Abbas 'Ali translated Katharina Mommsen's *Goethe und die arabische Welt* as *Juta wa-al-'Alam al-'Arabi* (Kuwait: Majlis al-Watani li-al-Thaqafa wa-al-Funun wa-al-Adab, 1995).

125. See Anil Bhatti, "Iqbal and Goethe." Iqbal's *Payam-i mashriq* (1923) is the most widely received engagement with Goethe's *Divan* in the Persian language. The *Divan* was translated into Persian by, among others, Shojaeddin Shafa, *Divan-i Sharqi: Qata 'at-i Muntakhaba* (N.p.: Kitabkhana-i Suqrat, 1949) and by Kurus Safawi, *Divan-i Gharbi-Sharqi* (Tehran: Intisarat-i Hirmis, 2000).

126. Annette Freiin von Droste-Hülshoff, *Klänge aus dem Orient*, in *Das Geistliche Jahr und religiöse Dichtungen. Gesammelte Werke* (Vaduz: Liechtenstein, n.d.), 1:340–56.

127. Maria Tatar, *The Hard Facts of the Grimms' Fairy Tales* (Princeton: Princeton University Press, 1987); Jack David Zipes, *The Brothers Grimm: From Enchanted Forests to the Modern World* (New York: Routledge, 1988); George S. Williamson, *The Longing for Myth in Germany: Religion and Aesthetic Culture from Romanticism to Nietzsche* (Chicago: University of Chicago Press, 2004).

128. Anke Bosse, "Orientalismus im Frühwerk Ludwig Tiecks," in *Ludwig Tieck: Literaturprogramm und Lebensinszenierung im Kontext seiner Zeit*, ed. Walter Schmitz (Tübingen: Max Niemeyer, 1997), 46.

129. William Thomas Beckford's novel *Vathek* was originally written in French in 1782 (published in 1787) and published in 1786 in an English translation by Reverend Samuel Henley. The tale was also titled *Vathek, an Arabian Tale* or *The History of the Caliph.* The English translation of 1786 appeared without Beckford's name as *An Arabian Tale* and claimed to be translated directly from the Arabic. Beckford successfully merged Oriental themes with elements of the gothic novel, such as those found in Horace Walpole's *The Castle of Otranto* (1764).

130. With regard to the use of Oriental metaphors, see Alev Tekinay, "Der morgenländische Bestandteil im 'Wunderbaren Märchen von einem nackten Heiligen' Wackenroders," *Archiv für das Studium der neueren Sprachen und Literaturen* 218 (1981): 323–30. Birgit Tautz argues the tale's use of Oriental metaphors allows the author to "link . . . tradition and innovation" and to articulate a Romanticist vision of autopoiesis. See "Wack-

enroder's 'Ein wunderbares morgenländisches Mährchen von einem nackten Heiligen: 'Autopoiesis of World, Rhetoric of 'the Orient,'" *Monatshefte* 95, no. 1 (2003): 59.

131. Wilhelm Heinrich Wackenroder, "Ein wunderbares morgenländisches Mährchen von einem nackten Heiligen," *Sämtliche Werke und Briefe,* vol. 1, ed. Silvio Vietta and Richard Littlejohns (Heidelberg: Winter, 1991), 201.

132. See my discussion of Hofmannsthal's tale in *Orientalismus, Kolonialismus, und Moderne,* 165–259; for a list of other works by Hofmannsthal that engage the Orient, see my overview in *Orientalismus, Kolonialismus und Moderne,* 168.

133. See Mechthild Rausch, "Eine seltsame Scheherezade," afterword to Paul Scheerbart, *Der Tod der Barmekiden: Arabischer Haremsroman* (Munich: edition text + kritik, 1992), 217–36; Michael Matthias Schardt, "Berlin-Roman im orientalischen Gewand," afterword to Paul Scheerbart, *Tarub, Bagdads berühmte Köchin: Arabischer Kulturroman* (Paderborn: Igel, 1992), 298–324.

134. Regarding Mann's extensive research on ancient Egypt from the perspective of an Egyptologist, see Alfred Grimm, *Joseph und Echnaton: Thomas Mann und Ägypten* (Mainz: Philipp von Zabern, 1992). Also from the perspective of an Egyptologist, see Jan Assmann, *Thomas Mann und Ägypten: Mythos und Monotheismus in den Josephsromanen* (Munich: Beck, 2006).

135. Polaschegg, *Der andere Orientalismus,* 415.

136. Polaschegg, *Der andere Orientalismus,* 442.

137. Polaschegg, *Der andere Orientalismus,* 448–49.

138. Said, *Orientalism,* 7.

139. Karoline von Günderrode, "Mahomets Traum in der Wüste," in *Karoline von Günderrode. Sämtliche Werke,* 1:75.

140. As Solbrig has shown, Günderrode was familiar with some of the same sources as Goethe but uses the material quite differently. "Die orientalische Muse Meletes," 311–20.

141. Achim von Arnim, "Isabella von Ägypten, Kaiser Karls des Fünften erste Jugendliebe," *Achim von Arnim Werke in sechs Bänden,* vol. 3: *Sämtliche Erzählungen 1802–1817,* ed. Renate Moering (Frankfurt am Main: Deutscher Klassiker Verlag, 1990), 740.

142. Wilhelm Solms, "On the Demonising of Jews and Gypsies in Fairy Tales," in *Sinti and Roma: Gypsies in German-Speaking Society and Literature,* ed. Susan Tebbutt (New York: Berghahn, 1998), 97.

143. Wilhelm Hauff, "Abner, der Jude, der nichts gesehen hat," in *Wilhelm Hauff Werke,* ed. Bernhard Zeller (Frankfurt am Main: Insel, 1969), 2:142–43.

144. Wilhelm Hauff, "Jud Süß," in *Wilhelm Hauff Werke,* ed. Bernhard Zeller (Frankfurt am Main: Insel, 1969), 1:506. The story of Joseph Süß Oppenheimer was picked up later by, among others, Lion Feuchtwanger (1917, 1925) and Veit Harlan whose violently antisemitic film appeared in 1940.

145. See Florian Krobb, *Die schöne Jüdin: Jüdische Frauengestalten in der deutschsprachigen Erzählliteratur vom 17. Jahrhundert bis zum Ersten Weltkrieg* (Tübingen: Niemeyer, 1993).

146. In the German the term reads "orientalisches Fremdlingsvolk." C. W. F. Grattenauer, *Erklärung an das Publikum über meine Schrift 'Wider die Juden'* (Berlin: Johann Wilhelm Schmidt, 1803), 36.

147. Quoted in Mommsen, *Goethe und die arabische Welt,* 233.

148. Johann Wolfgang von Goethe, *West-östlicher Divan, Hamburger Ausgabe in 14 Bänden,* vol. 2: *Gedichte und Epen II,* ed. Erich Trunz (Munich: Beck, 1998), 258.

149. Zafer Şenocak, "Literarische Übersetzung: Brücke oder Schwert?" *War Hitler Araber? IrreFührungen an den Rand Europas* (Berlin: Babel Verlag Hund und van Uffelen, 1994), 49.

150. Kontje, *German Orientalisms,* 132.

151. See "The Making of a Cultural Obsession," in Marchand, *Down from Olympus,* 3–35.

152. Marchand, *Down from Olympus,* 32.

153. Marchand, *Down from Olympus,* 33.

154. Polaschegg, *Der andere Orientalismus,* 253.

155. Polaschegg, *Der andere Orientalismus,* 248.

156. Müller's son is the famous linguist and Indologist Friedrich Max Müller (1823–1900).

157. See, for example, *Chants helléniens,* trans. in 1828 by Hippolyte Carnot.

158. Müller, "Der Mainottin Unterricht," *Werke, Tagebücher, Briefe,* vol. 1: *Gedichte I,* ed. Maria-Verena Leistner (Berlin: Gatza, 1994), 241.

159. Müller, "Byron," *Werke, Tagebücher, Briefe,* 1:228–32.

160. Müller, "Die Veste des Himmels," *Werke, Tagebücher, Briefe,* 1:272–73. The Ottoman army was indeed reinforced by troops from Africa, namely, from Egypt, which in Müller's poem appear as "hordes of Negroes." Polaschegg, *Der andere Orientalismus,* 257.

161. Annette von Droste-Hülshoff, *Die Judenbuche* (Stuttgart: Reclam, 1975), 54.

162. Holub, "Narrator of Realism," 168.

163. Holub, "Narrator of Realism," 169.

164. See my discussion of May in *Orientalismus, Kolonialismus und Moderne,* 41–164.

165. Tom Cheesman, "Das Türkenbild als Eigenbild im Bänkelsang des 19. Jahrhunderts," *Gender-Culture-Poetics: Zur Geschlechterforschung in der Literatur- und Kulturwissenschaft,* ed. Andrea Gutenberg and Ralf Schneider (Trier: Wissenschaftlicher Verlag, 1999), 151–71.

166. See Yahya Elsaghe, *Die imaginäre Nation: Thomas Mann und das "Deutsche"* (Munich: Fink, 2000).

167. Thomas Mann, *Wälsungenblut,* in Thomas Mann, *Frühe Erzählungen 1893–1912, Große kommentierte Frankfurter Ausgabe vol. 2.1,* ed. Terence J. Reed and Malte Herwig (Frankfurt am Main: Fischer, 2004), 429.

168. Yahya Elsaghe has identified the implicit characterization through physical features as a significant feature of Thomas Mann's portrayal of Jewish figures. "Juden und Jüdinnen," in *Thomas Mann und die kleinen Unterschiede: Zur erzählerischen Imagination des Anderen* (Cologne: Böhlau, 2004), 141–258.

169. Heizer, *Jewish-German Identity,* 71.

170. See, for example, the following quote describing a scene in which a French military officer expresses his desire to visit the site "wo der Splitter einer christlichen Nation sich vierzig Tage lang gegen barbarische Übermacht behauptet hatte." Franz Werfel, *Die vierzig Tage des Musa Dagh* (Frankfurt am Main: Fischer, 2000), 942.

171. Heizer, *Jewish-German Identity,* 80–81.

172. Ludwig Tieck, *Alla-Moddin,* in *Ludwig Tieck's Schriften* (Berlin: Reimer, 1829), 11:367–68.

173. See Geoffrey Winthrop-Young's discussion of Günderrode's play in "Mahomed, der Prophet von Mekka (1805)" in *Lexikon deutschsprachiger Epik und Dramatik von Autorinnen (1730–1900),* ed. Gudrun Loster-Schneider and Gaby Pailer (Tübingen: Francke, 2006), 185–86.

174. Ferdinand Freiligrath, *Sämmtliche Werke* (New York: Friedrich Gerhard, 1858), 1:39–41, 146–48, 226–30, 239–41.

175. Necdet Sakaoğlu and Nuri Akbayar, *A Milestone on Turkey's Path of Westernization: Sultan Abdülmecid* (Istanbul: DenizBank, 2002), 274.

176. Bettina Arnim, *Gespräche mit Dämonen: Des Königsbuches zweiter Band,* 2nd ed. (Berlin: von Arnim, 1853), 368.

177. See Mounir Fendri's chapters "Heine und die Dichtung des islamischen Orients" and "Heine, Muhammad und der Koran," *Halbmond, Kreuz und Schibboleth,* 95–188, 189–241.

178. See, for example, Ritchie Robertson, "Heines orientalische Masken," in *Internationaler Germanisten-Kongreß in Tokyo,* ed. Yoshinori Shichiji (Munich: iudicium, 1991), 10:126–32.

179. Heinrich Heine, *Almansor: Eine Tragödie, Heinrich Heine Säkularausgabe,* vol. 4: *Tragödien, Frühe Prosa, 1820–1831,* ed. Karl Wolfgang Becker (Berlin: Akademie, 1981), 15.

180. See "*Almansor* im Lichte seiner Quellen," in Fendri, *Halbmond, Kreuz und Schibboleth,* 42–60.

181. Fendri, "Heine und die Orientalische Frage," *Halbmond, Kreuz und Schibboleth,* 244–57.

182. Fendri, "Heine und die Orientalische Frage," 282.

183. For a comprehensive study, see Jonathan Frankel, *The Damascus Affair: "Ritual Murder," Politics, and the Jews in 1840* (Cambridge: Cambridge University Press, 1997), which includes several references to Heine.

184. Fendri, "Heine und die Orientalische Frage," *Halbmond, Kreuz und Schibboleth,* 299–306.

185. See Else Lasker-Schüler, *Der Prinz von Theben,* in *Gesammelte Werke II: Prosa und Schauspiele,* ed. Friedhelm Kemp (Munich: Kösel, 1962), 133. See my discussion of Lasker-Schüler in *Orientalismus, Kolonialismus und Moderne,* 260–345.

186. Heizer, *Jewish-German Identity,* 53.

187. Heizer, *Jewish-German Identity,* 56.

188. See Ingeborg H. Solbrig, "Literarischer Orientalismus im Expressionismus: Der *Mohammed*-Roman Klabunds," in *Im Dialog mit der Moderne: Zur deutschsprachigen Literatur von der Gründerzeit bis zur Gegenwart,* ed. Roland Jost and Hansgeorg Schmidt-Bergmann (Frankfurt am Main: Athenäum, 1986), 246–60.

189. See Paul Levesque, "Mapping the Other: Lion Feuchtwanger's Topographies of the Orient," *German Quarterly* 71, no. 2 (Spring 1998): 145–65; also Shaswati Mazumdar, *Feuchtwanger/Brecht: Der Umgang mit der indischen Kolonialgeschichte: Eine Studie zur Konstruktion des Anderen* (Würzburg: Königshausen und Neumann, 1998).

CHAPTER 5

1. On the history of the reparations treaty and payments, see Lily Gardner Feldman, *The Special Relationship between West Germany and Israel* (Boston: Allen and Unwin, 1984), 49–121.

2. Austria's culpability in Nazi crimes and its approach to reparation remains the topic of intense discussions. See Brigitte Bailer, *Wiedergutmachung kein Thema: Österreich und die Opfer des Nationalsozialismus* (Vienna: Löcker, 1993). With regard to Switzerland's problematic relationship to the Nazis, see Philippe Braillard, *Switzerland and the Crisis of Dormant Assets and Nazi Gold,* trans. from the French by Denys Crapon de Caprona and André Lötter (London: Kegan Paul International, 2000).

3. Werner Kilian, *Die Hallstein-Doktrin: Der diplomatische Krieg zwischen der BRD und der DDR 1955–1973: Aus den Akten der beiden deutschen Außenministerien* (Berlin: Duncker und Humblot, 2001), 18–19.

4. See Rüdiger Marco Booz, *"Hallsteinzeit": Deutsche Außenpolitik 1955–1972* (Bonn: Bouvier, 1995), 35–37, 78–87.

5. William Glenn Gray's *Germany's Cold War: The Global Campaign to Isolate East Germany, 1949–1969* (Chapel Hill: University of North Carolina Press, 2003) provides a detailed analysis of West Germany's far-reaching attempts to prevent recognition of East Germany. Alexander Troche's *Ulbricht und die Dritte Welt. Ost-Berlins "Kampf" gegen die Bonner "Alleinvertretungsanmaßung"* (Erlangen: Palm und Enke, 1996) explores the issue from the East German perspective.

6. Hannfried von Hindenburg, *Demonstrating Reconciliation: State and Society in West German Foreign Policy toward Israel, 1952–1965* (New York: Berghahn, 2007), 2.

7. Hindenburg, *Demonstrating Reconciliation,* 3.

8. Hafez, *Orientwissenschaft in der DDR,* 23.

9. Booz, "*Hallsteinzeit,*" 80–87.

10. For official announcements regarding political events in the Middle East, see documents published in *Die DDR und die arabischen Staaten: Dokumente 1956–1982,* ed. Wolfgang Bator and Angelika Bator (Berlin: Staatsverlag der Deutschen Demokratischen Republik, 1984).

11. Martin Jander, "Vereint gegen Israel? Die DDR und der westdeutsche Linksterrorismus," *Deutschland Archiv* 41, no. 3 (2008): 416–22.

12. Gabriel Gorodetsky, "The Soviet Union's Role in the Creation of the State of Israel," *Journal of Israeli History* 22, no. 1 (2003): 4–20; Yaacov Ro'i, "The Deterioration of Relations: From Support to Severance," *Journal of Israeli History* 22, no. 1 (2003): 21–36.

13. Angelika Timm, "Ideology and *Realpolitik:* East German Attitudes towards Zionism and Israel," *Journal of Israeli History* 25, no. 1 (Mar. 2006): 205. Regarding the differing relationships of East and West Germany toward the Shoah, see Jeffrey Herf, *Divided Memory: The Nazi Past in the Two Germanys* (Cambridge: Harvard University Press, 1997).

14. Timm, "Ideology and *Realpolitik,*" 213.

15. On the relationship between Brandt's *Ostpolitik* and his government's policy toward Israel, see Fink, "*Ostpolitik* and West German-Israeli Relations." See also Markus

A. Weingardt, *Deutsche Israel- und Nahostpolitik: Die Geschichte einer Gratwanderung seit 1949* (Frankfurt am Main: Campus, 2002), 180–240.

16. Weingardt, *Deutsche Israel- und Nahostpolitik,* 241–375; Timm, "Ideology and Realpolitik," 203–22.

17. Neither Austria nor Switzerland ranked among the top ten trading partners of, for example, Turkey. Selin Sayek and David D. Selover, "International Interdependence and Business Cycle Transmission between Turkey and the European Union," *Southern Economic Journal* 69, no. 2 (Oct. 2002): 213.

18. Sven Olaf Berggötz, *Nahostpolitik in der Ära Adenauer: Möglichkeiten und Grenzen, 1949–1963* (Düsseldorf: Droste, 1998), 134.

19. Berggötz, *Nahostpolitik in der Ära Adenauer,* 134.

20. Berggötz, *Nahostpolitik in der Ära Adenauer,* 54.

21. Sayek and Selover, "International Interdependence and Business Cycle Transmission," 213, 223.

22. Berggötz, *Nahostpolitik in der Ära Adenauer,* 135.

23. *Statistisches Jahrbuch für die Bundesrepublik Deutschland* (1979/1980): 647–50.

24. Hans-Joachim Spanger and Lothar Brock, *Die beiden deutschen Staaten in der Dritten Welt: Die Entwicklungspolitik der DDR—eine Herausforderung für die Bundesrepublik Deutschland?* (Opladen: Westdeutscher Verlag, 1987), 254.

25. Alexandre Afonso, "Immigration and Its Impacts in Switzerland," *Mediterranean Quarterly* 15, no. 4 (Fall 2004): 147, 159.

26. Sabine Kroissenbrunner, "Islam and Muslim Immigrants in Austria: Socio-Political Networks and Muslim Leadership of Turkish Immigrants," *Immigrants and Minorities* 22, no. 2–3 (July 2003): 188–207.

27. Karin Hunn, *"Nächstes Jahr kehren wir zurück . . .": Die Geschichte der türkischen "Gastarbeiter" in der Bundesrepublik* (Göttingen: Wallstein, 2005).

28. Hunn, *"Nächstes Jahr kehren wir zurück . . . ,"* 29–33. Turkey was consistently listed as part of Europe in West German government statistics.

29. Hunn, *"Nächstes Jahr kehren wir zurück . . . ,"* 32, 52, 65.

30. Hunn, *"Nächstes Jahr kehren wir zurück . . . ,"* 57.

31. Hunn, *"Nächstes Jahr kehren wir zurück . . . ,"* 71–99.

32. See references in Hunn, *"Nächstes Jahr kehren wir zurück . . . ,"* 71 n. 2.

33. Hunn, *"Nächstes Jahr kehren wir zurück . . . ,"* 72.

34. Hunn, *"Nächstes Jahr kehren wir zurück . . . ,"* 68.

35. To name only a few of the large corpus of analyses on the subject, see articles in the special issue on "Immigration and the Emergence of Right-Wing Violence in Unified Germany," ed. Daniel Maier-Katkin, Susanne Stemmler, and Paulin Stretesky, *Crime, Law, and Social Change* 24, no. 1 (Mar. 1995): 1–75; and Klaus J. Bade and Lieselotte Anderson, "Immigration and Social Peace in United Germany," *Daedalus* 123, no. 1 (Winter 1994): 85–106.

36. Serdar Sayan, "Guest Workers' Remittances and Output Fluctuations in Host and Home Countries: The Case of Remittances from Turkish Workers in Germany," *Emerging Markets Finance and Trade* 40, no. 6 (Nov.–Dec. 2004): 69.

37. Sayan, "Guest Workers' Remittances," 73.

38. Prodosh Aich, *Farbige unter Weissen* (Cologne: Kiepenheuer und Witsch, 1962), 17. By 2005 the percentage of foreign students in Germany had reached 11.5 percent. *Internationalisierung des Studiums: Ausländische Studierende in Deutschland, Deutsche Studierende im Ausland. Ergebnisse der 18. Sozialerhebung des Deutschen Studentenwerks durchgeführt durch HIS Hochschul-Informations-System,* ed. Wolfgang Isserstedt and Judith Link (Bonn: Bundesministerium für Bildung und Forschung, 2008), 3.

39. The author defines "farbige Studenten . . . [als] diejenigen . . . , die auf Grund ihrer Hautfarbe und/oder ihres Aussehens sofort als Nicht-Europäer zu erkennen sind." Aich, *Farbige unter Weissen,* 17.

40. Khairallah Ahmad Assar, *Arabische Studenten an einer deutschen Universität: Eine Untersuchung an der Universität Heidelberg* (PhD diss., Heidelberg University, 1964), 1, 231. Regarding the socioeconomic status of the students, see 19–21.

41. See Assar, *Arabische Studenten,* 25–31. Regarding social status and motives of international students in the 1960s, see also Hans Eich and Hans Frevert, *Bürger auf Zeit: Junge Ausländer unter uns* (Baden-Baden: Signal-Verlag Hans Frevert, 1967); Björn Pätzoldt, *Ausländerstudium in der BRD: Ein Beitrag zur Imperialismuskritik* (Cologne: Pahl-Rugenstein, 1972).

42. See, for example, case studies in Eich and Frevert, *Bürger auf Zeit.*

43. Figures according to Statistisches Bundesamt, IB Bildung, Forschung und Entwicklung, Kultur, Rechtspflege, comp. Apr. 2009.

44. *Statistisches Jahrbuch der Deutschen Demokratischen Republik* (1981–82): 297.

45. Spanger and Brock, *Die beiden deutschen Staaten in der Dritten Welt,* 237.

46. Roselyne Crausaz, "Higher Education in Switzerland," *European Journal of Education* 14, no. 1 (Mar. 1979): 40.

47. Figures provided by Département Fédéral de l'Intérieur (DFI), Office Fédéral de la Statistique (OFS), Section Processus de Formation, Neuchâtel, Switzerland, Apr. 8, 2009.

48. Klaus J. Bade, *Ausländer, Aussiedler, Asyl: Eine Bestandsaufnahmen* (Munich: Beck, 1994), 92.

49. *Statistisches Jahrbuch für die Bundesrepublik Deutschland* (1989/1990): 59.

50. Figures provided by Bundesamt für Migration und Flüchtlinge, Apr. 27, 2009.

51. Orhan Pamuk, *Snow* (New York: Knopf, 2004), 59.

52. Rita Polm, "Iraner/Iranierinnen," in *Kleines Lexikon der ethnischen Minderheiten in Deutschland,* ed. Cornelia Schmalz-Jacobsen and Georg Hansen (Munich: Beck, 1997), 73.

53. See, for example, Farideh Jeddi, *Politische und kulturelle Auswirkungen des Auslandsstudiums auf die iranische Gesellschaft im 19. Jahrhundert, unter Berücksichtigung der iranischen Stipendiaten in Westeuropa (1812–1857)* (Frankfurt am Main: Lang, 1992). For a case study that considers the situation of international students in the late 1970s and early 1980s, see Yousef Abu Laila, *Integration und Entfremdung: Eine empirische Studie zur Situation ausländischer Studenten am Beispiel Clausthal-Zellerfeld und Göttingen* (Göttingen: Edition Herodot, 1981).

54. The need for innovative approaches to living arrangements for international students was also documented in Friedhelm Neidhardt's detailed study, *Studenten im in-*

ternationalen Wohnheim: Gruppendynamik und Sozialisation (Tübingen: J. C. B. Mohr [Paul Siebeck], 1963).

55. See, for example, Hamdallah Neserat, "Aspekte sozialen Wandels in der arabischen Minderheit in Israel," *Traditionelles Wissen und Modernisierung: Beiträge zu einem interkulturellen Wissenschaftsverständnis und zur Reintegration,* ed. Karl Fritz Heise and Kyaw Tha Tun (Frankfurt am Main: Verlag für interkulturelle Kommunikation, 1991), 206–20.

56. For a more detailed discussion of the organization, see Nina Berman, "Multiculturalism, Reintegration, and Beyond: The Afrikanisch-Asiatische Studentenförderung in Göttingen," *South Central Review* 16, no. 2–3 (Summer–Fall 1999): 34–53.

57. Bassam Tibi, *Europa ohne Identität: Die Krise der multikulturellen Gesellschaft* (Munich: Bertelsmann, 1998), 180–83.

58. See the roster of active members, which includes only few Tunisians: http://www.deutsch-tunesische-gesellschaft.de/dtg/struktur.htm.

59. https://www.d-a-g.org/default.asp.

60. http://www.daeg-hannover.de/index9.htm.

61. http://forum.konsulate.de/deutsche-frauen-in-tunesien-t-3503.html.

62. http://dpg-netz.de/index.php?option=com_content&task=view&id=25&Itemid=65.

63. http://www.araby.de/.

64. Kenan Önen, *Die politische Rolle türkischer Organizationen und ihre Relevanz für die Integration türkischer Familien in der Bundesrepublik Deutschland* (Freiburg: HochschulVerlag, 1997), 114–35.

65. Fikret Aslan, Kemal Bozay, et al. *Graue Wölfe heulen wieder: Türkische Faschisten und ihre Vernetzung in der BRD* (Münster: Unrast, 1997).

66. See organizations listed at http://www.laenderkontakte.de/arabische-laender; see also http://www.marokko.net/links/Vereine/.

67. For an incomplete list of Turkish-German soccer clubs, see http://www.deutschetuerken.de/service/tuerkische-fussball-vereine-in-deutschland .htm.

68. http://www.scpersia.de/.

69. See "Deurabika—Diversity Management Consulting," http://www.deurabika.de.

70. Yasemin Karakaşoğlu, "Turkish Cultural Orientations in Germany and the Role of Islam," in *Turkish Culture in German Society Today,* ed. David Horrocks and Eva Kolinsky (Providence, RI: Berghahn, 1996), 166.

71. For a discussion of key organizations on the federal, state, and local levels, see Thomas Lemmen, *Islamische Vereine und Verbände in Deutschland* (Bonn: Friedrich-Ebert-Stiftung, 2002). See also Thomas Lemmen, *Muslime in Deutschland: Eine Herausforderung für Kirche und Gesellschaft* (Baden-Baden: Nomos, 2001); Marfa Heimbach, *Die Entwicklung der islamischen Gemeinschaft in Deutschland seit 1961* (Berlin: Klaus Schwarz, 2001).

72. It should be noted that membership figures for the various organizations are difficult to verify; scholars generally agree that a total of about 10 to 12 percent of Muslims are members of the major organizations. Heimbach, *Die Entwicklung der islamischen Gemeinschaft,* 164.

73. Werner Schiffauer provides a study of the most extremist of the Islamist organi-

zations in Germany, the community around Cemaleddin Kaplan. See *Die Gottesmänner—Türkische Islamisten in Deutschland: Eine Studie zur Herstellung religiöser Evidenz* (Frankfurt am Main: Suhrkamp, 2000).

74. http://zentralrat.de/2594.php.

75. Tariq Ramadan, *To Be a European Muslim* (Markfield, United Kingdom: Islamic Foundation, 1999).

76. Mathias Rohe, "The Legal Treatment of Muslims in Germany," in *The Legal Treatment of Islamic Minorities in Europe,* ed. Roberta Aluffi Beck-Peccoz and Giovanna Zincone (Leuven: Peeters/Fieri, 2004), 87.

77. Religionswissenschaftlicher Medien- und Informationsdienst e.V., http://www.remid.de/info_zahlen_grafik.html.

78. Regarding the history of the Islamic community's legal status in Austria, see Johann Bair, *Das Islamgesetz* (Vienna: Springer, 2002).

79. Maja Sticker, *Sondermodell Österreich? Die islamische Glaubensgemeinschaft in Österreich (IGGiÖ)* (Drava: Klagenfurt, 2008).

80. Anna Strobl, *Islam in Österreich: Eine religionssoziologische Untersuchung* (Frankfurt am Main: Lang, 1997), 31.

81. *Volkszählung 2001: Hauptergebnisse 1—Österreich,* ed. Statistik Austria (Vienna: Statistik Austria, 2002), 77.

82. Anna Strobl, "Einzigartiger rechtlicher Status: Die Muslime in Österreich," *Herder Korrespondenz* 4 (2006): 200.

83. An overview of Islamic institutions is given on a Web site maintained by the Islamische Glaubensgemeinschaft in Österreich. See http://www.derislam.at/islam.php?name=Themen&pa=list_pages_categories&cid=5. See also Strobl, *Islam in Österreich,* 46–69; Nikola Ornig, *Die Zweite Generation und der Islam in Österreich: Eine Analyse von Chancen und Grenzen des Pluralismus von Religionen und Ethnie* (Graz: Grazer Universitätsverlag, 2006).

84. Forschungsgruppe "Islam in der Schweiz," *Muslime in der Schweiz: Identitätsprofile, Erwartungen und Einstellungen* (Bern-Wabern: Eidgenössische Ausländerkommission EKA, 2005), 15–16.

85. For a list of organizations, see http://lexikon.calsky.com/de/txt/i/is/islamische_organisationen_in_der_schweiz.php.

86. Regarding the legal status of Islam in Switzerland, see contributions in René Pahud de Mortanges and Erwin Tanner, eds., *Muslime und schweizerische Rechtsordnung—Les musulmans et l'ordre juridique Suisse* (Freiburg: Universitätsverlag Freiburg, 2002).

87. Forschungsgruppe "Islam in der Schweiz," *Muslime in der Schweiz,* 18.

88. Contributions made at a symposium regarding Turkish and German attitudes toward religion illustrate this issue and are documented in *Religion—ein deutsch-türkisches Tabu? Türk-Alman ilişkilerinde din tabu mu?* (Hamburg: Körber-Stiftung, 1996).

89. Iman O. Khalil, "Arab-German Literature," *World Literature Today* 69, no. 3 (1995): 521–27.

90. Hamdi el Attar and Elisabeth Heer, *Al Fann—Die Kunst: Zeitgenössische Kunst in den islamischen Ländern* (Kassel: Projektgruppe Stoffwechsel, Universität Gesamthochschule Kassel, 1995). See also Hamdi el Attar, *Türkische Kunst heute am*

Beispiel der Universität Mimar Sinan Istanbul (Kassel: Projektgruppe Stoffwechsel, Universität Gesamthochschule Kassel, 1990).

91. *Die Tageszeitung* Sept. 18, 2004, http://www.taz.de/index.php?id=archivseite&dig=2004/09/18/a0211.

92. Recent Web-based booksellers include alkutub.de–Buchhandlung für arabische Bücher, which was founded in Oct. 2005.

93. See Kira Kosnick, *Migrant Media: Turkish Broadcasting and Multicultural Politics in Berlin* (Bloomington: Indiana University Press, 2007).

94. See Konuk, *East West Mimesis.*

95. *Über das Leben in Bitterland: Bibliographie zur türkischen Deutschland-Literatur und zur türkischen Literatur in Deutschland,* ed. and annotated by Wolfgang Riemann (Wiesbaden: Harrassowitz, 1990).

96. Wolfgang Riemann, *Das Deutschlandbild in der modernen türkischen Literatur* (Wiesbaden: Harrassowitz, 1983), 18–31.

97. Riemann, *Das Deutschlandbild in der modernen türkischen Literatur,* 32–37.

98. Abdo Abboud, *Deutsche Romane im arabischen Orient: Eine komparatistische Untersuchung zur Rezeption von Heinrich Mann, Thomas Mann, Hermann Hesse und Franz Kafka, mit einem Überblick über die Rezeption der deutschen Literatur in der arabischen "Welt"* (Frankfurt am Main: Peter Lang, 1984). See also Abboud, *Hijra al Nusus: Dirasat fi al-Tarjama al-Adabiyya wa al-Tabadul al-Thaqafi* (Damascus: Ittihad al-Kuttab al-'Arab, 1995). Abboud discusses interactions between German and Arabic literature and language on 88–201.

99. Mustafa Kamal, *Yawmiyyat Rihla min al-Ra'smaliyya ila al-Ishtirakiyya* (Cairo: Dar al-Thaqafa al-Jadida, 1976).

100. Fu'ad Badawi, *Warda min Birlin* (Cairo: n.p., 1974); Ahmad Musa Salim, *Sibaq al-Mustaqbal bayna al-Din wa-al-Shuyu'iyya: Min Mudhakkirat Muslim fi Mujtama' Shuyu'i* (Beirut: Dar al-Jil, 1976).

101. Gaby Strassburger, "Transstate Ties of the Second Generation: Marriages of Turks in Germany," German-Turkish Summer Institute Working Paper No. 7/2001 (Bremen: Institut für Interkulturelle und Internationale Studien, 2001), 6.

102. Hartmut Esser, "Interethnische Freundschaften," in *Generation und Identität: Theoretische und Empirische Beiträge zur Migrationssoziologie,* ed. Hartmut Esser and Jürgen Friedrichs (Opladen: Westdeutscher Verlag, 1990), 187.

103. Paret, *Arabistik und Islamkunde an deutschen Universitäten,* 3.

104. Hafez, *Orientwissenschaft in der DDR,* 1.

105. http://www.goethe.de/ges/phi/prj/ffs/ueb/enindex.htm. Other relevant magazines include *Der arabische Almanach: Zeitschrift für orientalische Kultur,* founded in 1991.

106. http://www.qantara.de/webcom/show_softlink.php/_c-360/_lkm-2881/i.html.

107. Aly discusses this connection in *Das Bild der islamischen Welt in der westdeutschen Presse,* 1:192–210.

108. Gernot Rotter, *Allahs Plagiator: Die publizistischen Raubzüge des "Nahostexperten" Gerhard Konzelmann* (Heidelberg: Palmyra, 1992).

109. Verena Klemm and Karin Hörner, eds., *Das Schwert des "Experten": Peter Scholl-Latours verzerrtes Araber- und Islambild* (Heidelberg: Palmyra, 1993).

110. Kenneth M. Lewan, *Der Nahostkrieg in der westdeutschen Presse* (Cologne:

Pahl-Rugenstein, 1970); Sami Fayez Khalil Musallam, *Zum Araberbild in der bundesrepublikanischen Presse am Beispiel des IV. Nahostkrieges* (PhD diss., Rheinische Friedrich-Wilhelms Universität, 1976); Richard Blank, *Soraya, Farah und der Schah: Deutsche Schicksalsberichte vom Pfauenthron* (Munich: Rogner und Bernhard, 1977); Hub, *Das Image Israels.*

111. Hafez, *Die politische Dimension der Auslandsberichterstattung,* vol. 2, 145.

112. Hafez, *Die politische Dimension der Auslandsberichterstattung,* 177.

113. Hafez, *Die politische Dimension der Auslandsberichterstattung,* 30, also 56.

114. Hafez, *Die politische Dimension der Auslandsberichterstattung,* 239.

115. Rita Chin, *The Guest Worker Question in Postwar Germany* (Cambridge: Cambridge University Press, 2007), 13.

116. Orhan Gökçe, *Das Bild der Türken in der deutschen Presse: Eine Inhaltsanalyse der Berichterstattung zum Besuch des türkischen Ministerpräsidenten Turgut Özal im Herbst 1984 in der Bundesrepublik Deutschland* (Giessen: Schmitz, 1988).

117. Teraoka, "Talking 'Turk,'" 105.

118. Teraoka, "Talking 'Turk,'" 106.

119. Teraoka, "Talking 'Turk,'" 127.

120. "'The Lowest of the Low' No More," Deutsche Welle, Oct. 21, 2005, http://www.dw-world.com/dw/article/0,,1746801,00.html.

121. Thofern, *Darstellungen des Islams in* Der Spiegel, 136.

122. Thofern, *Darstellungen des Islams,* 138.

123. See references to a substantial number of studies regarding Islam in German media in Hafez, *Die politische Dimension der Auslandsberichterstattung,* 16–28. See also *Der Islam in den Schulbüchern der Bundesrepublik Deutschland,* ed. Falaturi. Similar publications are also available with regard to Austria and Switzerland.

124. Kamaluldin, *Das Bild des Nahen Ostens,* 115–18.

125. Kamaluldin, *Das Bild des Nahen Ostens,* 88.

126. Kamaluldin, *Das Bild des Nahen Ostens,* 126.

127. Elias Canetti, *Die Stimmen von Marrakesch: Aufzeichnungen nach einer Reise* (Munich: Hanser, 1967), 40.

128. David Simo, *Interkulturalität und ästhetische Erfahrung: Untersuchungen zum Werk Hubert Fichtes* (Stuttgart: Metzler, 1993), 267.

129. Kamaluldin, *Das Bild des Nahen Ostens,* 56.

130. Dagmar C. G. Lorenz, "Dismantling Islam: Orientalism and the Women's Perspective in Barbara Frischmuth's Novel *Das Verschwinden des Schattens in der Sonne,*" in *Barbara Frischmuth in Contemporary Context,* ed. Renate S. Posthofen (Riverside, CA: Ariadne, 1999), 278.

131. Christoph Gellner, "Grenzüberschreitungen zwischen Orient und Okzident: Literatur, Multikulturalität und Religionsdialog," in *Barbara Frischmuth, Fremdgänge: Ein illustrierter Streifzug durch einen literarischen Kosmos,* ed. Daniela Bartens and Ingrid Spörk (Salzburg: Residenz, 2001), 236.

132. Kamaluldin, *Das Bild des Nahen Ostens,* 133–35.

133. Botho Strauss, *Gross und Klein: Szenen* (Munich: Hanser, 1978).

134. Franz Xaver Kroetz, *Furcht und Hoffnung der BRD: Das Stück, das Material, das Tagebuch* (Frankfurt am Main: Suhrkamp, 1984), 73–77. The play also contains a scene dedicated to Kemal Altun, who in 1981 sought asylum in the Federal Republic

and, faced with potential deportation in 1983, killed himself by jumping through a window in the courthouse in Berlin (70–72).

135. Adelson, "Opposing Oppositions," 313.

136. Sabine von Dirke, "West Meets East: Narrative Construction of the Foreigner and Postmodern Orientalism in Sten Nadolny's *Selim oder Die Gabe der Rede,*" *Germanic Review* 69, no. 2 (Spring 1994): 64.

137. Adelson, "Opposing Oppositions," 305–30. B. Venkat Mani follows Adelson's lead in his exploration of the novel in *Cosmopolitical Claims,* 44–86.

138. Ülker Gökberk, "*Culture Studies* und die Türken: Sten Nadolnys *Selim oder Die Gabe der Rede* im Lichte einer Methodendiskussion," *German Quarterly* 70, no. 2 (Spring 1997): 97–122. Mani gives an overview of the scholarship on *Selim* in *Cosmopolitical Claims,* 51–53.

139. Susan C. Anderson, "Outsiders, Foreigners, and Aliens in Cinematic or Literary Narratives by Bohm, Dische, Dörrie, and Ören," *German Quarterly* 75, no. 2 (Spring 2002): 150–51.

140. Petra Fachinger, "Orientalism Reconsidered: Turkey in Barbara Frischmuth's *Das Verschwinden des Schattens in der Sonne* and Hanne Mede-Flock's *Im Schatten der Mondsichel,*" *Studies in Twentieth Century Literature* 23, no. 2 (1999): 239–54.

141. Arlene A. Teraoka, "Detecting Ethnicity: Jakob Arjouni and the Case of the Missing German Detective Novel," *German Quarterly* 72, no. 3 (Summer 1999): 270.

142. See Teraoka, "Detecting Ethnicity," 274–76, for a review of the quite amusing obsession with Arjouni's identity.

143. Teraoka, "Detecting Ethnicity," 274.

144. Akbulut, *Das Türkenbild in der neueren deutschen Literatur,* 208–11.

145. Sander L. Gilman, *Jurek Becker: A Life in Five Worlds* (Chicago: University of Chicago Press, 2003), 177.

146. Gilles Deleuze and Félix Guattari, *Kafka: Toward a Minor Literature,* trans. Dana Polan (Minneapolis: University of Minnesota Press, 1986), 16.

147. Cheesman, *Novels of Turkish German Settlement,* 33–39.

148. Cheesman, *Novels of Turkish German Settlement;* Mani, *Cosmopolitical Claims.*

149. "Liste deutsch-türkischer Schriftsteller," http://de.wikipedia.org/wiki/Liste_deutsch-t%C3%BCrkischer_Schriftsteller.

150. Aifan, *Araberbilder;* Omar, *Exotisches und Ästhetisches.*

151. See http://www2.mcdaniel.edu/german/arab-german/index.htm.

152. *Lyrik deutschsprachiger Perser: Eine Anthologie,* ed. Bouzard Parsa-Nejad (Cologne: SOHRAB, 1989).

153. Figures are based on data about individuals who are not German citizens, as provided in *Kleines Lexikon der ethnischen Minderheiten in Deutschland,* ed. Cornelia Schmalz-Jacobsen and Georg Hansen (Munich: Beck, 1997), and estimates about naturalization and intermarriage. The number of individuals from Arabic-speaking countries, as listed in *Kleines Lexikon,* amounts to about 320,000; the group of Iranians consists of 106,979 people (both figures exclude the 350,000 to 550,000 Kurds, who may be from Iranian, Arabic, and Turkish areas). Given the high percentage of men among Arab and Iranian immigrants (fluctuating between 65 and 80 percent in the various subgroups), intermarriage rates are considerable. Taking naturalization and bicultural chil-

dren into consideration suggests that the total number of Arab Germans and Iranian Germans is potentially higher than the number of those without German passports.

154. Omar lists thirty-eight writers of Arab descent who live in Germany and who wrote at least one longer prose text. Twelve of these authors write exclusively in Arabic. *Exotisches und Ästhetisches,* 207–8.

155. Göktürk, "Turkish Women on German Streets," 67.

156. *AufBrüche: Kulturelle Produktion von Migrantinnen, Schwarzen und jüdischen Frauen in Deutschland,* ed. Cathy S. Gelbin, Kader Konuk, and Peggy Piesche (Königstein: Ulrike Helmer, 1999); *Morgen Land: Neueste deutsche Literatur,* ed. Jamal Tuschick (Frankfurt am Main: Fischer, 2000); *Spricht die Subalterne deutsch? Migration und postkoloniale Kritik,* ed. Hito Steyerl and Encarnación Rodríguez (Münster: Unrast-Verlag, 2003).

157. Franco Biondi and Rafik Schami, with Jusuf Naoum and Suleman Taufiq, "Literatur der Betroffenheit: Bemerkungen zur Gastarbeiterliteratur," in *Zu Hause in der Fremde: Ein bundesdeutsches Ausländer-Lesebuch,* ed. Christian Schaffernicht (Fischerhude: Verlag Atelier im Bauernhaus, 1981), note 1, 134–35.

158. Biondi and Schami, "Literatur der Betroffenheit," 128–29.

159. Suhr, "*Ausländerliteratur,*" 80.

160. See Chin, *The Guest Worker Question,* 64–85, 105–40, for a discussion of the early phase of German minority writings and literary organizations.

161. Exceptions are mostly workers who published in the Turkish language, such as Bekir Yıldız and Fethi Savaşçi. Sargut Şölçün, "Literatur der türkischen Minderheit," in *Interkulturelle Literatur in Deutschland,* ed. Carmine Chiellino (Stuttgart: Metzler, 2000), 136. See also *Über das Leben in Bitterland,* ed. Riemann.

162. Rafik Schami, "Zwischen Traum und Straßenbahn," in *Zu Hause in der Fremde,* ed. Schaffernicht, 38–44.

163. Fahri Kaya, "Gedanken zu Deutschland," in *Zu Hause in der Fremde,* ed. Schaffernicht, 68–72; Zehra Çırak, "Tatsächlich," Alev Tekinay, "Du machst dich, Mädchen!" in *Freihändig auf dem Tandem: Dreißig Frauen aus elf Ländern,* ed. Luisa Costa Hölzl and Eleni Torossi (Kiel: Neuer Malik Verlag, 1985), 88, 89–97.

164. Habib Bektaş, "krank in deutschland," trans. Yüksel Pazarkaya; Aras Ören, "Bahnhöfe," trans. Yüksel Pazarkaya; Semra Ertan, "ich habe gesehen," "wofür lebe ich," in *Zu Hause in der Fremde,* ed. Schaffernicht, 73, 87, 98; Sabriye Cemboluk, "Nacht in einem fremden Land"; Şiir Eroğlu, "Abschied," Alev Tekinay, "Das Kind am Anlegeplatz," in *Freihändig auf dem Tandem,* ed. Hölzl and Torossi, 51, 114, 115–23; Alev Tekinay, "Ali Stern"; Özgür Savaşçı, "Unsere Lage," in *Das Unsichtbare sagen! Prosa und Lyrik aus dem Alltag des Gastarbeiters,* ed. Habib Bektaş, Franco Biondi, Gino Chiellino, Jusuf Naoum, and Rafik Shami (Kiel: Neuer Malik Verlag, 1983), 79–84, 118.

165. *Zu Hause in der Fremde,* ed. Schaffernicht, 136, 213.

166. *Freihändig auf dem Tandem,* ed. Hölzl and Torossi, 37–41, 56–59.

167. Among works and anthologies from the period that focus on social and economic questions are *Wir sind fremd, wir gehen fremd,* ed. Guillermo Aparicio, Bernd Böhm, and Suleman Taufiq (Aachen: Klenkes, 1979); *Zwischen Fabrik und Bahnhof,* ed. Franco Biondi, Jusuf Naoum, Rafik Shami, and Suleman Taufiq (Bremen: Con-Edition, 1981); *Dies ist nicht die Welt, die wir suchen: Prosa, Lyrik und Fotos von Ausländ-*

ern, ed. Suleman Taufiq (Essen: Klartext, 1983). For a review of mostly Turkish German writers publishing in Turkish and German in the late 1960s to early 1980s, see Cheesman, *Novels of Turkish German Settlement,* 82–85. See also Riemann, ed., *Über das Leben in Bitterland.*

168. Melek Baklan, "Das Korsett," in *Freihändig auf dem Tandem,* ed. Hölzl and Torossi, 124–48.

169. Hamid Naficy, "Phobic Spaces and Liminal Panics: Independent Transnational Film Genre," in *Multiculturalism, Postcoloniality, and Transnational Media,* ed. Ella Shohat and Robert Stam (New Brunswick: Rutgers University Press, 2003), 217.

170. Chin, *The Guest Worker Question,* 171–90.

171. Yüksel Pazarkaya, "deutsche sprache," Schaffernicht, *Zu Hause in der Fremde,* 123.

172. Heidrun Suhr, "*Ausländerliteratur:* Minority Literature in the Federal Republic of Germany," *New German Critique* 46 (1989): 87.

173. Rita C.-K. Chin, "Imagining a German Multiculturalism: Aras Ören and the Contested Meanings of the 'Guest Worker,' 1955–1980," *Radical History Review* 83 (2002): 56.

174. Fakir Baykurt, *Frau Dumàn,* trans. Helga Dağyeli-Bohne and Yıldırım Dağyeli, in *Das Unsichtbare sagen,* ed. Bektaş et al., 10–19.

175. Mehmet Ünal, "Neue Freunde," in *Das Unsichtbare sagen,* ed. Bektaş et al., 125.

176. Personal interview in Leipzig on July 1, 2008.

177. Aifan, *Araberbilder,* 167, 171. Karasholi also evoked the image of the "Syro-Sachse" in a personal interview in Leipzig on July 1, 2008.

178. See Adel Karasholi, *Umarmung der Meridiane* (Halle: Mitteldeutscher Verlag, 1978); *Daheim in der Fremde* (Halle: Mitteldeutscher Verlag, 1984).

179. See, for example, Adel Karasholi, "'Wir sind nur so fremd, wie man uns als Fremde sieht,' Aus der Begrüßungsansprache im alten Rathaus anläßlich der zweiten Chamisso-Tage in Leipzig 2001" (Leipzig: n.p., 2001).

180. Karasholi, *Umarmung der Meridiane,* 65–67.

181. See, for example, Aysel Özakin, *Zart erhob sie sich bis sie flog: Ein Poem* (Hamburg: Galgenberg, 1986), 57.

182. Aysel Özakin, *Du bist willkommen: Gedichte* (Hamburg: Buntbuch, 1985), 53–68.

183. See Cheesman's discussion in *Novels of Turkish German Settlement,* 53–58.

184. Her first publication was *Die gläserne Heimat* (1989).

185. Said, *Wo ich sterbe ist meine Fremde* (1983; Munich: Kirchheim, 1987), 42. An early example in which Said comments on exile is the story "Ein Märchen." Said, *Ein Märchen,* in *Das Unsichtbare sagen,* ed. Bektaş et al., 88–92. Another early example for Said's focus on exile is the poem "Im Exil." In *Das Unsichtbare sagen,* ed. Bektaş et al., 97.

186. Yêhat, "Wir werden zurückkehren," in *Zu Hause in der Fremde,* ed. Schaffernicht, 144.

187. Rafik Schami, *Ein Kassiber,* in *Das Unsichtbare sagen,* Bektaş et al., 63–70.

188. Aifan, *Araberbilder,* 172.

189. See Haimaa El Wardy, "Die Bedeutung bzw. Rolle des Märchens in der

abendländischen europäischen und der orientalischen arabischen Kultur: Ein Vergleich," in *Das Märchen und das Märchenhafte in den politisch engagierten Werken von Günter Grass und Rafik Schami* (Frankfurt am Main: Lang, 2007), 29–96.

190. See Clinton Bailey, *Bedouin Poetry from Sinai and the Negev: Mirror of a Culture* (Oxford: Clarendon, 1991).

191. See Omar's discussion of oral narrative aesthetics in the works of authors of Arab origin in *Exotisches und Ästhetisches,* 165–98.

192. Aifan, *Araberbilder,* 265–68.

193. See my analysis of Alafenisch's narrative *Das Kamel mit dem Nasenring,* in which I assess the richness of the text's political and cultural trajectory. Nina Berman, "German and Middle Eastern Literary Traditions in a Novel by Salim Alafenisch: Thoughts on a Germanophone Beduin Author from the Negev," *German Quarterly* 71, no. 3 (Summer 1998): 271–83.

194. *Das Unsichtbare sagen,* Bektaş et al., 29–33.

195. For analyses that relate Schami's narrative techniques to the subject matter, see Magda Amin, "Stories, Stories, Stories: Rafik Schami's *Erzähler der Nacht,*" *Alif: Journal of Comparative Poetics* 20 (2000): 211–33, special issue, "The Hybrid Literary Text: Arab Creative Authors Writing in Foreign Languages," ed. Ferial Ghazoul; Seyhan, *Writing Outside the Nation,* 40–50.

196. Rafik Schami, "Als der Angstmacher Angst bekam," in *Der Fliegenmelker: Geschichten aus Damaskus* (1985; rpt., Kiel: Neuer Malik Verlag, 1993), 39–52.

197. See Khalid al-Maaly, *Eine Phantasie aus Schilf: Gedichte,* trans. Stefan Weidner and Khalid al-Maaly (Berlin: Das arabische Buch, 1994); Fadhil al-Azzawi, *Auf einem magischen Fest,* trans. Fadhil al-Azzawi and Heribert Becker (Berlin: Das Arabische Buch, 1998).

198. Mustafa Al-Slaiman, "Literatur in Deutschland am Beispiel arabischer Autoren—Zur Übertragung und Vermittlung von Kulturrealien-Bezeichnungen in der Migranten- und Exilliteratur," in *Literatur der Migration,* ed. Nasrin Amirsedghi and Thomas Bleicher (Mainz: Donata Kinzelbach, 1997), 94–96.

199. Jarrod Leslie Shepherd, "Translation of Culture in Emine Sevgi Özdamar's *Das Leben ist eine Karawanserei*" (Master's thesis, Ohio State University, 2006).

200. Seyhan, *Writing Outside the Nation,* 99–124.

CONCLUSION

1. Theo van Leeuwen notes that the analysis of multiple representations of the same social practice "opens up the field to all kind of studies; to looking at ways in which social practices and events are represented, bottom up, not top down, looking for contradictions rather than coherence, and studying the factors that structure the relationship between social practices and discourses" (*Discourse and Practice,* 6).

2. Walter Benjamin, "[N7a,5]," *The Arcades Project,* trans. Howard Eiland and Kevin McLaughlin (Cambridge: Belknap Press, 2002), 471.

3. See, for example, the case studies in *Cultural Exchange in Early Modern Europe,* vol. 4, *Forging European Identities, 1400–1700,* ed. Herman Roodenburg (Cambridge: Cambridge University Press, 2007). Studies on translation are crucial in this

context; see, for example, contributions in *Cultural Translation in Early Modern Europe,* ed. Peter Burke and Ronnie Po-chia Hsia (Cambridge: Cambridge University Press, 2007).

4. David A. Sousa, *How the Brain Learns,* 3rd ed. (Thousand Oaks, CA: Corwin Press, 2006), 81.

5. Sousa, *How the Brain Learns,* 81–82.

6. Sousa, *How the Brain Learns,* 136.

7. Sousa, *How the Brain Learns,* 137–38.

8. Sousa, *How the Brain Learns,* 24–25.

9. The project *Kaaba* was carried out in cooperation with the Verein zur Förderung von Kunst und Literatur e.V. and the *Kunsttempel.* Zaki Al-Maboren was honored for the conception, planning, and execution of the project with the prize of the Dr. Wolfgang Zippel Stiftung, which was awarded in September 2007 by the Kulturamt der Stadt Kassel. The project was on display from June 13 to July 8, 2007.

Name Index

Subject Index